DI DI DAW DAW DI DI

AF251552

?

By

James E. Horn

Because I care

Copyrighted

All Rights Reserved

Quotes and excerpts from this text are permissible with attribution to this as the source.

The author can be contacted by writing to:
P.O. Box 2335
Menifee, CA 92586

The opinions and characterizations in this book are those of the author, and do not necessarily represent official positions of the United States Government.

ACKNOWLEDGEMENTS

My wonderful wife, best friend and partner, Nam-Yong has stood with me for so long. Without her devotion, encouragement, and support, this never would have been written. The unselfish caring and encouragement from my sons Frank and Ken are a treasure.

In memory of my beloved and devoted mother, Kathryn Loraine Berner, my fabulous beloved grandmother, Emma Stina Berner, and my fantastic, loving, caring, and very beloved aunt, Margaret Berner Smith; and uncles who cared, and treated me well: Richard and Russell Berner, and my aunts Eugenia Berner, Joyce Berner.

Chris Christenson who was an incredible man's man and role model who knew more about life, war, courage, and life's struggles than most.

My devoted teacher, Arvid K. Simmons who worked so hard to teach his young charges at Minneapolis' Edison High School that the real world out there where we were soon to go was not always such a nice place.

Others present and past who are forever in my memory: Jimmy, Ken Haas, Tom Geankopolis, Steve, Jutsuku, Loren, Ae-Suk KI, Reverend Lystig, Ellen, Donnie, Diane, Boghdan, Alan, Ned, Gerrard, Mr. Bower, Mickey, Ari Wolf, Will, Chantal, "Jack", Ambassador Manfull, Robert Wolf, Mamie, Joe, Ed, Nancy, John Wayne, Bonnie, Lloyd, Melvin Bates, Mr. Drage, Mr. Kottom, Mr. Bauer, Pete Guzzy, Dr. Zakaria Botros, Miss Sorenson.

"What thou seest, write in a book,
and send it unto churches which
are in Asia; unto Ephesus, and unto
Smyrna, and unto Pergamos, and
unto Thyatira, and unto Sardis, and
unto Philadelphia, and unto
Laodicea."
REVELATIONS, I:11

Disclaimer

This book is about ideological, intolerant, colonial Islam, a politically expansive and violently imperial Islam in its many manifestations, the U.S. Government's responses and how it functions, and other religious responses to Islam.

Anyone reading this, about my understanding, my truths, my opinions, my concerns, these words, and who after reading them pretends to be adversely affected or offended must understand this: If you have an inferiority complex, before you read this book, check first with your friends, family, politicians, bureaucrats, priests, rabbis, imams, mullahs, and other spiritual and political leaders; your psychics, favorite rappers, lawyers, union bosses, psychiatrists, and anyone you feel to be wiser, smarter, or better than yourself to get approval to expose yourself to these words.

The First Amendment to the Constitution of the United States of America protects the rights of freedom of expression, allowing its sovereign citizens to explore their opinions and viewpoints. There are some who, based on their pitiful ignorance and hatred of genuine freedom, will label this book as hate literature. This book is not hate literature, it is an expression of fundamental truths. Understand, please, that most truths are very, very often politically incorrect, and that's a fundamental truth.

Hate is a harsh word. I do not hate the religion of Islam. I do indeed fear the encroachment of the ideology of imperial political and social Islam and I do so with serious justification, but I will not be cowed by Islam or those who hate in the name of Islam. I am Islam-averse. I am Mohammed-averse. Above all, I am Islam-aware.

Some people may disagree with my opinions and conclusions. So be it! The publishers, agent or agents, distributors, bookstores and booksellers, libraries, and others offer this for informational purposes only.

An autonomous American, this book is my choice of, and assemblage of words. If after reading it you find that your are thus better informed, educated, wiser, and more able to understand and deal with this changing, increasingly complex and dangerous world we live in, so be it. If after reading this, you find its truths to not suit you, so be it.

This book is not a scholarly treatise. It is my knowledge and understanding of Imperial Islam based on my considerable personal experiences and independent learning. For excellent scholarly readings, there are great experts whose books and studies I recommend: Bill Warner, Robert Spencer, Steven Emerson, Serge Trifkovic, and Andrew Bostom to name just a few.

The United Nations Charter grants people who are under threat (the right) to defend against illegal, hostile occupation. We Americans must defend ourselves now and in every way!

About the Author

James E. (Jim) Horn was born in a U.S. Army hospital near Kansas City, Missouri shortly after the outbreak of Word War II.

He grew up living in his grandparents' home in Minneapolis, Minnesota. With little money in the home, Jim learned early to be productive with his first paying job at $0.09 (nine cents) per hour stuffing small tomato plants into tarpaper pots. He was nine, and has seldom been unemployed since.

He attended the same high school that his mother attended, and at that time, the tough 'Nordeast' Edison High School hosted grades 7 – 12. Good with his hands, he took industrial arts courses, and enlisted in the Navy days after graduating by the skin of his teeth. He wanted to be a machinist.

Rather than take advantage of his industrial arts training and skills, the Navy in its infinite wisdom put him into radio communications and taught him Morse code and how to sit at a typewriter, which sent him in an entirely new career and life path.

Jim served one enlistment, with time served on a troop transport, at a naval air facility in Sicily, and ending at the Navy's Atlantic amphibious forces headquarters, on the staff of Admiral, 'Cussin' John "Hot Dammit" McCain. After the navy he took a few courses at the University of Minnesota, and held a number of short-term industrial and construction jobs before joining the Foreign Service (Department of State). He served overseas for two dozen years, spent some time in 'purgatory' in Washington, D.C., and retired after thirty years of government service. After many world-wide assignments, the State Department offered him a position in Somalia in 1992, and he decided to retire rather than have to send his two young sons off to a boarding school in Europe. [Jim's career advancement potential had otherwise became poor at best because of two episodes where he blew the proverbial whistle on crooks in the State Department.]

Jim had entered the Department of State as a member of the Staff Corps (equivalent to the military's enlisted class), and earned a commission as a Foreign Service Officer through a Mustang program. At the time of his commissioning, he was one of just two officers whose formal, documented education was limited to high school. Jim held the highest levels of TOP SECRET security clearances with code word access to restricted, and sensitive compartmentalized intelligence. He earned a number of awards, among them a (rare) civilian award for Valor for actions taken while under hostile fire in Cambodia.

Jim and his wife, Nam-Yong, reside in Southern California.

INDEX

DiDiDawDawDiDi

INTRODUCTION

I started this book a few months after the razing of the World Trade Center in New York. I have worked on it intermittently completing it early in 2009, and I submitted it to federal authorities for review. The final censoring was completed six months later and the manuscript was returned to me in the fall. The more than six month wait has been agonizing.

Naturally, the world has continued to turn and events have occurred, some of which I bring forth in this text.

> *We are in a war that we must sustain*
> *to the very end, to prevail, to survive.*
> *If we don't, the enemy will persist to our*
> *ultimate demise, and the end of civilization.*

Following my morning routine on September 11, 2001, I sat down to eat my cereal and turned the TV on to catch the headlines. The American people had no inkling of what was changing our lives that morning.

The TV screen came on and the first image I saw showed roiling smoke spewing from the upper levels of a tall building. The narrator was saying that there were reports that an airplane had crashed into the building, one of the Word Trade Center towers. Seconds later, I saw the second jetliner banking as it sped into the other World Trade Center tower.

In a split second, my emotions went from placid curiosity to seething rage. I bypassed dismay, and had no need to ask why -- the implication of what I saw was crystal clear. What millions witnessed was an outrageously successful act of war accomplished by taking jumbo jets loaded with fuel and innocent people and crashing them into two buildings.

Everyone says it was a terrorist attack. It was an act designed to terrorize Americans.

America remains under attack in ways that it has never experienced before. America (in particular, our political, academic, religious, business, and judiciary) is having great difficulty coming to grips with the terrible and very formidable imperialistic enemy forces arrayed against us.

This book discusses among other things, so-called religious fundamentalism. What I discuss herein is meant to educate and inform about the true meaning of the ideological plague of colonizing Islam and what it bodes for America. This is an intent to inform people about Mohammed (aka Muhammad), Mohammedism (aka Islam), the Koran, Islamic tradition (history) - the Hadiths [of which there are reportedly about 6,000 sunna -- reported utterances, rulings, teachings, pronouncements and so forth of Mohammed that were only codified centuries after Mohammed's death..... They were supposedly memorized with "flawless" accuracy and passed on from one man to another over a dozen generations until someone decided to write them all down. How many and which of those are factually and truly purely precise, exact, honest, accurate, or contrived? Yet, the 'flawless' Koran and Sunna guide Moslems in every aspect of their lives.

There are many, a true fifth column, who are working diligently to keep Americans from learning or knowing the whole truth, the unpleasantly stark truths about the absolute evil embodied in Islam. Some of those fifth columnists are in the highest offices of our government, judiciary, economic, theological, and political leadership.

THE ATTACKS OF O9/11/2001 WERE JUST
AS THINGS SHOULD BE
Unidentified Philosopher

At 9:59 AM New York time on 9/11/01 many millions of Moslems began dancing and cheering in the streets of the world, some on American streets.

We Americans are right and justified to be furious about the horrific deed that murdered 3,000 genuinely innocent people. Our sustained anger directed at those perpetrators is justified, but some serious inward reflection is also in order. The actions or better, the inactions of the United States Government invited the attacks.

Let there never, ever be a mistake in believing that the perpetrators of this attack were a gang of loners. They are part of a centuries old world-wide fascist empire building conspiracy and they were working with the full support of a vast organization that included nation states such as Afghanistan's Taliban, and the government of and with the knowing assent and support of the house of Saud - Saudi Arabia, Iran, and others. Not only did these murderous Mohammedans receive support from outside of the United States, they were aided and abetted by like minded supporters right here, in the United States. None of the local or federal police or intelligence organizations have been able to or in some cases been allowed to publicly identify all of those supporters or to take action against them. We ought to ask why....

Betrayal

My rage was and is directed at and beyond those devoted Moslem perpetrators of that horror. I am also furious with those who enabled this.

What I realized that morning was the result of a profound failure of the public trust, an abject failure of responsible elements of the United States Government to even have an inkling of or foreknowledge of the attacks. Combating terrorism and protecting the American people is a federal responsibility. Someone (a lot of someones) had been grossly and irresponsibly, negligent, and a decade later, things have not really changed.

Led by the Central Intelligence Agency (CIA), the national security and intelligence community had utterly and dismally failed the American people.

That betrayal of the public trust cost 3,052 innocent civilians their lives on September 11, 2001. That failure of the public trust has and continues, and will continue to cost more lives for a long time to come.

As we move forward, much has been being said about the failures of the CIA (and FBI) and how to make their job easier, etc (how about more effective?). Among the changes are elimination of a stupid rule virtually prohibiting the CIA from exploiting and using as human intelligence sources nasty people probably guilty of illegal acts. That is one element that deserves thoughtful, considerate, intelligent change - something I suspect that is a challenge for our politicians and leaders to address.

Another element of the failure is the dismal communications between the CIA and the FBI, and the FBI and others which existed for decades, and probably continues to this very day. This has been brought up by others, and while some improvement is claimed, let's hope that this can be truly improved.

A third and vitally important element has not yet been mentioned. I doubt that the CIA in particular as well as anyone else in authority is even aware of this weakness. Some readers will be unable (or unwilling) to comprehend the meaning of the problem, but until this is addressed as well as other critical weaknesses, the CIA and others will continue to fail. One short-term CIA boss (Director, Central Intelligence) in Porter Goss was a step in the right direction. It's too bad that he fizzled. Dozens of senior CIA officials resigned whining about Goss' broom and cudgel approach to his new job. Hell, the CIA was ineffective due to its very inept leadership and mismanagement. What did those jokers expect? Did they want the new DCI to continue with the status quo of letting those inept morons run the ship further aground?

An example of CIA moronic leadership was one of those given the boot by Porter Goss, AB "Buzzy" Krongard who believed that it was better off for the U.S. to NOT capture or kill Osama bin Laden. Krongard expressed his belief that a power struggle within al Qaeda would bring about an unleashing of a string of terror as terrorists vied for the top leadership position to fill bin Laden's void. This, from the third highest ranking CIA official! What an utterly and foolishly total moron! What did this dipwad think was going to happen when bin Laden eventually dies of kidney failure or old age? He ignored the fact that thousands of sociopathic terrorists have tried to either emulate or to impress their idol, bin Laden with their 20,000+ acts of imperialistic Islamic terrorism since 9/11. And, this guy, Krongard, was hired by George Tenet, a great self-promoter, but who was otherwise not able to rub many genus brain cells together. How stupid can a senior official be? Krongard should never have even been considered.

Once upon a time people with a university degree had actually received an education, credentials, expertise, and were thus capable of independent critical thinking. Perhaps this holds true in some areas, but increasingly so-called intellectuals are really quite the opposite, especially in higher levels of government, the media, and academia. They are often ignorant, irrational, but politically correct dopes who are unfortunately lacking in genuine competence, morality, and character.

Charles J. Hanley of the Associated Press filed a report telling that a prominent terrorism researcher saw potential for endless war. OK so far. Then, this researcher, an ex CIA analyst opined that by invading Iraq, the United States took a big step backward, claiming that we're now at the point where jihad is self sustaining. It's good that this guy was broomed out as a part of Porter Goss' housecleaning. If after his reported decade of being an "expert", he had yet to discover that imperialist Mohammedan conquest -- jihad has been ongoing for fourteen hundred years. He needed to be "broomed" out the door. Another CIA so-called expert "broomed" out was a Lord Chamberlain type of quisling who had headed the CIA's bin Laden unit for nearly a decade and who claimed that the only way to appease (yes, appease, just like Chamberlain did with the Nazis) the imperialistic Mohammedists is for the United States to abandon Israel, and sever ties with Arab oligarchs. The report included reference to Bruce Hoffman, a veteran RAND Corp specialist who correctly refuted Administration claims of al-Qaeda's back having been broken. However, Hoffman reportedly joined with other "experts" claiming that we need to address underlying causes by improving economies, political rights, and education in Moslem countries. I agree: Improved political and civil rights regardless of gender or religious affiliation along with real (as opposed to Mohammedist) education, freedom of choice, and inculcating other civilized values will help work to cure economic problems. Such, however is not THE cure.

These guys have been a total waste of taxpayer money. We need hard headed, honest people who understand the dark, murky depths of Islam. Then, we can begin to deal with Islamic fascist terrorism.

Every day, bin Laden is being held up by thousands of Imams, Mullahs, politicians, hacks, teachers, and so forth as an icon, an idol to be emulated, as someone who could command the killing of thousands with impunity. His face is on every recruiting poster, CD, video, and whatever else is used to recruit jihadists desirous of killing Americans. Contrary to the Bush (43) administration's self aggrandizing but phony claims, al-Qaeda has, like a hydra, grown, morphed, and prospered. Al Qaeda is a capillary network organization that is resilient, diverse, and very dangerous. Their recruits have gone to Iraq where they have been trained, gained experience, built relationships, created additional cells, and are preparing to move on when the time comes to ever greater and bigger things. Saudi officials admitted that over 2,500 Saudis went to Iraq, and like the Americans, after serving for a while they are recycled back to Saudi Arabia (or other places) for their onward and upward assignments, etc.

President Bush said, and repeated again and again the fact that the United States is involved in a protracted war against the organized use of imperial terrorism, and that the solutions will be neither quick nor easily obtained. Cabinet officers correctly echoed this at every opportunity, because we, the American people need to become better informed and prepared for this deadly and vitally important effort. This is the greatest challenge America has ever faced and if we fail, the alternatives are not good. [Within weeks of being installed in Washington, the "blame America first" Barak Hussein Obama gang declared that the war on terror was over, an indication of their capitulation, or worse, joining those who want to destroy America.]

American authorities from the federal to the state and local levels continue to make pronouncements aimed at reassuring us that all is well. They issue comforting statements about their preparedness to deal with emergencies, etc. They are either lying and know it, or like a trusting President Bush regarding the Weapons of Mass Destruction in Iraq, are being misled by liars.

Jihad

Many on the other side, the Islamic side, of this conflict see this as a continuation of the continuing fourteen centuries' world wide imperial holy war against civilization and the Christian West. Religion has been a part and parcel of many if not most world conflicts, and will continue to be so in this conflict because religion plays an important role on both sides. So, yes, in a sense it is a religious war.

There has in fact been a world-wide civil war going on between the minority modernizing wing of Islam and the majority primitives of imperialistic Islam. The modernizing side is losing, fast.

The conflict is also cultural. It is the mostly civilized western society that we know vs. primitive but powerful and controlling elements of a less developed and willfully backward Islamic culture.

Christians have been involved in many conflicts, both ancient, and in modern history, and throughout these conflicts, many have involved wars with or against Mohammedans.

However politicians try to couch and want to minimize it, this conflict is between the civilized western culture dominated on one side by forward looking Judeo/Christian ideals, decency, laws, humanity, and ethics, and on the other a dark, primitive, vulgar, brutal, repressive and deceitful Arab culture dominated by Mohammedans bent on imposing their will over the whole world. There are pockets of decent moderates (educated, sensible, reasonable, and responsible) in the midst of the Islamic culture but they are a diminishing few who are vulnerable to intimidation and even death.

Moslem, defined

A Moslem, an Islamist, or a Mohammedan is one who adheres to and worships the system established by Mohammed. A Moslem is a person who follows the Koran and Hadiths, and abides by Sharia law. Some use the word Muslim, which is the same as Moslem, just different spelling. Nobody seems to be able to make up their mind as to which spelling to use, not even Moslems or Muslims. Mohammedan or

Muhammedan is an accurate term for a devout fundamentalist follower of, and one who patterns his life after Mohammed. Islamist is a polite term for a Mohammedan, both are militant. I use the two throughout this text.

In all sincerity, I believe that there are very few truly secular or nonsectarian Moslems. In my determination, a secular Moslem is one who fell to his knees on 9/11 and wept tears of anger and frustration, and directed his or her rage towards those evil devotees of Mohammed who perpetrated this outrage (and thousands of other hateful outrages every day). A secular Moslem has genuine honor, a sense of ethics, morality, and integrity. A secular Moslem is rare. My anger directed at Moslems does not include the few truly decent and good secular Moslems.

GOD is indeed great!

A message to the Arab/Moslem World: God is great. God is wonderful. God has lovingly and generously bestowed his greatest blessings on the United States of America. God has made the United States become the mightiest and wealthiest nation in the world, the greatest nation of goodness, charity, religious and political freedom, decency, and honor on earth. Yes, I give thanks to God for all of those wonderful blessings.

There is only one God by whatever name we mere mortals use in our confused and insignificant tongues.

The one true, living God is indeed great!

God is God, and allah is allah. The two are NOT the same.

President George W. Bush

I praise President Bush in his dealing with the 9/11 attacks. He demonstrated leadership by taking the responsibility of dealing with enemies of the United States.

Conversely, I shudder at the thought of what our response would have been with someone as inept as the impeached Clinton or as feeble as Carter (or John Keary). None of these had or would countenance a strong cabinet of capable, competent people, and neither could they have taken appropriate action. Early indications from Obama were that he planned to capitulate early to Islam in accordance with his Islamist beliefs. Does this reflect the unaccounted for millions of dollars in political donations that came from the Middle East? Obama has affirmed in many ways including bowing to Moslem royals, slips of the tongue (?), and several clear statements that he is Moslem.

During his first major overseas trip to a G20 meeting in London, Barak Hussein Obama bowed down deeply in an obeisant manner and seemed to genuflect as he supplicated himself before the Saudi royal disciple of evil. I felt betrayed, violated by this indecently shameful act by an elected American President. (I am proud that I did not vote for him, and actively supported those opposed to him.) Later, in Istanbul, Obama contemptuously claimed (a false claim) that the United States is not a Christian nation, nor a Jewish nation, nor a Moslem nation. What utter poppycock! Obama does not deserve to be President of the USA, and for me he is less than honorable, decent, or patriotic. I am proud to be an American, but I am terribly ashamed of this jerk in the White House. I note without pleasure that those who voted for him are discovering the meaning of buyers' remorse, and will unfortunately experience it much more before Obama's term expires.

Now that I've said that, President Bush, and the Bush family relationships with the Saudis was incestuous. It would seem clear enough to some that he may simply have declared war on Iraq for personal reasons, or just to please his Saudi pals (or possible paymasters) who felt threatened by Saddam Hussein.

Bush's presidency could have been better, and he has been blamed for every failure of government during his tenure, even when he was not culpable

Barak Hussein Obama

Early in 2009, it was too soon for some to tell about Barak Hussein Obama who took great strides to deflect charges that he is ineligible for the Presidency and to block access to information that would clarify the issue. By hiring teams of lawyers and spending tons of money to block that information, it was clear to rational people with any level of cognitive skills that his eligibility to take the seat of the President was more than merely questionable. Seyyed Obama flim-flammed the American people into electing him.

Id did not take long for a few oppositional patriots to quickly grow to more than half of the American population.

Seyyed Obama received millions of dollars in political donations from out of the country. Every dollar of these donations is questionable, and the Federal Election Commission has been cowed into not even investigating a portion of these donations. Reportedly Obama received over three hundred million dollars from the Middle East (Saudi Arabia via Pakistan, etc.) that nobody wants to talk about. This is worse than fishy. What is Obama obliged to do in return for these hundreds of millions of illegal, or questionable at best donations? Obama will fulfill those obligations in ways detrimental to the welfare of the USA and American citizens. Elsewhere in this book, I address the mastermind of the 9/11 attacks, and the treasonous role Obama is playing to get KSM sprung from the grips of justice.

Obama's Moslem familial ties, and his personal Islamic history rightfully cause clear thinking Americans great concern. His Islamic education, along with his pre-election statement to the effect that when things got bad between the Arabs and Israelis, he would automatically side with the Moslems. This anti-Semitic attitude is disconcerting. B. Hussein Obama condemned the only functioning democracy and genuinely civilized nation in that part of the world. Would he do the same in a Christian vs. Moslem conflict? I believe he would side with the Moslems against Christians just as Clinton did in the Balkans.

Barak Hussein Obama's 'spiritual mentor' for over twenty years, 'Reverend' Jeremiah Wright was or remains a Moslem. Reportedly he rarely even referred to Christ in his many sermons. Wright is clearly anti-Semetic, and anti-American and an uncompromising racist. He referred to God, as in: 'god damn America!' With this understanding combined with any reasonable understanding of Islam and Islamic strategies, I suspect that Wright's references to 'god' in his sermons was just using the word 'god' deceptively as a substitute for allah.

Obama's appointments to important national security positions during his first one hundred days showed a very clear bias towards Islam. About 15% of those appointments were reportedly Moslems or Islam supporters, clearly America haters, and clearly a disproportionate representation of the American population. His other appointments further established that his presidency would be little more than a Jimmy (Cracker) Carter disaster.

If things get tough between non-Moslems and Moslems here, in the United States, will he side with the Moslems? That seems likely. Subsequent to his election, video clip after video clip surfaced showing him proudly proclaiming his status as a Moslem, one who despises America and the American people.

With his getting elected in November of 2008, many patriotic Americans and their private organizations started moving underground out of legitimate concern that Obama may loose his own jack booted thugs and goons (led by his lackies, Eric Holder and the rogue, Janet Napolitano) on honest, non-criminal, civilized, decent families who are patriotic and concerned about America's future as a civilized nation.

Barak Hussein Obama's first 100 days were predictive of what his tenure will bring upon America:

-Go soft on terrorists and even reward enemies of America.

-Shoveled a massive stimulus plan through the congress. Billions of those dollars were pure payola to those who pulled whatever stunts they could to get him elected, including Moslems (millions in undisclosed donations) who are pulling his strings as they collect.

-Appointed more liars, criminals, and cheats than any other chief executive.

-Tried to appoint discredited former Senator Daschle to Health. Daschle was to implement Obama's national medical plan which had as its first point amassing all medical information on every American into one central database. Obama's Daschle had declared that health-care reform would not be pain free; and that senior citizens should be more accepting of the

conditions that come with age instead of treating them. That was clearly an announcement that euthanizing people to save money would be an important part of Obama's fascist system.
-Broke his promise to bring our soldiers home from Iraq in a short time. He decided to leave 50,000 troops there.
-Pledged a billion dollars to Gaza (Hamas).
-Humiliated British Prime Minister Brown. He brought great humiliation on the American people and great personal shame on himself when he bowed, scraped, and nearly prostrated himself before the Saudi king.
-Condemned actions taken by insurers and banks that he had earlier encouraged to take the very actions that ruined the American economy; and who paid substantial contributions (protection money) towards his various campaigns.
-Had his homeland security chief launch a hunt for American citizens such as decorated war veterans, religious conservatives, activist patriots, gun owners, and others to list as potential terrorists.
[Based on various reports, lists (medical records, patriots, war heroes, etc.), and so forth, the Obama crew is assembling a list of people to euthanize if they get ill, to deny medical care and other rights and benefits for political reasons, deny rights to travel for ideological reasons, etc., as he assembles his fascist empire.]

NEVER NEGOTIATE WITH TERRORISTS
President Ronald Reagan

Retired USAF General Richard Hawley succinctly pointed out: "Limp, panicky, half measures lead to more violence." "However, complete, fully thought through professionally well educated violence never leads to more violence because you see, afterwards, the other guys are all dead."

Chapter 1

A Short Background and History

Born during World War Two (W.W.II), I was too young to be aware of the involvement of two uncles and an aunt in the armed forces during that war. I didn't understand that going shoeless during the summer was because of rationing – so that my single parent mother could 'shoe' me during winter.

My first awareness of a "world" beyond my little boy's world was when I didn't finish a dinner and was admonished: "Think of all of the starving children in China! Clean your plate!" My response suggesting that my cold peas be sent to those children was not well received, and that plate of cold, drying peas appeared before me every day until I ate them.

Later, another uncle went away during the Korean War. My mother and I lived in the same house with her parents and this uncle. He was just ten years older than I and when he went off, I really missed him.

I was taught to hate and fear the "Reds", the "Commies", and the "Gooks". And, Jap, Kraut, and Chink were a part of this youngster's crude learned vocabulary.

In elementary school, we had A-bomb drills where we were taught to crawl under our desks for protection, etc. I learned to identify the symbols for nuclear fallout shelters and other related stuff considered important to survival. This was before I could read.

I never learned then why the Russian and Chinese Communists hated us. All I knew was that America was good, so "they" were necessarily bad. The "Commies" and the "Reds" were the enemy. Alcohol besotted right wing Republican fanatic, Joe McCarthy caused terror in the minds of many decent people during his witch hunts for Communists.

Later, in ninth grade, circa 1957 when I was about fourteen years old, I had a teacher, Mr. Simmons, who passionately tried to teach me (and the other kids) about the big, wide world -- the not so amicable world out there beyond Northeast Minneapolis. He had been a Marine infantryman combatant in Korea and hated the Communists. He was zealous about getting us kids to understand some of the reasons why things were as they were. His objective was to overcome our youthful ignorance and to teach us to be aware of things and he even had the audacity to teach us to actually develop critical cognitive skills. He made us (me) read books such as Orwell's 1984 which (in 1957) scared me silly; THE WAR OF THE WORLDS brought home a realization that Minneapolis wasn't the center of the universe; and THE UGLY

AMERICAN indelibly fixed the understanding in me that stupidity and ignorance can be incredibly hurtful --- a valid reason why some people hate America today, our stupidity and ignorance.

That passionate, caring teacher railed about American soldiers who fought in Korea who didn't know or understanding why they were there doing what they were doing. Because of their ignorance, those who became prisoners of war were susceptible to being easily brainwashed into supporting the Communist North Koreans, Russians, and Chinese; and who did just that after returning after the war. Now, in the face of Islamic advances, far too many Americans are unaware and unable to comprehend that their future, and the future of their children is close to extinction, that their children may soon be slaves, or worse.

I learned to understand. I learned that the (rapidly liberalizing) educational system would fail me (and others) in important ways; that the 'media' as we call it today would not always be truthful or even accurate let alone tell the complete story. I became aware that I would need to find truths by educating myself in many, sometimes unique ways. I did that.

Terrorism

TERRORISM. What is it? A dictionary definition: use of terror and violence to coerce, intimidate, subjugate, etc., especially as a political weapon or policy.

Islamic (Mohammedan) terrorism is all of the above.

There are differing degrees and levels of terrorism that range from school yard bullies to the Taliban of Afghanistan; and from the horrors of the Nazi death camps to America's firebombing of Dresden; and our use of the Atomic bomb to quickly end Japan's war against the United States and our allies thus saving millions of Japanese and allies' lives.

Milder forms of terrorism are applied to intimidate and coerce, such as police issuing traffic tickets to maintain rules of order and safety, building inspectors to assure building safety and durability, and the threat of the authority of the IRS to compel us to pay our taxes.

When I was in first grade, two older boys from a second grade class used to terrorize me by chasing me home from school whenever they saw me. The more I ran away, the more they chased me. If they caught me, I'd get a thrashing.

One afternoon, my mother's cousin was visiting (recuperating from a surgery to repair a WWII wound) and caught me as I breathlessly rushed into the house. He admonished me: "Jimmy, as long as you run away, they'll chase you." "Now, go out there and punch the biggest one in the nose, and after that, they'll leave you alone." He opened the door and pushed me out of the house to face my tormenters. He turned to speak to my mother and they both heard the sound of wood (a 2X4) connecting with a head. Scared shitless and desperate, I had decided that a wood board was an even better equalizer than a fist. The nails on the other end improved on even that.

It was true. Neither of the boys ever chased me again, especially the one who wound up in the hospital with a nail imbedded in his skull........

After that incident got settled, my mother forbade me to fight for years. By fifth or sixth grade, it was well known that I was the Waite Park Elementary School's punching bag. Even kindergartners punched me out.

By the time I entered Edison High School (grades 7-12 at the time), I was getting beaten on too often, and my regularly coming home in tatters became a new issue. I was so terrorized and demoralized by the end of that 7th grade year that I could barely function.

My mother decided that a change of policy was necessary for my survival. Over the summer, she hired a professional boxer, a prize fighter (on parole) to teach me to box. I had three two hour lessons per week, and he first taught me to box -- and then, more. He taught me how to fight mean, nasty, and dirty, and to win.

The second day back at school in the eighth grade, the biggest nastiest terrorist (bully) in the school launched an attack on me. It took three attempts by two teachers before they managed to pull me off of that guy. After he got out of the hospital and his concussion healed enough for him to return to school, he was terrified of me. For the next five years, nobody in that school tried to terrorize me. They were terrified of confronting me even though I never pushed my weight around. The 'history' of my pounding the snot out of the bully (terrorist) sufficed.

I understood that I had no need to "prove" anything to anybody, and thus had no need to bully anyone or pick fights. I was a model student - as regards my citizenship.

Two types of terror were employed. Bad terror - the bully picking on me; and good terror - my eventual pounding the snot out of the bully which caused him to stop bullying.

Immediately after graduating from Edison High School, I enlisted in the NAVY, did my thing in boot camp, was sent to a technical school, and joined the fleet. In boot camp a white boy kicked a black kid in the face in order to establish by terror his superior position. I didn't like it, and I 'neutralized' the bigot by establishing that I was more terrifying than he was.

My first overseas trip aboard the vintage WWII troop transport, the USS General George M. Randall was a poignant introduction to another form of terrorism. We had been (on May 1st, 1961) in a NATO port - Naples, Italy, when a Mayday crowd of rowdy Communist demonstrators came careening down the pier, and we were compelled to cut our lines and steam off.

That Communist led demonstration was an act of terrorism -- intimidation that succeeded in making an American military ship run away. It was my first up close personal exposure to impersonal terrorism. I didn't like it.

Later, I joined the Foreign Service and, in 1966 was assigned to the American Consulate in Istanbul (formerly Constantinople), Turkey. During my more than two years there, I experienced and learned more about terrorism. While not all of it was directed at me on an individual basis - it was more intense and therefore more frightening.

This was my first exposure to a Moslem culture and an Asian society. I took the time and spent the effort to observe, study, digest and sort information, analyze and make determinations, and learn.

Serving in Turkey was one of the greatest and most interesting experiences of my life. I came away understanding that there are (as in every country) Turks who are just wonderful folks, and there are those who are really jerks. I encountered and dealt with both kinds.

Chapter 2

Post World War II Terrorism

Terrorist acts have occurred since the end of world war II. The use of terrorism is an effective tool in maintaining control of elements of societies. Stalin used it in the USSR, often in dealing with rebellious minorities or factions. He used his military to ruthlessly suppress fundamentalists and zealots and to maintain discipline in a huge, sprawling nation.

China uses terror, for the same purposes, to maintain order, and Islam was (and still is) seen as a challenging and disruptive influence. The Chinese have done what the Moslems have done in earlier centuries, ruthlessly wiping out entire populations that were uncooperative, disruptive, and hostile to their established society and culture.

CAR BOMBING

In 1948, Zionist terrorists establishing a modern Jewish state used a car loaded with explosives to blast a hotel in Jerusalem

Former Israeli Prime Minister Menachem Begin was one of those early Irgun Zionist participants in that terrorist event. Lessons were learned from that and copycat Palestinians have used that again and again.

The United States was delivered its first modern car bomb in 1968, when a Citroen sedan loaded with explosives blasted the American Embassy in Saigon, Viet Nam.

TERRORISM'S ESCALATION

I was in Istanbul in 1966-7 when demonstrators against the American involvement in Viet Nam demonstrated. The first Anti-American event was outside of the gates of the American Consulate and we were locked in for a while until the noisy demonstrators calmed and went home.

A few months later, with my car parked on a pier alongside of the Bosphorus, another noisy demonstration occurred. I was out on a boat and expected that I'd never again see my American Chevrolet with distinctive license plates identifying it as American Consular official's car. When we were able to return to the dock hours later, the car was there, unscratched. Nearby, during that demonstration, some Turkish police got stoned and clubbed.

Demonstrations got progressively ugly. A rowdy one developed and when they came by the Consulate we got stoned and many windows were broken. I was caught out during that one, before the mob reached the Consulate. I was in an Embassy Jeep Wagoneer driven by a wise old Turk, Hari. I had some diplomatic pouches and we were headed for the airport when we rounded a corner onto a boulevard and were confronted with the large, passionate mob. At the vanguard of the mob was a large caricature banner of Uncle Sam with President Johnson's face, blood dripping from his fanged mouth, and shredded and bleeding Vietnamese bodies strewn at his feet. The unruly demonstrators, many carrying clubs, were about fifty yards away and moving in our direction. I was in serious trouble. With cars on all sides, there was nowhere to back up or to turn out and drive off.   [[xxxxx this portion has been censored by the Department of State and/or the CIAor the CIA xxxxx]]   ......[[xxxxx this portion has been censored by the Department of State and/or the CIA xxxxx]]   ....[[xxxxx this portion has been censored by the Department of State and/or the CIAxxxxx]]   ......

Hari reached over, mussed my hair and stuck a cigarette in my face, and told me to slouch in my seat and to remain calm, to look like a Turk, to scowl and appear surly. I did as best I could.

Hari got out of the vehicle and spoke to the driver behind us and jumped back into the Wagoneer, and pulled forward, touching the bumper of the car in front of us. The driver behind us came forward and bumped into us. In this manner, Hari got covered or concealed the special Consular license plates identifying the Wagoneer as a diplomatic vehicle.

The ugly mob of several thousand came surging by us and went on.

Hari saved my life right there.

Many people (Turks) were injured during that demonstration, some very seriously.

The Administrative Officer of the Consulate, my supervisor's boss, chewed me out for getting caught up where there was a demonstration. As if I could have done something about it...... He should have rewarded Hari and when I suggested that he do so, the horse's ass just ranted some more.

The Consulate's windows were repaired and wooden shutters were installed to protect the glass windows. Thrown stones bounced off of the shutters during the next couple of demonstrations which were otherwise contained by the police. While some police were banged up pretty badly and some students got killed, we were safe in the Consulate, about two miles from Istanbul University, the center for Istanbul's often violent student unrest.

The office I was in, Communications, was in one of those situations where there was too much work for one person, but not enough for two, so I had leisure time while at work. The Consulate had training funds and I had the opportunity to study Turkish for a couple of hours every day. When out doing my duties, I practiced with the various motor pool drivers, especially Hari. I also got to know some Turks outside of work and would meet with them and practice my Turkish.

Some of these new friends were in fact students at Istanbul University. I asked one of them how he and others could call themselves my friends at the coffee house in the evening, and the next day riot outside of the Consulate. The response was that they really did like me, and even liked most Americans as far as that went, but were hostile to America's policies towards the third world.

I awoke on a June (1966) morning and my radio, tuned in to the British Broadcast Corporation (BBC) announced that the Arabs had attacked Israel. [Like most Americans that I knew, I almost always listened to the BBC for prompt news. The Voice of America was lousy.]

My Israeli neighbor, Ari stopped by on his way to the airport and asked me to keep an eye out for his wife while he was away. A Major in the Israeli army reserves, he was being called home to defend his nation. Turkish police stationed themselves outside of our apartment buildings, and Ari's wife and child were safe throughout without my intervention.

American Embassies throughout the Middle East under attack by mobs were being evacuated as all hell broke loose. For a few days, I found myself living at the airport with a rented furniture van. Whenever a plane landed, I would race over to see if an American Diplomatic courier was on board, and if so, I gathered up their many diplomatic pouches for transfer to another courier headed towards a safer place, or the pouches were to be hauled back to the Consulate for storage. Later, I would sort and forward or return those pouches which contained all of the most important and sensitive secrets of most of the American Embassies throughout the Middle East.

Turkey did not involve itself in the 1967 Middle East war. I was told once, by a knowledgeable American that when the Turks were asked by the Syrians (who got whupped early) to join in, the Turks reportedly responded that if they sent forces over their borders, the purpose would be to re-establish the Ottoman empire, not fight with the Israelis. That threat sent the terrified Syrians (and others) running with their tails between their legs.

When I asked my Turk friends about this, I was told bluntly that Turks are Turks, not Arabs and the only thing they had in common with Arabs was their religion. The Turks did not and do not like Arabs. The Turks dislike Americans, British, Germans and the French, and a few others, including one-another. The Turks hate just about everybody else. If one is merely disliked by the Turks, one is seemingly in a position of favor...... However, being brothers in Islam, the Turks will do whatever they can to further the Mohammedan cause.

TURKS AND JEWS

During the Spanish Inquisition, the Sultan extended an invitation to all of the world's Jews to come to and to live in the Ottoman Empire in (dhimmitude) peace forever. Of course, that peace was on Moslem terms. The Turks therefore have no serious gripe with the Jews so long as they understand and keep their place.

Following the collapse of the Ottoman Empire after World War One, the great Turkish leader, Kemal Attaturk, dragged Turkey into the twentieth century kicking and screaming every inch of the way. He outlawed the fez, the turban, and the veil. He converted the language to the Latin alphabet, dressed Turks in western garb, and assured women the vote. Attaturk also established a secular government based on a constitution respectful of law, which until recent years has been jealously protected by a powerful military. My old friend, Betty Carp played an influential role in Attaturk's circle of advisors. She was more than just an advisor, and she described to me some of her and Kemal's midnight horseback rides along the Bosphorous in Istanbul.

Recently, the Mohammedans have gained sway, and the relative peace (on Moslem terms) and dignity accorded to their non-Moslem minorities are rapidly being eroded. The only thing protecting those minorities today is the fact that the Turks are seeking entry into the European Union. If and when this fails, or even succeeds, the minorities' situations will ultimately deteriorate.

ESCALATING VIOLENCE

Towards the end of my assignment to Istanbul the violence directed at us Americans had escalated. Molotov cocktails started being used and they burned the wooden shutters on the building, which were then upgraded with light metal shutters. Subsequent escalations led to drive by shootings at the Consulate and the light metal shutters got holes blown through them.

This was not unique to just Istanbul. It was happening all over the Middle East where Moslem passions were running strong.

In subsequent years the light metal shutters (Embassies and Consulates all over the Middle East) were replaced by steel plate shutters and armored glass, and heavy guns and rocket launchers were brought into play and, forget about the steel plate shutters and bullet proof windows, these bigger weapons were used to blast holes in the walls of embassies. Satchel bombs were tossed into lobbies and other more nasty and more powerful weapons of terror were employed, ultimately escalating to powerful car and truck bombs. Terrorists actually preferred Chevrolet Suburbans, or medium Mercedes trucks which are reliable and sturdy enough to haul a ton or more of high explosives.

The rule has been one of escalation. Whatever terrorists have done, we have responded with escalated levels of security. The terrorists have simply escalated their levels of violence, sophistication, and deadliness.

As we hardened certain targets and reduced their vulnerability, the terrorists in turn sought softer targets and new opportunities to spread their violent, hateful devotion to Islam. While Embassies (targets) in close proximity to the Middle East core became hardened, the ones geographically more remote were left less protected, and became new "soft" targets. Thus, the congressionally mandated vulnerable Embassies in Dar-Es-Salaam and Nairobi remained vulnerable, and were later successfully targeted by Al Qaeda.

Well funded, and growing in numbers (Saudi funded Madrassas preparing and recruiting thousands for jihad), these hard core Moslem terrorists have expanded, and continue to expand.

Not since our wars with the British, Mexicans, and Japan has the United States been so viciously attacked on our own soil. Not during World War I. Not during the Korean or Vietnamese wars. Not during the Cold War.

Now, however, the expanding ideology of Islam has come onto, has invaded the shores of the United States, and killed innocent defenseless Americans. Attacking the Taliban and whupping Saddam is not the end of this conflict. Those acts have just caused the Mohammedans to move around and regroup, to develop new plans.

American laws and institutions protect these murderous terrorists even as they strive to destroy us. The United States has become a nation that foolishly tolerates the intolerant even as they work to enslave and destroy us. Will we be tolerant unto our own demise?

We need as a nation, as a civilized society to become less tolerant of radicals and murderous zealots regardless of their ideological Islamic foundations. Their goal is to take away all of our freedom and to impose their harsh and intolerant will on the American people.

Chapter 3

MY EARLY INVOLVEMENT IN THIS
COUNTER TERRORISM THING

I did not get heavily involved in the protective aspect of this stuff during my early years in the Foreign Service, in Turkey, or at my subsequent assignment in Belgium.

The Central African Republic

My third Foreign Service assignment, in 1971, was at the American Embassy in Bangui, the Central African Republic, a remote, isolated place few have heard of.

There were nine of us Americans at the Embassy. In Bangui, there were three American business people, and the remainder of the Americans were a few dozen missionaries. The missionaries were of two camps, the first were what I'd consider moderates, whose mission was to educate, improve health, and convert to Christianity. The other group was similarly focused, but were intolerant of any Americans who didn't adhere to their narrow values.

Keep on Truckin!

The Ambassador's residence had a nice pool that the Ambassador permitted the staff to use. Taxpayer funded, it was about the only recreation available to us. My ambassador's predecessor had permitted the missionaries to use the pool on Sundays, and the intolerant conservatives had taken over.

My Ambassador enjoyed his Sundays and liked to spend them at the pool's side while he read his month old New York Times' and Washington Post, and sipped on a martini or two.

He found that he could not comfortably do this with the disapproving glares of those tetotalling missionaries glaring at him and had to retreat into his house for his martini/s.

Being somewhat rowdy and non-conformist in those days, I showed up at the pool one Sunday sporting a new tee-shirt I had just received. It was one of those 1970's things with bright colors, an illustration of an overly endowed jiggly lady in an undersized tank top and a man with his eyes bugging out of his skull. The inscription read: Mother trucker! Keep on Truckin! I ignored the missionaries and had my relaxation and fun.

The next morning, a delegation of disapproving missionaries came to the Embassy, to my supervisor, a worldly and perceptive guy. They came, of course, to complain about my T-shirt, and when he pressed them to clarify their objections, they claimed the inscription, "Mother trucker", was offensive and obscene. He asked what was wrong with motherhood and trucks? They responded that the phrase could be mispronounced and then mean something "dirty". He again asked what was or could be dirty about motherhood, while he agreed that trucks could get muddy.

Those missionaries wanted him to forbid my wearing that T-shirt, and he responded that I had First Amendment rights and he was not about to forbid me from anything not illegal. Unsatisfied, they left, and made an appointment to see his boss, the Deputy Chief of Mission (DCM) the next day.

The DCM was a fine, sober man who attended church regularly with the missionaries. He discussed this issue with my boss and the Ambassador, and the result was that he reluctantly affirmed my First Amendment rights to the missionaries. The unhappy missionaries, still pursuing the issue, made an appointment with the Ambassador, which took place two days later.

The Ambassador, the DCM, and my boss all discussed the issue (my boss kept me informed of all proceedings - he was having fun), and when the missionaries came to meet with the Ambassador, he sent them home with the promise that he would discuss this now infamous T-shirt with me.

When they had left, he summoned me to his office, where he, the DCM and my boss were. He recounted the previous days' proceedings and then the DCM and my boss left. The Ambassador explained how he really liked sipping his martinis poolside, and that my T-shirt presented just that opportunity, and he asked me to please wear it at the pool every Sunday.

He fulfilled his promise to the missionaries to discuss my T-shirt with me, and I happily complied with his request. Outraged and offended, the missionaries stayed away and we enjoyed our Sundays much more. (The American embassy operated on a six-day workweek in Bangui.)

The American missionaries had attempted to impose their will on me and others - to intimidate (terrorize) us into complying with their wishes and conforming to their view of things.

Ultimately, they were so terrified of my exercising my First Amendment rights supported by the Ambassador that they quit coming around altogether.

Their intolerance and hostile actions backfired.

Had they come to me directly and asked in a civilized manner, I probably would have cooperated with their request. They didn't.

ENGLISH SPEAKNG

We Americans were the only English speaking people to have an embassy in Bangui. Nobody else cared.

Heck, there were not many other embassies in Bangui. The French maintained an embassy there in their former colony, of course. The Soviet Union and Communist Chinese were present as well as a few others, including the Israelis.

Six months into my assignment, a Palestinian contingent appeared. A few families came to Bangui, rented houses, and threw us and the Israelis in to a tizzy. The Palestinians were mostly able bodied young men who were "traders". But there was no business for them, and no obvious means of gainful employment. We buttoned up on our security at the American Embassy and I worked on re-enforcing the communications vault, where I worked. The Israelis really got serious about their security too. Just for fun, I got involved with them and suggested a capacitive discharge type (livestock) fence charger, and gave them a catalog where their Washington embassy could get the items and forward them in their diplomatic pouch. The Israeli Embassy staffers added a wire fence atop of their seven foot high wall along with the charger. Within weeks, one of the Palestinians got jolted and knocked silly late one night, and returned to Palestine with a leg in a cast.

I got my payback. A package of documents was delivered to President Bokassa containing forged documents indicating a plot to kill him (Bokassa) and that I was the designated assassin. After a couple of tense weeks while we worked to disprove the report, everything settled down. That package was a form of terrorism.

When I was preparing to leave at the end of my assignment, one of the Palestinians approached me to purchase my stereo system. It was a nice component system that included a short wave receiver. We agreed on a price and he gave me a down payment, promising to pay the rest later.

Each week for about six weeks, I checked with him, and he promised to pay soon.

After I had packed all of my effects and they had been shipped, I reminded him again, and he promised to pay the day before I was to leave.

On the morning before my departure day, he promised to pay me the following morning just before I departed. I agreed. I then opened the stereo amplifier and removed a couple of strategic transistors, moved a couple of capacitors and resistors around, took a vital part out of the turntable, some pieces out of the tape deck, and more out of each speaker, rendering everything useless, and then packed the components neatly in their original cartons. I kept those components in a little baggie.

In the morning, this lying Arab called to tell me that he was tied up, but would come to the airport with the money before I left, but would I please let his 'brother' pick up the system. "Reluctantly", I agreed.

When I arrived at Le Bourget airport in Paris, I dumped the vital components in the trash as I exited the airport. The Arab had a worthless stereo system.

Korea

From Bangui, I was assigned, in 1973, to Korea for a four year assignment. The American Embassy in Seoul was a large Embassy in a very secure environment where Embassy security was not a great issue as far as anti-American terrorists were concerned. I loved Korea, but my assignment was cut short because of my involvement in a complex brouhaha (another story), and I was transferred to Cambodia in 1974.

Cambodia

In Phnom Penh, I worked in the Embassy's Communications Section as the Code Room supervisor for a while until one day when the Embassy's Maintenance Officer, following a close call with an incoming rocket decided to retire, that very day.... He told people that he was retiring and was gone within a couple of days.

Over the next couple of weeks, three different people were assigned to replace him in the Maintenance job in Cambodia. All three retired rather than take on the assignment.

I asked for the job as part of a career mobility program. The request was approved and I found myself closing the Embassy Code Room one night, and opening the Maintenance Office in the morning.

Within hours I was really immersed in physical security. We were finishing up on a program to "harden" the Embassy lobby. All windows and the interior access doors were about three inches thick using layers of Lexguard and safety plate glass mounted in really heavy steel frames.

Always loving a challenge, I became a quick study in ballistics and concluded that a satchel charge in the lobby could still cause a lot of hurt. So, I modified the heavy windows facing the street placing special hinges in strategic places; and even removed parts of the brick wall and replaced them with hard packed sand. My reasoning was that a bomb going off inside of the lobby, like gasoline in an automobile engine's combustion chamber would create lots of pressure needing someplace to vent. Rather than let the pressures work like pushing a piston down (or a door in, or a ceiling up), I established high pressure exhaust points (the light window hinges and sand packed holes in the wall) to give blast pressures an easy exit.

The Embassy was an old French colonial building six stories tall. With very high ceilings on each floor, it was about eighty feet to the top of the roof. The tall Embassy was an easy target for rocket propelled grenades (RPGs).

RPG's detonate on contact, and when one hits a window or an old, not too sturdy mortar wall, they can cause a lot of damage, and people on the other side will suffer terribly.

We fashioned framework and installed a chain link fence sloping from the roof top all of the way down to the ground in some areas, and in layers in other areas. Basically any RPG would thus make its first contact with the chain link fencing and blow up, splattering its shrapnel against the walls and shuttered or ballistic windows.

The Khmer Rouge were also firing a lot of 107MM rockets into town. These are great weapons of terror. They are easily transported on the back of a porter; one porter, one rocket. They can be set up, propped against two pieces of bamboo and are ignited by a flashlight battery. As strategic weapons they suck as they can not be reliably targeted or counted on to strike a given target smaller than two or three football fields in size.

With their contact fuses, they can detonate when striking a twig in a tree and splatter shrapnel all over the place. When enough are fired off, sooner or later they will hit something, as was evident with a gapping hole in the wall of the former American Embassy not too far distant.

If one indiscriminate 107MM rocket chanced to come down on the Embassy's roof, very serious damage to its vital classified communications systems would occur and lots of Americans could be killed.

So, we installed a series of false roofs over the top of the Embassy. The first was sheet metal on which the falling rocket would, with its contact fuse, detonate. The second layer down was steel plate against which the shrapnel would splatter, and the real roof (and the people inside of the building) would thus be protected.

I learned a great deal about ballistics, about sandbagging things, and building bunkers. I had had a rapid on-the-job training course where I could ascertain results quickly if not immediately. I built a bunker in every occupied bedroom of every house or apartment that Embassy American staff lived in. I put huge, oversized, ugly ballistic metal roof racks on motor pool vehicles, so the raining shrapnel from rockets hitting trees wouldn't come through the roof or windows and kill someone.

I bunkered an inside storage area in the warehouse (away from the Embassy) where I had my office. The area I bunkered was where we stored hundreds of tanks of propane that we used for cooking fuel at our staff housing. My purpose was to direct any possible blast away from where we had people and offices in that warehouse. Reportedly, this propane supply was struck by an artillery round after we Americans left, and that a pieces of the warehouse landed on the western bank of the Ton Le Sap (Mekong) river, about two miles from the warehouse's location.

By the time we Americans pulled the plug and ran away from Cambodia, I was eating, sleeping, and dreaming bunkers and ballistics. One might say I had become an expert.

Emergency planning

Every American Embassy has what is called an Emergency and Evacuation (E&E) Plan. It is a comprehensive plan detailing levels and sources of threats against the Embassy, stages of awareness, along with available resources both in the Embassy, in the country, and in the region, etc. It is reviewed and updated by Embassy officials every year and certified by the Ambassador. Every four years it is supposed to be substantially revised taking into consideration changes in threats, technology, governments, attitudes, and much more.

There are good plans and not-so-good plans.

There are good officers and Ambassadors who do their jobs responsibly, and there are officers and Ambassadors who fail.

The American Ambassador in Saigon, Vietnam, in 1975 refused to do his job in spite of what his staff advised. Officials at the State Department and other agencies in Washington didn't have the courage to override the Ambassador who in fact refused to plan.

When the stuff hit the fan in Saigon, the Embassy was ill prepared to deal with the emergency. The result was a disaster with terrified mobs assaulting the Embassy, terrified refugees being blown off of the wings of sky bound airplanes, and so much that is abundantly documented.

The Ambassador's poodle took priority over desperate people on the aircraft when the Ambassador finally turned tail and fled.

A stupid jackass of an Ambassador refusing to accept reality and plan cost thousands of people their lives and freedom, and the credibility of the United States suffered another unneeded setback.

In Cambodia, next door to Vietnam, the situation was different. We were a smaller Embassy and contingent. Everyone was familiar with our E&E plan and each understood their role if and when the stuff hit the fan, everyone complied with the plan. Every office was allowed so many lineal inches of classified records holdings. Not, feet, not pounds, lineal inches, and the rule was enforced. Even the Ambassador complied. He didn't consider himself above any rules, even home generator fuel rationing.

When I complained that I wasn't in the equation as regards destruction of the several file cabinets I had of maintenance work orders and contract documents, some people chuckled. That stuff wasn't classified and contained no information of strategic or national security value. When I brought this up with the Ambassador stating my concern: That I felt the Khmer Rouge would kill everyone whose name was listed (several hundred Cambodian workers and contractors, plus correspondence records with hundreds of others such as landlords and utility officials, etc.) in any of our work orders, etc., he agreed and placed my unclassified records in a priority after SECRET and before CONFIDENTIAL documents.

While everyone was relying on fancy electric powered shredders (which did two or three paper clip and staple free pages at a time) and forced air incinerators, I built a crude cage device, referred to as a 'squirrel cage'. In appearance it looked like a giant, elongated exercise wheel such as used in hamster cages, ten feet wide by five feet in diameter, with a twelve foot extension to the handle, and a heat shield to protect those cranking the handle. I used steel bars and angle iron for the framing, and chain linked fencing materials. It had two doors through which an entire file cabinet drawer of documents including accompanying staples, paper clips, and even metal fasteners could be dumped. It permitted lots of air flow and space for the ashes to fall away. I was met with scorn and derision for making it, but when the crunch came, attitudes quickly changed.

We followed the Embassy E&E Plan guidelines and when certain trigger events took place, we reacted.

We sent nonessential American and Cambodian staff off in an orderly manner. This included Cambodian employees who wished to leave, along with their immediate family members.

The Americans in Phnom Penh were a mix of single and many married. Several had Cambodian girlfriends, some live-in. Some were hookers and got paid. Some were more serious relationships. The Ambassador announced in no unequivocal terms that he would not authorize, and in fact forbade using seats on government aircraft (owned, leased, chartered, whatever) to move these "ladies" of the night out of Phnom Penh. There was a lot of grumbling but his orders where his orders. I had been contacted several weeks earlier by an American who had earlier finished his assignment and he asked me to get his former live-in out. I was trying to locate her when the Ambassador's ruling was passed on to me. So, I dutifully gave up on that quest and went about my business.

We even packed and shipped employee personnel effects out, along with pets (including my Doberman), long before the "crunch" came.

When we were certain the Khmer Rouge would soon be upon us, we began destroying documents.

While everyone (officers, secretaries, etc.) with all of their classified documents developed scores of paper cuts removing paper clips and staples and then stood shredding a few sheets at a time, or about two hours per 2' file cabinet drawer, I went on with my home made 'squirrel' cage device. I would unload five drawers into my cage, strike a match, and let it burn, using the handle every couple of minutes to turn the cage once or twice to knock the ashes free and stir the documents. I was able to destroy an entire cabinet (twelve tightly packed lineal feet) of documents in twenty minutes or less, every piece of paper in my section in a few hours, including bound manuals.

By the time I was done, nearly everyone who had ridiculed my 'cage' was standing in line to use it having abandoned their shredders and with bandages on their shredded fingers.

It worked, and was the most effective document destruction device around. It was crude, hot, sooty, and dirty, but it worked extremely well and fast.

The E&E plan was adhered to, and by the time we pulled the plug and bailed out of Phnom Penh, we sent empty helicopters back to the ships. The Khmer Rouge came into the Embassy and found a true paper-free office. Not a scrap was left behind.

After everyone was out of Phnom Penh, and we had all arrived in Bangkok, there remained some money from the Phnom Penh embassy employee commissary and recreational fund. A decision was made to expend it on a party aboard one of the Oriental Hotel's river sight-seeing boats was chartered for the catered event. When I got on the boat for the party, I observed that most of the CIA guys had brought their Cambodian "ladies" with them from Phnom Penh. This, those CIA people had done in direct contravention of the Ambassador's instructions. (Yeah, sure, the CIA chief had declared all of these "ladies" to be intelligence assets, which was patently false.) Clearly, the CIA people believe there was a set of rules for them and another set of rules for the rest of us regular people. That was an outrage, and a lot of people were very, very angry.

Bangladesh

From Cambodia, I was assigned to Dacca (now Dhaka), in Bangladesh, the former East Pakistan. I was there as the Transportation and Supply Officer, and filled in as and when needed in the Contracting, Procurement, and Buildings & Maintenance areas.

The main Embassy was housed in the top two floors of the Adamjee Court, an ancient, five story high building in the center of Dhaka. A feature of the building was its big, open rotunda, about thirty feet across with rooftop skylights that lit the ground floor far below.

Our physical security there was awful, not completely due to bad planning, but the physical facility itself was dismal.

While we had steel gates and locks to secure our portion of the building, the building's rotunda was open from ground floor to domed ceiling, so anyone determined to get to the Embassy offices could, with a grappling hook, climb right on up and in. Or, if acrobatic enough, could simply scale the walls, as happened one night.

My boss, the Administrative Officer, was a wonderful guy. Elderly, he was a tall, robust, white haired, one eyed ex marine with an attitude who hailed from an Irish background. Dubbed "Wild Bill" he was a character, the type of which legends are made and I loved working for him. He let me do my job, he let me get things accomplished. He appreciated me too, because I got things done expeditiously, lots of things, and they were done well, solving a lot of problems, eliminating a lot of his headaches.

After an interloper scaled into the Embassy late one night and assaulted (not with any luck) the Embassy's Marine Guard (who spared the unfortunate screwball his life), "Wild Bill" asked State Department "Security" experts for help in preventing such incidents. Their response was to close in the rotunda using cement. Engineers nixed that because the building lacked the strength to support such an addition -- of several unsupported tons of concrete. "Wild Bill" didn't like this and asked these "Security" experts for more help, and was simply told that the best solution would be to build a new Embassy. With that, the so very professional and concerned 'security' 'experts' got on the next plane and flew off leaving us to fend for ourselves. That new embassy building quip was out of the question without funding from the Congress and a several years long bureaucratic exercise. "Wild Bill" was very unhappy (an understatement) as was everyone else in the Embassy.

After cogitating about that situation for a few days, I went to "Wild Bill" with an idea that had germinated. After explaining my thoughts, "wild Bill" readily agreed. On the following weekend, I brought in a crew of our Bangladeshi maintenance men along with some angle iron, steel rods, welding gear, paint, and ropes. We crafted a frame and a structure, and then laid chain link in place, which a hanging worker, suspended by ropes and pulleys, welded all into place, and we painted it. I designed (cobbled is a more apt term) it in such a way that it actually strengthened the building and the framework supported itself. It worked, blocking access to Embassy spaces, yet allowing light entry, and air to flow.

From the Ambassador on down, everyone was happy, feeling far more secure than before.

Before long, as it happens in the Foreign Service, one of us was transferred off to another assignment. I had only been at Dhaka for a year or so. It was Bill, who had been there for over two years, and he was transferred to the American Embassy at Tehran, Iran.

In the late 1970's, the situation was getting tense with the Islamic fundamentalists strongly against the modern, progressive, civilized government of the Shah. The United States, of course was backing the Shah as we had been since we placed him in power in the 1950's.

Because of our relationship with the Shah, the American Embassy was the target of demonstrations that were increasingly hostile.

"Wild Bill" was the Embassy's Executive Officer -- in charge of administrative and related operational activities, which included supervision of Embassy Security. "Wild Bill" recognized that there were serious problems and asked the Security officials to put together a plan to improve what he believed was a weak, vulnerable security program. They couldn't come up with anything that he was satisfied with.

"Wild Bill" contacted the State Department at Washington, D.C., asking that I be immediately transferred to Tehran and that I be assigned to develop a comprehensive and effective security program. He wanted me right away because he was certain that the existing security plan sucked and that trouble was coming soon.

The Ambassador at Dhaka got wind of "Wild Bill's" request, and moved quickly to squash any consideration of my being assigned to Tehran anytime soon. He refused to allow me to be taken away from his Embassy at Dhaka because there were things needing doing, and he felt I was the only one who could get them done, and done well. So, I remained at Dhaka, even though I had let people know that I was willing to be assigned to Tehran.

As is well known, the Embassy in Tehran was overrun about a year and a half after "Wild Bill" tried to get me to go there to overhaul the Embassy's inadequate security facilities.

Besides having an inadequate protective security program, the Embassy's Emergency and Evacuation (E&E) plan was both inadequate and/or not adhered to (not due to "Wild Bill's efforts). A good E&E plan allows Embassy managers to see troubles coming and take steps to evacuate people in advance of trouble. A good E&E plan would have permitted the Embassy to destroy all of its classified documents. "Wild Bill" didn't get the support (from above) or help (from peers and subordinates) that he needed.

[[xxxxx this portion has been censored by the Department of State and/or the CIA xxxxx xxxxx this portion has been censored by the Department of State and/or the CIA xxxxx xxxxx this portion has been censored by the Department of State and/or the CIA xxxxx xxxxx this portion has been censored by the Department of State and/or the CIA xxxxx xxxxx this portion has been censored by the Department of State and/or the CIA xxxxx xxxxx this portion has been censored by the Department of State and/or the CIA xxxxx xxxxx this portion has been censored by the Department of State and/or the CIA xxxxx xxxxx this portion has been censored by the Department of State and/or the CIA xxxxx xxxxx this portion has been censored by the Department of State and/or the CIA xxxxx xxxxx this portion has been censored by the Department of State and/or the CIA xxxxx]]

Fifty-four Embassy officials were captured and held hostage for 444 days.

When I think of that disaster and that I could have made a difference, I pause to wonder if things might have been very different in Tehran. In fact, I believe deep down in my heart that had I gone to Tehran to work on the security situation (and the E&E Plan), we could have avoided being overrun so easily, having the Embassy staff seized and held as hostages, and the forfeiture of sensitive intelligence resulting in so very much incredible pain, terrible suffering, and the horrible deaths of decent Iranians.

After the hostages were taken and Khomeni took up residence sitting on his ass at the holy city of Quom, I advocated loading several USAF C-141's up with bladders full of fermenting pig manure and urine and then flying them over Khomeni's palace and dumping that pig manure all over. It didn't happen, but my sentiments remain unchanged.

Article

Somewhere along the line, I found an undated article written by one Hossein Askari titled _The U.S. the Muslim World and Iran_. Askari is a proponent of Islam who teaches at George Washington University.

Below, I reproduce his article and include my parenthetical italicized commentary to his statements:

Begin:

Muslims, especially those in the Middle East, attribute many of their problems (dictatorial regimes, regional turmoil and civilizational and economic failure) to the U.S., either because of U.S. actions or inactions. _(Yep, it's all America's fault, we are damned if we do and damned if we don't. The Muslims over there are, of course without fault.)_ This is a region where one Muslim country, Iran, has had national elections that "might" be considered as somewhat free and open to both male and female voters. _(But, the voters had no choice in selecting candidates to vote on.)_ This is a region where real per-capita income has <u>declined</u> while globally it has doubled over the last twenty-five years even though many of the countries have had significant revenues from oil with little work input. Oil revenues have been embezzled _(stolen)_ or squandered, especially on the military; and Iran may be in a position to develop a nuclear bomb and long-range delivery capability. These countries increasingly blame the U.S. for the Palestinian impasse. _(Yep, it's America's fault because we haven't abandoned the only true democracy and civilized nation in the Middle East, Israel, so that the Arabs can slaughter them and steal all of the wealth that Israel has created.)_ The war on terrorism and the invasion of Iraq have exposed the U.S. to criticism of hostility toward Islam and toward Muslims. _(But, it's OK for Moslems to be hostile towards the U.S.)_ The U.S. has become isolated even from its traditional European allies. _(France and Germany's leadership were corrupted by Saddam, and the Spanish readily submitted to dhimmitude after terrorists attacked them. Everyone else seems to feel fine with the U.S.)_ During the fall of 2003, in two General Assembly votes on the Middle East, the U.S. and Israel were on the short end by 144 to 4 and 133 to 4. _(This affirms the level of corruption in the UN.)_ The U.S. and Muslim countries invariably find themselves on opposite sides on high-profile issues. _(There are many other Americans besides I who understand the true meaning, goals, and objectives of Islam.)_ Islam and the U.S. are on a collision course and it sure looks as if the U.S. <u>wants</u> to head towards a clash of civilizations. _(Islam is the one who is the aggressor here, and has been for the past fourteen hundred years, and another clash of Islam and civilization is just an ongoing saga. Moslems like Askari are hysterical because the_

U.S. is refusing to drop to its knees and submit.)
The Elements of a New Approach

 First and foremost, the United States needs a good dose of humility. *(Such as?)* The U.S. cannot afford to be intoxicated by its military and economic power. *(Why not? We've got it, why not use it?)* We cannot alienate and fight the whole world. *Who is alienating whom? By confronting the consummate evil that is Islam, we are winning more friends than we are losing).* We, like other countries have no choice but to function in this world as it is and can only change it by persuasion (and not by confrontation and invasion). *(But, it is OK for Islam to confront and invade, eh?)* Phrases such as "bring 'em on" do nothing to further U.S. interests and only fan the flames. *(So say you.)* Yes, we have the power to change governments, but at what cost and with what future political and economic implications? *(Changing the governments in Germany and Japan after WWII were really a bad deal, eh? Ending the cold war on our terms was a disaster, right?)* We have needlessly created enemies and terrorists with our hubris and with our use of unnecessary feel-good phrases. *(Who attacked the United States on 9/11/01? We are darned well entitled to respond in kind against those who attacked us, and are entitled to say what we mean, too.)* Humility on the part of the U.S. will go further than anything else to win the hearts and minds of average Muslims in Iraq and around the world. *(The greatest humility was after WWII when we created in good faith the UN, which in bad faith has stabbed the U.S. in the back again and again. Winning the hearts and minds of Mohammedans in Iraq and around the world is a distant, lower priority to preserving our civilization.)*

 To regain the respect of the world, the U.S. should disavow regime change and interference in the internal affairs of any country as national policies. *Sorry, pal, but you are wrong. Brutal, inhuman, savage, ugly regimes like the Taliban and Saddam need to be eliminated, and the UN has proven itself useless in taking care of such business. The Tehran regime, one which is so evil that, for example holds to a government policy instituted by Ayatollah Khomeni requiring repeated rapes of female prisoners prior to execution or death and while being interrogated, to assure they go to Hell, has no right to exist. Another thing the Khomeni did was to change the legal age for marriage of women to nine (the age of Mohammed's child bride Aisha), thus legitimizing pedophilia and child rape.)* Regime change is up to the citizens of a country. *(If the poor victims of such evil villains have the wherewithal, they can and do make change, as the countries of the Iron curtain recently did. When they are so badly abused and intimidated that they can't stand up, they need help from civilized countries.)* Independent democratic regimes come about as the result of internal struggle and not from outside intervention. *(A little outside intervention can always help, as did France's help during America's struggle for independence.)* Another problem with regime-change-as-foreign-policy is that, because of its nature, it will be applied selectively and when it is convenient. *(That's a good idea!)* This is the painful reality as seen by Muslims. *(Yes, it is painful when we help some of those most in need, and let others wallow in their well deserved self-pity as we do with the Palestinians.)* To appeal to the Muslim world, the U.S. must be consistent in the conduct of its foreign policy. *(Yeah, we've been a bit inconsistent at times, and that may be regrettable, but that comes with regular free and democratic elections of new presidents on a regular basis.)* It should withhold its support from corrupt undemocratic regimes, which ironically it has not done. *(Agreed, we have unfortunately supported a few undemocratic regimes while we have encouraged them to effect change.)* Only under exceptional circumstances should regime change be adopted and then only by the world community (through the United Nations) to confront egregious regimes. *(Yeah, like the UN has worked to establish regime change in Somalia, North Korea, Cuba, right? Moslem entities within and outside of the USA and the UN are working for regime change in America, too.)* We must stress that, like the UN, we in the U.S. are committed to protecting the territorial integrity of each and every country – those who want to maintain their legitimate borders. This can be an elastic concept. *(The UN claims to be committed to protecting territorial integrity of each country? Taqiyyah! What has the UN done to protect Israel? Zip! Africa has borders not created by themselves, but by the colonial powers of Europe. The concept of borders in Africa ought to be much more elastic.)*

On a related point, we must emphatically state that we will not interfere in the internal affairs of any country and that we will not support corrupt undemocratic rulers. *(Boy, Askari wants us to let evil despots roll on but not support them.)* Even adherence to this simple commitment *(which is after all, what we espouse)* will win us considerable support. *(I bet the North Koreans love and support us for letting them suffer and starve, and the non-Arabs and non-Moslems in the Sudan really support what we've not done for them.)* Ironically, it is for this reason that the Middle Eastern country where the U.S. is most popular is Iran, a country that has had little contact with the U.S. for nearly thirty! *(Sorry, chump, but we get more popular support from Israel, while Iran's government instrument, the Pasdaran controlled Hezbollah has, with the exception of recent events in Iraq, murdered more Americans in the Middle East than any other scumbag outfit.)*

If we want to play a positive role in the Middle East, we must act as an honest broker in the Arab-Israeli conflict. *(We are about the only honest broker in the Arab-Israeli conflict.)* If we cannot do this, we would be better served by a hands-off policy. *(Askari seems to sincerely believe in his twisted, atypical Moslem thinking that we ought to stab the Israeli's in the back to thus be considered an honest broker by Mohammedan terms.)*

Finally, appreciating the synergy of policies is essential. We need a number of simultaneous policy initiatives in order to succeed. At the same time, it is essential that we incorporate the broader ramifications of each and every policy. Tunnel vision is not a viable option. *(That is some gobbledygook - right out of the textbooks. The tunnel that Askari wants to lead the U.S. into is a very narrow, twisted one, indeed.)*

In sum, the U.S. need to do three things to win the hearts and minds of Muslims around the world: promote democracy in the Islamic world (in deed as well as in words), act as an honest broker (Arab/Israel, Iran/Iraq, etc.), and embrace Islam as it does other religions. *(The U.S. has long promoted democracy (along with universal suffrage, freedom of religion, etc.) and we have been repeatedly kicked in the face for our efforts. With the Koran as the instrument of government and law, there is no way that true democracy can be established. The U.S. has been the most honest broker in the Middle East, one of the most back stabbing, treacherous regions on earth where we often get tripped up by those pretending to be our friends. And, the U.S. does permit freedom of beliefs as regards Islam, as it does other cults. The U.S. must never, ever embrace Islam.)*

Why Iran is Key

There are a number of reasons why Iran may afford a unique opportunity for at least a good start in the effort to win the hearts and minds of Muslims and to turn things around in Iraq. If it wishes to engage Iran, the U.S. must pursue rapprochement, as opposed to isolation and containment, as its new policy toward Iran. *(No! Iran must first be an honest broker vis-à-vis Iraq, quit practicing deception as regards its effort to develop nuclear weapons, and quit interfering in Iraq, Afghanistan, and Kurdistan, drop its support for Hezbollah, cease oppressing women and minorities, permit a free press, permit freedom of religious choice, and drop its hostility towards Israel. Then, rapprochement can be considered.)*

Iran's population is larger than the combined population of Bahrain, Iraq, Jordan, Kuwait, Lebanon, Oman, Saudi Arabia, Qatar and the United Arab Emirates. Iran's population is young, with over 50 percent aged eighteen and under. *(It looks like Iran's government has to get its butt going in the right direction to deal with those millions of frustrated, unemployed young people.)* Sandwiched between Afghanistan and Iraq, Iran is strategically located and could play a positive political and economic role as a market for regional exports and for the trans-shipment of oil and gas from a number of former Soviet republics. *(Wishful thinking.)* Iran has vast natural resources, including the second largest gas reserves and the fourth largest oil reserves in the world. *(Agreed.)* With more enlightened economic policies, Iran could become an economic giant in a span of ten years and, as a strong economic partner, it could afford hope to poorer Muslim countries. *(Iran needs enlightenment in more than economic policies. What has Iran done for poorer Moslem countries over the past three decades?*

46

Nothing! What did Iran do for Indonesia after the tsunami? Nothing! Iran needs to remain isolated until it decides to behave in a civilized manner and is ready to join the world.) Iran has had its revolution. *(Yes, and thus moved backwards a couple of centuries. The majority of Iranians consider the Islamic revolution to be an unmitigated disaster.)* It has a constitution, flawed though it may be. *(Based on the Koran.)* Iran is unlikely to have an upheaval on the scale of its revolution -- something that might still occur in a number of neighboring countries, including Iraq, Saudi Arabia and Syria. *(With its fascist styled government, it butchers anyone who gets too far out of line -- and we all know that Iran is very aggressively fomenting trouble in neighboring countries.)* Iranian institutions and human rights policies do not yet live up to Western standards, but they are way ahead of their regional Muslim counterparts. *(A good admission, that they do not have very good human rights policies. Being way ahead of their regional Muslim counterparts ain't saying much. They are all primitive.)* Although the vetting of candidates for political office does not live up to our expectations (a policy this regime will have to change if it wants to survive), Iran does hold fair elections by regional standards. *(Everyone vets candidates, it's the criteria used that is the problem. Regional standards are dismal.)* It is up to Iranians to force a change in their electoral laws to eliminate the veto power of the Council of Guardians. *(Agreed.)* Still, Iran affords much more of a basis to build on than do other Muslim countries in the Middle East. *(That isn't very much!)* From a practical standpoint, it is worth repeating the fact that the majority of Iranians were born after the Revolution and do not blame the U.S. for their own shortcomings, ironically affording the U.S. a more receptive audience for cooperation. Through its engagement of Iran, the U.S. could be successful in changing Iran at the margins and pushing it toward a more democratic system. *(Who do the Iranians blame for their shortcomings? The United States rightfully is holding Iran at arm's length because of its treacherous government.)*

Arguably, our worst relationship with any country is the one we have with Iran, a member of the "axis of evil" as coined by President Bush. *(Iran's own premeditated actions earned it the justly applied evil title.)* Iran is a large Muslim country that is seen as hostile to U.S. interests. *(Iran is in fact, action, and deed very hostile to U.S. interests.)* Iran is a country that commands a good deal of respect in the Muslim world; in large part because of its past problems with the U.S. and the way it has stood up to the U.S. *(It commanded far more respect before the Ayatollah Khomeni turned it into the disaster that it is today.)* Iran is a country that can help the U.S. in the current situation in Iraq, in Afghanistan, in the Middle East peace process, in the struggle to win over the hearts of Muslims and in the fight against global terrorism. *(If Iran quit meddling in her neighbor's affairs and stopped sponsoring terrorists, it would help the U.S., the world, and civilization in general.)* In the case of Iraq -- whether the Administration likes it or not -- Iraq will be Shiite governed. *(That's why I believe Iraq will break up, whether the administration, Iran, or anyone else likes it or not.)* While Ayatollah Sistani is first and foremost an Iraqi and is unlikely to adopt the political posture of his Iranian counterparts, he will listen to their views and advice. *(Sistani is a Moslem, first and foremost.)* The Kurdish issue in Iraq can be ameliorated or fueled by Iran. *(The Americans have far more traction with the Kurds than do the Iranians. That is irksome to the Iranians.)* In Afghanistan, the veterans of the Northern Alliance and warlords of western regions have close relations with Iran. *(That is regrettable, but probably true as it is fueled by the drug trade.)* In the Palestinian territories, important factions have both ideological and religious connections to Iran. *(That's the outcome of considerable Iranian meddling and influence buying, nothing more.)* An amicable rapprochement will impress Muslims of honorable U.S. intentions. *(Taqiyyah!)* Cooperation with Iran, given Iran's perceived radical Islamic credentials, will win us support among disparate groups of Muslims. *(Here we go again, demanding that the U.S. play a dhimmi role to the Iranians who are in fact and deed radical, not merely perceived as radical. No, Iran ought to cooperate with the U.S. to establish a lasting, honorable peace between Israel and the Arabs.)*

There is no better time for us to adopt a new policy approach outlined above to reestablish relations with Iran. *(Iran needs a new policy approach to the civilized world, not us.)* So-called experts on Iran, who reside in Washington, who have not visited Iran since the Revolution, who have not engaged a representative sample of Iranians or who have had any significant exchange of views with senior Iranian officials have been saying the same thing for nearly twenty-five years; they advise against rapprochement because the regime in Tehran is on its way out. *(Sounds fair enough to me.)* Wishful thinking -- an unfortunate malady in Washington -- will do us very little good. *(It's working just fine in this instance.)* Iran can play a positive role in the Muslim world and in the region from India to Algeria. *(They can begin at any time.)* A balanced U.S. policy would do much to encourage Iran to play such a positive role. *(How about a balanced, sane Iranian policy?)* Such a policy should be bold and comprehensive, as opposed to timid and narrow. *(I think we ought to nuke Iran's nuclear facilities, as opposed to timidly wringing our hands.)*

How to Deal with Iran

The U.S. should unequivocally apologize for its interference in internal Iranian affairs between 1945 and 1979, and especially for its role in the overthrow of the populist Prime Minister Mohammad Mossadeq in 1953. *(Horsepookey! We did what we did in post world war II for good and valid reasons pertinent to those times)* We should apologize for supporting Iraq during the gruesome eight-year war between Iran and Iraq (above all for saying little and doing nothing while we watched Iraq use chemical weapons with impunity, killing and maiming tens of thousands of Iranians). *(We did what we did to maintain a balance of power between two evil regimes who would have otherwise committed far more mischief than we wanted or were prepared to deal with.)* We should settle financial (FMS or Foreign Military Sales) claims outstanding at the U.S.-Iran tribunal at the Hague in a fair and expeditious manner. *(When the time is ripe, we'll consider that.)* We should not use the Mujahedin e Khalq (MEK) as an instrument against Iran. *(It's working. Iran can stop using terror against the United States first, then we'll consider stopping.)* The MEK who even supported Saddam in his brutal suppression of Shiites in southern Iraq, is unpopular with Iranians of every persuasion. *(Good. The Iranian sponsored and controlled Hezbollah is unpopular with all civilized societies and decent people throughout the world.)* We must make it clear to Iran and to the world that we will not do anything to undermine the regime in Tehran, recognizing that this is an internal Iranian matter. *(When Iran lays off of its neighbors, we may reciprocate. As long as Iran participates in evil deeds, we have every right and also have a responsibility to decency to undermine that which is evil and uncivilized.)*

We should not be "soft on Iran" but should make it clear that to the extent that they play a responsible role in the world and adhere to generally acceptable principles of democratic and diplomatic behavior, we will support them in their policies. *(We should continue being tough on Tehran until Tehran begins to play a responsible role in the world and begins to adhere to civilized standards.)* We should use the carrot as well as the stick. *(We need to apply an even bigger cudgel.)* Above all, we should demonstrate humility and stop the use of pejorative phrases to describe Iran and, by association its people. *(Hey, aren't they calling us the Great Satan? Civility is a two-way street.)*

Iran, in turn, must apologize for the taking of U.S. hostages, disavow any connections to terrorism, divorce itself from interference in the affairs of other countries through surrogates such as Hamas and Hizbullah, and be ready to support a fair and just peace between Palestine and Israel. *(Here! Here! They can begin the process at any time. I am sure the United States will reciprocate.)*

At the same time we should not forget the lessons of post-WWII Europe. *(We haven't.)* Economic and political cooperation among the countries of the Middle East (Muslim and Israel) offer the best possible hope for a peaceful, stable and prosperous region. *(We've been promoting that all along.)* We should actively promote cooperation and integration, as opposed to isolation and containment as we have done in the past, and especially in the case of Iran; many of these U.S. actions have appeared as vindictive, not only against the government of Iran but also against the people of Iran. *(It's up to Tehran to stop the vindictive stuff, to be magnanimous and for a change, to initiate the good stuff.)* We should not wait until conditions worsen in Iraq. If we wait, our options will become even more limited. *(Iran's government can do a lot to make the conditions in Iraq better.)* To cut and run is not an option. *(I agree on that. We need to continue using the cudgel.)* If we do so, the Middle East will be thrown into even more turmoil than before, no Muslim will ever trust the U.S. again and the U.S. will be powerless to act in the Middle East for years to come. *(Don't worry, we'll hang in there as long as someone has oil to sell. After that, we'll leave all of you to your Koran, your sand, your camels, your dates, and the impoverishment that is certain to follow.)*

It is time to swallow our pride, discard policies that might be beneficial in the next election and do what is in the long-term interest of the United States. *(We are trying to do what is truly in the best interests of the United States, and in the best interests of the long term survival of Western civilization.)*
END

Subsequent to the above, the Iranians, in 2005 "elected" a hateful cretin named Ahmadinejad as "President" who was probably an ideal for the writer and pro Mohammedist professor, Askari, at George Washington University. The new regime was even more bellicose than its predecessor. A call (repeated) went out to wipe Israel -- and the United States from the map. Ahmadinejad has called for a holocaust to eliminate Israel and the United States, two first steps towards world domination.

Naturally, all of the Islamist governed nations, and many others remained mute after Ahmadinejad's call for more hate, murder, and evil in the name of Mohammed.

And Askari wants the USA to have a dialogue with this cretin. And, Hussein Obama said that he would do just that.

In 2009, Ahmadinejad "won" re-election in a rigged election and when Iranian freedom seekers took to the streets, he unleashed the worst of his thugs to 'neutralize' the demonstrators with some well applied mayhem and murder. He silenced the freedom seekers.

It seems to me that Mr. Askari would better serve humanity by directing his lecturing and writings at the very ugly, dangerous, evil, repressive regime in Tehran. But then again, while we Americans tolerate outrageous idiots, morons, and fools like Askari, the Iranian government would likely have him killed if he were at all honestly critical of them.

Algeria

From Dacca, I went to Algeria while the American hostages were being held in Iran. Our physical Security at the Embassy was just fair, but the layout of the place was such that not a great deal could be done without a huge infusion of cash which was not forthcoming while I was there. While I tried, I was not allowed to do much for Embassy security, although I was the Embassy Security Officer. Washington didn't have funding for what I wanted, and the Ambassador was an even bigger obstacle.

The Algerian police were a large presence all around us, both to protect us and to keep an eye on us.

The Ambassador had a few screws loose and to me, didn't seem certain about his sexual orientation, so my greatest security headache was him,   [[xxxxx this portion has been censored by the Department of State and/or the CIAxxxxx]]   [[xxxxx this portion has been censored by the Department of State and/or the CIAxxxxx]] [[xxxxx this portion has been censored by the Department of State and/or the CIAxxxxx]]   .

Algeria's president, Houari Boumedienne was very sick, and the Algerians approached us for help (after all of the Arab world and Soviet physicians failed). We did, big time, with a C-141 containing a MRI scanner, teams of physicians and so forth, but it was too late and Boumedienne died. The Algerians were impressed with our efforts to help.

Algerian security faced a daunting task with Boumedienne's funeral and delegations coming from over ninety countries, some of them hostile to one-another, etc., and local Palestinian 'refugees' (20,000 of them) were stirring things up plenty. I met with a lead Algerian security official and we worked together on some of the issues he faced. A day or so later, some American intelligence was fed to them (not from me), which apparently proved helpful, and the funeral took place without incident.

After the dust cleared from the funeral,   [[xxxxx this portion has been censored by the Department of State and/or the CIAxxxxx]] [[xxxxx this portion has been censored by the Department of State and/or the CIA xxxxx]]   [[xxxxx this portion has been censored by the Department of State and/or the CIAxxxxx]]   Western Algeria in conjunction with my periodic visit to the American Consulate in Oran. American contractors were building a huge facility where natural gas, pumped from the Algerian desert, was processed into liquefied form (Liquefied Natural Gas, or LNG). The project represented billions in loans and investments, etc. My purpose was to review security with the American company officials, and "perhaps" do a reconnoiter on my own. I did, and what I found was disturbing.

I was able to walk into the complex undetected. I was able to get to several sights strategically overlooking the complex. From any of these vantage points, a person with a rocket propelled grenade (RPG - bazooka) could hit the complex. A more powerful weapon such as an anti-tank missile could have penetrated the LNG storage tanks, or ships when they were taking on their loads of LNG.

I queried some of the American LNG experts and learned that nobody knew exactly what would happen if one of the 800,000 gallon storage tanks was hit. The expert opinion amounted to speculation that a fire with the violent equivalent of an explosion lasting several minutes would occur and to fuel the fire a suction of air at speeds of about 200 miles per hour would ensue. It would probably suck a nearby town (three miles distant) off of its foundations and into the conflagration.

The report I prepared was classified at a high level, received lots of attention in Washington, and parts were excerpted and presented to Algerian officials, who quickly moved a division of troops into the area to provide security. It was ultimately their investment of billions of dollars that were at stake.

My Ambassador, a Jimmy Carter political hack/appointee was very unhappy with me for other reasons, much related to his gross mismanagement, fraudulent bent, and gross ineptitude; and my assignment was "curtailed" and I moved on to another assignment.

Following my departure, the Algerians paid us back for all of our help. They stepped up to the plate and went to bat for the United States and worked towards getting the American hostages released from Iran. The election of President Reagan played an important role too.

An airliner was hijacked by Palestinians and flown to Algeria where passenger/hostage, U.S. NAVY Diver, Robert Stetham was murdered in cold blood, with a bullet in his back and his dying body thrown out of the airplane onto the tarmac.

Burma

The time I spent at my subsequent assignment in Rangoon was relatively tranquil regarding terrorist threats and physical security. The Embassy was in its own building and security was judged adequate for the times and the place.

I did harden the lobby with the use of steel plates, and other materials so that an attack would be contained in the lobby.

There was, during my last year at Rangoon one incident involving a sign found attached to the gate of the house where I lived that caused some consternation. It was put up sometime during a night and had a heading that said: "Wanted, Dead or Alive!" Below this were the initials "C.I.A." superimposed over photographs of three people. I was the only American to be singled out in this way, and that bothered a few people. For the remainder of my time in Rangoon, Burmese authorities staked out my house with a protective security detail.

While I was in Rangoon, a terrorist - a suicide bomber in Lebanon drove a stolen Embassy SUV loaded with Propane into the American Embassy in Beirut and blew the place up. A good friend, Ken Haas was murdered in that blast.

Shortly thereafter another terrorist drove a truck laden with explosives right down a straight path and into the Marine barracks and killed 241 Marines. There were no barriers or obstacles for him to overcome. Some stupid Marine officer invited this terrorist act that cost so many lives, and the American response was to tuck tail and run away. This in fact encouraged militant Mohammedans to commit more such acts.

United States

After seventeen years assigned abroad, the powers that be in Washington, D.C. determined that it was time for me to return and become re-Americanized. I agreed - I needed time in the USA.

I was assigned to a mid-level officer's career development training course, with some specialized programs and stuff. Among them was a course which set me up as one of a small cadre of officers schooled and prepared to act as hostage negotiators.

I did not have an assignment to any specific office in Washington after my career development course. I was told to go and find something to do. There are always vacancies in a number of departments, and anyone showing up looking for an assignment is often welcome. I asked around and was told to go and talk to a man, Bob Blackburn, who headed an office called A/SPL = Special Projects and Liaison, a place where my talents and experience might prove useful.

I did as was suggested and within a day I was locked in to the assignment as a "Program Manager". The office, A/SPL, was an anomaly within the bureaucracy. Normally, there is a long, bureaucratic chain of command between whatever and wherever and the Secretary of State or other offices of authority. A/SPL was indeed special. We had one level between us and the Secretary of State.

A/SPL's role was to make about five dozen American Embassies, which had been determined to be extremely vulnerable, truck-bomb proof.

Now a counter terrorist project manager, my job was to assemble and lead teams of experts to designated high threat embassies, where we would thoroughly assess the threat/s, analyze the situation and determine the best way to provide security (harden the target), and then sell (an easy sell in most cases) the program to the Ambassador. On our return to the USA, I prepared a comprehensive report with recommendations and ran it through various offices within the State Department,   [[xxxxx this portion has been censored by the Department of State and/or the CIAxxxxx]]   , Department of Defense, etc., to get approvals and concurrence.

If anyone balked or delayed, I could make a visit to my boss, and within a day or two Secretary of State George Schultz (one of the few credible Secretaries of State that we have had in recent years) would be having a discussion with some other official, and the balking or delaying generally ceased. It wasn't the best way to make friends, but it certainly did influence people. Lazy jerks were inspired to get off of their butts and do their jobs. Things got done. It felt good to be able to accomplish important things expeditiously.

I was given training in ballistics, shock waves, blast effects and deflection, etc, and soon became an authority on explosives and their effects, etc.

There were a few projects that had been ongoing, had gotten bogged down, and were incomplete, and I was told to pick them up, revive and get them back on track. They were fairly big, complicated, and difficult, and I worked hard to get them back up and running. One involved the Embassy in Pakistan (which had been burned out in earlier riots), and our four Consulates. A lot had been done, but without completion, the work was useless, and I twisted a few arms and got the ball rolling again, and the projects got fired up and were completed. One of the projects of greatest concern was the Consulate in Karachi which had no setback from the street to speak of. A setback is desired because of the physics of blasts. Every foot of distance from a blast is significant in that the blast pressures reduce dramatically, etc. We did the best we could with re-enforced building walls, a super heavy perimeter wall and lots of attention to the glass and doors with plenty of ballistic and shatter proof glass, etc.

On June 12, 2002, the work at the Consulate in Karachi was tested by a powerful blast. A van was used so that more explosives could be used. A hole was blown in the perimeter wall and debris from the blast rained down as far as a half of a mile away. At the Consulate, an American Marine Security Guard and about five employees were injured by some flying debris. There were no deaths, and the limited damage is directly attributed to the work done to "harden" the consulate. I am proud of my work.

I had great support from my boss, Mr. Blackburn, and the people I worked with on a daily basis were also dedicated, and we worked successfully to overcome differences and maintain our focus on preserving lives.

Other Embassies or consulates on my project agenda were in Baghdad, Kuwait, Manama, Abu Dhabi, Dubai, Muscat and Oman, Tunis, and Algiers. I was budgeted for up to five million dollars per Embassy. I "turned to" as they say in the Navy, and within eighteen months all were done or well underway. Eighteen months in the Bureaucracy where the normal process is closer to ten years for anything of a magnitude equaling what we were doing was remarkable. Most were done using less than half of the $5 million budgeted per project. I wasn't interested in spending the money, I was focused on developing effective, safe and secure Embassies that had proper evacuation plans that would work if and when needed.

It wasn't all smooth going, and we ran into a few idiots along the way, but we managed to deal with them.

In one Persian Gulf country where I worked, the front of the Embassy opened onto a football field sized area where a very large hostile mob could gather easily. Also facing onto this open area was a large mosque. The scenario was not good, and when we were discussing possibilities and probabilities with the Ambassador, his deputy opined that if a mob came at the Embassy, he'd deal with them. He had a 9mm semi-automatic pistol. When he said that, my hair actually stood on end. Here was a fool who would take a piss-ant 9-shot pistol to a mob of thousands of impassioned people, and he actually believed he could stop them. In reality, all he would do if he used that pistol would be to really fan their passions.

Our team's focus was to modify or upgrade (harden) the exteriors of Embassies so they could withstand   [[xxxxx this portion has been censored by the Department of State and/or the CIAxxxxx]] an onslaught using battering rams and so forth while the staff got out of there. Also, we established ways to control or restrict vehicular access to or near Embassies so that a truck bomb would NOT take the place down.

While we hardened Embassies, we were also focused on ways for the Ambassador and staff to evacuate out through hidden or camouflaged passageways between buildings, crawlways across rooftops, and even tunnels to various safe havens, or escape routes.

Along with all of this, we developed limits to the volumes of classified documents to be held at each Embassy, and emergency document destruction systems that would permit rapid and complete document destruction in case of an attack on an Embassy.

None of the Embassies we were assigned to upgrade were the ideal candidates for easy accomplishment of objectives. They were not new or modern buildings built of steel and re-enforced concrete with a 200 foot gap between them and any street or other building, etc. They were in urban areas, were small, vulnerable, and built of native materials.

One Embassy building, in Bahrain, was 450 years old and had been built of native materials consisting of woven bamboo, sand, straw, and camel dung. When we wanted to make substantial changes to its walls and stuff, the owner's representative nixed everything we wanted to do. He was adamant in his refusal. I tried to pressure the local government to no avail. I tried to locate the owner and circumvent the 'agent'. No dice.

After several brews late one evening, one of our team members, a very talented architect, came up with an idea which he drew on a napkin and saved. After coffee in the morning and giving our heads some time to clear, we reviewed the napkin and decided the idea was a winner and went work on it that morning. Within days the Embassy was ringed with "flower pots". They were planter boxes a meter high, a meter deep, two meters wide, were built of steel re-enforced concrete with 60 cm walls.   [[xxxxx this portion has been censored by the Department of State and/or the CIAxxxxx]]   [[xxxxx this portion has been censored by the Department of State and/or the CIAxxxxx]]   [[xxxxx this portion has been censored by the Department of State and/or the CIAxxxxx]]   We filled them with sand and dirt, planted flowers and shrubs and set them up for irrigation. When done, each pot weighed well over three tons. The design was later tested in the USA using a ten wheeled military (deuce-and-a-half)

` truck loaded with sandbags and driven into two planter 'flower pots' at 55mph. The truck was demolished. The planter pots were moved around and damaged, but held.

Within a year, the White House in Washington, the Capitol Building, Supreme Court and a host of other buildings had a variety of "planters" strategically placed around them. They are aesthetically more attractive than raw concrete, are blended into the architecture, and many are rounded and covered with marble, but they are the "flower pots" that will stop speeding trucks loaded with high explosives.

In other areas, such as the White House along Pennsylvania Avenue, a series of "dragon's teeth" (bollards) made of heavily re-enforced concrete aggressively defend approaches.

As our work in A/SPL drew to a successful end, the office was transferred into the mainstream of the bureaucracy and assigned to the State Department's Diplomatic Security Division. I didn't fit with that group and I was thus reassigned to another job.

In that new assignment, where I managed the world wide inventory of State Department (and Embassy) vehicles, I got involved in an armored vehicle program. Two American Ambassadors had been assassinated (in Lebanon and Afghanistan), so, the Congress threw some money at the State Department and a decision was made to put a fully armored vehicle (FAV) at every Embassy in the world.

While the idea was sound, foolishness was involved. At a quarter of a million dollars a copy, a fully armored vehicle is a huge purchase, and is enormously costly to operate and maintain.

Someone in the Security Division had gotten in touch with the Cadillac and Lincoln division of their respective corporations about doing a special run for the program. Lincoln didn't respond. Cadillac was very responsive, wiling do anything we wanted.

Someone in Security wanted big 400+ horsepower racing engines installed, and I balked. I knew that in Embassies, a local (native) employee typically is the Ambassador's chauffeur and not many third world drivers understand the physics or the dynamics of driving an 11,000 pound car with a 400+ horsepower engine. I could visualize a scenario with some unsophisticated driver trying to take a corner at 100 mph, rolling over, and taking out a dozen houses or a few buildings. I could also visualize some ambassador and his wife rattling around in there like peas in a matchbox. I suggested a V-6 engine which after ridiculing guffaws brought a compromise of a small V-8 with special (deep) gearing that would allow the FAV to run quickly and easily up to 65-80 miles per hour, but not run 150+ mph.

Cadillac built them with special a chassis and suspension to hold the weight, along with truck axles, suspension, transmission, and brakes, etc. When they were delivered, they looked like off road vehicles with lift kits. After the armoring company finished its work, they sat properly, looked good, and rode well in spite of their six plus ton weight.

Chapter 4

THE ENEMY

Religious fundamentalist/fascist zealots hate and fear what
President Abraham Lincoln said at Gettysburg,
That: *"Government of the people, by the
people, and for the people, shall not perish
from the earth"*.

Not all Arab people are the enemy. Not all Moslem people are the enemy. Very, very few of them are our friends either. Neither also are all Americans, Europeans, Africans, and Asians necessarily with us, nor are some so-called Christians friends of America.

The enemy we face is an entrenched faction or factions, groups and individuals, many in positions of power, leadership, and authority. The enemy is religious zealotry. The enemy we are dealing with now and will deal with for a long time *is Mohammedan, Islamic, Moslem fundamentalism* which has as its goal the enslavement of and subjugation of everyone on earth to a deadly, regressive dark age of repression, terror, ignorance, and poverty, all in the name of allah. The enemy in America is controlled by the American Moslem Brotherhood. Anyone or any government entity that does business with the Moslem Brotherhood is performing traitorous acts no less treasonous than doing business with the Nazis or Communists.

During World War II, if anyone joined the Nazi party, they were considered traitors, to be shot. During the Korean War and Cold War, anyone proven to be a Communist suffered the consequences of traitors including death. In this same vein, any Americans joining Islam (as a convert) is likewise a treasonous traitor, who should be shot.

The enemy is the hydra headed al Qaeda, all of those Islamist fascists and more; it is Al Fatah; it is the pathological liars – the many Arafats; it is Iran's proxy to the world, Hezbollah; it is Hamas, Islamic Jihad, and the list of evil goes on by hundreds of other names. It is all of these -- and more, born of ignorant hatred, feelings (knowledge in fact) of inferiority, especially willful ignorance -- the kind of willfulness that burns books, and one that relishes poverty along with bigotry and plain stupidity, and wallows in self-pity based on its non-competitiveness.

The list of names goes on, and on, and on. There is a web site that has a comprehensive list of individuals, groups, organizations, and nations that target the United States. It takes more than 1.3 megabytes of computer space to hold all of those names, etc.

While we are currently and rightfully focused on one major, predominant enemy represented by Mohammedan fundamentalists, we must remember that the enemy are also the fanatic Tim McVeigh's, idiotic Eric Rudolphs, and insane Ted Kazynskis here at home, and others yet to crawl out from under their rocks.

The greatest, most fearsome enemy of all, of our entire history, and one that threatens our very survival as a nation and culture is the Islamization process of making everything Islamic. It is Islamic Mohammedism, which represents all of what is truly evil.

Radical, militant, Moslem fundamentalism is technically a Myth. Islam is by nature radical in its hatred of all else and its universal Mohammedist objective to dominate the world. This is a fundamental reality.

The Mohammedists, Moslems are not and have barely ever been competitive with any other civilization, especially the western civilization, places of freedom, prosperity, joy, creativity, and individual rights. Their visual art is limited. Musically they are just drum beaters (Mohammed didn't like music and nearly outlawed it). They don't know what theatre is although they are dramatically theatric in their antics. They did well in math for a while, but otherwise have no original sciences to speak of and they have contributed virtually nil to modern medical science. Their literature is limited to and by Islam, and their culture and society is backward, ignorant, primitive, savage, and brutal. Because they cannot develop and apply skills necessary to legitimately compete, their singular article of faith is to destroy and remake the world Moslem, where every person on earth submits to their one set of depraved, repressive, ugly, biased laws and rules. Because they cannot win hearts and minds through respect, love, charity, decency, and goodness, they are compelled to convert people by subversion or force, using fear and intimidation, terrorism.

The fundamentalist Mohammedan government of Iran is a vile enemy, but not all Iranians are enemies.

Iraq was fascist but not a fundamentalist Islamic government, and Saddam Hussein was a committed foe of the United States. It is telling that a CIA officer, Bob Baer was sent to Northern Iraq with instructions to encourage the overthrow of Saddam Hussein, and was later recalled and nearly prosecuted by the FBI -- for doing his job and following orders..... Is the FBI a friend or foe? Under the Bush presidency, the hostility and distrust between the CIA and FBI was somewhat subdued. After Barak Hussein Obama took office and installed his team of jackals at the Justice Department and the CIA, and turned some of them loose to investigate CIA officials involved in aggressive interrogations of murderous terrorists, everyone at the CIA went into hibernation. The word was out: Do your job, and you WILL suffer unhappy consequences.

In war there is no substitute for victory.
Douglas MacArthur, 4/19/1951

We must hunt the fundamentalist terrorist enemy down and neutralize them, and this can best be accomplished on their own terms, not ours, even when some of them are us. By dealing with those who are not Americans on their own terms, in ways that are unequivocal, decisive, and delivered in a manner they clearly understand, they will cease to exist.

**When you see a rattlesnake poised to
strike, you do not wait until it has
struck before you crush it.**
Franklin D. Roosevelt, 9/11/1941

We face many enemies both without as well as within. We need to work to avoid becoming completely paranoid. While a little paranoia is healthy, too much can be destructive.

Some of these very many religious and terrorist organizations are anarchists whose objective is not only to conquer, but to destroy civilization as we know it.

Among them are the Muslim Brotherhood, an organization with ties to the extremist hard-line Saudi Wahabi Moslem sect that is dedicated to bringing their puritanical version of the kingdom of allah to earth, to impose their disgustingly sick version of purity and religious domination to bear on every person on earth. Besides targeting the United States and most of Europe, they have targeted the governments of Syria, Jordan, Egypt, Kuwait, and many other Arab nations, even to some extent themselves.

The senior royals of the Saud gang include a very few pragmatists who have discovered to their dismay that they, themselves, are actually behind terrorism. Incredible, eh? Their own Saudi funded charities and radical anti-Western Madrassas located all over the world have for fifty years worked to spread Wahabism. Their billions and billions of dollars have graduated tens of thousands of terrorists who have come home and struck them in their own gardens. So the royal household suddenly started an anti-terrorism campaign. Unfortunately, they themselves are the terrorists, but in their willful ignorance they can't fathom this. Very senior members of the Saudi royal family in fact are resisting the new campaigns against terrorism.

For those few moderates in the Saudi government and leadership, their newfound efforts are not likely to bear much fruit. At least not immediately. They have decades of Wahabism to reconcile with and to overcome before they can begin to clean up their own house.

The quarrel Syria has with the Untied States was initially because of Israel. Now, however, Syria has joined the ranks of terrorist sponsors, harboring, funding, training, financing, and participating in terrorist activities and events directed at the United States. In the war on fundamentalist terrorism, Syria has only pretended to support the

United States.

In 2004, an American citizen observed some upsetting behavior by some fellow travelers and reported this to authorities. A brouhaha resulted and I sent, as a private citizen, the following letter to the Syrian Ambassador:

Quote: With interest, I have been following accounts about an air traveler's experience on a recent Detroit to Los Angeles flight, where she observed strange and upsetting behavior by a number of passengers. These passengers were Syrians who seemed to be conducting a dry run of some sort, and whose unusual and suspicious actions were properly brought to the attention of authorities who took appropriate action.

It has been revealed that these Syrians were criminal lawbreakers. Their visas had expired and they should have left the United States before the expiry of their visas. You have reportedly claimed that these Syrian criminals were innocent musicians who had played at some various venues which is false information (a lie) because they had not been on those stages.

You had the irrational and typical Mohammedan temerity to accuse the American citizen woman (who expressed her concerns) of being a racist, of racist profiling, etc. This American citizen had every right to do what she did.

I wish to reaffirm to you that Syria is a country that foments and sponsors international terrorism, and that all Syrians are thusly properly held to be suspected terrorists, including yourself, and all members of your staff. Accordingly anything that you say is to be considered a lie, because you don't know the truth, and would never know the truth even if it was in front of your face. Having lived in Islamic countries for over a decade, I understand that you and most other Moslem Arabs are often dismayed when people don't believe your lies, but that's the way it is. Unquote

I never received a response to my letter from the Syrian Ambassador or anyone on his staff.

Egypt's leadership (for whatever it's worth) is at risk. Led by Hosni Mubarak (who came into power after the courageous moderate Anwar al Sadat was murdered by fundamentalist Mohammedans) who has barely fought off the fundamentalists. As long as necessarily very tough men like Mubarak hold sway, Egypt can survive, but never, ever progress. Egypt is a spawning ground for Mohammedan radicals.

Egypt's government has to deal with overwhelming poverty, a by-product of Islam - fertile grounds for fundamentalists, and indeed Moslem Brotherhood (founded by Hitler admirer Hasan al Banna) fundamentalists (supported and funded by the Saudis) have killed past Egyptian leaders.

In 2005, a Coptic church in Alexandria presented a drama that was based on factual history, but the Moslems found that its basis (on historical truth) was offensive (naturally) to Islam (because most

Moslems are often offended when being presented with facts about their own history) and riots took place, churches were burned and Christians abused and murdered.

Jordan has long been led by a moderate, progressive, civilized monarchy which does not support or sanction terrorist organizations, fundamentalist or otherwise.

Kuwait's government owes its existence to the United States, but that means little as Kuwaitis are involved all over the map against the United States.

Another enemy is the insane leadership of North Korea who continue to starve their people while developing nuclear weapons and long range missile technology. It is possible or even probable that mutually beneficial (based on hostility to the West) links to fundamental terrorists are in place.

Here, at home, there are hundreds of Islamic, Moslem or other organizations that have as a singular goal the subversion of the United States. Some are secret, operating underground. Others operate under false fronts, smiling in our faces while sliding a rusty, dull knife into our backs.

Under American laws, these radical groups are even able to hold conventions and preach hatred right here in the American homeland. Their right to preach hatred against your and my friends, neighbors, and I are protected under the First Amendment to the Constitution. The FBI and other law enforcement agencies are in many cases powerless and are not allowed to monitor such groups because of legislative restrictions. We need to establish private militias of civilized citizens who should attend these meetings and rallies and to monitor and report (publicize) these groups. This too is protected by the Constitution.

A lot of the characters involved in these groups are scruffy, unshaven, slovenly dressed, often smelly, almost always scowling, and clearly Arab type middle easterners, relatively easy to identify. Others are oriental, black, Latino, and white, are clean and presentable, and are harder to detect, but their evil little hearts are the same. Still some other individuals and groups work hard to appear mainstream, even civilized. One of these slime bag outfits is the large, well-funded and very insidious nationwide group of pathological liars called the Council on American-Islamic Relations (CAIR). The CAIR is as anti-American or anti-civilization, anti-freedom, anti-joy, and anti-independence of an organization as can be found. It is unquestionably the Moslem equivalent in hatred and bias as is the KKK. But, their members, their spokesmen appear at Republican, Democratic, or other meetings, at universities, churches, rallies, 4th of July picnics, all over the place. Well funded by the Saudis (Wahabi) and very well trained, they are clean shaven, have neat hair cuts, are generally very clean cut, dress well, wear shoes properly, and they even smell good – very similar in appearance to modern Mafiosi. They are well spoken graduates of charm schools and are easily accepted by the many gullible fools they reach out to. They preach a phony message claiming Islam is a religion of universal human rights (in fact Islamic "universal" rights apply to Moslems only, with far lesser rights for non-Moslems), freedom of religion (as along as it's Islam), freedom of choice (choices that the Imam makes for one), protection against the powerful (until they are defeated), the rule of (Sharia) law, and the protection of property rights (selectively, under Sharia law), and other balderdash.

CAIR will not, in any way, condemn Mohammedan gangsters, thieves, liars, fanatics, terrorists, butchers, killers and hate mongers, but readily condemns civilized, honest Americans who dare condemn Mohammedan beasts, declaring them bigots and racists. CAIR can't bear hearing the truth, so they attack, fulminate, criticize and lie.

CAIR has offices established in nearly every state, several in larger populated states. They work at getting a moderate message (packages of lies and false propaganda), and have plenty of money to do this. They also act as spokesmen lying for Mohammedans who stupidly get themselves in trouble.

An example (one of thousands of actual case files) is when an illegal Mohammedan (a genuine lawbreaker) threatened to blow up a Florida Best Buy store because he was unsatisfied with a rebate. He was arrested for terrorist threats. The CAIR jumped in claiming that a very humble member of the Moslem community was being jailed for asking questions about a rebate (nothing about his threats of violence and lawbreaker status). Then, when a judge wanted to have the crazed illegal, law breaking criminal Mohammedan immigrant subjected to a psychological evaluation, the CAIR wanted to have the judge removed. Why? Probably because such an evaluation would have validated the fact that the guy wasn't actually nuts, but a true Mohammedan terrorist, which is, ah, err, ahem, probably certifiable as nuts.....

The likes of CAIR are successfully playing many gullible Americans for suckers and fools because they do know us far better than the majority of us know them.

CAIR conducted a poll and "discovered" that a third of Americans (only a third) hold negative stereotypes of Moslems and believe that Islam encourages oppression of women (true); that Islam teaches violence and hatred (true); that Moslems value life less than other people (true); and that Moslems teach their children to hate blacks, Christians, Jews, Buddhists and others who are not Moslem (true). If the proverbial shoe fits........

CAIR reports on the status of Moslems in the United States and is the chief whine factory of Islamic taqiyyah (balderdash). CAIR reports mere rumors as if they were factual incidents of bias, and whines about such offenses as flyers or posters with what they consider offensive or degrading statements about the Koran or Mohammed, even when or even especially if they are historically accurate and represent the truth. Some of CAIR's complaints don't even pass the laugh test, such as a complaint against a school regarding Moslem girl being unable to compete in sports because of her long, flowing hajib (head-to-toe garment). They, of course wanted to put all girls into the same garb so they could then be competing on an even playing field?.?.?.?....

CAIR insists that employers such as DELL computers (my next computer won't be a Dell) submit to dhimmi status to honor Moslem demands with special accommodations for their religious practices on the job. That is in fact providing preferential treatment for a particular religious group. Where is the ACLU here? Shouldn't the ACLU step up in favor of the businesses being attacked, and keep religion out of the workplace? Neither the Mohammedans nor the slimy ACLU care a whit that this causes hardship for non-Mohammedan employees and may even break companies involved plunging everyone into poverty. Poverty is fine if not preferable with the Islamists anyhow.

CAIR wants to teach (indoctrinate) Americans about an untrue version of Islam, and strives to oppress anyone who want to teach real truths and facts about Islam. They have sued the founder of an organization called anti-CAIR because of its activities. Anti-CAIR has documented that CAIR is a front for Islamic terrorist organizations and received funds from the same, and CAIR can't stand the scrutiny. At lest two of CAIR's employees or former employees have been indicted and arrested for participation in terrorist activities. Others have been named but not indicted for their involvement in such as committing terrorist acts in the United States

The Senate Judiciary Committee on Terrorism, Technology, and Homeland Security in its investigations reportedly has developed enormous amounts of evidence in examining Saudi Arabia's role in exporting Islamic terrorism around the world, including or especially to the United States. Deviant CAIR, since its 1974 creation, has been a major beneficiary of the Saudi funds and largesse, and is a major supporter of terrorism in the United States. CAIR is intimately linked with Hamas, and a CAIR Community Affairs Director, Bassem Khafagi, has pled guilty to visa and bank fraud charges regarding his role with the Saudi funded (and controlled) Islamic Assembly of North America, a group advocating violence in and against the USA, etc.

The dots are being connected, and they paint a very clear (and ugly) picture.

I have no doubt that the CAIR will declare me a 'hostile' by virtue of this book and other activities that I am involved with and probably report me to the police calling the contents of this book a hate crime. In fact I am indeed hostile to CAIR and others of their slimy ilk, and I really do hate liars and criminals. I do oppose Mohammedan expansionism and I ain't even Jewish.

Reportedly when one speaks out against Mohammedans, the fine fellows of CAIR tend to brand them as "Jews' which is reportedly their nitwit way of insulting one who opposes them.

TRUTH AND LIES

*When a follower of Mohammed's teachings
says "trust me", the next words out of
his mouth will assuredly be a lie.*

and

BETRAYAL

**Only in the Middle East (can) you
"betray" someone by refusing to
accept the lie he told you.**

*by Robert Baer,
(author of SEE NO EVIL)*

A fundamental truth: Arabs/Moslems have a penchant for denying the truth, reality, or simple facts. It's a part of their teachings, their culture, their society, and is approved by their belief system.

Iraqi Information Minister Mohammad Saeed Al'Shaf (dubbed Bob by TV spoof artists and late night talk hosts) stood before a camera scoffingly demanding: "What American troops at the airport?" "There are no Americans at the airport." "What American troops in Baghdad?" All this while, on the TV screen an American battle tank made its way down the street just yards away. It seemed hilariously funny to us, but Moslems take this fantasy world of theirs seriously.

Al Jazeera TV is a greater world of fantasy than Disneyland, Buffalo Bob, and Clara Belle. It makes Dan Rather's pre-retirement foolishness look positively saintly.

In 1993, an American of Arab extraction said "trust me." He was addressing a group of people I was with. What he proceeded to tell us was a lie and when I later called him on it and circulated (hand delivered to homeowners of a housing tract) a rebuttal letter debunking his "trust me" lies, he reportedly threatened to kill me. He had expected everyone to accept his "truth" and dumbly go away, and when his lie backfired, he was outraged. How dare I challenge his lie?

Whenever a Moslem/Arab/Palestinian "spokesperson" or talking head appears on TV, takes a breath and begins pontificating, my by now well-honed built-in horsepookey detector sounds internal alarms. It has become automatic for me. It just happens based on my many years of personal experience, knowledge, and understanding.

Dr. Sami Al Arian was reportedly a man who many called a liar when he claimed he was not a terrorist fund raiser. He told us that we should just "trust" him at his word. In his own mind, in a typically Mohammedan/Arab manner, he sets aside and won't acknowledge this reality. He shuts his duplicitous mind and becomes conscious only of a few thousand dollars raised for the Red Crescent, but blanks his mind about the thousands or millions that he raised for terrorism. This bald faced pathological liar was caught up in his lies and faced true American justice and jail when his deceit and lying was finally uncovered, and it was proven that he in fact funded, supported, and even helped terrorists plan their acts, some of which caused the deaths of innocent Americans. He provided material support to terrorist organizations, participated in actual racketeering in this context and conspired to kill Americans. Naturally al-Arian and his defense team want to argue all sorts of silliness not related to the charges, to claim that their killing of innocents in Israel is justified as warfare, etc.

Al-Arian had a good defense, and the prosecutors weren't up to the task of effectively prosecuting Arian at his trial. While they demonstrated his evil, they were not able to convince all members of the jury. The jury failed to find him guilty of some of the most egregious charges.

An Egyptian pilot drove his aircraft into the sea and killed everyone on board. Cockpit recordings have him repeating "Insha'Allah, Insha'Allah, Insha'Allah" as the aircraft plunged. When civil aviation authorities, following their exhaustive investigation, suggested that the crash was no accident, that the Egyptian pilot had intentionally flown the plane into the ocean, Egyptian officials ranted and raved at the audacity of the American investigators to say such a thing -- to speak the truth.

After the Saddam regime fell in Iraq, U.S. troops killed Saddam's sons Uday and Qusay Hussein. Then, there were DNA records, dental identification, and other (medical) records as well as visual identification by dozens of people who personally knew them. In spite of this, thousands of Arabs steadfastly refused for months to acknowledge the factual proof of their deaths. This is another example of the profoundly stupid and moronic ability of Moslems to remain fancifully and willfully ignorant.

Moslems/Arabs have the most audacious ability to deny truths and to pathologically lie in the face of reality and fact. In 1966, following a series of homicide bombings, an American born Mohammedan militant drove his car into Israeli civilians waiting at a bus stop in Jerusalem, killing one and wounding twenty-five. After Israelis opened fire and shot the terrorist dead as he tried to flee, the American based Muslim Public Affairs Council (MPAC) issued a press release accusing Israel of a "terrorist" act for killing the murderer.

Terrorist, Yassir Arafat said, in English that he was willing to share the land of Palestine and to live alongside of Israel. In Arabic he turned around and called for the annihilation of every Jew, and refused to accept any condition of Israel's existence. Arafat was a despicable, but typically two faced liar. Most Mohammedan Arabs lie (to us, in English) about their acceptance of Israel, and turn on their Arabic tongue and call for the death of Jews and Christians. When these lies are brought to their attention, they deny their own written, recorded, and documented pronouncements. The newest head of the

Palestinian/Arab band of snakes, Abu Mazen aka Mahmoud Abbas is also a renowned liar who says nice out of one side of his face and preaches about the destruction of Israel and every Jew out of the other side of his face. Their Hamas has vowed to keep fighting until Israeli 'occupation' of Arab lands ends. That means, let me remind those of limited memory or intellectual capacity (primarily liberals, anti-semites, the willfully ignorant, and their fellow travelers), that they (Hamas and the Arabs) won't stop until every Jew is dead.

Dr. Sami Al Arian was a liar when he adamantly denied that he was a terrorist fund raiser. He told us to "trust" him at his word. In his own mind, in an atypically Arab manner, he sets aside and won't acknowledge this reality. He shuts his duplicitous, bipolar mind and becomes conscious only of a few thousand dollars raised for the Red Crescent, blanking his mind about the millions raised for terrorism. Professionals would call that schizophrenia.

Al Arian, when he was arrested declared: "It's all politics." For a change he was being honest. It was about his Islamic/Mohammedan taqiyyah.

Truth and reality as we westerners know it is irrelevant in the mind of the Arab/Islamist. Myths and lies are more powerful to the Islamist than truth. The mental process churning along in Mohammedan minds are so completely different from ours as to be incomprehensible to rational people. That is what is so frustrating and impossible about trying to reason with and/or deal with these characters. Logic, statistical facts, evidence, proof, truth, none of this really registers …..or matters. These Arabs/Islamists aren't thinking in the same realm as we are. Or, as some would say, their mental elevators don't stop on floors corresponding with the numbers being displayed.

If Israel disappeared from the face of the earth today, the Mohammedans would not be satisfied. Happy with the end of Israel, yes, but the Islamic world would not be satisfied. They would next want America to leave the face of the earth, then Europe, and any other Christian society, followed by everything Buddhist, Hindu, etc., until they achieved world domination. That is what Islam is all about.

There are Americans and Europeans who live in worlds of their own, or who "march to different drummers" who are considered to be "loonies" or are in fact clinically delusional. We need to understand that this is atypical of most Islamists/Mohammedans. They are delusional.

We Westerners - Americans especially, and in particular the "liberal elite" and their related utopianist do gooders are likewise delusional in a witless belief that all of the people in the whole wide world are able to reason just like us. It ain't so, folks. There are fire ants, wasps, hornets, vipers, scorpions, centipedes, and other nasty killers in them there fields of honey, daisies, and peach trees.

Egos, Stupidity, and pure Ugly Nastiness

I came across two dogs that some young Moslem (Turkish) men had caught on a street in Istanbul. These nasty, slimy, sick creeps had taken a piece of shoe lace and died the two dogs' testicles together and then whipped the dogs. Screaming and howling in pain, fright, and confusion, the dogs were torturing one-another as the several young princes of Islam laughed and celebrated their vicious nastiness. Had I more than just my two hands vs. a dozen of those dirt bags, I'd have joyously shed their worthless blood right then and there.

Another time, while riding with three men, (Moslem locals of the country I was in Turkey) driving down a country road, I observed far ahead a poor beast of burden heavily laden with an enormous pile of sticks and branches. It was on the side of the rocky dirt road, staggering under its load as a man walked alongside whipping and flailing at the poor beast of burden. As we drew nearer and then passed by, I saw that the unfortunate suffering, struggling beast had but two legs, a woman........

An American whom I worked with and knew well was driving home from work one evening in Istanbul. He slowed to turn into the street where he lived, and was rear ended. He was driving a Chevrolet Corvair and was hit pretty hard by a local (native) Turk who was obviously fairly well off and was driving a Mercedes Benz. Yeah, the Benz driver was a Moslem. They went to court. The judge handed down judgment. My friend was 60% in the wrong and therefore liable for 60% of the damages to both cars. Twenty percent was just for being there. "Insha'Allah", if a person (or his property) just happens to be there, they are 20% responsible – if they weren't there, it wouldn't have happened to them. Great reasoning, eh? Another 20% was allocated because he was an American. The last 20% was allocated because his skin was black, and that Moslem judge declared (in the courtroom) that he didn't like blacks (he used the N word).

Rule: Don't have an auto accident in Turkey.

Another American in Istanbul was driving in a congested area of town. He slowed for a pedestrian, and was rear ended by a Turk. The damage was substantial. When the American got out of his car to look at the damage and do the civilized thing of exchanging driver license and insurance information the Turk just clubbed him over the head with a jack handle. When the American's wife got out of the car to come to the aid of her husband, the Turk kicked her in the crotch. He kicked her so hard that he broke her pelvis, then spat on her as he drove away.

I was driving in Istanbul on a major road, three lanes each way with a curbed median in the middle. I was heading away from town and the traffic on my side was light. The traffic coming into town was heavy and jammed up. I was in the left lane passing a taxi stopped in the middle lane, next to a stopped bus in the right lane. Suddenly, a car lurched over the median, and onto the road I was on, headed right at me. I skidded to a stop as did the oncoming driver, just a few feet apart. Relieved, I smiled and laughed - the wrong thing to do - and started to back up. He jumped out of his car and came to me declaring that I was an infidel in his country and he therefore had the right of way, and that I (the infidel) should not even be in his way. My smiling and laughing at him was humiliating, and then he slugged me. He hit me pretty hard and I fell sideways in my car. My glasses flew to the rear window deck. He had three other guys in his car, and I knew better than to take him (them) up on the offer (bearing in mind the beating my colleague and his wife had been treated to). I backed away again to get room to maneuver and drive away, to get out of there. As I put my car into first gear, he jumped in front of me, and I drove on, banging into him and he rolled off of my hood as I took off. He got into his car, turned and followed me. My six cylinder Chevy was not a match for his Mercedes and I was not able to outrun him.

About two miles along, I turned into the street of my destination. In my rush, I had taken the wrong turn and worse, it was a dead end street. There was nobody around.

I had already learned to not drive unprepared in the Middle East, especially in Turkey. I turned and headed back the way that I had come and the Mercedes came up and stopped, blocking the road. I was the first out of my car, and had my five foot length of stout logger chain clipped together by a heavy padlock. The ass who had punched me, the driver, was first out of the Mercedes and I slammed the chain into his head. He dropped and didn't move again for a while. The driver side back seat passenger was next out and I kicked him in the groin and then smacked the lock onto the back of his head and he too went down. The front passenger was big and fat, and as he was struggling out of the car, I reached over the roof with a roundhouse swing that caught him in the face and stopped him. The fourth man was coming around the back of the car with a big knife in his hand. I threw the chain into his face and then kicked him in the groin with so much force that he rose into the air. (In my mid-twenties at six feet tall and 220+ relatively fit pounds with some boxing experience, experience playing as a center/middle linebacker on a football team, and a background that included road construction, working a grinder in a foundry, and in a steel yard, I had enough strength to cause hurt.) He was stunned and I grabbed his knife hand and broke his wrist, then I spun his arm out of his shoulder socket, and on his way down, I broke his elbow over my knee. What a rush that was!

The fat guy had gotten up and came around the car, and using the chain, I smacked him in the face again, and then worked him over really hard until he quit screaming. I returned to the knife wielder and broke several of his fingers (both hands). I used the knife on the Mercedes' tires, and then the chain on all of the windows, much of the body work and the grill and radiator. I then got into my car as the Mercedes' driver was starting to rouse, and I drove over his legs as I left. He made lots of noise as I did that, and I just felt wonderful. I had not only survived, I had prevailed and I was on an adrenaline high that I couldn't believe (my pulse raced for days.). I got out of there and didn't look back. I didn't report this incident, to my diplomatic colleagues or my boss because they probably would have made sure I got screwed one way or another over this.

American Conservatives and Liberals

The liberals in America as well as conservatives are hung up on their own agendas and seemingly have forgotten or abandoned the real American people. For years and years American Presidents have been unable to appoint the best judges to the federal benches. Appointees have to pass a litmus test based on liberal or conservative ideals, not on ideals based on serving the American people.

Both sides champion different viewpoints to the extreme, and work to enact laws or appoint judges who will legislate from the bench to further liberal or conservative objectives. The American people - those of us caught in the middle, the American people are being jockeyed and jacked around continuously.

Laws have been passed or legislated into standing that hurt Americans more than they help them, but provide immense benefit and countless opportunities to those who hate and want to destroy us. It is gross stupidity run amok. While some of it has come from so-called conservative judges, the vast majority of these bad rulings have been generated by egotistical, flaky, out-of-self-control mostly liberal judges to serendipitously support Mohammedan causes.

Moslems are resistant to assimilation in the civilized nations of Europe, the United States and the Orient, regions that generously opened themselves up to host the Moslems and to welcome them. These Moslem jackasses are rejecting the hospitality of their civilized hosts and are now trying to impose their own loathsome rules on civilized people. It is reasonable to expect that those unwilling to assimilate with their hosts be forcefully repatriated to their Mohammedan homelands.

In parts of Michigan, noise abatement laws have been deleted to enable Mohammedan mosques to use powerful megaphones announcing their offensive multiple daily calls to prayer. This is flat wrong! This is a first step in Mohammedism's imposition of their offensive and uncivilized rules on Americans in the United States.

Sharia permits male members of a Moslem family to beat their women, and the Hadiths of Mohammed even prescribe the methods. A young girl in Madison Heights, Michigan, was severely beaten by her brother, with the approval of their parents because she had a non-Moslem boy friend. When she complained of being in pain, her parents refused to get medical help for her. It turns out that she had a broken back. Had she died, it would have been OK by Islam's Sharia. But, that level of uncivilized behavior is not OK in the United States.

Mohammedans in other parts of the country are working to

establish Sharia rules and laws in the neighborhoods in which they reside. Establish Koranic rule on America? This is an outrage, but these people and their fellow travelers think this is great.

A Mohammedan filed a suit against a Delaware school district claiming harassment when a teacher taught an honest, truthful lesson that the Koran teaches war and hatred. It's true!

Former Supreme Court Justice Ginsburg opined that the opinions, laws, and practices of foreigners and foreign laws are applicable to US law and the Constitution.....??? Does she mean that it is OK to impose Sharia laws on Americans in the United States? This is the highest order of foolishness run amok. It affirms that Justice Ginsburg is either insane or just an outrageous idiot. Perhaps I'm just being redundant.

A simple minded President Bush has established foolish faith based welfare programs that funnel taxpayer money into conservative, even reactive or militant religious organizations (both Christian and Mohammedan) that work against American ideals and principles. Some of that taxpayer money is finding its way into terrorist organizations whose objectives are against American interests.

Conservatives are pushing hard to further religion (a Christian theocracy?) in government as opposed to keeping government free from religion. This is stupid, and eventually will be used to destroy the free America that most of us treasure. The ultimate beneficiaries of this foolishness will be the Mohammedans whose goal is to establish a Moslem theocracy in America. The Mohammedans will exploit this faster than the simple minded conservative Christians can blink.

Liberal attitudes in academia open the way for Mohammedans to come in with their lies and balderdash, stuff that the silly liberals think is neat -- anything to go against the religious Christian conservatives. While the liberals are enjoying their myopic serendipity, the Mohammedans are preparing to eat them alive. The naive mostly liberal fools believe they can be palsey-walsey with the Mohammedans. Fools! When the sadly silly and willfully ignorant liberals wake up to this fact it will be too late because the dirty, dull, sabers and cutlasses will be at their throats sawing and hacking away.

If the Liberals and conservatives are too stupid to wake up to the world around them, they will blunder into a Moslem theocracy where nobody will win, and everyone will lose.

Here's what we can expect when the Moslem theocracy takes over America and throws the Constitution and all that comes with it out:

The Constitution would be burned - all copies. Anyone caught with a copy would be hung.

Raping nine year-old girls would not be a serious crime.

Raping nine year old boys would be encouraged.

Only creationism would be taught in schools. That ought to please the Christian conservatives, eh?

Wife beating would not only be OK, it would be encouraged. OJ

Simpson and Robert Blake's killing of their wives would never have been brought to trial. In fact wife beating is strongly encouraged and the instructions are even laid out by Mohammed in the Hadiths. Little Moslem boys are even allowed to slap, kick and hit their mothers and sisters. It's on-the-job training for when they have their own wives.

Michael Jackson would never even have been indicted or much less tried for being a pedophile. That is an established and honored practice for Mohammedans. Michael Jackson would be a national hero. Subsequent to his California trial for child molestation, he left the United States for a new life in an Arab/Moslem haven where he can pursue his passion for children without fear of prosecution.

The American Civil Liberties Union: The first time one of these jerks opened his or her yap against any Islamic laws, practices, or rules, the whole crew along with their supporters would be rounded up and slowly fed into shredding machines --after other tenderizing ministrations were completed.

Janet Jackson would have been stoned to death for her "wardrobe" malfunction.

The Pope would be hung for being a heretic along with all Cardinals and Bishops. Pedophile priests would qualify for immediate conversion to ranking Imams.

Churches would be required to pay a special, high tax, or be confiscated and turned into mosques. Every man, woman, and child would need to learn the direction of Mecca and get a little rug to roll out five times a day so they could get down on their knees five times a day with their asses propped high in the air while they say their Alahu Akbars.

Judges? Who'd need them? Jury trial? What's that? Sharia law would prevail and an arbitrary Imam would be your judge.

Congress? Senate? Abolished. The grand mufti would establish laws.

Military conscientious objector? Yeah sure. Branded a coward, it's time to cut another throat. The Koran doesn't allow for this nonsense. Flash a peace sign and get fingers chopped off.

Libraries? Pure blasphemy - they'd all be burned.

TV? Al Jazeera news and Koranic preaching 24-7 on all channels. It's all you'll need or be allowed.

Fashion boutiques? Try sack stores.

Music? Only drums for Moslem religious events. All else would be sinful - outlawed.

Liberals and like minded airheads would be delighted to see the NRA abolished. Gun ownership would be permitted for Moslems only. There would be no penalty when a gun is used against a non-Moslem.

In December, 2005, I was listening to a popular conservative radio program and the host's bubble headed assistant opined that guns should be outlawed because: "If there were no guns, there would be no crime." She is obviously one of those incredibly naive pie in the sky types who believe that by outlawing guns, the nearly one billion in existence on earth would instantly be turned into plowshares or SUVs and everybody would commence being nice to one-another. I am sorry to say, sweetcakes that your head is on another, very distant planet in this regard. Under Islamic rule by decree, you would be treated differently, your ideas would be ignored, and you could hide your foolishness in your head-to-toe burka.

Conservatives would be delighted to see the amoral ACLU abolished . There would be no more foolishness called civil rights. In fact, the ACLU which has become better known as the defenders of pederasty, sodomy, and anything that is anti-God will probably fare well if and when the Islamists take over. In fact, they'll only need to grow longer beards, learn the routine of five daily prayers, and they'll fit right in.

Women voting? Don't kid yourself.

ART? Only two kinds would be permitted: Calligraphers to write fancy gilt scriptures and architects for pretty mosques. Picasso's etchings and such would be burned.

Pensions and retirement? Your children will take care of you, or you're on the streets.

Charity? How devout of a Moslem are you? Zip for non-believers.

Drug Abuse? Public intoxication? Know what a bull whip is?

Health care? Yeah - for the Mohammedan elites first, and then -- how much will you be willing to pay. For women? Hah! Care for the mentally ill? How 'bout 'Hit the road jack!', or: "Here's a bomb vest to go blow yourself up."

And here's one for you: Hamas has actually introduced legal consideration law in the territories that they control, to re-introduce the medieval practice of execution by crucifixion. How'd you like to see your mother or your child crucified?

**We (Islamic and Judaeo-Christian cultures) are
fundamentally, diametrically opposed
as cultures, and conflict is our destiny.**

In the Orient and in the West, there is a clearly defined separation of church and state in countries where people enjoy (with the exception of China and North Korea) political and religious freedom, economic and educational liberties and freedoms, and choice. This is our strength. This is the true meaning of civilization.

In Islam, there is no distinction between, or separation of church and state. Their Koran is their constitution. Domination of the world is their goal. This is a permanent deficit at the same time that it is a clear and ever present threat to civilization, honor, decency, joy, independence, and freedom, and all that is good.

Tinseltown

Patriotism is an honored thing in most of America. In Tinseltown (Hollywood), a strong patriotic theme is not on the current agenda. Nor is there a theme that honestly includes or depicts Mohammedans/Arabs and their anti-western political agendas.

John Wane is probably rolling over in his grave.

If the weenies of Tinseltown had any courage at all (seemingly very unlikely) they would spawn some intellectually accurate silver screen pieces about apologists. I'm not going to hold my breath.

Question: What is it about generous quantities of cash in the pockets of so many self-centered, preening silver screen and TV figures that they are suddenly self-declared "authorities" about that which they open their yaps? This list of ignoramuses includes the likes of horse's patooty Alec Baldwin (a true moron, liar, and promise breaker who reaffirms his idiocy as often as he can), Ted Danson, Martin Sheen, Whoopi Goldberg, and other feeble minded fools who spew their willful ignorance at every opportunity. They are protected in their actions by the First Amendment as am I when I offer my single finger salute to them and their harebrained, pinheaded opinions.

One "summer of 2002" movie depicted a terrorist nuclear device in a football stadium as being a right-wing neo-Nazi plot. Hey, tinsel weenies, try being a little, just a teeny, itsy bitsy honest and show plotters as Islamists and/or Arabs, the real enemy. It worked in WWII movies.

Another piece of dribble, "Syriana", was likewise false to the truth, and "Munich" soft pedaled Mohammedism terrorism all of the way.

Self-centered, sometimes photogenic, silver screen and boob tube denizens of "Hollywood" and environs declare themselves experts and espouse their wisdom for all to hear. Barbara Striesand spoke of Saddam Hussein as the President of Iran. Iran? Sorry, 'Babs' but your embarrassingly gross ignorance is loud and clear. Then Striesand added to this the misspelling of the name of the Congressional House Minority Leader (Dick Gephardt). Babs is so smart that she misquotes Shakespeare to support her positions. And, she's so proud of herself that she does this on stage, in front of audiences.

There are dozens of them out there embarrassing themselves daily. I don't bother to try to remember all of their names or even spend my precious time to list their names. I have things that I feel are more important to clutter my mind with. Then there a larger numbers of much better and therefore smarter actors and actresses who are more likely civilized, wise, and moderate who chose not to make fools of themselves. And we have good guys too, mostly civilized people who usually tend to do the right thing.

Of course, on the right wing of the spectrum, we have the often demagogic but incredibly accurate Rush Limbaugh, the awesome passion of Glenn Beck, the great Michael Savage, and the deceased evangelist Jerry Fallwell.

Then, there are the pacifists, a bunch of mostly despicable, cowardly, pseudo intellectuals and phonies who want the United States, the most powerful and decency focused nation on earth to bow down and show humility to the Mohammedists. Let's all understand very clearly that showing humility to a Moslem is a show of weakness only to be exploited.

Prisoners of War

It is illegal for us Americans to torture prisoners of war. This is a very important principle that dates back in American history. Notwithstanding this it is true that Americans have often been subjected to the most egregious forms of torture. There are treaties and conventions that prohibit torturing of prisoners of war which have been violated by our opponents in the past, in recent times, and this is occurring today, and will be inflicted on Americans in the future. In a few, rare, well publicized instances there have been instances of Americans doing this as well. Americans are in prison for these violations. However, torture is commonly used by Mohammedan Arabs who have a very low threshold for what they consider courage, and that they take great pride and pleasure in abusing prisoners of war. Yeah, abusing the helpless is really courageous, just ask any Arab.

Torture is physical torments such as beatings, burnings, breaking bones, whippings and flogging, dismemberment, and general inflicting great amounts of physical pain. There are other forms of torture including extreme psychological torments designed to break down one's ability to resist. For Arabs and Mohammedans this includes joyously raping females as well as males and even small children in the presence of their loved ones.

This is wrong, and is what is done by savage, uncivilized brutes. In past conflicts, even modern conflicts such as in Korea and Vietnam, in compliance with the Geneva Convention, we worked to refrain from torturing prisoners that we held, hoping for reciprocity. Did we get reciprocity? Ask Senator John McCain. Ask the hundreds of others who endured inhuman suffering, pain, and degradation in North Vietnamese prisons. And, please, let's not forget for one moment the eighty-four+ American aviator prisoners-of-war in Vietnam who were tortured so terribly that they died--were murdered in captivity. Captured Americans in Iraq, Somalia, and Afghanistan have been subjected to the most unspeakable forms of human torment.

When Mohammedans have kidnapped Americans in the Middle East, have they refrained from torturing them? When Mohammedans have gotten their hands on Israelis, have they been nice to them, or even to one-another?

So much for the Geneva Convention.

Then, we have Abu Ghraib, and the infamous photographs of

naked Iraqi prisoners. The flaky quisling western dhimmi press led by the New York Pravda.....er.....Times, the Guardian, CNN, and others had a field day with that. Even the Mohammedans were able to make a fuss about it.....and I'll bet they had a hard time keeping straight faces in front of their fawning western liberal press. Some self-important twitter brains (again amongst the most ignorant Americans on earth) claimed that this was the worst thing that America had ever done. Ahem, America didn't do that, a couple of ignorant, poorly trained soldiers who suffered under terrible leadership got out of line. All of this could, of course, have been avoided by not taking any prisoners......

In the Iraqi incidents, and even in Afghanistan, some American Army enlisted personnel were found culpable for a few irresponsible acts, and were subjected to disciplinary actins for their misdeeds. These soldiers while guilty of transgressions were also scapegoats of senior non-commissioned and commissioned officers who failed completely in their oversight, mentoring, and supervision of those younger troops. The rungs of the ladder of those who really should be held culpable ran right up the chain of command to former Army General Karpinsky whose attainment of that ranking position was based not on competence but risk averse political correctness. Disgraced, she was quietly relieved of command, demoted just one rank, and allowed the dignity of retirement while her much lower ranking subordinates were sent to prison for her abhorrently poor management and inept leadership. This is horsesh.....balderdash. Karpinsky and her entire chain of command should all be in the slammer. Whenever a younger trooper screws up, we need to look at her or his superiors, and deal them the same levels of discipline for their poor leadership.

It is sickening that every chance they get, some pinheads go into conniption fits whenever the treatment of prisoners comes up even when the treatment is excellent. The U.S. is one of just a few nations that have worked to abide by the Geneva Convention. American soldiers were tortured and mistreated by the Japanese in World War II, by the Chinese, by Soviets, and North Koreans during the Korean war, and what the North Vietnamese did to Americans in and around Hanoi was insanely cruel. Americans do not abuse their vanquished who always fare well whenever in captivity by us. However, Americans rarely receive the same levels of humane and decent treatment.

There are some who feel that enemy combatants who are not uniformed soldiers of a sovereign nation ought to be delivered of the same treatment that Americans receive on a reciprocal basis. There are others who disagree. The treatment of combatant prisoners at Guantanamo has been excellent, far better than any American captives have been treated in Iraq or Afghanistan.

In some situations, our treatment of enemy prisoners should include at least using drugs in interrogation along with mind games to get the information we want. There is no inflicting of physical pain or maimings here, and let's leave it at that. When a subject of interrogation gives up the information we want or need, he or she has to deal with it in her or his own mind.

Enhanced interrogations are not nice, and on his third day in office, Barak Hussein Obama signed an executive order outlawing this practice as well as renditions or transfers of prisoners to countries where blatant torture is used to extract information. He also determined that he would empty the detention facility at Guantanimo Bay, and that some of those terrorists would be released on the streets of the USA. Thus, it is deemed OK if not even appropriate to sacrifice American lives based on Obama's flaky liberal standards. I sincerely hope that when terrorists strike next, they murder liberals, because that would be most appropriate. I also pray that the terrorists miss murdering genuine patriotic Americans.

It's feel good politics to dump on America patriots who do the dirty work to protect our country and its citizens, even those unworthy of protection.

Chapter 5

MIDDLE EASTERN NEIGHBORS

There are none so blind
as those who will not see....

Israel is not blind. Israel is a nation that we can trust. We're committed to them and they are committed to us. Our destinies are intertwined. Some feel that we ought to abandon Israel; that the Israelis have been living off of the Americans long enough and that they ought to begin standing on their own. Very noble but ignorant, flawed thinking. These cretins refuse to consider that the Palestinian Arabs are not standing on their own, that they receive more assistance from Arab and other outside sources than do the Israelis from us.

Israel and Palestine

The Arab tribes of the Palestine Mandate (created in the Balfour Declaration of 1917-22) who call themselves Palestinians are a sorrowful lot of Arab rabble, not deserving of any more sympathy as a group (as individuals, yes, as a group-no, they have earned what they are reaping). They have worked hard for sixty years to screw themselves up even more. They devote their energy to sustaining their status quo of ignorance, fear, self pity, corruption, hatred, and anger. They receive assistance and encouragement from the rest of the Arabs in this continuing venture which has as its only goal, the destruction of Israel.

Of the Palestinians, they need to back up their claim of being a once proud and viable entity that goes back through substantial periods of recorded history:
-When was Palestine founded? Who? Why?
-Where are the maps of antiquity showing borders?
-What is or was the capital?
-What is its currency unit?
-What were the original, and intermediate languages?
-Give some significant historical points, and name important leaders, religion/s before Islam? Don't substitute etymology for history.

Since the 1967 war, the Philistines, as they call themselves in Arabic have, by their continued hostility and intransigence encouraged Israelis to build settlements if for no other purpose but to defend itself. These Arabs are in fact nothing more than a sorry band of hated and hateful ragged residents of the Gaza strip and the West Bank of Trans-Jordan. Wallowing in self-pity, they call themselves refugees. Refugees from what? They are refugees of their own creation, nothing more. They have in fact abandoned and forfeit the rightfully Jewish land of Israel's forefathers, the home of Christianity. That land is NOT theirs, they only took it when they did by killing off the Jewish and Christian populations who were there before the bloodthirsty, rapacious Islamist raiders and thieves rolled out of the Arabian desert.

Before the Jews returned to their homeland, the area was a wasteland with just a few impoverished residents. Jews started migrating there from Spain and North Africa and by 1750, the area began to thrive. Like bees going after honey, the Arabs followed sucking up whatever they could scavenge. The flow of Jews increased significantly after World War I. Naturally, the Arabs wanting like the beggars and thieves that they are to take it all for themselves began protesting the Jewish presence.

In 1930's Germany, the monologue was very clear:
Jews, Get out of here (Europe) and go to Palestine!
--- then ---
When the Jews did, survive, and even thrived,
the Europeans monologue changed to:
Jews, leave Palestine.......

In 1947, Arabs attacked and slaughtered Jews in Aleppo, Syria, and destroyed the entire Jewish community. The few Jews who survived moved to the one place where Jews were working to protect Jews, and to create a secure future for Jews: Israel and Jerusalem.

In 1948, Arab leaders told their people to get out of the newly formed state of Israel so they, the Arabs could attack the Jews and drive them into the sea. The stupid, foolish, and boastful Arab leadership promised their people, telling them that they would soon return to their homes. The Jews in Israel in fact asked their Arab friends and neighbors to remain as friends, colleagues, and neighbors. Well, the Arab "leadership" failed their people in 1948, and continues to fail them ever since by perpetuating their racist myth of their return and the destruction of Israel.

The Arabs, aided and abetted by the totally, reprehensibly irresponsible 'Palestinian' Arab leadership have held those people (whom they encouraged to flee from their homes) in the squalid camps ever since. Their Arab brothers (Egyptians, Saudis, etc.) exploit the desperation of those people when they should, could, even can, but won't help them.

The UN established the UNRWA to take care of the Palestinians, who are now in their fifth or sixth generation (depending on how young they marry their daughters off for breeding purposes) of being generational parasites demanding more in time, attention, and funds than any other refugee group in the world.

Suppose you were insane.
And suppose you were a follower of Islam.

Insha'Allah, it's allah's true blessing on them that they are paranoid psychotics, insanely irrational, willfully stupid, poor, disenchanted, have crooks for leaders, and are repeatedly dumped on by their Arab brethren. They are incapable of raising the standards of truth and justice. The Palestinian/Arab people have been betrayed repeatedly by a succession of Ali Baba dens of thieves who have been personally enriched at the Palestinian/Arabs' expense. The Arabs need to be held to a genuine moral standard of decency and charity that they are unwilling to stand up to. Instead, the Arabs are swine using victims as only swine will.

There are twenty-some 'Arab' nations, and with the exception of Jordan (which has had little choice) none will permit even one Palestinian to emigrate. Twenty selfish Arab nations refuse to charitably welcome any brother Arabs, and will not accept them. This shows their true character.

The Arabs are not interested in peace with Israel, except on their own, despicably hateful terms. Their terms do not include co-existing with or allowing Israel to survive. As long as the Mohammed worshiping Arabs remain uncharitably dedicated to the total destruction (first) of Israel and every Jew in the Middle East, and then (secondly) the destruction of the entire civilized world, they can, should, and will continue to suffer.

Late in the 20th century, the Israelis, after a deluge of hashassins murdered far too many innocents, started building a wall between themselves and the Arabs. The Arabs naturally went goofy because the walls thwarted their ability to smuggle explosives and assassins in -- which proved the effectiveness of the barricades and walls. Naturally, the UN condemned the walls for other stupid reasons, denying that the walls actually protected and saved the lives of innocent people from wanton murderous Arabs.

To get the Israelis to consider or accept anything, the Israelis must first have an absolute guarantee to infinity of peace which includes unreserved recognition of and acceptance of Israel (in every language and country on earth). Only the so-called Palestinians and other Arabs can provide such a guarantee, not the USA, not Russia, not China, not Europe, and especially not the Useless Nations. Only Arabs themselves can accomplish lasting peace. But, because the Arabs are such abject failures at keeping promises, they naturally blame everyone else for the failures -- that's their nature. It's an Arab thing -- blame someone else for your failure. If anything is consistent in Arab culture, it's scapegoating -- blaming someone else for their own uselessness and failures.

Further, we all understand that Mohammed instructed his followers to never keep promises with non-Moslem people. So, any agreement worked out will be hollow (as all have been) and meaningless, and soon ignored. Should we ever be surprised when the Arabs betray their word? Anybody who is surprised when betrayed by an Arab is a fool, an idiot, or a chump. Or, perhaps, he or she is just beginning to learn about the true Islam

In 2005, the Israelis under Sharon pulled out of their holdings in Gaza, and a couple of places in the West Bank. This was apparently to appease and strengthen the liar, Abbas, as he tried to govern the Arabs. The various factions of Arab gangsters and murderers in the Arab territories unable to send their youth into Israel strapped with explosives started turning, like rats in a cage, against one-another, establishing new levels of anarchy. With fewer targets in Gaza, they fought over the spoils the Israelis left behind. With hollow leadership, they were unable to govern themselves and maintain a semblance of civilized law and order.

The Arabs need to do something they are not accustomed to doing, and are probably incapable of doing. They need to be honest with themselves and face facts. That's a very, very tall order, an impossible challenge -- being honest and dealing with truths, facts, reality. They need to pull their heads out of the proverbial sand, or from where the sun doesn't shine..... And learn to compromise, to earn the right to settle in territories not yet settled by Israelis. They must honestly make internationally recognizable promises and then keep them. Yeah, sure......., in its 1400 year history, Islam has NOT ever kept any promises with real people. Anyone who believes this can happen now is insanely naive.

Let's consider a fundamental truth: The Israeli - Arab conflict is NOT a conflict over borders, or land, or water. It is a clash of cultures and the goal of one (Islam) is the elimination, the total annihilation of the other, of Israel and all Jews. In fact, this cause -- the destruction of Jews (and next, the whole of civilization) is a specific obligation, an article of faith of all Moslems. It's a duty and responsibility laid out in their laws, their constitution, the Koran.

Since Israel's inception, American political leaders have, one after another been humbled again and again by the Arabs. They all honestly worked at peace -- the useless appeasement of the Arabs who deceitfully only want and demand more and more, leaving negotiations, treaties and agreements to just die. To the Arabs, negotiations or a dialogue is just an opportunity for another charade, to lie and beg, to lie and wheedle, to lie and plead, to lie and harangue, to lie and accuse, to lie and divert attention whilst they sharpen their knives in preparation to plunge them into our backs. That is not just an opinion, it is a historical fact of one-thousand-four-hundred-years. Dialogue is an Islamic Trojan Horse.

One of the better Secretaries' of State, Colin Powell made a few genuine attempts at doing something but only got humiliated for his honest efforts, and wisely backed off for the last two years of his tenure. He simply knew that he was wasting his time and energy. Wisely, he saw that there was no future in beating his head against an unyielding Islamic wall of stubbornly willful ignorance, stupidity, hatred, self pity, and deceit. He confirmed what he had already learned, that Arab agreements are in fact only tactical ploys, lies, deceit, and nothing more. He knocked that waste of time, resources, and energy off.

Just after her confirmation as Secretary of State, Condoleeza Rice trundled hurriedly off on her first pilgrimage to the Arab lands of deceit, lies, falsehoods, and humiliation. Hopeful that with the recent death (reportedly from HIV/AIDS) of the murdering liar, Arafat, that she could have better luck than the others, she struck out and came home a confirmed useful fool, a dhimmi.

The United States' policies in this regard are a continuing cycle of failure in spite of our sincere best efforts. The USA needs to look itself in a mirror and to recognize and accept that the futile pursuits of the past sixty years are a failure, and continuing to pursue this same path is simply a recipe for continuing failure. The clinical sign of insanity is doing the same thing over and over and getting the same negative results, and then trying again. We are not alone in this regard. We are not the only ones to have made fools of ourselves trying to resolve, to come to grips with the Middle East. The French hauled out of there with their tails between their legs after more than a century of hard work and effort. The British were confounded despite their best intentions and efforts of a couple of hundred years. The Russians didn't fare well at all, either.

Appeasement minded but feckless American intellectuals, leftists, and others of this discredited type have largely dominated the Washington diplomatic scene for over fifty years, since the time of John Foster Dulles. Is there any reason why some of the best and most effective leaders of this nation, people like Presidents Reagan, the Bushes, and Nixon had and so often have so little confidence in the Department of State and other liberal groups in and around Washington?

The United States needs a new strategy -- over a half of a century of "negotiations" that haven't brought any measure of Middle East peace is a gross failure by any measure. The United States must develop and adopt new policies based on reality, not foolish pub politically correct dreams and myths, not based on Arab lies and deceit, not based on half-witted or half-baked so-called intellectual thinking. We need realistic policies that have a chance of working. Any such policies will of necessity be harsh.

Firstly, no Secretary of State should ever venture off to any of these places on a "mission of peace". Any such travel will ultimately be another lesson in continuing humiliation.

When and if a Secretary of State or other cabinet officer, advisor to the President, or Presidential envoy travels to any of these places, it can be as a "goodwill mission" in which the traveling VIP will hand down advice or instructions, and to admonish (Arabs especially) and to encourage, but not ever to be admonished. When an Arab starts to admonish an American VIP, the only appropriate response is to immediately stand, turn his or her back, show the sole of his or her shoe and walk away, to leave, and to not return until the Arab makes an apology. We'll get much more traction by treating them on those realistic terms because we have learned that their terms don't work, ever.

Obama, weeks after his swearing in sent a patsy (who earns income from Arab clients) named Mitchell off to the Middle East with instructions to listen to the Moslems' whining, cajoling, lying, and crap. Then, his first major TV interview was granted to a Moslem TV propaganda organ. In that interview he emphasized his Moslem family ties and heritage (something he de-emphasized during his campaign). Within two weeks of taking office, Obama stepped forward as a weakling vis-à-vis Islam, and established his role as a useful fool sympathizer if not an out-and-out anti-American proponent of Islam.

Clientitis

The Department of State itself has another problem occasionally voiced by Secretaries of State (and others). This is the problem of American ambassadors "going native". "Going native" is a phenomena afflicting Ambassadors, both career Foreign Service Officers as well as political appointees. An ambassador assigned to whatever xyz republic seemingly within a few weeks of getting off of a plane and becoming "oriented" suddenly forgets that it is her or his job to represent the United States. Instead, they seem to feel that it is their duty to become that country's advocate in the United States, a job that the ambassador of xyz republic is supposed to do. All too often, the American ambassadors abandon their mission -- their duty to represent the United States' interests in xyz republic and nothing else. In my opinion, these ambassadors are betraying their sworn duty to the people of the United States.

Reportedly, Secretary of State (another of the very few good Secretaries of State – probably the best in recent history) George P. Schultz began a practice with newly minted Ambassadors. He'd meet them in his office and wander over to a map of the world and ask something like: "Where is your country?" The hapless appointee would immediately assume Schultz was just another dolt (as is true with most Democratic regimes' secretaries of state) and immediately point to the country they were assigned to. Schultz would then correct them by pointing to the United States and remind them that: "THIS is YOUR country!"

An example of the problem: Annually, the Department of State hosts experts from various agencies as well as the State Department itself for annual policy reviews. Naturally, the American ambassador of the respectful countries is included for their hands-on expertise in living in these places and dealing with the local governments on a day-to-day basis. The purpose of course is to plan for future endeavors, how to deal with different issues in different regions and countries such as the Horn of Africa (the Sudan Eritrea, Djibouti, Somalia, Ethiopia, etc.)

A 2005 gathering of such experts was convened regarding East Africa, but the American Ambassadors to Ethiopia and Eritrea were actually excluded because those two ambassadors had "gone native" to the extreme extent that the ambassadors' expertise was and judgment so compromised by their misguided "clientitis" loyalty to Ethiopia and Eritrea rather than to the United States that their presence would be worse than detrimental.

Another example was a letter to President Bush signed by about sixty former American diplomats complaining about the USG's support for the only democracy in the Middle East, Israel. This noxious dribble was pure anti-Semitic and anti-Israel bias at its best, and the effort was led by a former Ambassador named Killgore, another victim of clientitis and obviously a leading quisling useful fool dhimmi of Mohammedism.

The British don't have this problem, nor do the Australians, the French, the Germans, the Russians or any others, but there's something with many American Ambassadors who forsake their duties and sell themselves out becoming whores acting very contrary to the best interests of the United States.

We need a criteria that independently checks, monitors, and evaluates communications emanating from American ambassadors. The moment they start going whacko or native (as in clientitis) as regards their responsibilities, they should be recalled to the United States and reminded very firmly about their oaths of office. If they go off course again, they ought to immediately be pulled back to the United States and fired. This should be uniformly applied to both political hacks rewarded with appointments as well as career Foreign Service Officers.

The Arabs have, on occasion been able to understand and appreciate the value of honesty and guarantees only when they have been backed up by a generous wielding of the proverbial "big stick." And then, it's only temporary. We must ourselves understand clearly that the Arabs' unhinged, fundamental, immature, self-centered, generally insane and anti-civilization orientation equates to their single minded world of willful ignorance, hatred, and stupidity. That's where the Moslems live. When we learn to deal with them on those terms, terms they understand, then we can be comfortable.

Arabs work really hard at remaining (willfully) ignorant, and are internationally recognized as treacherous, and untrustworthy. They know this. We know it. It's no secret, even from them. They know it all too well, and thus treat one-another with this understanding. Why should we treat them differently?

As an example: One aspect of this (distrust of other Arabs) is reflected in their typically arranged marriages to tribal members -

cousins - they have no trust outside of the "clan." If a marriage is outside of the "clan" it is solely arranged to form an alliance with and bring another group into the "clan". That's how the current Saudi royal family managed to gain control of the Saudi peninsula years ago, with hundreds of arranged marriages to the Saudi Kings (Faisl and Saud) to bring different clans into alignment.

When we learn to properly and judiciously wield that big stick with dexterity and firmness, the Arabs will actually be more comfortable, responsive, and will be more likely to accept the outcome. They don't need to like it, just understand and accept.

"MANCHURIAN CANDIDATE"! That wasn't a Santa Suit that that a little boy was wearing in an Arab propaganda/training photograph the Israelis found during their takeover of Arab territories on or about June 26th, 2002. The Arabs had dressed a small child in a quasi-military suit with a suicide inscribed headband, and his body strapped with (hopefully) imitation explosives and then photographed. That photo was not for a family album. That unfortunate child, like so many thousands and thousands of children in Madrassas throughout the Moslem world was and is a Manchurian Candidate trainee in Islam's assault on anything and everything not Moslem.

Twisted indeed is the mind of a woman who would spawn children just so that they can become suicidal hashassins and go off and murder innocent people.

Syria, along with every other Arab nation is opposed to Israel's existence. Syria has done nothing to assimilate Arabs who ran out of what is now Israel in 1948 and became refugees. Syria does all that it can to harm Israel and the United States, and has harbored, funded, and trained terrorists who have murdered Americans and Israelis.

Syria pretends to be ready to accept things as they are. But, there is a major sticking point that prevents any serious settlement. The Golan Heights overlooking Israel were Syrian property (from which they could observe Israel, and for many years before Israel seized the Heights repeatedly launched terrorist rocket attacks) and were among the first objectives seized by the Israelis after Syria attacked Israel in 1967. Israel is not inclined to return the Golan Heights to Syria as long as Syria remains hostile. That's forever!

The Golan Heights could be made international for an interim period of at least a couple of hundred years. The Syrians and Israelis could share equally in the mutually beneficial economic benefits (tourism, agriculture, and water) of the Golan Heights, but administration needs to be under an international peacekeeping force made up of 25% Arabs (none of them from countries bordering on Israel), 25% European/American, 25% non-Moslem Asians, and 25% African/Latin American. In other words, the Golan Heights should be an international enclave and not a part or parcel of any one country.

Lebanon fought which has been called a civil war between Christians and Moslems that is technically over - they fought themselves out. The Mohammedans attacked the Christians in 1975 with a goal of eliminating or converting them to Islam, to spread the dominance of Islam. Until the 1970's, Lebanon was a democracy ruled by a Christian minority along with some Moslem moderates. It was a prosperous and beautiful country with trappings of a civilized nation. Now, falling further and further under Islamist control, it is rapidly deteriorating and becoming just another snake pit of pain, suffering, death, deceit, poverty, and disease.

Over in Jordan, the Palestinian Liberation Front's snaky, treacherous leader, Yasser Arafat decided that he had had enough of his host, Jordan's King Hussein and his relatively civil, decent, and moderate leadership. Arafat launched a civil war with his Palestinian rabble attacking King Hussein and his people. Arafat lost terribly, and was run out of Jordan. This conflict caused the death of more 'Palestinian' Arabs than Israel has killed during its 60+ years of existence.

The 'Palestinian' Arabs not killed flooded into Lebanon, which accepted them with hospitality, food, shelter, medicine, and the hosts suffered the consequence. The Palestinian Arabs quickly allied themselves with other Arab rabble, got assistance from Syria, and launched a holy war against the vulnerable Christians, their hosts.

Before the holy war started, Moslem farmers produced opium in the Bekaa Valley which they sold for profit to the Christians who processed the opium into base products from which heroin is derived. The Christians produced some heroin for sale and export, but also sent base products to Europe where it was refined into heroin (the French connection) which was then distributed to the United States and throughout Europe. Arafat the thief, wanted in on this, and the Moslem Lebanese opium growers never really had a chance. They were overwhelmed and taken over. These were, and still are controlled and funded by Syria, and others to lesser degrees for a while, until Tehran's Ayatollahs got themselves ensconced in Lebanon with their lackeys, Hezbollah.

The Lebanese "civil war" is not over. There have been lulls, and periods of hostility, but until the Christians are all killed off or driven out of Lebanon, it will not end, ever.

Opium is now processed fully from the poppy to the finished product, heroin in the Bekaa Valley from which it is exported to Europe and other places. The greatest share of the profits now go to support terrorist operations and to the Mohammedan politicians of the region. Lebanon has been chopped up and remains tenuously a nation divided between Christians and various Moslem factions, some purely fundamentalist, and others more ideological, if there's a difference.

The CIA of course has no real idea of what is going on.

Jordan, the Hashemite Kingdom in its third generation of Hussein rulers is moderate, progressive, and also got its butt kicked in the 1967 war against Israel. It was sucked into that war, and everyone knows that. Jordan has also fought wars with its Arab neighbors and partners to maintain its independence and integrity. The fiercest fight was with Palestinian Arabs who tried to take over the country. In spite of this, Jordan has been the most accommodating towards Palestinians.

The Palestinian "West Bank" is the territory of Trans-Jordan west of the Jordan river. It was not Jordanian property and has not been a major issue between Jordan and Israel.

Egypt is a large impoverished nation that borders on Israel. It is currently led by ruthless pragmatists who have barely been able to slow the effectiveness of the fundamentalists although the fundamentalists have managed to kill several of the nation's leadership.

American taxpayers have given Egypt, a country that is by no means our "friend" nor an "ally" more than $60 billion in direct aid (tribute), much of which goes into the pockets of its leaders. For all of that, we have received absolutely nothing in return. Egypt is one of the most anti-American and anti-Western, or anti-civilization countries in the world today. Egypt is a center of anti-Semitism and all of the wonderful promises made by its government about improving relations with Israel have never been honored. Egypt is a fraud, and neither the American nor the Israeli government have had the courage to call Egypt what it is, a worthless pit.

Egypt got its butt kicked in the 1967 war, and again in a 1973 attack. Lessons learned, Egypt's government is working hard maintain a moderate façade and pretends to work with Israel. Of course, the billions the United States sends to prop up the government is a major factor. No Palestinians are permitted to immigrate into Egypt however. The Egyptians much prefer to see their Moslem 'brothers' in the Gaza Strip continue suffering in poverty, as a front, a foil.

The Christians (who pre-date Islam) in Egypt are suffering terribly, and the United States and United Nations are oblivious of their contributions towards this suffering. This is stupid and wrong.

Iran, while distant from Israel, is a large, oil-rich nation ruled by militant zealot Moslem fundamentalist clerics who are so corrupt that they must foment trouble outside of Iran to keep attention focused away from their incompetent, inept selves.

These fundamentalists are purposeful in their expansionist desires, and are therefore committed to the destruction of Israel as a first step in the expansion of their rabidly insane form of Islam.

They are working overtime to thwart U.S. efforts at democratic nation building in Afghanistan and Iraq.

The Iranian people had a taste of relative freedom, at least freedom from oppressive religious theocrats when under the rule of the

Shah. The Shah worked hard to follow Kemal Attaturk (Turkey) and to pull the Iranian people (kicking and screaming) into the twentieth century and to join the civilized nations of the world. He partially succeeded, but when the he needed our help he was simply abandoned by the vacuous, inept and wildly goofy Carter and his gang of KKK oriented idiots. The civilization hating Carter gang allowed, even paved the way for the creation of Ayatollah Khomeni's radical Islamic regime with its accompanying depredations of the succession of ayatollahs. The Persian people are wise enough and have enough collective knowledge of civilization's ideals of freedom, honor, and independence to hunger for those once again. They would like to revive civilization in that country but their chances appear slim.

Of course, the Iranians won't allow, not one Palestinian to emigrate.

Also distant from Israel, **Libya** and its goofy leader, Muamar Khadaffi, is nevertheless committed to Israel's demise and supports and funds anyone and everyone allied against Israel. Khadaffi is wily and has taken steps to improve relations with the United States and the civilized world, but he cannot be trusted.

Iraq, like Iran is a country with plenty of oil wealth. The regime of Saddam Hussein is gone, replaced with instability brought about by the United State's disposal of that regime. Saddam had no viable heir apparent and the Iranians were poised to take over Iraq's oil fields if and when Saddam fell out of power or died. The United States could not tolerate such a situation and got rid of him using the valid premise that he was a monster and that he would use weapons of mass destruction against Israel at some point. When things settle down again, it is likely that the new Iraqi government will be unfriendly towards Israel, and will not permit Palestinians to emigrate.

After the first Iraq war, President Bush (the 41st) did not fail regarding the removal of Saddam Hussein. The decision at the time was to leave him (Saddam) in power because there was nobody who could fill the vacuum were he removed, except for the ayatollah's of Iran which were (and are) a more insidious evil than Saddam.

Saddam seemingly fooled the world regarding his 'weapons of mass destruction'. In the future when dealing with countries or dictators who play this game, we need to establish and follow rules, simple, direct and very clear. If and when it becomes necessary to 'inspect' for weapons of mass murder, and teams are out there doing it, if a site is denied to the inspectors, it should be assumed that weapons of mass murder/destruction/mayhem are there and the sites should be bombed into rubble. This is a simple and effective solution, because this is what gets their attention.

Kuwait owes its existence to Israel's main ally, the United

States and the sheik's who rule the tiny, oil rich country are on their temporary good behavior. Still, no Palestinian immigrants are welcome.

Bahrain, Qatar, the **United Arab Emirates**, and **Muscat and Oman** are not terribly involved in the fray against Israel so far, that we know of. But, what do we know for sure? No Palestinian immigrants please.

Soft target, Qatar is paying millions to al Qaeda every month in protection money--bribes, support, or whatever to assure that al Qaeda does not launch any attacks against Qatari interests, especially in Qatar itself. Qatar also permits Al Jazeera TV to operate with impunity, as a sop to the Mohammedans.

When a US report cited Qatar as being a violator of human rights, treating servants as slaves, engaging in human (slave) trafficking, the Qataris reacted with typically hysterical "dismay" and "shock" and so forth, all taqiyyah. They claimed (taqiyyah) that they know nothing of such activities, etc. So, if one Arab official claims, because of his balderdash, or willful ignorance, that something is untrue, the world is supposed to believe him, eh? This is just another example of an Arab/Mohammedan getting angry with someone for not believing his taqiyyah lies. The truth is still the truth to those of us civilized enough to see it.

Yemen is not much involved, but only because they are poor, right?. Yemen is moderate, right? The USA is supporting the Yemeni government in its war on terrorism, right? Because the Yemenis are now suddenly cooperating (at least they are pretending and have the Americans fooled) with the USA -- no doubt to avoid the Taliban's fate. The Yemeni government owned, operated, and controlled television station regularly broadcasts prayer sermons from the Grand Mosque in Sana, Yemen's capital on Fridays. The broadcast is fully sanctioned by the government. A typical message (this is not a one-time incident, but is typical) was a prayer on August 23rd, 2002: "O Allah, destroy the Jews and their supporters, and the Christians and their supporters and followers. O Allah, destroy the ground under their feet, instill fear in their hearts, and freeze the blood in their veins!" Christians are described routinely as vile kufar, to be annihilated.

In its ongoing lawmaking, the Yemeni government has reformed their freedom of the press laws to include the death penalty for journalists. That will assure that journalists in Yemen report honestly and accurately on happenings in Yemen.

A Yemeni woman who, at the age of sixteen (and already the mother of two children) was tortured into confessing that she killed her husband was sentenced to death. However, her guards raped her and made her pregnant before the execution could be carried out, so she was allowed, in accordance with Shari 'a law, to live until the child was two. Then the execution went forward even though credible witnesses stated repeatedly that her husband was killed by his own cousin over a land dispute. That doesn't matter however to these inhuman Mohammedan savages.

Many Moslem states of the former USSR whose names all seem to end with **'stan'**), as well as the **Pakistanis, Algerians, Moroccans, Bangladeshis, Malaysians, Tunisians,** and others are uniformly hostile to Israel. These nations tend to have some form of make believe nonsectarian governments that are presently claiming to be non-fundamentalist, and who are therefore being helpful, if only marginally so in our "war on terrorism". That all will come to a screaming halt when (if) the leadership of the United States discovers their long forgotten courage, and acknowledge that Islam has declared war on the United States and we must, for our survival fight to drive those Mohammedans back.

Indonesia: Hostile to Israel. You bet. Indonesia has oil, so the United States government in violation of its own laws provided weapons and munitions to the Indonesian government over the decades. First, they were used for ethnic cleansing, to kill and drive out millions of ethnic Chinese. Then, after thousands of ethnic Chinese were murdered off, they were unleashed to murder more than a half million Christians and other non-Moslems as Indonesia's Mohammedans spread their corrupt, evil rule out to other islands in the archipelago. The Indonesian government supported and sanctioned Islamist Laskar Jihad and other Mohammedans have murdered tens of thousands of Indonesian Buddhists and Hindus. They have forcefully converted (convert or die) tens of thousands to Islam, and have demolished hundreds of Christian churches as well has Buddhist and Hindu temples. The Moslem Indonesian government which is secretly wholly supportive of the Mohammedan terrorists has no interest in protecting their minorities, and only does so, resentfully, when pressured by the civilized world.

The lying Moslems in control of Indonesia claim that the country is a progressive Asian democracy. Yeah, progressive means murdering off the ethnic Chinese first, then the Christians, then the Hindus, to soon be followed by the Buddhists, and then any other non-believers. Before they kill or enslave the women of course, they like all good Mohammedan men gang rape them.

Non-Moslems who try to defend themselves are of course branded as terrorists and are then murdered.

Apes and Pigs
Sinful Viewing

Mohammed declared (it's in the Koran) that Jews and Christians are pigs. In Islam, pigs are dirty, not to be touched. But, according to

Mohammed, it is just fine to have sexual contact with 'pigs' when Moslems go out and rape young Christian and Jewish women and boys. Obviously Mohammed was a hypocrite, and his followers today are hypocrites violating their own Koran. It would be reasonable therefore to assume that like everything else that Moslems only adhere to the Koran when it suits them.

As evidenced in Afghanistan when we saw TV reports of women being thrashed for exposing an ankle, Mohammedism has declared it a sin to see a woman other than one's wife naked. Again, Mohammed had captive women stripped naked and marched through the streets, so it was OK to see women naked under these circumstances. Also, when committing rape, a woman is usually exposed to the rapist, so viewing a naked woman is again a sin, but it's still OK during rape (sanctioned by Mohammed).

There is a real cognitive dissonance here between different instructions handed down by Mohammed, and in his Koran. Clearly, Mohammed was suffering from schizophrenia, and this has been passed along and has become a part of the reality that is Islam. Islam is insane.

The **Malaysian** government is a Moslem dictatorship wearing a false front claiming to be a democracy. Malaysian 'Prime Minister' Mahathir called for the extermination of the Anglo-Saxon race. The Mohammedan Jemaah Islamiah terrorists in Thailand and Cambodia are directly supported by the Malaysian government along with their Indonesian counterparts under the control of the Wahabi al Qaeda. Since 9/11/2001, thousands of civilized Thais have been butchered by Mohammedans in southern Thailand.

Sudan, where Islamist terrorists murdered American Ambassador Cleo Noel. The Sudanese did not cooperate with the Americans investigating this murder. Don't trust them. Sudan is one of the most evil places on earth, especially for Christians and animists who are routinely slaughtered because of their beliefs, with the women and children becoming slaves who are sold and used however their purchasers desire. Sudan's 2005 peace accord with the Christian dominated south was just a ploy. Before long, the Sudanese government will again begin slaughtering innocents in the most horrible ways. They set fire to houses and shoot anyone trying to escape. They bury wounded alive. They cut off the opposing hands and feet of able bodied men and leave them to die. They dump dead bodies into wells thus poisoning the water. They enslave young women and children. Rape is standard practice.

Attacked and destroyed Christian and animist villages, churches, hospitals, and schools are not and never have been military targets, they are just the 'infidel'. Recent Mohammedan Sudanese atrocities have been taking place for fifty years, and anyone who says otherwise is either a liar, is very misinformed, or just willfully ignorant.

America's often haphazard response to these atrocities just encourages their continuation.

The Sudanese government has a new ally in their murderous Mohammedization of the country - China. Because of the cost of oil, the reserves in the eastern part of the Sudan are now worth recovering, and the Chinese have stepped in with resources to get that oil, oil the Chinese need for their economic expansion.

Afghanistan is a mess. Afghanistan is a fool's destiny. We Americans with all of our sophistication temporarily routed the Taliban. Wow! They were ugly, stupid, primitive cavemen with a few rifles and rocket propelled grenades. With the partial ouster of the Taliban, the drug trade again flourished, and its benefactors are the Taliban. Go figure. And, the United States Government has been instrumental in allowing this. What? Yes, we have. We held sway over Afghanistan and all that happened there to a large extent, including election of the Karzai government. We could have, and ought to have insisted as a first priority that the cultivation of opium cease. We didn't, and opium production remains king in Afghanistan, once again the world's leading supplier of opium.

The June, 2002 Afghani Loya Jurga council that formed a supposedly new government in Afghanistan basically re-created the defunct fundamentalist Moslem status-quo that the USSR worked earlier to oust. The Loya Jurga appointed or re-appointed surviving primitive, ugly, greedy war and drug lords to govern the nation. Many of these utterly corrupt jerks are even members of the Taliban.

Yes, we definitely blew it. We had an opportunity to have a lasting adverse impact on the illicit drug trade, and to help a nation move into at least the nineteenth century, and instead we give the thugs a pass. Apparently we were totally lacking in two important areas: -- The Central Intelligence Agency has no idea of who the good guys are nor who the bad guys are, enough to be able to put forth a list of characters that should have been prohibited from taking or holding any office in the new government. And, nobody in the U.S. Government had the fortitude and foresight to insist that the Loya Jurga prudently bring in people who would work towards creating a modern, civilized government that would serve the people rather than return a bunch of evil, ignorant, corrupt tribal war lords to power.

The British spent over a hundred years trying to bring civilization to Afghanistan and were handed their butts in a basket; the USSR invested, twenty years with a half of a million men in arms and were handed their butts on a platter. What are we doing there with a few thousand good men, no clear objectives or goals, and a president who wants to lose the war? What we are doing now is a pure waste of money, and most importantly the blood of decent men. Men fought and died so that Mohamed Karzai could take the leadership role in trying to bring a semblance to civilization to the country. In March of 2009, he signed into law the right of husbands to rape their wives, and new laws restricting females to their houses unless escorted by a male family member. Great progress here, eh? Karzai is a pig under a goatskin cap.

Our handling of Afghanistan can go one of three ways being mindful that the and the USSR were handed their own backsides.

1)   We've been putzing around there for seven years and Obama wants to send more troops over there to putz around some more. Putzing will only cost precious American lives as well as squander tons of money. How many dead Americans will it take before we decide to haul or backsides in the proverbial basket out? When we leave, the primitives will rule and we'll be back where we were in 2001.

2)   Slice and dice the place up among the various tribes and create a dozen or so little countries, each of them beholding to, and depending on us for survival. The Taliban will be neutralized, and we can play one against the other to keep the peace (divide and conquer). In this environment, we can enjoy successes in bringing a semblance of order and civilization.

3)   Go in and defoliate the opium crops using available herbicides that target just opium plants. [Rumor has it that the Bushies decided against such actions because it would upset their so-called allies; and that the Obama crew feel the same way. This amounts to trading American soldier's blood for opium that will kill American civilians. The only losers here are us. Perhaps defoliate the farms as well. Make everyone come to us for food, and do that at sites where we can then deal with them on our terms. Put planes in the air and blast anyone moving about with a weapon, and then impose new rules, start educating people (it will take at least four generations for the winning of hearts and minds to succeed), and tolerate NO nonsense.

Dong what we are dong now, option one is a clear loser. That is guaranteed! Option two has possibilities. Option three is draconian, follows their rules, rules they can understand and relate to. But, I doubt that America has the stomach to do option three, which is the best chance of really winning.

Somalia is barely what one would call a nation. It has no government, hasn't had one for decades, and consists of a bunch of brutal, savage tribals. This miserable place in the Horn of Africa is a haven for al Qaeda and all other terrorist groups.

The Somalis humiliated the inept President Clinton who along with his cabinet and advisers was so befuddled and cowardly that he couldn't bring himself to respond in any way to a bunch of savages desecrating the remains of eighteen brave American soldiers that he, Clinton abandoned and refused to support, condemning them to their brutal deaths.

The terrorists who attacked and blew up American Embassies

in Kenya and Tanzania staged their attacks from Somalia.

Somalia remains a haven for terrorists and terrorist organizations such as al Qaeda who are thriving in that place. But, U.S. authorities cannot confirm this because they have no "confirmable" intelligence. The CIA is ineffective in the area and therefore cannot confirm that which it does not know, even if it's happening.

Some smart American officials in the area, with experience in dealing with Somalia believe that the best thing that could or should happen to Somalia would be to 'vulcanize' the whole place.

Pakistan wisely sided with the United States in the limited war on terrorists where the first focus was on the Taliban and Al Qaeda in neighboring Afghanistan.

Pakistan, among all of the Moslem nations has an Atomic Bomb. There is no doubt that the fundamentalists would topple the moderate, pragmatic government in a heartbeat if they had the chance. And, there is no doubt that they are working hard towards this end.

Pakistan's creator of her atomic bomb was all too willing to sell what he had to the highest bidders.

What would the United States and India do if militant Mohammedan fundamentalists got hold of Pakistan's nuclear weapons? Does anyone think the Indians or the United States would or should sit on our hands and dither? Certainly, there are elements in America (such as Senators Kennedy, Keary, and others come to mind) that preferred to dither (as did Nevil Chamberlain) until the mushroom clouds appeared and then wring their hands because it happened. These, of course are the "liberal" elitists and their loyal but stupid followers.

Turkey is rapidly reverting away from Ataturk's dream of a civilized nation. Turkey is moving towards becoming just another backward Mohammedan pit. It is time for the United States, NATO, and the Europeans to reevaluate their relationship with the increasingly anti-civilization oriented retro-Mohammedan dominated Turkish government. Turkey's ability to ever be a modern, democratic, responsible nation is diminishing rapidly, and it's continuing as a secular democracy is increasingly in doubt. The ball is clearly in the Turks' court. Turkey must make the right choices now. Their decisions and choices since the United States actively started the process of eliminating the Saddam regime in Iraq have been uniformly bad which makes them increasingly unreliable and therefore irrelevant to any meaningful US-Turkish partnership. The Turk's continuing irrational, immature, and hostile attitude towards Armenia and the Greeks of Cyprus indicates how their continuing attitude towards Europe will evolve.

We must not forget the manner in which the Turks established their control over half of the island of Cyprus, and how we (NATO) cowed before the Turkish invasion of that Greek place. We ought to step up to the plate and insist that the Turks back out of Cyprus and let the Greeks take it back. By virtue of the fact that we haven't stood up to Turkish aggression, we have established that we are weak and ineffectual. We must support the Greeks and dump the Turks.

Jihad

The Islamists want us to believe that the translation of the Arabic word, jihad to English has nice meanings such as 'involvement' and other nice terms such as "spiritual struggle". This is a flat, boldfaced lie, taqiyyah! The true meaning of Jihad in any modern contextual meaning is: HOLY WAR. There is no other acceptable translation. Naturally, the uninformed, the ignorant, and the simple minded apologists want to believe that it has other meanings. Fools!

Islamists want us to pretend as they do, that people do not mean what they mean. Balderdash! When an Islamist uses the word "jihad" he means one thing and one thing only: Holy War against all infidels, you and I and our destruction, and the destruction of all that is decent.

According to the Koran, jihad is not something a Moslem can opt out of. It demands absolutely that all able-bodied believers unquestioningly join the conflict. Yes, there is always a conflict that Islam is involved with, somewhere. Nobody gets an out of jihad. The women, children, elderly, and the lame are required to give aid without compromise to the jihadists. They don't just go out and start slicing throats.

Madrassas

Quite a bit has been said about Madrassas, the fundamentalist Islamist schools that prey on the ignorant, mostly in Moslems, but also in other countries where children are brainwashed, and the jihadi were and continue to be recruited and trained for jihad against civilization.

Of course, the Madrassas (they are not really schools in the sense of civilized nations because they don't teach or educate in the traditional sense of reading, writing, math, sciences, etc., and what is needed to survive or thrive in the real world. Among other things, the Madrassas are political tools to indoctrinate and brainwash children and to create jihadis for the holy wars to come. They are funded with American and European dollars and Euros used to purchase oil from Saudi Arabia. A January 2005 announcement reported that the Saudis had opted to fund another 4,500 fundamentalist Wahabi Madrassas in Afghanistan, Pakistan, Bangladesh, and India. . I cannot fathom why India would permit Madrassas that teach hatred of Hindus, Buddhists, and Christians - in India.

The Madrassas recruit young boys from about the age of six, and they are put into 'training' for up to or even exceeding twelve years.

Brothels: For the first five years or so, the boys are locked away at night for their 'protection.' After that period, they are brought out and trained for other functions, as Boy-toys for the sexual satisfaction of first the Imams, and then the older boys and young men.

Taj Mahal

During the several centuries of Mohammedan rule over India, they managed to instill in Indians the subordinate acceptance of second class status of dhimmitude which survives to this day whether the Indians realize this or not. It has become part and parcel to their culture. An example is the Taj Mahal, one of the most beautiful structures ever created, and which is a major tourist attraction drawing thousands to India every year to see it's spectacular beauty. The Taj was built by an emperor at the Moslem Moghul capital at Agra. Sha Jahan built it in memory of his Persian Moslem princess, Mumtaz (among other names) Mahal who died after birthing her 14th child. Attributed to architect Ustad Isa, the Taj took over twenty years to be built by 20,000 serfs and slaves, and the tax burden imposed on the Indians was enormous. Reportedly, to make sure nobody duplicated it, Sha Jahan had the architects eyes ripped out and cut off a hand of the best artisans. Thus, mutilation was their reward for their faithfulness and creativity.

The Taj displays Koranic scriptures throughout, which is in fact paying tribute to Islam, by Indians, in India. I would suggest that the Indians remove the Islamic scriptures and other Islamic crap from the Taj, and claim it for what it is, a beautiful building built with Indian blood, sweat, and money.

Camels, Dates, Sand

The Saudis are another story. Before oil was discovered, like most oil rich Arab states all they had was their camels, dates, and sand. After the oil runs out, they will be left with their camels, dates, and sand. The Saudis know this and we know it. It's just not talked about. We pretend to be the best of pals.

The Saudis absolutely hate us for this reason: oil, or rather America's thirst for oil. Therefore and because the Saudis have nothing else and once the oil is gone or we move to another energy source, we depend on them, and they on us, and the United States therefore controls the Saudis' destiny in this regard.

American military forces protected the Saudis from both Iran and Iraq. If we were not there to protect the corrupt "imperial" Saudi government, they'd be hung out to dry, fast.

The Saudi Royals, in their own arrogance saw the U.S. in the 1991 war on Iraq that protected them from the depredations of Saddam Hussein as mere (dhimmi) hirelings doing their bidding.

The Saudis buy lots of military hardware from the United States, and occasionally from Europe. However, they are hopeless at managing, maintaining, and operating this stuff. (This is true of almost all Arab/Islamic nations.) Their military leaders are in their exalted positions because they are members of the Royal family or have other such connections, not because they are capable or competent. They need the USA absolutely and desperately. We know it and so do they although they will never admit this truth.

Naturally, when we went into action against the Al Qaeda (sons of Saudis) and their Taliban subordinates in Afghanistan, the Saudis forbade the use of their 'sacred' soil to stage our military forces from. We were obliged to fly our aircraft farther, at higher risk to our military personnel, and at a much higher cost.

One must ask why? The answer is because most of the al Qaeda in Afghanistan are Saudis. Many Al Qaeda are even members of the Saudi "royal" family. Osama is the scion of one of the wealthiest Saudi families, the bin Ladens, who did and do contract work for the United States government, American companies in Saudi Arabia, and of course for the Saudis. Those Al Qaeda who are not Saudis, get their money from the Saudis (remember the Wahabi funded Moslem Brotherhood who have killed many Egyptian leaders, and target other governments that are not fundamentalist).

Let's be reminded that Wahabism is a fundamentalist form of Mohammedism that is and always has been militant, is virulently anti-civilization, anti-democracy, anti-independence, and anti-freedom, and clearly against all other religions and political systems. The Wahabi laws as applied in Saudi Arabia forbid women from wearing comfortable garments in one of the most hostile climates in the world. Summertime temperatures in coastal Jeddah (for example) are well over 100 degrees, with 90+% humidity, and those women are given little respite.

American Air Force Lt. Col. McSwain sued the USG for acceding to the Saudis and forbidding American military officer who are female from wearing their authorized uniforms outside of U.S. establishments in Saudi Arabia, and the denial of their American rights as well. Good for her!

When Iraq invaded Kuwait and threatened Saudi Arabia, the 'royals' all hauled their wealth and their sorry fat backsides out of the country. But, it was OK for us Americans to place our sons and daughters lives on the line to protect them.

Yeah, it's OK for Americans to lay their lives on the line to protect Saudi, Kuwaiti, etc. interests, but when American interests are involved, we can forget it.

When, during the spring of 2002, the United States was trying to build support for a coalition to go into Iraq and remove Saddam Hussein and his rule, the Saudis intervened on Iraq's behalf. Twelve years earlier, the Saudis were in quaking fear of Saddam, and begged the United States to protect them. We did. Americans and our coalition partners died fighting Iraq -- protecting the quaking cowardly Saudis.

In 2002, the Saudis were dead set against removing Saddam. On April 26th Saudi Crown Prince Abdullah flew to President Bush's Texas ranch for a confab. Why? M-O-N-E-Y. The Saudis have us, because of our oil needs, by the proverbial short hairs and we both know it, at least the Saudis think they know it. They wanted to keep Iraq and the United States at odds with one-another. The Saudis understood that when we got Hussein out of power in Iraq, the new government might just be beholding to and perhaps even willing to accommodate the United States with a steady supply of high quality Iraqi oil at more reasonable prices. Iraq has enough oil to replace the Saudis as a major oil supplier. That wouldn't be good for the Saudis, even though it would be very good for the USA.

South of the Sahara

For a part of Islam's 1400 years, Islam in Africa south of the Sahara has at times been peaceful, moderate, and homogeneous with what was there, tribes that got along, and with mostly Coptic Christians willing to live and let live. Islam did not have a majority of population at first and was therefore temperate characterized by being an organization of tolerance and moderation - because they were in the minority. Moderates are considered to be apostates by the Wahabism and other radicals and therefore this peaceful version of Islam is being overcome and marginalized in the primarily Wahabi drive to radicalize Islam in black Africa. The very successful Saudi/Wahabi program for the radicalization of Islam in Africa has been underway for half of a century, since the colonial powers departed. When the Saudis, Libyans, and Iranians started rolling in their petro-dollars, they very actively pushed their hostile, militant versions of Mohammedism. This went slowly until the 1970s when OPEC was established and started blackmailing us Europeans and Americans because of our stupidity and need for energy. With their bundles of petro-dollars and petro-Euros, their programs both covert and overt have really accelerated.

They have been and are continuing to be very successful. Primarily, Saudi, (with Libyan and Iranian) money has collectively flowed into black Africa with the funding of mosques, Islamic centers, and Madrassas as well as numerous terrorist groups. Moderates are being pushed aside (or, if they resist, killed) so that with the money comes mostly Saudi Wahabi trained and controlled Imams, teachers, and bosses. The bosses are at the Saudi government funded and controlled Muslim World League (MWL), the World Assembly of Muslim Youth (WAMY) which has been controlled and run by the Saudi Ministry of Islamic Affairs, and the official Saudi Fund for Development (SFD).

In African countries where the Moslems are not (yet) the majority, these funds are directed and controlled so that they only benefit increasingly aggressive and radicalized Moslem minorities in those countries. Those countries are mainly Ethiopia, Eritrea, Kenya,

Uganda, Congo, Guinea, Chad, Mali, Cameroon, Gabon, Tanzania, Senegal, Malawi, South Africa, to name a few.

Mauritania is dominated by Arab Mohammedans, who have been systematically killing off and otherwise displacing free, moderate, decent Africans

The Madrassas being funded by this money are characterized by one Ethiopian journalist as jihad factories nurturing recruits for bin Laden and jihad against all non-Moslems.

Everyone more or less got along in Nigeria until the Wahabis started pouring money into the Moslem (Northern) parts of Nigeria. Iranian funded Hezbollah maintains terrorist training camps in Nigeria. The moderate Islamic parts of Nigeria not yet converted to radical Islamic sects are being ground down and will soon become radicalized. In many parts the lying radicals have taken hold: A polio epidemic started affecting people in the northern state of Kano. The Americans began providing polio vaccine to protect children from the disease in 2003. Mohammedist leaders in Kano declared that the vaccine was designed to infect Moslem children with AIDS and make women infertile and thus stopped the program. Because of this paranoid Mohammedist stupidity -- profound willful ignorance, the polio outbreak has spread to twenty-two countries and is now affecting millions of children.

Two countries in great jeopardy of rapid Islamist expansion today are Ethiopia and Eritrea located in East Africa at the Horn of Africa, an area that has traditionally received little attention from the Western security community. The two are Christian governed and fought a 30-year war before the Eritreans gained their independence from the Ethiopians. After their war ended, both signed an accord agreeing on allowing a Boundary Commission to adjudicate undefined border areas determining which few square miles of desolation and sand are to be awarded to which country. The Eritreans wanting peace and stability agreed to the judgments but the Ethiopian government denied them and threatened war, which guarantees instability for a long time to come. Within Ethiopia, the government is also waging another stupid war, this against other Christian groups/tribes. While the Christians are battering one-another, the Wahabis are quietly concentrating talent, money, and effort towards the Moslem groups in both countries, rapidly converting them from moderates to radical Wahabis. The Moslems are at 50% of the population in Ethiopia and about 60% in Eritrea. Naturally the United States government is beating up on both governments for suppressing religious minorities which include the Moslems. So, the United States' misguided actions regarding those two is in fact providing de-facto support to the Wahabis who are radicalizing those countries' Moslem populations. The USG needs to stop this type of stupidity, and begin funding, supporting, and arming the non-Moslems before they are eradicated, as already is being done with the Coptic Christians in Egypt and Libya.

A rather simplistic and naive February, 2005 editorial by Sophia

Tesfamariam in the official Eritrean government newspaper, Eritrea Profile, criticized a Christian Evangelical group's "Africa Quest Initiative" that figured out what the Wahabis are up to, and took an initiative to preserve East Africa's cultures and civilization. Tesfamariam criticizes the Quest's claim that HIV/AIDS, war, and the advancement of radicalized Islam have stripped Africans of hope. Tesfamariam confuses the growing radicalization of East Africa's Moslems with the general population growth throughout the area. Tesfamariam correctly points out the historic 1000 year tradition of the area's (Sufi) Moslem, and Coptic and Roman Catholic Christians' living in close proximity and harmony, erroneously claiming that it maintains that status quo. She is clearly ignorant of the stealthy progress of Wahabi radicalization of the area's Moslems.

In her full page editorial, the dhimmi Tesfamariam calls the Christian Quest movement a radical subversive group classified in the same category as bin Laden, and criticizes the Quest movement's offering to replace certain cult "Bibles" with real mainstream Christian books. Duuuhh! Bin Laden is a Wahabi Mohammedan, and the Wahabis are all over the place. The Quest movement is merely a pro-civilization organization trying to counter the radicalized Moslems because the local established Christians' fine old tradition of religious tolerance and harmony are operating totally ignorant of what is in fact happening all around them. The old time local Christians are foolishly welcoming a Saudi inspired radical Islamic Wahabi Trojan Horse movement with open arms.

The dhimmi thinking and opinion expressed by Tesfamariam, if it represents the true feelings of the people in East Africa, in particular those of Eritrea and Ethiopia who share so much in their rich, old, charitable, hospitable and very decent Christian cultures clearly indicates their sad but impending doom.

Personally, if this thinking and attitude prevails much longer, I give the two countries not more than twenty years before the Mohammedans take over and start slaughtering the Christians like the Moslems in Egypt are doing to the Copts; and the Sudanese Moslems are doing to the Copts, Animists, and even Black (moderate) Moslem Africans. The battle has been joined in stealth by the Wahabis, and the outcome is increasingly certain.

There is some hope because there are smart, experienced (with Islam) Christian groups who are aggressively challenging the Mohammedans. They desperately need help and support from Europeans and Americans in their quest to protect the African people from the dark violence and overwhelming evil of Islam.

Then of course, the elite policy wonk geniuses at the State Department actually wonder out loud why many in leadership positions within those two presently paranoid governments are so distrustful of the USA. Duuuhh!

AIDS in Africa

HIV/AIDS grew out of Africa. This is understood by most people in civilized nations. Of course the lunatic fringe declared that AIDS was created by white Americans to kill off Africans. This has been loudly and repeatedly proclaimed by Barak Hussein Obama's 'spiritual mentor' for twenty years, the crypto-Christian Reverend Imam, Jeremiah Wright. These rumors probably came from both white haters and Mohammedans because it is useful in causing widespread denial of HIV/AIDS in Africa, and has thus led to the deaths of millions of Africans. And, the Mohammedans didn't have to bloody their hands with one of those tragic non-Moslem victims.

It took many years for many African nations to accept the scourge of HIV/AIDS for what it is and to begin working to save and protect lives, but it was/is too late for millions.

In the Moslem areas where they deny their widespread homosexual promiscuity, they also deny HIV/AIDS which is killing thousands of Moslems off. Their answer to this scourge is Insha'Allah, it is the will of God.

Chapter 6

VISAS, IMMIGRATION, BORDERS

We Americans are despised and hated by so very many in Middle Eastern nations. Yet, the throngs of visa seeking people outside of the atypical American Embassy each morning never diminishes.

One must ask not just themselves, but our government: Why do we grant visas to people who hate us? We are more than fools to give these jerks visas. We are acting in our own worst interests and supporting our own demise.

Everyone entering the United States is supposed to have a Passport showing U.S. citizenship, or a foreign passport with an appropriate Visa. Some people from certain nations are allowed to enter on a visa waiver program because it is not considered to be a serious problem for citizens of these countries to become law breakers -- illegal aliens. This includes most European Union nations, Japan, Korea, etc. Given this, Mohammedan terrorists with British, French, Italian, Spanish, Swiss, or German passports, etc. can waltz right through an immigration station and into the United States. I am comfortable in stating that this infiltration has already happened, and these terrorists have joined their appropriate 'cells' where they are planning their mayhem, or performing other roles, and this is continuing to occur.

Undocumented aliens – criminals are another story. Undocumented, criminals should not be encouraged to cross over the borders and hold out as they have until some sort of amnesty is declared because the cowardly U.S. Congress is so screwed up and inept that it can't handle just this one glaring 30+ year running problem. There should be no more amnesty programs or declarations. Whenever an amnesty is even considered, it is clearly an acknowledgement that the sitting President along with the entire Congress are complete and total failures incapable of doing their jobs, and need to be removed from office.

Placing water, food, and other types of stations in the deserts of the American southwest should not be done. It only encourages and supports criminals in their lawbreaking acts. I understand that this is meant to be a humanitarian act, but those misguided humanitarians interested in such activities need to direct their good hearted efforts on the other side of the border -- to keep people from becoming criminals, before they come over.

Employers who hire criminal illegal aliens should be punished with increasing levels of fines and even closures of businesses, as well as imprisonment for repeat offenders.

The idiotic, moronic government of California (and other states) which considered giving drivers licenses and ID cards to undocumented criminals is stupid. I know and everyone else knows it is a blatant ploy of the pinheads to buy votes. For the same reason, criminal aliens can easily (and do) register to vote in California and other states. This is criminal fraud, and the elected officials of California (and every other state that permits this) need to be held up for both ridicule and accountability in this.

Other idiots are the local governments of San Francisco, Los Angeles, New York City, and others who have taken steps to prevent their police from identifying lawbreakers and reporting or turning them over to immigration authorities. This encourages even more lawbreaking, especially criminal enterprises to set up their shops in those cities because they feel protected by those cities' governments. Then, these same silly government officials whine about brutal, murderous criminal activities in the ghetto havens they have created for criminals. Duuuhhh!!!!

Visas

Visas are issued at American Consular Offices in Embassies or Consulates all over the world. Visas are issued and signed by Consuls or Vice Consuls. Consul and Vice Consul Commissions, or titles are authorized by the Congress, and signed by the President of The United states.

There are a few hundred Consuls, and several thousand Vice Consuls assigned at American Missions, and all have authority to issue (or deny) non-immigrant Visas. Other embassy officers do NOT have visa authority.

The issuance or denial of a visa is discretionary on the part of the Consul or Vice Consuls -- visa officers, who work the visa lines.

All junior Foreign Service Officers are normally obliged, early in their careers to serve a stint of duty "on the line" as a Vice Consul. Most junior officers "punch their ticket" and serve their first year or two years at a "visa mill" such as the American Consulate in Tijuana where thousands line up daily. Tijuana is one example of dozens of places where the local governments are corrupt, inept, and desperate poverty is the norm. Virtually everyone wants to get out of those cesspools and their objective is the land of milk and honey -- America. Serving on a visa line is normally perceived as an undesirable but necessary assignment in purgatory, a prerequisite to a bigger and better future as a Political Officer, Economic Officer, Commercial Officer, or something - anything else.

It is a given that while serving in such a position, with thousands of desperate "hopefuls" around the world lining up every morning, that more than a few lies will be told by applicants. Being a visa officer is akin to being a cop, where many if not most applicants lie in every way imaginable trying to secure entry into the United States. The duty of the

Visa Officer is to quickly determine whether the applicant is legitimate or otherwise. With hundreds lining up, the average applicant is allowed a brief amount of time to present his or her case, to convince the visa officer that she or he is not an intending (illegal) immigrant, and will not take advantage of the visa and burn his or her passport as soon as they clear immigration in the U.S.A.

Five percent (5%) of State Department visa officers are professional, career Consular Officers. The 95% who serve their "tour of duty", aka 'purgatory' have poor, don't give-a-damn attitude towards this odious duty, and a task of drudgery it often is, and where less than 100% of their attention is paid to their duties it is little wonder that visas are often issued to undesirables. This is a serious problem that the Department of State needs to overcome.

In some places, because of a shortage of visa officers, the inept Department of State slacked off and permitted local travel agents to screen travelers, and do the 'gofering' to get travelers their visas. Of course, travel agents will get everyone they can a visa because this sells tickets. These travel agents are not American citizens, and do not have America's best interests at heart. It is good that this corrupt, stupid practice ended and its chief perpetrator, a genuine politically correct pinhead, Mary Ryan, got canned for this and probably for other reasons. Oh, yeah, that's right she didn't get fired, she resigned, in thorough and rightful disgrace.

[Let's not forget for a moment that fifteen of the 9/11/2001 hijackers were Saudis. These murderers were not poor, did not emanate from deeply religious backgrounds, and all were 'educated' (but obviously not civilized), and they were clearly hateful of that which is civilized. Most of the 400+ early members of Qaeda were well-educated men from middle or upper class Arab families, in their mid-20's, considered psychologically stable (by Moslem standards), and healthy. [Assuredly, psychological stability in many core Moslems clearly is a pretty iffy prospect.] Many spoke several languages and had traveled widely.

Many electronic media elitist talking heads and experts asked what drove these guys to do what they did. Notwithstanding the analyses of so many "experts", the nineteen hijackers were first and foremost core Mohammedan devotees. Therefore, when they visited or tried to live in western cultures, they found themselves to be complete, total cultural and social misfits unable to fit in, to compete in a modern civilization. These jerks gravitated to one another because they discovered that they would never fit or be able to assimilate into a civilized society. While they did not, probably could not articulate their feelings, in their cores they realized collectively that they were not and would never be competitive. They took the next step. With the help, support, and guidance of fellow Mohammedans, they attacked what they believed was the core of modern western civilization, the United States, a leading symbol of what they feared.

Another aspect of this visa business that has a powerful impact on young, visa officers is both the U.S. Congress and senior officials in the embassies.

All too often, when a visa officer actually exercises due diligence and good judgment in denying a visa, a problem arises. Either the person denied the visa, or someone acting on his or her behalf (such as an attorney, a relative, or some sort of associate) gets on the case of a Congressman, a Senator, or some other ranking politician or official. In the cases of Representatives or Senators, the next thing that will happen will be receipt of what I call a 'nastygram' -- a message to the embassy that to all intents and purposes causes that visa officer to be hauled off for a session in the proverbial woodshed. Too often, the Ambassador or some other risk-averse reactive ranking butt kisser proceeds to "council" (admonish) the visa officer on his or her errant behavior. Subsequently, the case is "reconsidered" and a visa is often issued.

After being "counseled" a time or two, any young officer seriously considering a career with decent assignments and a few promotions before retirement will see the light...... You can understand that these fresh young officers' apprenticeships will result in issuing visas to a lot of unworthy or worse characters -- criminals, terrorists, and intending illegal immigrants. The alternative, diligently doing their duty, can be detrimental to their careers, or they can chose to bend way over and kiss their own as... -- er, careers goodbye.

This is how the State Department and the Congress corrupts all junior Foreign Service Officers right away. It's called character adjusting and molding. In reality, it's stupid mismanagement of valuable resources.

A solution to this problem: When a visa officer refuses a visa it needs to be a done deal. Done! Final! Over! Beyond review..... To protect the visa officer, a system needs to be established to remove the butt reaming woodshed options which foster visa issuances to the undeserving.

Thus, if some elite, effete, insignificant Saudi (for example) gets his prominent proboscis out of joint over a visa refusal, they can still appeal - to the Ambassador directly, or to another senior government or embassy official or to a politician as is often the established practice. Alternatively, of course, there are the list of attorneys, relatives, and sponsors or whatever honorific they appoint themselves calling Congressmen, Senators, or others to raise hell. Thus, after a thorough review by at least three independent people, an allowance can still be made to issue the visa. However, the visa issued under such an appeal MUST then bear the actual signature (no facsimile or other bullcrap) of the overruling Ambassador or Senior Official, the Senator, the

Representative, or other authorizing senior (white House) official, etc. If this means mailing the passport to Washington, D.C. for the required original signature, so be it, delays and all....

Send the hassle upstairs, not downstairs. Affix responsibility appropriately. With such a system in place, bogus visas being issued to people who want to do illegal things such as steal, commit murder, and or destroy us will be curtailed.

Then the ambassador, senator, congressman or other important, ranking official can rightfully and appropriately have his or her name tied to a hijacker, bomber, murderer, pedophile, drug dealer, or illegal. Not many of these high fauluting dignitaries want to have their names tied to crap like this.

If an effectively responsible system were in place in 2000 or 2001, some of those nineteen hijackers of 9/11/2001 would not have been here. The aforementioned senior official, Mary Ryan, in fact facilitated the 9/11 attacks with her policy of letting Saudi travel agents secure visas.

The murder of three thousand innocents are sufficient testimony justifying an overhaul of a convoluted, inefficient, and corrupted visa issuing system that punishes good visa officers for exercising diligence and good judgment. These officers need to be encouraged and supported in doing a good job, not punished.

In my own case, I luckily didn't get called on to "punch my ticket" with my visa line service until later in my career, at the American Embassy in Dhaka, Bangladesh. At that I was lucky. I was only periodically required to review applicants for a few weeks at a time while the regular visa officers were away on business or leave. Nearing retirement age in a dead career having already annoyed one too many bosses, I was not susceptible or terribly vulnerable to sessions in the woodshed. I therefore had no compunction about refusing visa applications that I felt were not legitimate or were questionable. I actually refused 100% of applicants for an entire week. The morning line up of a thousand or more "hopefuls" at the Embassy typically vanished when word was let out that "Mr. Horn" would be on the visa line that day......... Of the few visas that I did issue, everyone returned at the end of their visit to the United States.

The Principle of the Seven P's, or
Proper Prior Planning Prevents Piss Poor Performance

The (former) Immigration and Naturalization Service admitted that there were over 300,000 lawbreakers (in 2004) in the United States who had overstayed visas, and that was a lowball estimate, by a few million. The Department of Justice has no idea of who they are or where they are. If just one percent of them have terrorist links, we've got a problem ranging from 3,000 and upwards of criminals wishing you and I serious harm, and probably working towards this end.

We can hold the line in defense of the Homeland and keep intending terrorists out with a simple act or set of acts involving application of the seven P's. For instance, whenever a person in the USA applies for a government job, fills out a form for a security clearance, gets a drivers license, a passport, etc., we are asked to attest by signing that (the applicant) is not a member of any organization, etc., that advocates the violent overthrow of the United States.

We should require each and every visa applicant to sign such a form, and then seriously check it out...... before they get their visa. Not six months or a year later - not after they've killed you, your child, or I, or raped someone's wife or daughter. If they have to wait a while for their visa, that's OK. Those who are legitimate and do their seven P's should have no problem, and if checked out by an adequately staffed and managed embassy visa office, ought to get their visas forthwith.

While there are thousands of groups hostile to the United States, this is not such a difficult problem. Big? Yes. Insurmountable? No. Most of these groups have the names of their members on a database somewhere, and if there is a database, the CIA, DIA, FBI, State Department, DEA, INTERPOL, or other authority should be able to ferret these out and amass or link them into the VISA LOOKOUT list. The lists need to have all of the names, and aliases used by these characters. The list needs to be shared with airlines who should be fined when they let such a person on a plane coming to the USA.

Some new criteria have been established which further restrict visas being issued from countries listed by the State Department as state sponsors of terrorism, including Libya, Iran, Iraq, Sudan, and Syria. Later, Saudi Arabia was added to this list. Immediately the whine went out claiming that the list is unfair and intended to fuel prejudice against Muslims. Good! That is indeed appropriate. The list needs to be expanded to include Malaysia, Indonesia, Yemen, Somalia, and forty others.

Our European, Asian, and Latin American friends share the same risks and have problems similar to ours. If we work with them, we can develop and maintain an effective international VISA LOOKOUT list.

The State Department's VISA LOOKOUT list is not comprehensive, timely, nor well maintained. It is easily circumvented using false names and forged passports. We can deport a criminal one day, and with a trimmed beard and new passport under another name, he can be in an American Embassy a few days later obtaining another visa. We need to document every deportee and criminal into a database with appropriate (biometrics technology), finger prints, and other means of identification. Then, we need to use this to eliminate their ability to travel freely, not only to the United States, but anywhere in the world.

We must require that passports - all passports used by foreign nationals traveling to the USA be in compliance with certain high standards. These standards should be that passports be forgery resistant and comply with other requirements such as smart chips containing finger and retina prints, issuing country national I.D. registration information, and other unique identifying information.

Yeah, sure, some countries will cry fowl and whine and wail about sovereignty and so forth. That's fine. They can maintain their sovereignty, and also keep their fine, wonderful highly prized citizens at home. If they want something from us, they must comply. We can protect our sovereignty too. Passports that don't comply should not get American visas. That's a simple solution.

Further, we should establish a standard regarding names used in passports of travelers seeking visas to the United States. We know that many cultures allow a person to have one or more names or groups of names for whatever reasons they wish. That's fine. Those countries that give those names (including legal nicknames under their laws and practices) should be compelled to list all such names and aliases in a travelers' passport. We'll need to deal with others who use even other sets of names.

However, we can use each country's unique (national) system to verify identities and then, all by ourselves combine this information with biometric data and whatever else that works well. At present all we ask for is a valid passport, many of which are forged, or easily obtained with a bribe. Most if not all of these countries nevertheless have fairly strictly controlled national identity information along with drivers licenses, work permits, ration cards, etc. that carry their photographs as well as finger prints and other means of identification.

We can and ought to require, on a country-by-country specific basis that visa applicants provide three forms of such identification in addition to the passport. So, a Yemeni in Paris would need to provide a valid, compliant Yemeni passport and three other forms of Yemeni identification. If an applicant failed to provide this information, visa denial would be automatic.

Further, when the applicant's name or one of those names on the Visa Lookout list turns up - no visa.

As is the present case, when a visa is denied by an American Embassy or Consulate, an entry is made in the passport, and other countries peruse passports looking for such an entry. When such and entry from an American visa office is noted, other nations routinely refuse visas. It's a good way to protect ourselves. We need to encourage our partners to do the same, and then respect their similar notations in passports. This redundant screening will help keep the bad guys away.

The Department of Justice and former INS is supposed to control visas, and to handle all non-citizens once they reach the USA. They have failed in this miserably. They failed with the concurrence of the Congress.

The Congress (our elected representatives) of the United States has failed miserably in its lack of oversight and support. Now that the crap has hit the fan, some action is being taken, any and all which is good, whatever it is, because the INS was so screwed up that anything at all helps.

A tale about a visa officer

Junior, first tour Foreign Service Officers often go to embassies assigned as rotational officers not necessarily within their area of specialty. Typically, they'll work in four different sections of an embassy during a two year assignment, six months in each section, or a variation thereof.

In Bangladesh, I ran an embassy section that provided support and logistical services to the Embassy. I had several dozen Bangladeshis working for me, along with several contractors. Among the many issues and problems I faced, fraud was always an issue near the top of the list.

My friend, Ken Haas (later murdered by Islamic terrorists using a truck bomb at the American Embassy in Beirut Lebanon in April of 1983) ran the Consular section of the Embassy.

A newly minted junior Foreign Service Officer I'll call Fred was assigned to Bangladesh as a rotational officer. It was determined that for his first year, he would be assigned to the Visa Section and to my section. Ken and I agreed that we'd each keep Fred for a half of a day in each section.

Prior to coming out to an Embassy, it is customary to follow protocol with an introductory letter to the Ambassador expressing one's delight with the assignment, and to tell a little about oneself and expectations, etc. Fred's letter was open and good. He also set himself up for a real serious educational opportunity. A copy of his letter was sent to Ken and I. Fred's letter discussed his expectations for his housing and how he'd rather not be assigned to the standard fare of Embassy housing, but that he'd prefer it if we could find someplace where he could board with a Bangladeshi family. He apparently thought that Dhaka was some quaint college town or something.

Ken and I got together to plan Fred's proper introduction to the real world. We first agreed that Fred, just twenty-one years old, was very bright having passed the Foreign Service Officer exam on his first try. Fred was also clearly wet behind the ears and more than a trifle naïve. Ken and I plotted......

Normally, visa officers' housing was highly protected information - as protected as intelligence officers, if not more so in some circumstances. The reason for protecting this information? Visas to the United States – a sought after treasure in Bangladesh.

There is a historical, cultural precedent for people of the Islamic culture to accept and work within a totally corrupt society. More than a thousand visa seekers lined up outside of the American Embassy every morning knowing that the visa officers would only get around to interviewing a few hundred (how many minutes in a day?) every day and most of those applicants would be rejected. Accordingly desperate visa seekers worked to find the "back door" access to a visa officer where they hoped they could find a way to persuade the visa officer that they were worthy of a treasured, precious visa. If only one could get to the front of the line, past the guard, around the receptionist, they'd have a chance. Better yet, find out where the visa officer lived and make their entreaties, offers of treasure, or threats and demands separate and away from all of the other hopefuls.

First, I didn't accommodate Fred's desire for a boarding situation with a Bangladeshi family. Virtually no Bangladeshi family had a spare room or other western amenities. I instead assigned Fred temporarily to a small house in the city. Ken and I then 'leaked' the word that the new visa officer would be living at that house.

When Fred arrived, I greeted him planeside and escorted him through the terminal, picking up his luggage, clearing customs and immigration, the normal stuff. We then proceeded to the terminal gate where Fred got his first taste of desperation and poverty.

Armed police officers manned the terminal gate beyond which were throngs of beggars. When the two of us passed the gate, a crush of people surged forward, pawing and clutching at us. Fred, eyes bugging out was rapidly getting pretty concerned. I had come prepared with a pocket full of the local equivalent of one penny coins, and reached into my pocket and withdrew two hands full of coins and I threw them out over the crowd in two directions. Like Moses parting the sea, the scrambling throngs moved after the coins, opening a pathway for Fred and I to hustle through and into a rickshaw, not an Embassy car. We bounced, lurched, and swayed precariously off to Fred's house, where I had installed a supply of vittles. He unpacked and I took him to my house where we had dinner before returning him to his house.

Phones were unreliable and we each had a portable radio (about 20-pounds at that time) which I showed him how to use before I left for the night.

Early in the morning, Fred was on the radio frantically calling me for help. There were hundreds of people in the yard, and people were hammering on every door, demanding a visa. I rescued him that morning, but let him live there for two weeks where he had to deal with a mob every morning. When I quietly moved him into another place where he was secure from the mobs, he was grateful. His squeaky, youthful voice had also lowered an octave.

Over the next two months, Ken and I got Fred involved in his duties. We actually set him up. I had him working on researching, gathering information on and interviewing people involved with contractor fraud, and Ken was similarly escorting Fred into the realm of visa fraud. Fred was lied to at every turn by all of these princes of Islam. By the end of Fred's two month's initiation, his voice had dropped another octave, he sprouted hair on his knuckles, his peach fuzz turned into real whiskers, and the wetness behind his ears was gone.

Fred survived Ken and I, and went on to a very successful and rewarding career.

Immigration

The Immigration laws, policies, and practices of the United States; and the management of these must be reviewed carefully with a view to become more restrictive in allowing both immigrants and non-immigrants access to the United States.

There are the politically correct idiots or genuine fools who espouse the benefits of open borders, the open borders lobby (OBL), who consider immigration laws to be 'anti-immigrant'. These pinheaded morons are the terrorists' greatest friends (and allies), and are of course champions of AZTLAN, La Raza (the race), and other closely related racist anti-American organizations such as the Mexican style KKK - MEChA. They are well represented by criminal drug cartels, illegal smugglers, al Qaeda, and others from whom they derive a goodly portion of their support (money).

In fact, Mexican Coyotes (people smugglers) have been actively moving non-Latinos over the border into the United States by the hundreds. One of these was ranking Hezbollah murderer and convicted terrorist, Mahmood Youssef Kourani. Kourani's trip into the USA began with a visa to Mexico purchased from a corrupt Mexican visa official in Beirut, Lebanon. He was driven over the border from Tijuana into the USA in a car trunk,

Thank God for sensible, honest politicians like Representatives Tom Tancredo and James Sensenbrenner who along with other genuine patriots are working to keep America whole and civilized.

Immigration laws, rules, and regulations are a mess. The Congress needs to sit down and overhaul the laws. That's no small challenge. But it must be dealt with responsibly.

Whenever an illegal is caught, they need to be locked up immediately, and held in a lock-up until tried for violating U.S. immigration laws. When convicted, they ought to serve time. Afghanistan needs money and employment. Send the convicted illegals to a prison in Afghanistan for a couple of years, and then repatriate them to their home countries. If caught a second time, they ought to be imprisoned (in Afghanistan) for a longer period of time.

Whenever an illegal commits a crime and is arrested, deportation should be automatic at the end of their sentence whether it's a felony or a misdemeanor. Congressman Issa of California looked at this issue and believes the DOJ's Border Patrol can accomplish this by allocating personnel and resources to the prison systems. The personnel are available and can be removed from less productive duties and tasked and assigned to these roles where they can do the most good.

Asylum is abused. Every person seeking asylum ought to be held until a complete investigation of their case is expeditiously completed by the CIA and/or others as appropriate. If valid, they can then be granted a temporary visa, until their situation changes, at which time they ought to be repatriated. If they deliver babies, the babies should NOT get U.S. legacy baby citizenship. If they commit a felony, their asylum should be revoked immediately, they can then serve a prison term (in a prison in Afghanistan), and then be repatriated to their home country, or any other country that will take them. If their asylum claim is bogus (such as Palestinians murderers or terrorists merely trying to avoid being arrested and imprisoned by the Israelis), they ought to be imprisoned and then, when their sentence is served, be either repatriated to their home countries or extradited as appropriate to face justice.

Legal residents (Green Card holders) should be encouraged (credits or cash for courses completed satisfactorily) to learn English, study government, and take a real test (as was required in the past) to become legitimate citizens. They must accomplish this within five years, or off they go. If they commit felonies (while Green Card holders), they ought to be treated like criminals, serve prison sentences, have their Green Card revoked, and be repatriated to their home countries, and their legacy babies can go with them.

Our borders are porous, too porous. It is not possible to "seal" them absolutely as some xenophobes wish. However, by dealing sternly with those who come into the United States illegally, we can send a message that the good times aren't rolling anymore.

At present our borders, especially our border with Mexico are meaningless. Criminals by the thousands pass over those borders every day. American citizens living along those borders live in fear which is unreasonable and represents irresponsible government inaction. Our porous borders with Mexico are two thousand miles long allowing more than a million illegal crossings a year. They are so poorly guarded that busses drive to the border and let dozens off who just pour over the border.

Our porous borders are an invitation for mayhem in the way of Mohammedan terrorists. In just one month, October of 2003, 5,510 illegal aliens designated "Other Than Mexican" (OTM) were picked up crossing over into Arizona from Mexico. A significant percentage of those numbers did not speak Spanish, but did speak Arabic, Farsi (Iranian), and other Middle Eastern languages. Those numbers represent only those who got caught. If five Mohammedan terrorists per day got over the border (a very modest number), that would represent 1825 per year, and considering that many are insane enough to wrap themselves in high explosives, that is a growing and very dangerous army already massed within the borders of United States.

Travesty

One of the gravest travesties of our non-policy towards illegal immigration is that we are the ones responsible for causing so much suffering.

The Bush administration, Republicans and Democrats alike and other administrations before them all take and took big money from big companies that wanted to maintain the status quo so that they could get away with paying low wages, and having no responsibility for or towards the illegal workers.

This is irresponsible, reprehensible, immoral, and unethical and is supported by politicians and dirty money that drives them. Add to this the fact that because of their illegal status, these poor people are in the USA with no safety nets. If they get injured or sick, their employers don't bear or have any responsibilities, but we taxpayers wind up paying for their care.

Further, when they lose their income, there is no safety net, and some of these poor illegal immigrants have nothing to do but resort to crime at one level or another to survive. They tend to prey on one-another which some think is OK (it's not, it's wrong). Their illegal activities are many and include drugs, human trafficking, murder, and so forth.

U.S. Customs and Immigration enforcement

The inept Immigration Service under the reorganization of so many agencies was combined with the formerly efficient U.S. Customs Service to form an investigative and enforcement agency (ICE). Now, both are screwed up. This was contributed to by a totally inept, failed former Congressman and political hack, Asa Hutchison, the Homeland Security Undersecretary for Border and Transportation Security, the overseer of ICE.

When professional Customs and Immigration officers organized themselves and started to actually do their jobs, Hutchison intervened and stopped them, saying that what they were doing was not illegal but that they were in violation of policy. Hunh? Hutchison called a halt to officials doing their job, and doing it well because they were violating some unarticulated dopey policy? That's what the word incompetent means, and it applies to Hutchison, and as long as he and other dolts like him remain in office, the incompetence charge appropriately rolls up the line to the White House.

Hutchison's subordinate, Michael J. Garcia, another ICE bigwig was another failure in that job. Factual derogatory reports to the administration didn't seem to spur the Bushies to replace either of them with competent professionals. In this connection, the Bush administration is emulating their corrupt, inept, incompetent, idiotic, Mexican government counterparts.

The morale at ICE fell so low as to border on a rebellion. Their complaint: Nothing complex. Just LEADERSHIP FAILURE! Aside from writing to congressmen and working with their representatives, most working level ICE managers, supervisors, and their subordinates avoided exposing themselves too much for fear of retaliation. In the meantime, criminals went on a field day and remain so today.

Ice inspectors weren't even allowed to do the simplest part of their jobs, to perform verification inspections at businesses.

Two ICE employees, named Ramos and Compean did do a good job and shot a Mexican crook in the butt. The ICE employees, Ramos and Campion were prosecuted for doing their job, found guilty of some human error or infraction and were sent to prison. And the dolt (Bush) in the White House did nothing for them until his last day in office. This single act convinced me absolutely, that Bush was in fact deserving of just as much ridicule as the ultimate jackass, Jimmy Carter, as regards wrongheaded ignorance.

Bush actually protected a criminal, and sent two loyal, devoted patriots to jail. This is flat wrong. Ramos and Compean should have been rewarded. It is stuff like this outrage that causes good, decent people to really distrust government, and to encourage capable, competent civil servants to not do their jobs well, if at all. I suggest that people should demand hold-harmless laws for law enforcement officers who lay their lives on the line in the fury of conflict and should never be prosecuted for some resulting unintended infraction. In response to continuing public outrage, Bush commuted the sentences of these two men on his last day in the white House.

Vigilantes

Rightfully and justifiably outraged Americans are taking action where their unworthy government just won't to do the right thing, and when their elected leaders won't respond in a responsible manner. People are forming organizations to do what the government won't do to protect our borders and national integrity and sovereignty. One group, the Minuteman Project was a group of private citizens organized to patrol the U.S.-Mexican border in an effort to deter illegal crossings of the US-Mexico border. Is this vigilantism? No! It is patriotism in one of its purest and simplest forms. These fine citizens stepped up to do what their government was unwilling to do. Are politicians and government officials bothered by this? They ought to be. It points a finger at their incompetence, gross stupidity, and rank cowardice regarding doing what ought to be done. When President Bush thoughtlessly referred to these patriots as vigilantes, he showed that he was bothered alright, bothered by patriots courageously stepping up to do the right thing, something that he shirked. That will be one of President Bush's legacies, one of shirking responsibilities. Shirker-In-chief Bush.....

Naturally the America hating ACLU sent representatives to

monitor the American patriots. After consuming their ration of Mexican grown weed, or pot, they--the ACLU characters worked to harass the patriots and to create incidents. They failed.

Conscription

A solution would be to temporarily re-establish mandatory military service, conscription, the draft. American citizens or legal immigrants, on attaining the age of majority or graduation from their secondary school or university should be conscripted into the Border Patrol where they would serve for up to two years along the border inspecting inbound freight (ocean, truck, and rail) and luggage, building fences, barriers, and walls; manning checkpoints and outposts, etc. They would be armed and authorized to use lethal force to stop fence jumpers, and to shoot back when shot at. Some could even be assigned to visa offices in consulates and Embassies to help with that workload. Non-college graduates could serve for up to four years, and then get a free (GI bill type) college education. College/University graduates would get two years of post graduate studies paid for and/or other benefits.

Escape Valve

Yeah, yeah, I know, we're supposed to be an escape valve or pressure release for Mexico's lousy, slimy, corrupt, inefficient, crooked, and generally worthless government. By "permitting" millions of criminals to hop over our border, we are protecting the elite greedy, incompetent Mexican government. Protecting them from what? From serving their own people? This is bogus. We owe nothing to whoever sits in the Mexican President's seat. (Vincente Fox in 2003, acted against American interests in the war on terrorism, let's not forget that, ever.) Mexico's avaricious, treacherous leadership are likely assisting terrorists on a daily basis. We don't owe those elite jerks anything, nada, nil, rien, zip, zero, not even visitor or refugee visas when they get run out of office, like Vincente Fox.

I repeat: We should cease providing visas to all Mexican officials until they clean up their acts.

At the time that the American Minutemen Project started monitoring the border in the spring of 2005, the Mexican government actually published and began distributing a twenty-seven page booklet telling criminals how to cross their northern borders into the United States. This explained the best routes, the times of day, and how to avoid American Border Patrols.

Then the elitist, asinine Mexican government jerks condemned the fine, patriotic American people involved in the equivalent of a large or broad scale neighborhood watch, the Minutemen Project for protecting the integrity of our borders.

President Bush's calling those fine American citizen patriot volunteers vigilantes was dumb, really dumb. If Bush did his job in a responsible manner, this Minuteman project or subsequent border watches would not have been necessary. Bush's (and subsequently Obama's) willful neglect of his sworn duty to protect and to defend the United States may indeed cause Americans to begin taking the law into their own hands, to become genuine vigilantes, to protect our homeland. I applaud the patriots, their spirit, their integrity, and their patriotism. Every responsible American that I have talked to feels the same way.

Secretary of State Condoleeza Rice, fearful of upsetting the Mexican government thugs, who need to be upset - right onto their thieving, corrupt backsides or into hangmen's nooses, also degraded herself, calling those fine American patriots vigilantes. Rice should have done the proper diplomatic thing, and called the Mexican Ambassador onto the carpet and raised holy hell about his government's issuing a publication telling their countrymen how to break American laws, and she should have then encouraged American patriots to continue protecting our homeland. Rice was and remains a fool.

Mexican President Vicente Fox, in an address, used disparaging remarks as he referred to black Americans and was rightfully and righteously chastised by private Americans, but President Bush and his cohort remained mute, including Rice. Bush should have had his Secretary of State, Condoleeza Rice haul the Mexican ambassador onto the carpet for a butt reaming, and then sent him packing back to Mexico. Bush failed a large segment of America's population here, but any Democratic president would have probably done the same thing. Shameful!

Just months after el Presidente Fox's stupid, racist remarks, the Mexican government introduced postage stamps showing outright racist caricatures of blacks. When this was brought to their attention, they argued that this was OK, that this characterization of blacks as monkeys was acceptable and that we Americans had no business getting involved in this Mexican activity. Yeah, sure! To me, the Mexican government established their bonafides as genuine bigots, the whole lot of them.

Remembrance

Let's remember, in the name of Enrique Camarena, just how truly evil, rotten, and horrible our Mexican neighbor to the south is.

Camarena was a very competent American Drug Enforcement Agent working in Tijuana, Mexico, doing a good, diligent, and very effective job of thwarting drug trafficking into the United States. Apparently he did his job too well. He knew too much.

He was picked up by Mexican police working under the direction of ranking Mexican government officials. Camarena was subjected to some of the most terrible tortures known before he died. He did not die easily. In fact, he died several times, each time to be injected with ephedrine to revive his heart so the torments could begin again, and again, and again before he finally died and could not be revived. His torments included several broken bones, fingernails pulled out by a pliers, broken teeth, or teeth pulled by a pliers, a broomstick shoved deeply up his anus, crushed testicles, massive deep burns, and more.

An experienced senior American Drug Enforcement Agency (DEA) investigator, Hector Berrellez, was sent to Mexico to investigate Camarena's murder. Berrellez was one of the most capable, effective, and successful DEA agents in history, and also the most highly decorated. Berrellez was stonewalled by Mexican authorities, who did all that they could to thwart his investigative work. Barilla was more than a measure smarter than those arrogant Mexican authorities, and he found fingerprints on the syringe used to inject Camarena with ephedrine as well as on the tools and instruments used in torturing him. The fingerprints belonged to a Mexican government doctor.

Berrellez confronted the Mexican authorities and demanded the arrest and deportation of the doctor to the United States. Naturally, the Mexican government refused. The incrimination ran too deep and too high up in the Mexican government.

Somehow, the homicidal Mexican government doctor inexplicably found himself trussed up in the trunk of a car in the United States where he was 'discovered', arrested, and arraigned in the death of Camarena. The circumstances of that Mexican government official's circumstances were considered cloudy to a liberal judge in San Diego who turned that filthy murderous Mexican government's doctor loose so he could return to Mexico, and avoid facing justice in Camarena's incredibly brutal murder.

Humiliated by revelations of the truth, of their involvement in drug trafficking and the murder of an American official, the corrupt Mexican government issued a warrant for the arrest of the courageous DEA investigator, Berrellez. The eternally corrupt Mexican government naturally wants Berrellez so they can punish him or worse for his fine investigative work. That warrant remains outstanding today.

Any new treaty, agreement, or whatever, must include extradition to the United States of criminals such as cop killers, especially cop killers like the doctor and including the officials who directed him. Whenever the Secretary of State or any other official visits Mexico, extradition must be on the agenda. The same must be the case whenever Mexican officials visit the United States.

Until Mexico steps up to the plate, we Americans are rightly entitled to use disparaging remarks about Mexico being a third-world cesspool and the Mexican government and its officials flotsam in that cesspool.

NAFTA

The North American Free Trade Agreement (NAFTA) was

established to provide jobs in Mexico for Mexicans, the fine decent, honest, hard-working family oriented regular people. The treaty unfortunately took away jobs from thousands of decent, hard working American citizens and moved them to Mexico. The purported purpose of this was to provide employment for Mexicans so that they would stop hopping the fences to get jobs in the USA. It is a failed policy! The only thing NAFTA really did was enrichen corrupt Mexican officials, and avaricious American corporations who were and are able to get work done cheap and to avoid paying decent wages, taxes, health, medical, or retirement benefits. The biggest victims of NAFTA are decent, hard working Americans.

Neither the Mexican nor the American governments have done a thing to stop criminal invaders from coming across the border, and NAFTA did nothing to really benefit regular working class Americans. NAFTA in fact put thousands of able bodied, honest, hard working Americans out of work, nothing more. Barak Hussein Obama with all of his rhetoric in support of American unions is not doing a thing to help restore jobs to America by way of altering or cancelling NAFTA.

If Mr. Obama and the Congress were likewise genuinely caring of Americans, they would immediately call for the nullification or at least a heavy modification of NAFTA. They would pull those jobs back to the United States, establish reciprocal import/export taxes and restrictions on Mexican products and ownership of land in America, enforce trade and intellectual protection laws, and secure the border along with establishing proper work visas for decent, honest, hard-working, worthy, Mexicans where there are jobs for them.

Fences and Walls

Fences make good neighbors.

Israel, after years of being terrorized by Arab hashassins built a wall to fence themselves off from the Arabs. It worked. Insane, murderous Arabs were frustrated and thwarted from dong their evil deeds.

We need to fence Mexico off, to enable them to be a better, more responsible neighbor. We need to let that government deal with its own issues, not dump them on the United States. If the Mexican government can't or won't serve its people, then the Mexican people should hang or just shoot their so-called leaders and start over again. It would be the best thing to ever happen to Mexico.

Many Mexicans and American Latinos claim that Texas, New Mexico, Arizona, and California are just occupied extensions of Mexico and that the Gringos are 'illegals'. These are members of *"La Raza de Bronze"* a hateful racist organization with a fantasy of creating a Latino utopia called AZTLAN in the above named states. Yeah, sure, and if these states ever became a part of Mexico, folks would soon be climbing over the fences to seek jobs and a life in the United States, and to escape gross mismanagement and corruption, and all the crap that exists behind whatever borders of Mexico. Face reality folks: Those territories were sold to the United States by a then (as is today) indecently corrupt Mexican government following an honest, legitimate war that gave freedom to the people in those territories who sought freedom then, and who live in and enjoy freedom, prosperity, and security in those American states now.

The Mexican government is inserting itself into American internal affairs by distributing anti-American books and literature in the United States. Some on the American side wrongly ignore this, and others on the Mexican side claim they have a right to do this. Can you imagine if the Russians began distributing books in Germany that were ugly lies and anti-German propaganda, or if the Germans did so in Russia or France, or vice-versa?

By any shake of logic, this distribution of anti-American propaganda in the United States confirms that Mexico is a very hostile neighbor. The American authorities who have been aware of this for over a dozen years and by doing nothing but give it a pass are treasonous themselves and ought to be fired if bureaucrats, and voted out of office if elected officials.

In some areas, the United States has begun building high walls and fences to control the flow of 'illegals'. With this obstacle, the 'illegals' have moved to more remote and hostile areas devoid of water and where the terrain is difficult. More and more of these lawbreakers have died trying to sneak into the United States. [I pray for their souls and that their country might one day have some honest, legitimate leaders who actually care and work for the good of their people. That's all.] American pinheads are predictably up in arms and want to put out supply stations with food and water, and maps to help the criminals sneak along the way. That's stupid. It encourages ever more illegal acts. We need to extend those walls and fences all of the way.

However, with secure walls or fences, I would no longer be able to leave my campground along the border and stroll over into Mexico after my breakfast, drop my drawers, and deliver my due and appropriate respects to Mexico. That would be a sacrifice that I can deal with.

There remained near San Diego a long section of border that was not walled for some reason (reportedly to do with habitat) where hundreds of lawbreakers broke into the United States every day. Finally, in late 2005, judges cleared the final obstacles to building those walls, and when he learned of that, the Mexican el Presidente declared that this was wrong, yada-yada-yada. Who is he to tell us what is right or wrong when we act to protect ourselves?

Fortunately, the House of Representatives approved an additional 700 miles of fencing.

Mexican police and military authorities have been making illegal forays into the United States, even shooting at uniformed American authorities. This is precisely where forceful reaction is needed. We need warplanes and a fleet of helicopter gunships out there along those borders. When a Border Patrol Agent reports any such incursions, let the gunships deal with the invaders.

Also, if dozens of people can just saunter over the border from Canada or Mexico leaving tons of trash and debris in their broad foul wake, we have a problem of another nature.

While some politicians and wishful thinkers declare otherwise, it is obvious that our neighbor to the south, Mexico, is far less than a friendly neighbor and is NOT in any way a participating partner in anything other than exploiting the United States in the most egregious ways. Their authorities make incursions across our borders and shoot at us, committing acts of war that deserve an appropriate response, and our own elected leadership is grossly derelict when they fail to respond. Those illegal incursions are in support of abetting illegal immigrants, drug smuggling, and even helping terrorists intent on doing America and its citizens grievous harm. In 2005, when Mexican attorney general, Rafael Macedo de la Concha, proclaimed after "Mexican authorities had investigated", that no terrorists have come across the border from Mexico into the United States, he was flat out lying. If he wasn't lying, then he is incredibly stupid, and in fact is probably both.

Our national policies and actions need to be revised to reflect this reality. We need to seriously protect our borders, our sovereignty, and our security.

In Mexico, the Mexican national and local "policia" rip American tourists off whenever they get the urge. They are abusive and negligent. Any Americans who venture over the border and make such contributions to Mexico's largely illicit wealth are fools deserving of being ripped off by those Mexican scum.

There are many along the American/Mexican border who have beliefs, fears, and concerns that are reasonable. While their names may be of Hispanic origin, these people are Americans, loyal, faithful, patriotic Americans. These people just know that it is the corrupt Mexican government and many Mexicans in general who are challenging the sovereignty of the United States' borders with Mexico.

Besides the borders with Mexico and Canada, we have other border issues to contend with: Native American (Indian) tribal lands. Many of the tribal areas are along or even straddling the borders.

Tribal members can live wherever they wish in their tribal area and are allowed to cross at will. Many have no birth certificates and their actual nationality may (and rightfully should) be in dispute when they step outside of those tribal lands.

Because the tribal lands are tribal controlled, federal authorities are often not permitted to enter into tribal areas to do their business. This is also a problem for state and federal agencies. It ought not be so difficult.

If the tribal groups want to be sovereign and independent, we should uphold those rights. The solution is simple. We should put up fences along the borders with the tribal areas and let them have their open borders (with Mexico) and they can deal with the drugs, the smugglers, the 'illegals', and all of the problems stemming there from. If the tribal groups don't want to deal with that, then they need to step up and cooperate (join us) and let local, state, and federal authorities onto tribal lands to do what they need to do to protect U.S. sovereignty. Like President Bush declared: You are either with us or against us. This aptly applies to the tribal groups along those borders as well as to everyone else.   They can either cooperate and join us as loyal participating citizens, or be negative and against us. A big, ugly, fence ought to be the result.

Unmanned Aerial Vehicles

We need to incorporate the use of Unmanned Aerial Vehicles (UAVs) in securing our borders. Armed UAVs are an option that can serve us well. The armaments could be Harm missiles which could blast speeding boats running from Coast Guard patrol boats. They could be equipped with rapid firing miniguns to turn people jumping borders with Mexico and Canada into minced meat. Use UAVs to scrutinize borders and alert patrols to people who violate our borders and when or if they attempt to evade helicopter or ground patrols, the miniguns could be employed effectively.

Moslem Immigration

Political, social, economic, and cultural Islamization is the principal if not the only motive for much of the immigration from Moslem countries. The process of Islamization must be declared an enemy of the republic, and immigration of Moslems must be halted!

Moslems are doing everything they can get away with and protesting when caught. It is disgusting, especially what they falsely claim as profiling, even though Mohammedans are principal terrorist candidates, hijackers, and joyously suicidal bombers.

We need new visa and immigration policies vis-à-vis Moslems that employ severe restrictions. Some feel that this would widen the gulf between civilized and Muslim worlds. I think this is a great idea! Moslems certainly are refusing to accommodate us even a little. I welcome decent, civilized, people willing to assimilate into our culture, not those wanting to subjugate or to destroy our culture as that Moslems are wont.

The goal of Islam is to establish and maintain fascist style subjugation (control) -- they want to change America into an uncivilized, restrictive, and oppressive nation following Mohammed's depraved Ahadith (Hadiths) and uncivil Sharia laws. There's nothing complicated there. It's just our subjugation, our total and complete submission to

Islamofascism.

We clearly need severe restrictions on all non-immigrant visas, and finger printing, bio scanning, HIV screenings, and all manner of scrutiny of people from hostile pseudo regions -- specifically Moslems visiting the United States. Moslems are in fact an increasing danger to our society.

Chapter 7

TERRORISM

The goal of terror is to create an atmosphere of insecurity and fear, weakening the loyalty and trust of us in our government, in our institutions, in our society. There are many forms of terrorism.

We are confronted with "state" sponsored terrorism. The "state" we first saw with 9/11 was Afghanistan, and of course correctly included Iran, Iraq, and Syria. We have very short vision. Our leadership is impaired. The real "state" sponsored terrorism that we face is the political state of Islam.

While we have had military successes against the modern purveyors of anti-Western terrorism, we are NOT yet winning the so-called war on terror (A war which has no end, can't be "won" in the traditional sense, and is not a war on real terror, but on terrorists who are Moslems bent on the subjugation – the destruction of the civilized world.). To really win the war on terror, we first need to eradicate terrorist enemies without creating new ones; and then deny them the support of local populations at the grass roots levels as well as at the top of their feed chain. The real conflict that we are engaged in, one that our political "leaders" are having such difficulty grasping, understanding, or focusing on is the real world war III, the conflict with the immutable, ideological, theocratic fascist political and social system, Islam, which we must win. For, if we fail in the conflict with the Islamists, we will then become Islamized in the worst sense of being subdued.

Zeroing in on Terrorists

One thought circulated by naive fools is that some (Islamic) terrorists do these awful things just to get attention and that the world should understand their grievances and take action to solve their grievances, the root causes of their discontent. This stupid thinking is moronic and counterproductive. It is OK to try to learn about their grievances to understand that the only cause of their so-called grievances is a compelling political agenda that has as its objective the subjugation of civilization to Islam. Unfortunately, influential politicians like United States Senator and intellectually challenged Tom Kean want to try to understand the root causes of terrorism so that we can deal with them. Read it here, dude!

Others like whiner Simon Reeve believe that we should solve the Israeli-Arab (Palestinian) conflict. He thinks this would cure terrorism. What is his proposed solution - the same as the Palestinians - to kill the world's Jews off with another holocaust. Does he have a better solution? If he does, he needs to articulate it. He can't of course, so all he does is whine, it's all he and others of his pathetic ilk can do.

Here's a fundamental truth: If Israel did not exist, 1.5 billion Moslems would still hate and want to destroy us.

Reeve wants the US to solve the Israeli-Arab conflict -- presumably with the Arab desire of abandonment of Israel so the Arabs can kill all of the Jews off. What next? Naturally, the Arabs would then (sensing our weakness - something to take advantage of) pressure Europe and then the United States to pursue their and Hitler's solution, the extermination of all Jews on earth. Oh yeah, pogroms where fools like Simon Reeve would be compelled to run around the streets of his city seeking out and butchering Jews, innocent people, after first raping and then beating the women and young boys, just like the Islamists do.

According to the most senior Imams and Mullahs in Saudi Arabia and Iran, who lead the preaching and dictate Islamist sermons around the world, the Jews and Christians are allah's enemies and must be destroyed (killed, murdered, eliminated). This is regularly repeated (in Arabic, of course, not so often in English) by such as Sheikh Musa Al-Qarni, a leading Saudi preacher. He also preaches the Koranic gospel that the Jews and Christians are the enemies of the Muslims and of Islam, and that they must be destroyed. This is pure, pathological hate-mongering of the type that inspires Moslems to commit murder, and deserves appropriate responses, but never rewards. The sermons promulgated by these hate mongers are published on the internet for lesser imams around the world to download and use in their sermons, and are drawn from the Koran.

Three terrorist murderers have been given the Nobel Peace Prize. This is unconscionable. To anyone who appreciates or values a Nobel Prize, the knowledge that their work has been so denigrated by association with terrorist murderers should cause some to reject anything from the Nobel committee -- of terrorist supporters in actual fact.

Hmm, hmm, hmm Barak Hussein Obama was given the Nobel peace prize in 2009. For what? Jibber-jabber is all.

Our American war on terrorism has been very limited. The main focus of the government has been al Qaeda. They have arguably had limited success. Al Qaeda is still out there, plotting and killing Americans. More worrisome, Islam is still out there, and over here, plotting against us, working against us, using us, and working to destroy us.

We need to expand the war to other terrorist organizations, and need to consider their sponsor countries such as Syria, Iran, Saudi Arabia, Somalia, Sudan, and many others. The organizations we need to get after very aggressively are sometimes slick murderous outfits such as the Palestinian Liberation Organization (PLO), Hezbollah, Hamas, Islamic Jihad, and others such as Jemaah Islamiyah. How do we go after them? First, stop all foreign aid to each and every one of those countries that support them, all fifty-eight countries. Another way is to send out squadrons of bombers to vulcanize their terrorist (military) training camps, headquarters offices, and safehavens in places like Pakistan, Lebanon, Somalia, Ethiopia, Libya, Iran, Saudi Arabia, Egypt, all over the world, even in Europe (of course these vulcanizations would have to be covert operations). Then we must go after their finances, and wherever we find their supporters, members, and adherents, we must neutralize them or just kill them. We should clearly indicate that we would be regretful of anyone who suffered as a part of collateral damage, but at the same time point out that the best way of avoiding being collateral damage, would be to isolate themselves from the terrorist groups and move or be far away from them. We must use real diplomacy as well. Tell the Syrians that they will suffer terribly if they do not take out Hezbollah in their territories NOW, or suffer serious consequences. Then, let a ship blow up hugely in a Syrian port and choke it all off, or have unknown bombers take out a few Syrian embassies, claiming they are Hezbollah fronts. Then, tell (not ask) the Iranians to dismantle their Hezbollah, and when they don't, we should start by sending missiles, lots of them into Hezbollah camps, hotels, armories (mosques), downtown offices, everywhere, even under the skirts of women or the diapers of babies where they hide. Turn Hezbollah into pariahs that everyone wants to avoid and drive away. Then, we can focus on the next target.

We should heavily arm Christian, Hindu, and Buddhist communities in Indonesia, Ethiopia, Eritrea, Nigeria, Cambodia, Malaysia, Egypt, Sudan, Serbia, Kenya, the Philippines, Borneo, Thailand, the Balkans, Greece, Georgia, Armenia, and everywhere else where they are being murdered daily by Moslems. Let these good, decent, innocent people protect themselves. We, in the so-called civilized world are obliged to help them, but we all too often turn a blind eye to such atrocities.

When an Islamist country sues for peace, it must be on our terms, not theirs. Terms must include universal suffrage, women's rights, freedom of speech and the press, elimination of Madrassas, the cessation of persecution of religious minorities, and the establishment and official protection of Christian and other faith's places of worship throughout those countries.

Success of Arabs/Islam and Terrorism

Terrorism has had more successes vs. the USA than we have had against them. I haven't kept a precise score, but we are not faring well in spite of what our national leaders try to tell us.

HOSTAGES: The Iranians seized the American Embassy and held fifty-three Americans hostage for 444 days with impunity. Our President, Jimmy, the dunce Carter merely sat on his ignorant butt and wrung his hands helplessly. Only when President Reagan who promised retribution came into office did the Iranians turn the hostages free.

CIA agent William Buckley was kidnapped by a Hezbollah cell led by Imad Mugniyah, a Lebanese who was involved with Hezbollah, the Palestinian Liberation Organization, Hezbollah, and Islamic Jihad (a subsidiary of Hezbollah), and was in fact a paid agent of Iran's Pasdaran. Buckley was brutalized, tortured, and slowly butchered for over a year by Mugniyah, until he succumbed to pneumonia. Did the United States retaliate? No.

Iran provides millions of dollars to Hezbollah in direct support of its military and terrorist operations. Hezbollah has killed more Americans outside of America than any other Moslem terrorist group.

MARINES: US Marines were sent to Lebanon. Mediocre Marine Corps officers allowed 241 of them to be killed by a truck bomber who just drove into the building and detonated a fearsome and very sophisticated home made bomb. This was planned, organized, and initiated by Mugniyah with Iranian financing. What did the United States do? Led by Ronal Reagan, we turned tail and beat a hasty retreat out of Lebanon, thus encouraging more such acts.

1983 BOMBINGS OF EMBASSIES: The American Embassy in Beirut was blown up in April of 1983, another Iranian sponsored act carried out by Mugniyah. The Americans opened another Embassy building and it was blasted in October. Then, the Embassy in Kuwait was hit in December of 1983. Have we done anything to bring those Iranian sponsored and supported murderers to task? No. Are we that afraid of the Iranians and their Hezbollah minions? At least three significant Iranian targets ought to have been turned into ashes and dust in retaliation, even now is not too late. Add another, or two for the Marines murdered in Beirut.

MARINE OFFICER: U.S. Marine Colonel William Higgins was kidnapped, held for months and months, tortured terribly and finally hung, in all probability by Iranian controlled Hezbollah agents led by Imad Mugniyah under the direction of the government in Tehran. Our response: A big fat zero. That is shameful.

Much later, Mugniyah was finally killed, and nobody took credit for this act. I, for one celebrated this filthy swine's death. I went out and danced in the street.

PANAM 103: Pan Am Flight No. 103 was blown out of the sky over Lockerbie, Scotland. As soon as we were convinced that the Libyans (Muamar Khadaffi) were behind this, we launched a retaliatory air strike and spanked him. It was fairly effective as it raised havoc with the Libyans, and Khadaffi in particular. Nevertheless, Khadaffi still continued to thrive, albeit with his tail between his legs. After a protracted effort, and after too many people had lost interest, two Libyans were brought to trial for that terrorist act.

CIA officer Mike Baer in his excellent book, SEE NO EVIL, explains that while he was stationed in Europe, he put out the effort on his own time to gather intelligence information about the attack. While it seems that the CIA itself didn't make a genuinely serious, concerted, prolonged effort after Pan Am 103 went down, some information was collected and haphazardly left laying around. Baer gathered that information, went out and gathered more, and pained a more comprehensive picture. While the accused Libyan operatives perhaps did the bomb planting, this apparently was really a clever effort of misdirection organized and put together by the Iranian Pasdaran in retaliation for the earlier USS Vincennes' erroneous shooting down of an Iranian airliner in the Persian Gulf.

The Iranians are going on about their business unhindered other than being appropriately branded by President Bush as being part of an axis of evil.

We need to deal with the Iranians in a manner they clearly understand, but our leaders have been unwilling or incapable of doing so. Our response has been to dither and pussyfoot around the issues like feeble morons. This behavior only encourages them to continue. We need to understand that we are dealing with nasty, ugly people who are primitive creatures at best. The appropriate and reasonable responses to them should be what they clearly understand. A big stick, wielded liberally and firmly, repeated as often as necessary for an indefinite period of time.

AMBASSADOR Dobbs was assassinated in Kabul in 1989. What was our response besides tucking our tails low and pulling our Embassy out of Afghanistan? We ought to have blasted the Taliban apart right then and there, if we had an idea that they did it of course.....but then our intelligence services had no real idea.......and was in fact incapable of going out and learning anything.

Bin Laden's al Qaeda was active in Somalia where Saudi money had let the Wahabis create radicalized Islamic groups who ultimately took the American forces to task, killing several, dragging their desecrated bodies through the streets and humiliated Clinton, who both failed to support those men or to respond in any way other than showing his abject cowardice. The only thing that saves him from being the worst President in history vis-à-vis international relations, was the moron, Jimmy Carter, who seems to be surpassed by Barak Hussein Obama.

Imad Mugniyah reportedly organized the KHOBAR TOWERS bombing in Saudi Arabia which very likely involved Saudis who were protected by the Saudi government. To get such protection, one can only assume that Saudi royal family members participated, and are being given a bye by our 'friends'. All efforts by the FBI, CIA, State Department and others trying to investigate this were thwarted by Saudi authorities.

Embassy bombings in Dar es Salaam and Nairobi went largely unanswered with the exception of a few cruise missiles that proved more embarrassing than effective. The embarrassment was rightfully based on poor intelligence. A Saudi Embassy or two should have been blown up....because Saudis in fact funded the Al Qaeda who were behind those bombings. It's still not too late.

The USS COLE attack speaks for itself. We ought to have turned the port of Aden into an ash heap as soon as we pulled the Cole and our troops out of there. Reportedly, the so-called "President" of Yemen was fully aware of the planning of this attack, and refused to cooperate in the investigation of the attack until the USG threatened to bomb him. This creep and most of his government are al-Qaeda sympathizers if not full-fledged members.

The 9/11/2001 attacks have not been appropriately avenged. True, we partially eliminated the Taliban, but have no right to be proud of a partial defeat of a stone aged band of bandits, thugs, and bullies that had no real modern weaponry with which to defend itself. Besides, the Taliban didn't hijack those planes and fly them into the targets. None of the hijackers were Afghanis.

True, we've declared war on "terrorism", but we can't find them, can't kill them, and don't even know where or who they all are. Well, we do, but they have oil........ Then, Bush's successor regime declared that the war on terror was over. While the term "war on terror" was a stupid refrain, it at least gave some focus on our response. Nothing has been brought out to replace it which is a deception promulgated against Americans. While Islam has declared war on us, why can't we at least acknowledge this? It seems that Barak Hussein Obama has already capitulated.

Years later, we haven't killed or captured, nor can we verify the death of the Al Qaeda leader, bin Laden or even find him. A $25 million dollar reward for his capture languishes for a number of reasons. One of these reasons is that the American allies, the Afghan militias, or warlords as well as our Pakistani 'allies' in fact warn bin Laden whenever campaigns are being launched into areas where bin Laden hides. This was done for money as well as based on religious principle. This was one of the issues used in the 2004 presidential campaign by John Kerry when he criticized Bush for 'outsourcing' the hunt for bin Laden. This 'outsourcing' was the best we could do because our intelligence was lacking, and our being relatively if not completely clueless about jihadist loyalties -- loyalty past and present to bin Laden.

Besides killing 3052, the 9/11 attacks have had another victory -- of sorts -- American business in the form of insurance companies.

American insurance companies who routinely squander billions of stockholder and insured dollars on highly speculative exotic but mostly useless so-called art collections, are refusing to provide terrorism insurance without federal government (taxpayer support) in the form of the Terrorism Risk Insurance Act (TRIA). Without the TRIA to cover their mismanagement (as in ENRON, TYCO, and the mortgage industry) a consequence would be thousands of Americans (construction workers) being unemployed because developers wouldn't be able to obtain funding, ...because they couldn't get terrorism insurance, ...because insurance companies may have to sell (probably at a loss) some of their vast "art" collections to cover possible losses. Of course many of those fabulously precious and costly 'art' pieces are purchased from family members, friends, and acquaintances (illicit sexual partners, male or female) of those insulated but nevertheless corrupt and inept insurance company officials.

The ANTHRAX mailings had a significant success. The United States Government's own Postal Service is no longer trusted to deliver safe mail. Senate Offices, offices in the House of Representatives, and even the Supreme Court were shut down for various periods of time
The news media suffered mortal casualties and many prominent figures (as well as many workers) in the media are now terrified of their own mail.
Innocent civilians died too, and took years to determine who killed them.

Osama bin Laden

Osama bin Laden was trained by the CIA in the Afghani war against the Soviets, and after the Soviets were defeated, the CIA spun bin Laden loose. He quickly became public enemy Number One and all of the President's men couldn't get him. They followed him around but didn't get him.
The CIA tracked him using surrogates, and worked with surrogates to try to get him in 1997, 1998, and 1999. They were using Afghanis who were not very reliable, but with nobody else, the CIA had to rely on them. Several times, these Afghanis were set to go after bin Laden but then the White House (Clinton) equivocated. Then CIA Director George Tenet was given a go ahead and then faltered claiming that a given plan was 'flawed'. He had resources, and could have applied them to improve the plan and make it workable, but he and his risk averse senior managers didn't want to do the right thing.
The CIA had reams and reams of information on bin Laden's al Qaeda, but never bothered to collate it and make it available (got forbid such a blasphemy!) to other government agencies. This was either intentional or simply stupid, and probably both.
Clinton, pre-occupied through 1998 with his zipper problems

and Monica Lewinski, was unable to focus and think clearly (if he ever did), and his staff were thus ineffectual. This White House National Security Staff included the ineffectual Terrorism Czar, Richard Clarke who was retained by the Bush administration until just two months before the 9/11 attacks. One of his brilliant plans was to use consistently flawed or late CIA intelligence to launch a series of rolling cruise missile attacks wherever bin Laden was reported to be whether he was actually there or not, a crap shoot at best. The Secretary of Defense, Cohen and his staff felt that the effort would be unworthy because the cost of a cruise missiles was so high.?.?.?.???

At another point, bin Laden had spent a fair amount of time at a hunting camp in Afghanistan and reportedly visited that location for a few days with some Emiriti prince from the United Arab Emirates (UAE). Bin Laden reportedly visited this site often. When he learned of this, Richard Clarke phoned a UAE official to express his concern about fraternization between Emiriti officials and bin Laden. A week later, the camp was completely and forever deserted, erasing forever that possibility of getting bin Laden. Boy, Clarke was really brilliant, eh? Is there any reason to doubt that Condoleeza Rice was well justified in firing this utterly failed nincompoop.

Then, we have Clinton's National Security Advisor, the treasonous Sandy Berger, who, after the 'who screwed up investigations got rolling' crap hit the fan hustled off to the National Archives where he went in and deliberately, intentionally purloined sensitive classified documents. He stuffed them in his socks, shirt, underpants, wherever he could find a place on or even in his person, and then waddled out of there and destroyed them. When this came to light, he claimed that he only made a mistake, and the powers that be allowed him to get away with those blatant thefts of valuable, sensitive documents that would have shed clear light on him and the Clinton administration's factually abject failures. This is absolutely shameful. It is more shameful that the Bush administration let Berger get off so lightly (Perhaps they are looking for 'bye' when their time comes around.). If Berger were a lower ranking person (dare I say commoner), he would have been fried, prosecuted and sent to prison. This letting of Burger off is representative of a double standard giving privileges to the high and mighty, but which screws the lower ranking people in government. It is wrong, flat wrong. This is one of many reasons why so many Americans are rightfully distrustful of our own government, and why so many of us Americans are becoming more disrespectful, disapproving, and flat disgusted with our own government, even when our preferred parties are in the White House.

Western Europe

The expansionist Moslem culture has made major inroads that can be considered greatly successful. Middle Easterners have slowly but steadfastly made their imprint in the European Community.

European Islamists see Western Europe as though they were a bunch of defeatists acting like frogs in a pot of heating water, just sitting there until they cook to death.

With the new millennium however, some of the Europeans are finally beginning to wake up to the threats in their midst, and have even started taking action to protect their society and culture. It's almost too late.

The bringing of Turkey into the European Union would contribute to the end of the European Union. It would open Europe to greatly accelerated Mohammedan immigration and expansion much like when the Mohammedans took over North Africa and their subsequent total rape and complete destruction of that fine, long established Christian civilization.

Some say that Turkish desperation for membership was threatened by the German and French leadership (they, or rather, their political leaders were bribed by Saddam to take this course) when the Americans were seeking to use Turkey as a staging point for an invasion thrust into northern Iraq in 2003.

Turkey is not European. Turkey is in fact an adversary of Europe and western civilization. This is a historical fact of long standing, and has not changed.

Moslems have been allowed to infiltrate (migrate) in large numbers into Europe. Almost too late, Europeans have recently started taking note and are finally reacting more responsibly and pro-actively in their own self interests – their own survival. The non-competitive Mohammedans typically have started whining and crying foul.

Popular Dutch film maker Theo van Gough expressed himself in a realistic, thoughtful and truthful manner, and a fearful barbarian Mohammedan murdered him to silence his messages of truth.

The Dutch sat up and took notice and to the dismay of the Mohammedans began responding in a positive manner. Some prominent Germans are also beginning to see the light and are beginning to voice their concerns about the Islamization of Germany and the growing deterioration this is bringing about.

A London based anti-European, anti-civilization, anti-Christian so-called Islamic Human Rights Commission whined that their Mohammedans were feeling harassed and discriminated against. Gee, too damned bad. What about Islamic sanctioned harassment, discrimination, and murder of Christians and believers of other creeds and faiths in Mohammedan countries? What about reciprocity? That doesn't matter to Mohammedans, after all it's happening to non Mohammedans in those non-Islamic places.

Islamic leaders teach and work their wily ways to undermine democracy by taking advantage of those very laws to further their hateful cause. The greatly civilized, freedom loving and genteel Europeans are finding their values being exploited so as to spread

Mohammedism.

Wherever one finds Islamic concentrations living in Europe, they have become squalid ruins of their own creation. They are breeding grounds for the exploitation and radicalization of their own people. The Europeans need to eliminate this squalor and compel the occupants to move out and to integrate with free, civilized Europeans -- to become civilized, or to just get out of Europe. German officials have wisely considered requiring all Imams to preach in German. This is great and all European countries ought to require similar measures immediately. They should further require that all teachings to Islamic children be in European languages, and that all preaching and teachings be recorded and monitored for sedition and teaching of intolerance and hatred; and when a teacher or Imam is found to be truly seditious or hate mongering, kick his treacherous being out of the country by sending him or her back to her or their ancestral homeland and never allowed to return to that or any other free, independent, democratic civilization.

Moslems who refuse to integrate with civilized people need to be returned to their ancestral homelands where they belong.

The ongoing Mohammedization of Europe must be reversed. A growing, Islamization of Europe already has had some very bad effects, but unchecked will have drastic negative consequences in all areas of European society, military, educational, social, and intellectual.

Islam is incompatible with western civilization, and in Europe the goal of Islam is to impose their version of political intolerance. If the Mohammedamization of Europe is allowed to continue, the European Union will disintegrate and those countries will rapidly become as impoverished, uncompetitive, and backward as the Mohammedan countries.

Germany

Germany started importing 'gastarbeiters' (guest workers) from Moslem countries in the early 1950's, and many have remained. Their increasingly hostile, aggressive, and intimidating Moslem population is now very large. A result of this is that, in their own country, some of the Germans are in fact becoming increasingly cowed into submission to the Mohammedans, just like when they fell under the spell of Hitler's Nazism.

Germany has also determined that they should withhold and not share information on certain terrorists because they object to America's practices of Capital Punishment – the killing evil people. They claim that certain information may lead to the imposition of the death penalty on criminals and terrorists who have participated in the killing of Americans (and civilized Germans). They don't want to share information because it could upset some 'rezident' Moslems who might take up some sort of action to retaliate. This is shameful and cowardly. However, if necessary, the United States could establish a treaty with the Germans and others like them whereby we would agree to not impose capital punishment (death) of those they extradite to the United States. In such a treaty, we could agree to hard life sentences in special circumstance prisons.

Norway

The Norwegians are among the most hospitable and liberal people on earth. So much so that a group of Mohammedans (mostly living off of Norwegian welfare) felt free enough to publish a book in Urdu (Pakistan's main language) calling their hosts, the Norwegians barbarians and snakes among other things. These thieving beggar Mohammedans ought to leave if they don't like it there. Better yet, the Norwegians ought to withdraw the welcome mat and boot their unfriendly, racist, bigoted guests out. Yes, the Mohammedans - get them out of Norway, all of them. Those that shave, get jobs, reject their turbans and burkas, stop beating their wives (and limit themselves to one wife), begin bathing, and abandon Islam forever can be permitted to remain.

Italy

Italy has a lesser degree of Moslems in their midst, but depends on Libya for their oil. In spite of the inability of the Italians to elect a strong, positive government capable of taking a leadership role, they have been supportive of the United States. Moslems have pushed and pushed, and the Italians have proven themselves far more responsible than I might have thought. The Italians have started booting larger numbers of Mohammedans out, and have even torn down an illegal Mosque.

Journalist and writer, Oriana Fallaci railed and railed against the new fascists, the Moslems in her lovely nation. She was harassed and hated by the Mohammedists, but she made enough noise that her fellow Italians paid attention, and their actions from now on can save Italy, and even point the way for the rest of Europe.

France

France depends on Algerian Oil, and has permitted a large Moslem population to become well established. The Mohammedans in France are probably the most volatile and as a result, the fear of some French leadership of upsetting them borders on abject terror. Saddam Hussein purchased and owned the French Prime Minister, Jacques Chirac, and the support we have received from that mostly cowardly French leadership was far, far less than it ought to have been.

France once was glorious. They had men amongst them, great men like Lafayette and Rochambeau who contributed to America's war for independence from England. Clearly however they didn't really do it for America. They were French, and as French, they were helping the American Colonies only for the purpose of screwing the British.

The French have also fought long arduous wars for centuries, almost always on the losing side (the American Revolution being out of the norm). Their gene pool is thus limited. Nearly all French men (real men) who had courage and initiative eventually got killed off in the wars, and the ones who stayed back and hid behind skirts stuck around to take care of the women and do the breeding. Most of the genes having to do with courage have seemingly been killed off leaving many French genetically predisposed to cut and run rather than fight. Being weak and truly insignificant after being glorious and powerful is a terrible thing, and that's a good part of the reason why the French hate the Americans. French Foreign Minister de Villepin spoke of working with the Americans one day, and then stabbed Secretary of State Colin Powell in the back the next day at the United Nations. Typical liberal European stuff.....

Look at the Vichy French. All that they did for the Germans is in history books, but France's greatest act was to stick us Americans with Degaulle in World War II. If Hitler's first name had been Jacques, even Degaulle would have joined the Germans.

While France, especially Chirac was vilifying President Bush for going after Islamic terrorists and Saddam Hussein, others more honest and pragmatic and with a few of those remaining fighting genes started stepping up. To curb increasing problems of violence in French schools they forbade the open display of religious paraphernalia such as Jewish Stars of David, Christian Crosses, and Mohammedan headscarves on female students. Of course, the Mohammedans went bananas claiming infringement on their rights and other balderdash. While it was not reported in mainstream news media in the United States, Mohammedans in Paris later launched blatantly bigoted and anti-white racist anti-French campaigns. These included attacks on white children who were beaten up while being ridiculed for their race/culture. The French authorities did nothing.

In the so-called war on terror, we cannot always be confident that the pusillanimous French leadership will consistently support us to any extent. As modern warriors we need to be reminded that France succumbed to terrorists in Vietnam, Algeria, and other former territories. In World War II, they submitted to the Germans. They needed help in World War I, and before that, Napoleon was crushed. The French are effectively neutered. Were it not for the British and the Americans, France would be speaking German now.

The French fought and lost the Gallic wars, the hundred years war beat them down pretty bad, and they were saved under the leadership and courage of a woman, they lost to the Italians, to the Huguenots, the Franco-Prussian war, and just escaped annihilation in a dozen other wars. The only recent wars they have won have been when the Americans and British fought for them.

The one great mark for them was Charles Martel who earlier beat the Moslems away from Europe's gates and saved civilization. We need another Martel right now.

The fall of 2005 saw a Mohammedan uprising in France. Two very stupid, ignorant Moslem punk thieves ran from the police and tried to hide by stuffing themselves into an area populated by high voltage equipment. They got fried. The morons killed themselves, and the Mohammedans of France went on a rampage for a dozen nights, burning and destroying in very typical Mohammedan fashion. Chirac and his government wrung their hands believing that they needed to "accommodate" these Mohammedans even more. What Chirac ought to have done was call out the Gendarmes armed with machine guns and given orders to shoot to kill. That burning and rampaging crap would have stopped quickly. Then, Chirac and company should have rounded up the instigators of this rampage and exported them back to their Mohammedan roots, cancelled the issuing of further visas in those countries, and generally cracked down. But, sans gonads, Chirac & associates worked like good, frightened little dhimmi servants to appease the punks. This is more than a tragedy, it is a travesty.

Notwithstanding my polemics, some elements of the French government is in some ways working to help the United States - and more importantly, civilization with their work and support in the Paris based "Alliance Base" which has worked to apprehend and pass valuable and useful information to the United States regarding Mohammedan and other terrorists. This is good.

The recent elections and the ousting of Chirac have been a blessing to France, one which they need to take advantage of quickly.

Spain

Spain likewise has a large, intimidating Moslem population, and depends on the Middle East for its oil. Spain had a Prime Minister willing to support the United States but one terrorist shot from al Qaeda took care of that. With two hundred murdered Spaniards fresh in their graves, the cowardly Spanish voters rushed to establish their servility to Islam and to elect a coward as their head of state. This is surprising (that the Spanish won't take a stronger stance) considering the depredations of Islam during the six centuries they ruled the Iberian peninsula.

The Spanish inquisitions got rid of most Mohammedans who didn't flee when the Christian Queen Isabella and King Ferdinand took Spain back in 1492.

Now, the throngs of al Qaeda adoring Mohammedan immigrants in Spain are claiming that they want to "reclaim" Spain and to "return" to their roots. Their roots are NOT in Spain, but the foolish Spanish may lose their corner of civilization, freedom, and independence and be compelled to bow down before the caliph once again.

The Moslems must have established a permanent dhimmi gene in the Spanish people. A dhimmi is very much akin to a victim of a hostage taking who develops the "Stockholm" syndrome – wherein they work vigorously to protect their tormentors. The Spanish who had gumption and courage were killed off to a large extent, and those left behind lack this essential genetic makeup. In this context a quisling Spanish judge, Baltasar Garzon assumed the role of a defender of Islamist terrorism when he began indictment procedures against American citizens who expressed opinions about torture while they were on sovereign U.S. soil. This asinine jerk should be prohibited from travel to the USA, if he has enough brains to even find his way to an airport..

United States of America

Of course the USA's well deserved reputation for dithering doesn't help.

We are all fortunate that Osama Bin Laden, Muamar Qadaffi, Kim Jong Il, Iran, or others of their ilk don't have weapons grade Anthrax, or other weapons grade biological weapons deployed -- yet. If they did, it or their use would be far more widespread, and the accompanying mayhem and death fearsome to behold.

What ought to be of concern is the motives of the Anthrax mailer. Was he doing this to merely pass on a message to us that we need to be better prepared and aware, or what? Was it a preview, a sales demonstration? He had a high quality weapon, and a means of delivering it. If

I am just disappointed he didn't mail some samples to the dozens of anti-western terrorist groups deployed around Israel, like dogs around a fire hydrant, to Kim Il Sung, Iran, Muamar Khadaffi, Saddam, the Bin Laden clan, a couple of Saudi princes, the gang that rules the Arab occupiers of the land of Palestine, and Syria's leadership, to name just a few.

The major terrorism success of the 9/11/2001 hijackings probably took more than two years of planning, training, logistics, practice (dry runs), and more, by nineteen men who sauntered past an ineffectual security system onto four fully fueled airliners. Today airport security remains rudimentary at best, in spite of the hundreds of millions spent.

Politically correct TSA screeners (not the brightest and most sparkling bulbs around) do it by the numbers, harassing little old ladies and allowing robust men pass by, while making two-year olds take their tiny shoes off. They even harass well known figures such as known entertainers who aren't likely to blow planes out of the sky.

Amusingly, an Arab-American, tossed off of an airplane got his undies all in a knot and raised a fuss about being racially profiled. Nope. It wasn't so. He got tossed off because his gun caught security screeners' attention. This was compounded because the arrogant moron didn't fill out his documentation correctly. So much for being a Secret Service "professional".

Any self respecting terrorist/hijacker would make sure his

drivers license name and picture match his face and the name on his ticket, yet thousands of hours are spent checking up on this stuff.

Of course, the politically correct screening is because of morons who support stupidity. Racial or ethnic profiling is technically wrong, but it is done, and done successfully. Japanese travelers are scrutinized, or rather, their pinkie fingers are screened and Yakuza--gangsters are picked up and rejected.

The Israelis profile travelers on El Al airlines. They don't look at racial -- many Israelis can be misidentified as Arabs. They profile nuances of body language, eyes, and things that are important. This is very effective.

Yeah, the likelihood of an exploding shoe are not likely. Bombs in cargo holds or stashed inside of wings are a reality. Re-enforced flight deck doors and bulkheads combined with new procedures plus very much aware passengers have greatly diminished the likelihood of hijackers, yet stinger type anti-aircraft rockets are proliferating.

I pass through airports where reportedly millions have been spent for security, and I look around and cringe at the vulnerability I see where the Transportation Security Agency has been totally shortsighted and neglectful.

Large doors are available and open to a vehicle which could simply hop a curb and trundle right into a terminal building and blow itself up. Bollards can stop this potential bomb laden truck or car threat, but very few airports have installed them.

Large expanses of glass are undefended from even a small blast that could turn those glass panes into flying daggers. Blast curtains or other window/glass coverings could eliminate this terrible hazard but the TSA is seemingly blind to this.

In Los Angeles I observed a grungy, battered one-ton van pull up to a terminal, and a swarthy, shaggy unshaven (he looked like an Arab to me) man in his late twenties pulled a bale of newspapers out and onto his shoulder. He walked into the terminal just nodding at the security guards who returned his nod and he sauntered off with that bundle of newspapers up into the departure terminal. That van could have been loaded with explosives and while the guy could have dropped his bundle, went downstairs caught a cab and been miles away when the bomb went off. Or, he could have delivered that unchecked bundle with guns or explosives inside to a traveler or travelers enabling them to hijack a plane.

At Palm Springs, California, after a six plus million dollar 'security' upgrade, the airport's security protection and defenses are barely improved. The six million dollar upgrade provided a longer, beautifully landscaped sweeping approach that steers cars one way, and vans another past an area where drop bars and multi-thousand dollar pop-ups can be employed to control vehicles. One man monitors the several video cameras and has control over those seldom used controls, when he's there...... Passenger car parking is directed to parking lots a couple of hundred feet from the terminal, but one-ton smoked glass (obscuring inspection as to who or what is inside) passenger type vans, stretch limousines, and 'handicapped' marked vehicles are still able to approach and park unattended at the terminal where the vast expanses of glass are unprotected from blast effects. Back at the control booth, a separate driveway has a one-half inch thick wood drop bar where an explosives laden truck could easily crash through the flimsy wood bar, and drive up to, or into the terminal building.

Air marshals virtually wear an identifiable uniform, so potential hijackers easily know who they are. This may be desirable in curbing such acts, but also identifies them for terrorists to murder first.

The effects of these 9/11 hijackings was profoundly felt by the airline industry. People rightly became afraid to fly. They had no confidence in the government, or the airlines -- who didn't hesitate to cry fowl and beg for help from the taxpayers when their revenues fell.

It is little wonder that the airlines (long conditioned by the depredations of financial predators such as Carl Icahn), operating by design at the edge of financial ruin went over the edge. Lacking loyal, trusting customers (something one earns even today), a cash safety net, capable and competent executive leadership and management, the airlines demanded a taxpayer funded bailout. Carl Icahn & Co. should have been forced to fess up some cash. What Icahn did and does may have been legal in the sense of legality, but it was and is harmful, unethical, and very, very destructive.

We (the USA) are not only seen as ineffective, we have in fact been very much so. By dithering and not responding as we ought to have in the past, as we are capable of doing, we have seriously, clearly, and simply encouraged continuing and expanding acts of barbarism. So long as we remain spotty or lacking in our determination, we'll continue to be targeted.

Good uses of terror

Whenever I stand at the Cabrillo Monument at Point Loma (San Diego, California) and watch an aircraft carrier as it sails out of the San Diego harbor, I get thrills and chills. It is an awesome sight to behold.

Any super carrier loaded with its complement of over eighty aircraft on board represents the equivalent of being the eighth most powerful air force in the world.

An American aircraft carrier projects America's might wherever it goes. Along with its accompanying battle group of cruisers, destroyers, frigates, and submarines, each warship alone is a force to be reckoned with. A battle group is awesome.

I recall a NATO fleet visit to Istanbul many years ago. A couple of NATO destroyers and a large Cruiser had come into the Bosphorus and set their anchors. Bristling with guns fore and aft, and other hardware, they were impressive, especially a freshly painted French Cruiser. With special lighting for effect and all, they made for a splendid sight at night in their anchorage.

When I looked out onto the Bosphorus the next morning, the aircraft carrier, the USS America had just come in and dropped anchor. The French cruiser, now seemingly puny by comparison, sat in the actual shade of the USS America's flight deck.

We are America. We are the greatest nation on earth. We are not an expansionist nation gobbling up our neighbors. Our expansion has been with purchases of territory, and by free elections of people who desired statehood. We are the world's most powerful nation, and have consistently strived to use our great power for good, for the freedom of mankind. This is our destiny, and we need to accept this with honor and respect.

It is right and good for us to use these awesome forces in terrorizing those aggressors and oppressors who do gobble up their neighbors and work to impose slavery, either ideological or religious on the world.

Did I say terrorizing? Yes, we are purveyors of terror as well, but as long as we use our power for good, for economic, political, and religious freedom, it is good terror.

Guns in the United States

Those who hammer their guns into plows
will plow for those who don't.
Thomas Jefferson

We have another foe, right here, at home. The foe is those ignorant fifth columnists and seditionists who oppose the Second Amendment to the Constitution, the anti-gun crowd. Barak Hussein Obama is clearly a leading figure amongst those freedom haters!

Guns don't kill!

I've had guns for decades, one a 50-year old handgun inherited from my police officer mother. None of my guns have killed or shot anyone. Amazing!

More than eighty million Americans own guns. Many own more than one. There are about 1,500 accidental gun deaths per year, many among people who are licensed to carry (like politicians, actors and actresses, and their bodyguards), and law enforcement officers. Accidental means an accident without intent.

[Point: There are far fewer doctors in the United States than there are guns or gun owners. Doctors cause 9,000 times more accidental deaths per year, over 200,000 deaths. Ergo, doctors are more dangerous than guns. So, we ought to work to ban doctors because of the far greater dangers they pose to society, shouldn't we?].

The right of each and every upstanding American citizen to own guns is sacred and must remain so. It is this proper and good proliferation of guns that guarantees, supports, and ensures the First Amendment, and everything else in our Constitution, our very freedom. Seditionist and fifth columnist America haters fear this rightful and proper gun ownership as they rightly should. The Second Amendment was clearly established and put in place in case political leaders ignore the Constitution along with the other Amendments.

In fact, many cities are taking steps to re-enforce the need for citizens to have and use home defense guns. For twenty years people have been obtaining and installing home burglar alarms. A result of these are a commensurate increase in false alarms taking hundreds of hours for police to respond only to find that they've wasted their time. Cities' police forces are increasingly deciding to not even bother to respond to burglar alarms, which really renders them useless without a gun in a homeowner's hand to back herself or himself up. Without a gun, an alarm tells a person to get out of the way of the house invader, because the police won't respond -- until the alarm is backed up by a phone call to verify that it's a real emergency call, by then too late.

Only tyrants fear an armed populace

The leftists and fifth columnists are in league with Idiots, morons, and self-righteous elitist tyrants woefully lacking in basic good judgment and simple common sense who believe that they have the right to tell the rest of us how to live and who pretend that they don't like guns. They only dislike guns in the hands of free citizens. These weak minded pseudo-intellectual hand wringing socialists want not only to take away our guns and freedom, but they would only be too happy to take away (or give away) our liberty as well. They start with Barak Hussein Obama and his entire White House crew, and include political lightweight Henry Wexler; seditionist Senator Leahy, idiot Jimmy Carter, the unfortunate and misguided Sarah Brady and her phony Handgun Control Inc.; Rosie O'Donnell (the big mouthed hypocrite who armed her bodyguards and then ambushed Tom Selick (a genuine gentleman) on her TV show; the self centered diva, 'Babs' Striesand; and Jane Fonda of course. The list continues with the hundreds of liberal pinheads and politicians such as 'Chuckie' Schumer, an Icon of the Democratic party; Congressman Gerald Nadler; and of course the infamous hero of Chappaquiddick, Teddy Kennedy; and former Presidential wannabe Hillary Clinton; and the slime bag activist Tom Hayden. The list includes egotistical faux intellectual Tinsel weenies such as Ed Asner, pretty boy Richard Gere, Timmy Robbins and his sidekick, Susan Sarandon, Sean Penn, Rob "Meathead" Reiner, and Madonna who first threatened President Bush over her preferred Saddam Hussein and then started following Jewish leaders; and others of the gilded or gelded screen who have the ability to strike poses and parrot memorized lines before cameras, and other fundamentally willfully stupid fellow travelers who are grossly misguided. THE AMERICANS FOR GUN SAFETY is a malevolent zero membership 'organization' representative of those very few freedom haters who would suppress or take away our rights, who would enslave us, who hate our freedoms, especially that of gun ownership. They know, and you and I know that if and when the Mohammedans, the fundamentalists, the enslavers attempt to gain too much power, they will be neutralized by those guns wielded by free, civilized patriots.

Charlton Heston, a great man and a patriot, after many years a popular and very significant leader in support of freedom announced that he was afflicted with Alzheimer's disease. Responding to this tragic news, idiot pretty boy George Clooney mean spiritedly mocked Heston's affliction. Gee, George really showed his true (yellow) colors, and demonstrated to the world that he is a real intellectual midget and genuinely silly, immature, cruel pinhead. Heston, gentleman that he is did not take issue with Clooney, but Heston's spokesman, Bill Powers did comment profoundly that "class sometimes misses people".

There are other actors who do have tons of class, courage, and convictions, men, real men like James Woods, Bruce Willis, Stallone, and many others who stand tall, very, very tall.

The first bulwark of freedom of the world is the Second Amendment of the Constitution. That is a fundamental truth.

Supreme Court Justice Joseph Story in 1883 offered the following: "The militia is the natural defense of a free country against sudden foreign invasions, domestic insurrections, and domestic usurpation of the power by rulers. The right of the citizens to keep and bear arms has justly been considered, as the palladium of the liberties of the republic; since it offers a strong moral check against the usurpation and arbitrary power of rulers; and will generally....enable the people to resist and triumph over them.

Yeah, I like private ownership of guns. I like, love and most of all appreciate that they stand for -- **F-R-E-E-D-O-M!!!!!**

In July of 2008, after years of strategizing on both sides, the Supreme Court decided that the intent of the founders was unchanged: Individuals have a right to own and bear arms.

The anti-gun crowd failed to take away the rights of Americans to defend America as well as their homes. But, like bad pennies, they'll come rolling and roaring back, especially with gun hater and usurper of power Barak Hussein Obama in the White House who started a back-door program to disarm American patriots.

Chapter 8

THE CENTRAL INTELLIGENCE AGENCY

*Being politically correct is being
false to what is right.*

Tragically and sadly but not unexpectedly, the Central Intelligence Agency (CIA) failed the public trust miserably and totally as regards the events of 9/11/2001. So did the FBI and the rest of the intelligence community.

The CIA had failed in its critically fundamental mission to gather, collate, analyze, and disseminate critical information to protect the United States. The CIA didn't have any idea what was going to happen on 9/11/2001; that four (4) airliners were to be hijacked by several Saudis in a plot hatched long beforehand. The hijackings took detailed planning, communications, extensive logistics, funding, and coordination over a long period of time (at least a year if not two or three) among many people, groups, and cells within their al Qaeda organization.

Shortly after those horrific events, I wrote a letter to Senator John McCain offering to testify at any Senate hearings that might take place regarding these failures. Later, I sent a copy of this letter to Senator Joseph Lieberman, as well as courtesy copies to my Representative, Darrell Issa, and to Representatives Mary Bono (Mack), and Ken Calvert. I heard nothing from any of them. In all fairness, the letters are either still sitting in a barrel in some warehouse waiting for them to be sanitized from possible anthrax contamination, or were cooked to the point of crumbling to dust during the sanitation process.

I didn't bother approaching any of the big three news networks like ABC, CNN, or CBS. I don't have much confidence in them to do the right thing in their reporting.

I seethed for several weeks after those murders of 3,000 people. I could hardly talk coherently because of my burning internal rage.

Some of what I have to say here has not been publicly discussed in any venue that I, a private citizen no longer privy to classified government information at the time of those attacks, was aware of. What I have to say may hurt some people because they could be embarrassed and perhaps made to look foolish, rightfully foolish.

Some of this will annoy others because their pious righteousness will be rightfully challenged. It is a truth, my truth, a terrible, unfortunate truth, and the truth can be painful.

In April of 1983, the American Embassy in Beirut, Lebanon was blown up. I have a particular interest in this because a friend of mine was murdered in that blast along with many other fine people.

[[xxxxx this portion has been censored by the Department of State and/or the CIA xxxxx.....xxxxx this portion has been censored by the Department of State and/or the CIA xxxxx..... xxxxx this portion has been censored by the Department of State and/or the CIA xxxxx]]   All we knew for a long time was that a suicide bomber drove a truckload of explosives into the building. Who was he? Who recruited, sponsored, trained, and encouraged him to do this? Who paid for it? Who was behind it? The CIA didn't even seriously pursue this? Why? Why?

CIA Case Officer Robert Baer, when time allowed, on his own initiative pursued this over a period of fifteen years, trying to ferret out the information about those murderers. After several years, and lots of midnight oil (his own time), he deduced, probably correctly, that the Iranian backed Hezbollah probably did it. Indeed, the Hezbollah is an official but secret arm of the Iranian government, owned, controlled, and directed by the Iranian Pasdaran. Phony repudiations aside, Iran is also a major al Qaeda supporter, although the CIA isn't too sure about this. Al Qaeda terrorists move through southern Afghanistan and freely into, through, and out of southern Iran, where they are protected and well cared for by Iranians who facilitate movements to other countries such as the Sudan, Lebanon, Syria, Somalia, Libya, Egypt, Europe, and other places. In this, the Hezbollah and significant al Qaeda factions are clearly Iranian assets. Saad bin Laden, one of Osama's sons lives in Iran where he works and plans terrorist activities such as the 2003 Casablanca bombings. One of Osama's wives and other children enjoy safe haven protection in Iran.

Surprised

In 1990, the CIA was surprised when Iraq invaded Kuwait. Surprised! In 1990, the CIA had only   [[xxxxx this portion has been censored by the Department of State and/or the CIA xxxxx]]   Arabic speaking intelligence, or Case Officers.

In 1990, the CIA had thousands of officers who spoke Eastern European languages, AND Western European languages, AND romance, or Latin languages. In 1990 the CIA even had a few dozen, or perhaps even a few hundred Case Officers who spoke difficult East Asian languages such as Chinese.

A dozen years earlier, the CIA was caught with its collective pants down when the American Embassy in Tehran was taken over by a mob.   [[xxxxx this portion has been censored by the Department of State and/or the CIA xxxxx xxxxx this portion has been censored by the Department of State and/or the CIA xxxxx xxxxx this portion has been censored by the Department of State and/or the CIA xxxxx xxxxx this portion has been censored by the Department of State and/or the CIA xxxxx xxxxx this portion has been censored by the Department of State and/or the CIA xxxxx xxxxx this portion has been censored by the Department of State and/or the CIA xxxxx xxxxx this portion has been censored by the Department of State and/or the CIA xxxxx xxxxx this portion has been censored by the Department of State and/or the CIA xxxxx xxxxx this portion has been censored by the Department of State and/or the CIA xxxxx xxxxx this portion has been censored by the Department of State and/or the CIA xxxxx xxxxx this portion has been censored by the Department of State and/or the CIA xxxxx xxxxx this portion has been censored by the Department of State and/or the CIA xxxxx xxxxx this portion has been censored by the Department of State and/or the CIA xxxxx xxxxx this portion has been censored by the Department of State and/or the CIA xxxxx xxxxx this portion has been censored by the Department of State and/or the CIA xxxxx xxxxx this portion has been censored by the Department of State and/or the CIA xxxxx xxxxx this portion has been censored by the Department of State and/or the CIA xxxxx xxxxx this portion has been censored by the Department of State and/or the CIA xxxxx xxxxx this portion has been censored by the Department of State and/or the CIA xxxxx]]   .

The message was clear to all as to the fate they would receive if they did anything for the Americans.

Is it any wonder that the CIA now has an impossibly difficult time recruiting agents, or human intelligence sources in these places when they treat these people's lives in such a cavalier fashion? With the death of Johnny Mike Spann, another name was added to the CIA's book of honor - reportedly of seventy-eight Operations Officers killed in the line of duty. Is there an annex in the book of honor to acknowledge the sacrifices of the hundreds or thousands of non-American spies (human intelligence assets) who have died for our cause, or the additional thousands that the CIA has ineptly caused to be killed or die? Probably not.

Of course, the CIA is not alone in stupid pigheadedness. There is a case (probably one of many) where the Drug Enforcement Agency (DEA) agreed to protect a witnesses family, and then betrayed that trust. The witness, with the avowed promise of the DEA to protect his family testified and helped to prosecute and imprison criminals who had threatened his family members. Several unprotected family members, over a ten year period were murdered in direct retaliation for the man's testimony. The message is clear. Don't trust the DEA either because it will get your cherished loved ones killed.

White House executive orders had long ago been signed which forbade targeting heads of state. These were strictly adhered to for a long time. After all, a quid-pro-quo applied, and it was becoming clearly apparent that the CIA and therefore the intelligence community could not find much about anyone targeting the U.S. president. So, the Executive Order was signed, it was not classified and the information was disseminated to every nation in existence. If we didn't target their President, Prime Minister, Chief Honcho, Beloved Dear Leader, King, Top Dog, Big Ayatollah Swine, Chief Pig Imam, Emperor, President-for-Life, or whatever, it was expected, even understood, accepted, and really hoped that none of them would target the American President. It was a good deal until Saddam Hussein broke the rules, and probably others broke the rules too. Wisely, this unworkable deal was rescinded by President Bush (43).

CIA

Eleven years after their sad performance vis-à-vis the   [[xxxxx this portion has been censored by the Department of State and/or the CIA xxxxx]]   INVASION OF Iraq, on 9/11/2001, the CIA still had only [[xxxxx this portion has been censored by the Department of State and/or the CIA xxxxx]]   Arabic speaking case officers holding TOP SECRET security clearances. The CIA had been given more than ten years to become better prepared and able to deal with these issues and the CIA again failed.

It takes a very talented person more than two years to learn Arabic well enough to work in those countries. Two years of hard study and practice for a talented person with a very high language aptitude. If the CIA started training Case Officers in January of 2002, they would not be even starting to work in the field for two or more years. Then, they would need more time to get established and really start working, talking to people and getting to know them and learn their way around, earning the confidence of contacts. Given that, it would take about three additional years, or until 2005 or 2006 before a case officer could become rudimentarily effective or productive in getting useful and valuable human intelligence information.

The CIA has very few people who speak well the dozens of languages of 1.3 billion Moslem people. They need hundreds of proficient linguists speaking and understanding the languages and cultures of the many and diverse Islamic countries and societies. When, if ever will they fulfill that need?

When Johnny "Mike" Spann was murdered in Mazur-i-Sharif, Afghanistan, the CIA lost a significant portion   [[xxxxx this portion has been censored by the Department of State and/or the CIA xxxxx]]   of its case officers who spoke the language that he specialized in, that twenty million tribal Afghanis spoke.

Following revelations of the CIA's errors of negligence, they (along with the FBI and others) rushed headlong to hire as many Arabic speakers as possible regardless of the consequences. And, there was a rush of applicants as well. This effort was all about the numbers, just the numbers. They hired (and are still hiring) all kinds of Arabic speakers, who are in fact Arabs, and who were fluent. They are Moslems, many if not most not kindly disposed towards you and I, our America, and who are fifth columnists who will protect the bad guys so that they can hurt us. This is the worst kind of disservice that can be performed.

Christian Arabs and Jews who are fluent in Arabic or Farsi and likely to be far more loyal to American interests do NOT get hired.

Is there any doubt that al-Qaeda and other Islamists of their ilk aren't among those applicants and among those hired, and now being rewarded with access to the nation's most sensitive secrets? The intelligence community has an immense challenge here, to properly vet candidates, and then to track them carefully throughout their careers, and then when ferreted out, either neutralized or used most ruthlessly for our (civilization's) purposes. For those most sensitive jobs, the intelligence community ought not to consider any other but American citizens of non-Islamist backgrounds and invest the time and effort to educate those people in Islamic languages so that they can serve and protect America.

LEGISLATION

As a former government employee, I posses some insider understanding if you will, of how the government operates. Often, federal agencies will work to formulate and propose favorable or beneficial legislation that is passed into law by the Congress. That's how a lot of stuff works.

Certain elements of the CIA (and others) found the very idea of dealing with criminals, murderers, your basic scum bag to be distasteful. Anyone who would betray his nation, his people, is essentially a scum bag. They (the CIA purists) wanted to avoid dealing with impure people.

After the Vietnam War ended and the Watergate scandals ran their courses, the CIA was reformed, initially under the helping hand of Frank Church, and then under Stansfield Turner. The CIA leadership necessarily got into this reformation too, and probably worked with friendly legislators to formulate and pass into being a law that forbade recruiting, or dealings with known or suspected terrorists, criminals, thugs, murderers, "individuals of dubious ethical standing" or whatever one wants to call them. Was this dumb? Did this tie their hands?

Like Roger Ayles' FOX television news claims -- let the reader (or viewer) decide......... For example, Bill O'Reilly is one of America's greates patriots and I believe, one of the finest TV journalists in the world. I am often thrilled by his no-nonsense dealings with exploitive, phony, fraudulent, fetid, flotsam like Barney Franks who is one of the most corrupt and nasty politicians in history. Clearly, O'Reilley does not suffer fools gladly. Unfortunately, I also believe that O'Reilley has been mugged or muzzled and is now constrained and tightly controlled because of one of FOX's major investors and stock holders, a Saudi Prince (Al-Waleed bin Talal) who invested hugely in Fox news, presumably so that he could silence O'Reilley. Accordingly, not even the 'spin stops' here's Bill O'Reilly dares to raise certain issues that are taboo with the Saudi (sixth richest

148

man in the world thanks to Yankee petro-dollars) who effectively controls who signs checks at FOX.........]? [When somebody has that much potential or power to in fact censor and exert undue control or influence ($$$$$$), over what we read, see, or hear, should we not be skeptical? Bill O'Reilley regularly reported and ranted about Saudi royals and their peccadilloes, for a while. Then he suddenly stopped, just after the Saudis bought into FOX, and began censoring Bill and others at FOX.]. Yes, FOX's Bill O'Reilly has sadly been compromised and neutered.

No other network TV commentators or news anchors seem to dare to report on the Saudis either. So, in these self censorship activities, O'Reilley is just one of the pack of cowed and controlled TV personalities.

Speaking of censorship, a great outspoken man is being censored: Michael Savage's name is hardly, if ever mentioned on FOX or any other network, even though his keen analyses and sharp tongue are correct about 99% of the time. Some years ago, his sharp tongued outspokenness about gays distressed some delicate egos and he was banished from NBC. I wonder what he has done to offend O'Reilley, Hannity, Limbaugh, and others so that they refuse to even speak up on his behalf when a British official banned Savage's travel to England. This is cowardice. She claimed that Savage was a security risk. Savage has never hurt anyone, never threatened anyone, never acted against England, or anything of that manner. He is outspoken and some people may be offended by his presence, and the cowardly leftist British government is so terrified of its residents that they refuse entry by one of the greatest intellects in the world. This is shameful. So much for sticking up for freedom of speech.

After all, when one seeks to recruit or "turn" someone in a government, military organization, terrorist organization, or whatever, who or what is the kind of person who can be turned? A person who will turn against his or her nation, homeland, fatherland, family, friends, is likely a lowlife. They are often scum bags such as the several Americans who have wound up selling secrets to the USSR and others over the years. The types of people who would sell their countries (or sell out their organizations such as Hezbollah, the Mafia, the KKK, the KGB, Al Qaeda, the FBI or the CIA, etc.) are typically nasty criminals themselves. The CIA didn't want to get their hands dirty dealing with such fowl, distasteful people. Oh, my goodness, it might have rubbed off and tainted someone. Better to avoid that at all costs. How? Use the gullible Congress to pass dumb laws.

President Carter's appointee, Stansfield Turner, apparently with not enough brains to find his way out of a short tunnel with lighted doorways at both ends, focused on his version of the best way of gathering intelligence. It was to be by just using spy satellites. He didn't want to even talk of any other methods. He actually focused farther away than ever from human intelligence.

Turner started his serious destruction of the CIA by pushing out the best and most capable real (human intelligence and decent managers) spies. All of his successors (yeah, all of them, under Reagan, Bush (and Bush (41) was also one of the perpetrators of this colossal screw-up), and Clinton) let that growing damage keep on rolling. Unwittingly (or perhaps not) they did more to damage or even destroy the efficacy of the CIA than the Soviet Union's KGB ever hoped to do.

Turner and his successors (all of them, from all administrations), and their senior CIA advisors are responsible for the CIA's move away from doing the nitty gritty nasty work of gathering absolutely essential human intelligence.

Complicit in all of this were the Senators and Congressmen who had oversight responsibilities and utterly failed to fulfill their responsibilities to the American people. People with status, prestige, authority, and the ability to make things happen, these jackasses sat on their duffs during two (plus) decades of near pogroms in the intelligence communities, and let this terrible, destructive evisceration happen.

So, with friendly, self-imposed legislation preventing the CIA from dealing with "individuals of dubious ethical standing", who was there left to deal with, to recruit, to use as HUMINT? Many probable defectors who for ideological or related reasons just walked into an Embassy willing or even wanting to turn over 'tons' of information were actually turned away because of possibly unsavory pasts or tainted relationships. Yeah, **invaluable sources of human intelligence were actually turned away and driven off.**

Who was the CIA with it's 2,500 field operatives left to deal with? Nobody, that's who! That was just the way the puritans wanted it. Safe. No matter that it was and is ineffective, and a terrible waste of taxpayer dollars (billions)

Feckless is the appropriate word for it. This type of moronic nonsense was initially promulgated under President Carter, and was sustained and even enhanced by each and every administration since -- until the murderous attacks of 9/11/2001 brought some of us to our collective senses.

CIA Roots

The CIA's roots go back to the days immediately following World War Two and the Office of Strategic Services and the legendary "Wild" Bill Donnovan.

"Wild" Bill and his group were on occasion a group of wild and woolly, rough and tumble people - smart, capable, successful and courageous, warriors who took on high risk opportunities and had some significant successes, and also faced grave embarrassment and dangerous consequences when they didn't succeed.

The high risk included using or dealing with people, dangerous, nasty, unscrupulous, bad people. The risks included some of their turned HUMINT sources being of questionable reliability. Some of the HUMINT sources they exploited and worked were rough and tumble turncoats, crooks, alcoholics, wife beaters, drug users, pimps, simply insane, smugglers, and more. Some were ideologically on our side too. They represented some of the good, and all of the bad and the ugly.

The high technology represented by U-2 spy aircraft were good at first, but became risky. Francis Gary Powers was shot down during one of his photo reconnaissance missions, and the embarrassment went all of the way up to and adversely affected the President of the United States. Heads rolled. Risk aversion became a new and important element of CIA careers.

The CIA careerists and bureaucrats moved towards lower risk operations and technology met some of those needs. The higher, faster, better SR-71 'blackbird' came into being. Then it was followed by satellites taking pictures that the Black Bird could no longer take because Soviet technology was closing the gap and the risk of having a Black Bird shot down was growing.

With satellites coming into service, powerful and sophisticated signal receiving technology, and over-the-horizon radar and other goodies, we were able to listen in on radio, radar, and telephones, and collect volumes of information. This is called SIGINT, Signals Intelligence, and is carried out jointly by elements of the CIA, Defense Intelligence Agency, National Security Agency, and others.

The CIA had agents, operatives, and case officers, many left over from WWII who had characteristics that no longer seemed to properly fit into the gray flannel suits with white shirts and blue ties. Many of those tough veterans and heroes were a little too colorful and rough around the edges, but they could identify and go after vulnerable or susceptible targets. Once targets were identified, these rough-around-the-edges CIA Case Officers would go out and work those targets and recruit (turn) them. They could relate to them, emphasize, deal with them and their foibles, they could handle them. They were good at managing those human intelligence assets, and thus obtained valuable, important, useful intelligence. But there was always a risk involved and people got injured, got shot at, and the USG faced embarrassment at times.

It is a dirty business, obtaining human intelligence.

Risk aversion took over. The colorful, rough-around-the-edges CIA Case Officers got old, retired, and new, younger much more ethically challenged and risk-averse men came into power. They were polished and poised, had good Ivy League educations, were cautious, prudent and clean, squeaky clean. They fit a mold. They found it frighteningly distasteful to work with the types of people one needs to work with to obtain human intelligence.

Finally, in the late 1970's and 1980's, these younger people came into power and they abandoned collecting intelligence from human sources. It was dirty, untactful, distasteful. No matter that it was productive and incredibly valuable. They didn't want CIA Case Officers who used four letter words, smoked tobacco products, consumed alcoholic beverages, patted pretty girls' behinds, could tell lies, or who were willing to mix it up in a street fight. The new squeaky clean and fast rising in the proper mold, now senior officers didn't want rough and tumble case officers who weren't as risk averse as they were. Gee, they might even succeed where the squeaky guys obviously failed. No, they wanted nice, clean, squeaky officers who taught bible school, were scout masters, were deacons in their churches.

The CIA was left with a bunch of officers talking to themselves, and doing just the same as State Department officers, meeting with foreign nationals at cocktail parties and trading gossip. Their best sources were the rare walk-ins. These were high risk sources because they were all too often foreign agents working to flush out who the CIA agents   [[xxxxx this portion has been censored by the Department of State and/or the CIA xxxxx]]   ..... [[xxxxx this portion has been censored by the Department of State and/or the CIAxxxxx]]   were. In a few cases, they were legitimate, but that was rare. A lot of walk-ins were nut cases and took time, resources, and were sometimes dangerous too.

In gathering intelligence in Arab/Moslem countries most spooks don't even speak the language. They rely on police officers (intelligence officers) of host countries, who have motivations not entirely in the U.S.'s best interests, so their information has been mostly unreliable or not useful, especially in the war on terrorism. Our bombing of a pill factory in the Sudan   [[xxxxx this portion has been censored by the Department of State and/or the CIA xxxxx xxxxx this portion has been censored by the Department of State and/or the CIA xxxxx]..... [[xxxxx this portion has been censored by the Department of State and/or the CIAxxxxx]]   .

In the 1980's and on into the 1990's, the clean, polished, mostly Christian managers went on a pogrom, a genuine witch hunt to weed out and eliminate CIA officers who had a rough edge or two. Impure officers who cussed and may have had other impure proclivities became untouchables because they perhaps smoked tobacco, knew a story or two that didn't fit in genteel, mixed company. They drank good whiskey, and didn't go to church. Some, god forbid may even have possessed special or rare talents, skills, or abilities such as clairvoyance, unique spiritualness, or whatever that the religious purists didn't understand or couldn't control or use for their own selfish reasons.

To get going in the right way, we need to change and to develop those unique and very special abilities to get HUMINT. We need people with an inane ability to identify, ferret out, recruit, and sustain clandestine HUMINT sources. They have or must be able to develop and work with instincts - gut feelings, talent, linguistic abilities, raw inane intellect, area knowledge, fortitude, an understanding of human nature, a willingness to disagree or take appropriate action when they 'just know'. They will be dedicated, and must have managers and leaders who will support, mentor, and guide them to take wise, well thought out risks, to win.

Then we need to keep them away from the risk-averse failure prone types, who are all too often ethically challenged in their own right.

To succeed, special HUMINT managers need secure careers with performance evaluations by peers, not self-aggrandizing mismanagers.

A few CIA adventures
and misadventures

The CIA worked successfully in 1953 to install the Shah of Iran after a CIA arranged a coup d'état. Iran became pro-American and this was good, especially at the time when the USSR was seeking to flank NATO and gain access to a warm weather port by using Iran for those purposes.

The CIA was involved in the overthrow of a Communist leaning government in Guatemala in 1953. This was good, because the USSR would have used Guatemala to spread Communism throughout Latin America.

Successes weren't always in the cards.

The CIA failed to predict the Berlin Blockade in 1948.

The CIA failed to forecast the 1950 North Korean surprise attack and invasion of South Korea. The CIA also failed to predict and downplayed the Chinese Communist entry into the Korean War. This failure resulted in a disaster with large numbers of South Korean, American, and allied losses.

The CIA did not predict the split between China and the USSR

The CIA was unable to forecast the speed of decay of the British Empire.

The CIA in its economic forecasting never predicted the rise of Japan's economy.

The Bay of Pigs fiasco in Cuba speaks for itself.

The CIA predicted wrongly about the Soviet Missile buildup in terms of their power, their numbers, and accuracy.

The CIA totally miscalculated the amount of GDP the Soviets were investing in their military.

The CIA's ignorance compounded by the rank ignorance of others in positions of authority and leadership led the United States into Viet Nam in support of a Christian minority (3% of the population) against a nationalist majority that was 97% Buddhist. They ignored Ho Chi Minh's earlier pro-American history, and actually drove him to seek increasing support from the Communist Soviet Union, to become

Communist.

Then, the increasingly politically correct but inept CIA was allowed to run the war in Viet Nam.

In 1988, when India detonated its first test nuclear weapon, the American Administration, the President of the United States learned of it via an Indian government press release. What a stunner! Working at night and under clouds, the Indians were able to hide their excavations and a few wires and cables (buried underground,) so that expensive intelligence photo satellites couldn't see them. The CIA was unable to predict the test blast, and was left totally befuddled.

Throughout the 1980's, the CIA continued to promote the idea of the USSR's strong threat to the USA. Reportedly, the CIA was collectively flabbergasted by the rapid sequence of events that culminated in the final collapse of the USSR. With all of their millions of dollars worth of satellites and photographs, and signal intelligence, the CIA was completely blind to actual events.

There was some success in Panama against Noriega, but this was brought about not only by the CIA, but with help and support from the Drug Enforcement Agency and others. It was too little, too late for some things, notably to prevent President Carter's foolishly relinquishing authority and control over the Panama Canal, which is now an asset belonging to and controlled by the Chinese government, not the Panamanians.

After the collapse of the USSR, the CIA lost whatever interest it had in placing case officers in the new Russia. Even when there were legions of disgruntled officers and men in the Russian military which, by the way, still has lots of nuclear weapons capable of obliterating the United States, the CIA had no interest. Now, the new Russia under Putin and Medvediev is more aggressive in its intelligence activities directed at the United States than the Soviets were during the Cold War, and the CIA is grabbing its proverbial a.....backside with both hands. The incompetent CIA doesn't have necessary HUMINT assets to help American leaders to understand what's going on and what to do about it.

When war broke out between Chechnya and the Russians, the Americans, led by the left ranted against the Russians for their tough tactics. The Russians are not known to play life and death games gently and responded without restraint against those who showed no restraint in their attacks on Russians.

In 1999, Clinton launched a 'police action' to "protect" Bosnian and Albanian Moslems from the Serbians in the former Yugoslavia. These Bosnians and Albanians were in fact actively engaged in growing numbers of egregious terrorist activities in support of Moslem ethnic cleansing taking place against the indigenous (Serb) population who had lived in that location for centuries before the invasions of the Moslem Turks. Those indigenous people are the Orthodox Christians. By 'protecting' Bosnia, we ignorant Americans (Clinton followed by

Bush) in fact unwittingly – or is it witlessly - created a Mohammedist stronghold in Europe; and horrible suffering and decimation of Christians who ought to be our allies, but who now do not trust us and have no confidence in us.

Owing to a combination of faulty CIA intelligence, feckless ignorance and gross stupidity in the Clinton Administration (Madeline Albright, Sandy Berger, and not least of all, the 'perfumed prince', General Wesley Clark at NATO) this action in the Balkans represents another major American failure. Led by impeached President Clinton, these hapless Keystonian Kops clowns jumped into internal Yugoslavian issues and concluded wrongly that the Orthodox Christian Serbs had initiated a campaign of ethnic cleansing. The Serbians failed to educate the Clintonites (if they were in fact educable) to the real facts that the Yugoslavian Moslems were raising money, training terrorists, and had already started a Taliban styled ethnic cleansing campaign against the Serbians. In the run up to the Serbian reaction, the Moslems had for years been raiding the Christians, murdering, raping, and killing hundreds and hundreds of innocent Serbian civilians. In defense of their lives in their corner of civilization, the Serbians initially took measures to try to separate themselves. The Moslems resisted, and this drove the Serbians to take control of their own destiny, and the Serbian response then (and only then) began. Some of the methods used were barbaric, right out of the lessons provided by the Moslems themselves in earlier periods in the region's bloody history. The Serbians were merely trying to protect themselves, and our stupid leaders sided with the Moslems. Go figure.

In one action, we sent a cruise missile, targeted by the CIA, into Belgrade to "punish" the Serbians. OOPS!!! The missile was directed at a target that three years earlier had been a Serbian government building, but was now occupied by the Chinese Embassy. So, the clearly clueless CIA didn't even know, or have it sorted out in their system, about the location of the Chinese Embassy in Belgrade. The Chinese are important and we don't even know the locations of their embassies, not even in sensitive areas. The Chinese response to this attack on their sovereign territory was muted. They didn't want to raise too much of a ruckus because it might have caused the CIA to clean up their inept act. Having a totally inept CIA is clearly in China's best interests.

We are stuck with a stupefyingly ignorant and uninformed policy initiated by the Clinton/Albright Keystonian Kops that concluded that the Serbs were 'bad'. The Clintonian Kops launched military actions that killed thousands of genuine innocents, helped the wrong side – the bad guys, the side of evil, and this perfidy earned us the enmity and distrust of millions of those whom we need on our side. We ought to pull back, repudiate our stance in the Balkans, and re-align ourselves with the Serbians as far as their dealings with Moslems are concerned. By helping the Mohammedans, we got nothing from them at all other than more knives in our backs.

The CIA had no idea who was really involved in the 1993 bombing of the World Trade Center, and denied that Iraq was involved even when perpetrators had transited Iraq, and used Iraqi travel documents.

During the 1991 war against Iraq, NAVY aviator, LCDR "Mike" Speicher was shot down. He was listed as missing in action until November of 2001, when his listing was changed to "possible" Prisoner of War. "Possible?" What the hell does that mean?

It means that the CIA, during a ten year period of time was not able to confirm whether the guy was alive or dead. The possibility that LCDR Speicher was alive was attributed to information being volunteered by defectors and so forth. Where the hell was the CIA? What were they doing to ascertain accurately the whereabouts if alive, or to confirm the death of this brave aviator? I know. They were out back singing kumbayah.

A William Safire editorial in April of 2002 told how the CIA, and its director, George Tenet were duped by Palestinian aid to Yassir Arafat, Jabril Rajoub, the head of the Palestinian Office of Preventive Security. This guy had Tenet convinced that he was a good guy - a moderate who was actually helping the CIA, etc., etc. When the Israeli Defense Forces went into Palestinian (Arafat's) offices, they recovered documents indicating that this guy (Rajoub) was actually supplying weapons and explosives, and disguising assassins and suicide bomber-murderers of Israelis. Tenet and the CIA swallowed this guy's bullcrap, hook line and sinker for years. The pitiful CIA did not have any sources to independently verify or dispute what Rajoub was feeding them – bullcrap and stinky bait.

Likable George Tenet had been bamboozled and was in over his head - deeply so.

Many will agree that the CIA in particular and the rest of the intelligence community failed us dismally. Others claimed that the CIA's too-few operational Case Officers were suddenly being allowed to do their work. That's arguable.

Without knowing what people are talking about, what's on their minds, what their dreams, plans, goals and objectives are both individually and collectively we will never, ever, be able to deal successfully with those who are arrayed against us. The proof of this is the 9/11/2001 attacks by humans who spent a lot of time talking, planning, preparing, and practicing to murder 3,000 innocent civilians. These twenty perpetrators had to have been recruited from among hundreds of candidates, were provided extensive training, preparation, logistical support, money, guidance, and mentoring for two or more years.

In recent years up to 90% of the CIA's intelligence came from open sources such as TV and radio, and the printed news media; and ten percent from multi-billion dollar SIGINT and KEYHOLE spy satellite programs. What percentage came from HUMINT?

While the abandonment of clandestine HUMINT intelligence activities really got rolling under President Carter and Stansfield Turner, some media reporters and/or investigators have blamed this on the liberals claiming they alone gutted U.S. intelligence capabilities. Not so. This decimation of the intelligence function continued through the Reagan and first Bush administrations as well. Reagan and Bush (especially Bush who had been the DCIA) could have and should have stopped this but they failed.

Elitists supported by Turner - and subsequent Directors of Central Intelligence gladly moved away from facing up to their responsibilities and doing their jobs, involving leadership, the exercise of sound, practical, and honest judgment. Among these inept CIA management elitists are a powerful cabal of puritan, religious fundamentalists, and they, under the reigns of "born again" Christian and anti-Semite President (KKK) Carter and continuing under the "Crusader" President Reagan gained the upper hand in running the CIA. These pious puritans are a major cause of the CIA's deficiency. Over the years they have systematically and thoroughly conducted pogroms, aimed at getting rid of people capable of doing the real tough jobs dealing with clandestine HUMINT. People who didn't fit the effete, puritanical mold stopped getting promotions or worthy job assignments, and many quit or became old enough to retire, and did so, or were simply railroaded out of the CIA.

The CIA's religious puritans simply hate and cannot accept or tolerate impure, colorful operatives who go to rock concerts rather than Bible study classes, and the few who may consider it a sport to have more than one bed partner. The puritans want bible thumpers, and that's who they have been hiring and promoting over the past three decades. Those NOT inclined to teach Sunday school are not welcome.

I knew of a senior CIA officer, fluent in two difficult languages who was singled out for elimination. He was well liked by most of his subordinates as a thoughtful and considerate mentor who was skillful, capable, and successful in the HUMINT field. He smoked, told an occasional joke, appreciated good whiskey, and enjoyed intellectually stimulating conversation and company. He was very, very smart and competent. He was a genuinely good guy, a good, faithful, loving husband and father, and a genuine patriot.

He insisted that his subordinates do their jobs, and didn't expect them to try to religiously convert everyone they talked to. Their jobs were to develop spies and gather intelligence.

However, he had his faults: He didn't go to church. His wife was foreign born. He was tainted. He was impure! It mattered not that he was doing his job well, and was very professional and competent.

The CIA's puritans didn't want him in their way. They went to an officer in a position to take certain actions and/or make administrative management recommendations. The puritans pushed him to do their dirty work, and to cause the good man's career and reputation to be destroyed. They pushed this other officer to condemn him so that he would be declared unfit for duty, relieved and transferred away -- condemned to oblivion.

The officer didn't feel good about this, being tasked to do someone else's dirty work. He was being asked to abuse his authority; that he was being called on to compromise his own ethics and principles. The puritans urged him to falsely condemn a good person for no other reason than that he didn't fit the puritans' mold. The chosen officer refused to kowtow to the CIA's puritans desire to screw over a good officer in their purge. That refusal really annoyed the puritans. The puritans hold grudges, and a short time later in, that very decent, ethical officer ultimately found himself in a position that compelled him to leave the CIA himself.

I was at a small Embassy where we had a really silly   [[xxxxx this portion has been censored by the Department of State and/or the CIA xxxxx xxxxx this portion has been censored by the Department of State and/or the CIA xxxxx xxxxx this portion has been censored by the Department of State and/or the CIA xxxxx xxxxx this portion has been censored by the Department of State and/or the CIA xxxxx xxxxx this portion has been censored by the Department of State and/or the CIA xxxxx]]   officer who was a character straight out of the SPY vs. SPY pages of MAD magazine. His duty (among other things) was to work on Russians, to meet them, talk to them, to recruit them. He didn't smoke, cuss, or drink whiskey. At cocktail parties, he would get a martini glass, have the waiter put water and an olive in it, and then he'd stand along a wall, faux martini in hand, rigidly in place, with a silly, sly grin on his face. He would face straight ahead, but his eyes would sweep from side-to-side. He was so obvious that the Russians made jokes about him. He was a devout Christian and took his kids and wife to Church every Sunday. He was thrifty too. His kids were stick thin, usually ravenously hungry, and I often fed them because there wasn't food for them at their home. He never got into any kind of trouble (embarrassing to the USG), never recruited a Soviet, never gathered real intelligence or caused the Embassy the slightest bit of concern or consternation. He never recruited anybody to work as a spy, and as far as I know, he never won a convert to Christianity either. But, he got promoted.]

In Burma, I ran the embassy's housing and logistics operation among other things. I got things done. I understood and worked the system, and got money approved to fix and correct long neglected government owned properties, and to even make minor improvements. I even got extra money to do nice and good things beneficial to the USG, and which enhanced the morale of people who lived and worked there, in that very remote place. In Burma, there was/is little for the Embassy and its staff in the way of life outside of work. There are no malls, movie theaters, TV, football, hooters, parks, few suitable restaurants, concerts, museums, and so forth. We had a couple of compounds where staff with families lived in houses, and an apartment building for single staffers.

At one of the compounds, we had a small, simple recreational facility that consisted of a small pool, a club with a little eatery, and a small bar. Outdoors, there were a couple of tennis courts and a half-basketball court. The recreational facility had to pay for itself and was self governing with an elected board of directors, each of whom served for two years. Half of the board was elected each year, (actually two on even numbered years, three on odd numbered years, or something like that) It was basically the only recreational show in town as far as foreigners were concerned. We permitted (and this was permitted by the Burmese authorities) two members from the embassy of each country represented in Burma. There were perhaps twenty friendly Embassies, which brought in forty additional dues paying associate members, essential to the economic viability of the club.

During the May through October Monsoon season, it rains, or more accurately drizzles for days and days on end. The concrete tennis courts, walkways, and the basketball court grew a slimy moss that was treacherously slippery.

With the Foreign Service being as it is, about a third of the American staff at the Embassy in Rangoon turned over every year on reassignment. Most of the transfers take place during school vacation times, so their kids can start a new school (wherever) at the beginning of the school year. People without kids have more flexibility and can be transferred at different times.

A new   [[xxxxx this portion has been censored by the Department of State and/or the CIA xxxxx]]   (I'll call him BCK) came to Rangoon after I had been there about a year. He decided that he wanted to serve on the recreation association's board of directors, and lobbied hard with everyone around (and reportedly ordered all of his subordinates) to vote for him. He got elected to the board after he had been there for only about six weeks. He didn't know everyone in the Embassy very well, but he sure had his opinions and a set of objectives.

The Sunday afternoon after the election, BCK came into the clubhouse. I was inside, quietly having a hamburger and a beverage. BCK came in, and invited himself to join me (I was also an elected board member) at the table, located next to a window overlooking the small pool. He immediately began lobbying me about his plans for the club. He had a personal agenda to fulfill. He wanted to make some changes immediately, and as he was saying this, a young Asian girl walked past the window. As she walked by, BCK indicated towards her and that she represented one of the changes he wanted to implement: "First of all, we've got too many of 'them' around here, and we should not allow any more of 'them' to join the club." Thirty seconds later when that pre-teen oriental girl walked up to me, her brother-in-law, and asked for a coke, he, BCK, was taken aback. Shocked, he departed the scene, his personal agenda and mission unfulfilled. I made sure that he never got that one done. Naturally, I became one of those he considered a traitor, because I had married outside of my white race.

So, the   [[xxxxx this portion has been censored by the Department of State and/or the CIA xxxxx]]   had sent an anti-Asian over-the-top redneck Christian zealot and racist to head its station in Burma, a place where there were many Chinese with ties to Communist China, and a basic reason for that   [[xxxxx this portion has been censored by the Department of State and/or the CIA xxxxx]]   being there. The Burmese and other indigenous people are Orientals, too.

There was little for our children to do during the interminable monsoon rains, especially the five-to-ten year olds who didn't play tennis, chess, or want to be in the pool all day long. When weather permitted, they'd gather on the basketball court and do what kids do. They couldn't do this very often during the monsoon rains.

I had worked long and hard and after some time justified a project to improve Embassy staff morale, to put a cover over the basketball court, high enough for basketball, and with a broad enough overhang to keep the rain off of the court. It took a year of arguments and justifications with headquarters to get the funds loosened up for this.

At the new board's first meeting, I announced that the funds had finally come through to build the cover over the basketball court. BCK (he didn't have young children) immediately chimed in that he wanted to use the money elsewhere. I said no, that the money was designated for one purpose and that was it. He challenged me with who was I to determine where the money was to be used. I got right in his face quickly and affirmed that by virtue of my job I was in fact the club's landlord, and that I had determined where that money was to be used, and had gotten it approved by our Ambassador and from Washington for just that purpose, and that was exactly how those funds would be used.

Needless to say, BCK next told his   [[xxxxx this portion has been censored by the Department of State and/or the CIA xxxxx]] staff that I was persona non grata and that they were to avoid me...... They were not allowed to socialize with me or any of my family members.

I had a good relationship with the Ambassador and very soon, we had a nice, private discussion about BCK, my wife's sister, the club, and a few other things that had come my way. One of those things was about one of BCK's   [[xxxxx this portion has been censored by the Department of State and/or the CIA xxxxx]]   officers who was married to a lady, a fourth generation American citizen of Chinese extraction; and another   [[xxxxx this portion has been censored by the Department of State and/or the CIA xxxxx]]   officer who was half Asian himself who was married to a woman of European extraction. BCK considered both of those men to be traitors, had said so, and I had heard of this.

Ordinarily, the   [[xxxxx this portion has been censored by the Department of State and/or the CIA xxxxx]]   in Rangoon stays on the job there for a full four years. It's a nice, cushy job. BCK didn't last two years.....

Shortly after BCK was transferred away (against his wishes), things   [[xxxxx this portion has been censored by the Department of State and/or the CIA xxxxx]]   were different, and I could tell because the morale of the station's staff improved greatly. I was the proverbial landlord of all housing for the Embassy, and the whining and complaints emanating from that section dropped off significantly. People, the officers, their spouses, and their kids were happy and were no longer looking for things to complain about.

Nevertheless, there were the annual transfers out of Rangoon, and a new crop of people arrived.

Many years later, an ambassador with an agenda to discredit the Bush administration, Joe Wilson, went to extremes regarding the so-called 'outing' of his attractive non-African linguist, white, blond, CIA wife, Valery Plame, who was stationed in Niger. Prior to her being assigned to Niger, she was an overt CIA officer at CIA headquarters in Washington for five years. It was well known, and publicly documented that she was a CIA employee.

Joe lied, claiming that the Vice President sent him to Niger to do research on Iraqi attempts to purchase materials for his nuclear weapons program. In fact, Wilson's wife had arranged for his trip (a $10,000 boondoggle at taxpayer expense) so that they could conduct their research under the bed sheets, nothing more.

Had liar Joe's wife, the   [[xxxxx this portion has been censored by the Department of State and/or the CIAxxxxx]]   done her job well and diligently (how a blond, white, non-linguist female spy can move around unnoticed in black Africa is an unanswered mystery), or if she had her underlings gather information to be reported back to analysts in Washington, Joe would not have had a need to go and "gather" information, or to conduct "research". The information should have been available to analysts in Washington for immediate delivery to the Vice President or any other official, with just a few minutes notice.

[[xxxxx this portion has been censored by the Department of State and/or the CIA xxxxx]]

[[xxxxx this portion has been censored by the Department of State and/or the CIA xxxxx xxxxx this portion has been censored by the Department of State and/or the CIA xxxxx xxxxx this portion has been censored by the Department of State and/or the CIA xxxxx xxxxx this portion has been censored by the Department of State and/or the CIA xxxxx xxxxx this portion has been censored by the Department of State and/or the CIA xxxxx xxxxx this portion has been censored by the Department of State and/or the CIA xxxxx xxxxx this portion has been censored by the Department of State and/or the CIA xxxxx xxxxx this portion has been censored by the Department of State and/or the CIA xxxxx xxxxx this portion has been censored by the Department of State and/or the CIA xxxxx xxxxx this portion has been censored by the Department of State and/or the CIA xxxxx xxxxx this portion has been censored by the Department of State and/or the CIA xxxxx xxxxx this portion has been censored by the Department of State and/or the CIA xxxxx xxxxx this portion has been censored by the Department of State and/or the CIA xxxxx xxxxx this portion has been censored by the Department of State and/or the CIA xxxxx xxxxx this portion has been censored by the Department of State and/or the CIA xxxxx xxxxx this portion has been censored by the Department of State and/or the CIA xxxxx xxxxx this portion has been censored by the Department of State and/or the CIA xxxxx xxxxx this portion has been censored by the Department of State and/or the CIA xxxxx xxxxx this portion has been censored by the Department of State and/or the CIA xxxxx xxxxx this portion has been censored by the Department of State and/or the CIA xxxxx xxxxx this portion has been censored by the Department of State and/or the CIA xxxxx xxxxx this portion has been censored by the Department of State and/or the CIA xxxxx xxxxx this portion has been censored by the Department of State and/or the CIA xxxxx xxxxx this portion has been censored by the Department of State and/or the CIA xxxxx xxxxx this portion has been censored by the Department of State and/or the CIA xxxxx xxxxx this portion has been censored by the Department of State and/or the CIA xxxxx xxxxx this portion has been censored by the Department of State and/or the CIA xxxxx.

Jobs for American employee dependent spouses are often difficult to get, especially in countries where the unemployment is high. The embassies try to help by providing some form of gainful employment in various temporary or part-time positions, but there are never enough jobs to go around.   [[xxxxx this portion has been censored by the Department of State and/or the CIA xxxxx xxxxx this portion has been censored by the Department of State and/or the CIA xxxxx xxxxx this portion has been censored by the Department of State and/or the CIA xxxxx xxxxx this portion has been censored by the Department of State and/or the CIA xxxxx xxxxx this portion has been censored by the Department of State and/or the CIA xxxxx xxxxx this portion has been censored by the Department of State and/or the CIA xxxxx xxxxx this portion has been censored by the Department of State and/or the CIA xxxxx]]   .

At one embassy where I served as the Personnel Officer, we had over twenty dependent spouses registered and awaiting an opportunity to work in an Embassy position. All jobs were opened for competition in a very formal, structured, and transparent way. Three of these unemployed spouses were qualified nurses. The lady working in that position departed with her principal employee spouse and the position opened up. I advertised for the position, and the three women applied, the   [[xxxxx this portion has been censored by the

Department of State and/or the CIA xxxxx]]   chief's wife among them. She had good credential and years of experience, and she felt the job was rightfully hers. So did her husband.

[[xxxxx this portion has been censored by the Department of State and/or the CIA xxxxx xxxxx this portion has been censored by the Department of State and/or the CIA xxxxx xxxxx this portion has been censored by the Department of State and/or the CIA xxxxx]]

When I selected another spouse for the job, the proverbial stuff hit the fan. The   [[xxxxx this portion has been censored by the Department of State and/or the CIA xxxxx]]   came roaring into my office demanding that I retract the hiring and just "give" the job to his wife. I refused and he went to the Ambassador (a complete wuss of a man) who called me onto the carpet to "explain" myself. I responded that I would not abide by the I   [[xxxxx this portion has been censored by the Department of State and/or the CIA xxxxx]]   ..... [[xxxxx this portion has been censored by the Department of State and/or the CIAxxxxx]]   demand   [[xxxxx this portion has been censored by the Department of State and/or the CIA xxxxx xxxxx this portion has been censored by the Department of State and/or the CIA xxxxx xxxxx this portion has been censored by the Department of State and/or the CIA xxxxx]]   . The [[xxxxx this portion has been censored by the Department of State and/or the CIA xxxxx]]   refused [xxxxx this portion has been censored by the Department of State and/or the CIA xxxxx]] and I refused to consider   [[xxxxx this portion has been censored by the Department of State and/or the CIA xxxxx]]   .

Serious

I took my job seriously, and had a few criteria that I stuck to. In an isolated, remote place like Myanmar (Burma), morale can be a problem, and I did all that I reasonably could to make sure employees' families were happy. Happy wives with happy children sent happy husbands to work where they could be more productive. Happy staff remained longer, so the (taxpayer funded) high expenses of frequent international moves was reduced.

Coffins were a necessary part of my all encompassing jobs. I had learned of an incident, actually two of them, years earlier that held my attention. One was where an American had died in a far away place. He had been a tall (what else) basketball player. That Embassy had only one coffin (a special type of body transfer case that can be sealed to prevent fluids and gasses from escaping) and it was a standard six feet long. The dead man was nearly seven feet long. To get him in, his legs had to be cut off, and when his family got him, they were upset to say the least. The other was where a 300+ pound man died, and that embassy had only one standard sized coffin, and the dead man had to be gutted in order to stuff him into the coffin and sent home.

Wherever I went, I made it a point to have a good supply of coffins, including long, wide, and infant sizes.

Back to my story. A new officer that I'll refer to as TM arrived late in the summer, assigned to the Rangoon   [[xxxxx this portion has been censored by the Department of State and/or the CIA xxxxx]]   . It was his first overseas assignment.

TM was at my office, in a compound in an industrial part of town, a few miles from the Embassy, checking in and getting oriented. We were, at one point, walking from my office to a shop area when a Russian military vehicle came wheeling noisily into the compound and came to a swirling, dusty stop in the dirt driveway. Two Soviets got out and I went forward to greet them. They asked for me by name and when I identified myself, they told me that they were there seeking a favor. I introduced TM and we all went into my office. The Russians (good intelligence on their part) didn't ask if we had what they wanted, they simply stated that they needed two of our coffins, on loan, or to purchase, whatever.

While I had my staff pull two coffins from the warehouse and load them into the Russian's vehicle, we and had coffee and chatted for a short while. When the coffins were loaded, the two Russians left, but not before inviting TM and I over for a few "drinks".

During this exchange, TM barely uttered a word. He was all gawky at encountering his first real Soviets.

As soon as the two Soviets left, he rushed back to the Embassy, obviously to report this encounter   [[xxxxx this portion has been censored by the Department of State and/or the CIA xxxxx]]   .

Being a TOP SECRET cleared official, I knew that I had a responsibility to file a detailed contact report (a royal pain in the butt, but wise and necessary) each time I had a significant contact with any Eastern Block official. Later that day, I went on to the Embassy for my normal activities, and to file my report with the Security Officer.

When I entered the Embassy, the Marine Guard said that Mr. ....[[xxxxx this portion has been censored by the Department of State and/or the CIA xxxxx]]   wanted to see me before I returned to my office.

[He and I already had a good relationship (much better than I had with BCK). We both liked and respected one-another. This had been cemented just a couple of weeks earlier when the lock to his safe failed and brought in expert   [[xxxxx this portion has been censored by the Department of State and/or the CIA xxxxx]]   locksmiths (safe crackers) couldn't get it opened. At the time of their visit, they had given up trying to cajole it open, and called me at my compound office and asked that I please bring a couple of sledge hammers and crow bars to them at the Embassy. When I had brought them into his office, I had asked   [[xxxxx this portion has been censored by the

Department of State and/or the CIA xxxxx]]   what was wrong, and he pointed at his safe and explained the problem. I looked at it, and I asked for the combination, which he gave to me – there was no compromise here as the   [[xxxxx this portion has been censored by the Department of State and/or the CIA xxxxx]]   "locksmiths" were preparing to rip it apart anyhow. I sat down, fiddled with it for a while, and opened it. He was astonished. So were the professional   [[xxxxx this portion has been censored by the Department of State and/or the CIA xxxxx]] safe crackers. I then held a class and the   [[xxxxx this portion has been censored by the Department of State and/or the CIA xxxxx]]   experts went home with a brand new trick in their bag.

[Over the years, I became known as a "friend" of the CIA. I never said anything to dissuade them of this. A one-time radio operator (Morse code at 24 words per minute on a standard key, 44 words on a speed key) and a licensed amateur (HAM), I had been asked to install, update, repair, and operate clandestine radio set ups for the CIA in various parts of the world. Somewhat technically inclined, I was (I believe) the only non-CIA person ever allowed to repair super sensitive CIA cryptographic cipher machines.)]

TM had told his   [[xxxxx this portion has been censored by the Department of State and/or the CIA xxxxx]]   of our encounter with the two Soviets.

When I entered his office   [[xxxxx this portion has been censored by the Department of State and/or the CIA xxxxx]]   told me that the night before, two Soviets had been decapitated when a car they were in ran into a parked truck. The truck had been parked, lights off in the middle of the road, which is typical in remote backward parts of the world. Besides, such roads typically have no "shoulders" to pull over onto. One of the Soviets killed was a senior KGB officer, and the other had connections with the Soviet military intelligence, the GRU. That was why the two soviets had come to us. They knew (good intelligence) that we had appropriate airline approved body transfer case-coffins, so they could send the bodies back to Russia when the next AEROFLOT flight came to tropical Rangoon, in about five days. (In many countries, embalming is not practiced, and such facilities are not available.) These two Soviet officers that had come to my office represented the dead, one was KGB and the other was GRU.

The   [[xxxxx this portion has been censored by the Department of State and/or the CIA xxxxx]]   , TM, and I discussed the motive behind the two Soviets' invitation, and TM's and my participation.

The   [[xxxxx this portion has been censored by the Department of State and/or the CIA xxxxx]]   and I knew (from experience), and we taught TM that the get together for drinks would be a serious drinking bout. Drinking binges were a Soviet modus operandi, to get people drunk enough to lose their inhibitions in a setting they controlled and which was most probably wired with microphones and/or more. At the end of the meeting with the   [[xxxxx this portion has been censored by the Department of State and/or the CIA xxxxx]]   , it was agreed that I would take TM under my wing and "show him the ropes."

I told TM how to prepare himself for the drinking marathon, mind and body, how to prepare himself to deal with large quantities of booze.

I did prepare myself, and when I went to pick TM up, I asked, and was very disappointed to learn that he hadn't followed my guidance. I'd soon know why. I didn't know earlier that members of his Latter Day Saints religion aren't supposed to drink alcoholic beverages, and that he adhered to this rule. Other Christians I had known did drink coffee and beer. They were, like me, obviously impure.

At the appointed time, we pulled up to the gate of the house (it was the KGB Station Chief's house) and our two new friends cheerfully greeted us and escorted us on into the house and directly upstairs to a room especially prepared for the event. There was a buffet loaded with foods and bottles of wine, liquors, and hard booze - mostly vodka and scotch whiskey. On one side, two comfortable chairs, side-by-side facing a coffee table and two more identically situated chairs on the other side.

The obvious senior ranking of the two Soviets, a Major in the GRU took the seat alongside of me, and the other, a Captain in the KGB sat next to TM.

We immediately started with a vodka (straight shots) toast to Soviet-American friendship. A minute or two later, another toast, to our personal friendships, and next a toast to our health, then a toast to the weather, then to Burma, and so forth. We chatted between toasts, and after about the fifth or sixth shot, TM turned his glass down and refused any more drinks. That left me vs. the two Soviet intelligence officers, engaged in a serious drinking bout.

Later, three bottles of vodka, three bottles of wine, two bottles of scotch, and half way through a magnum of cognac the first contestant succumbed. The KGB Captain folded his arms across his chest, his head dropped to his chest, and he started snoring. The GRU Major nudged me and commented "Fu..ing KGB - inferior, they can't handle it." He leaned across the coffee table, unbuckled the KGB Captain's pants and poured the contents of an ice bucket into the guy's pants. He grunted once and barely twitched as his genitals were bathed in iced water.

We then toasted to the inferiority of the KGB, the superior capacities of the GRU, TM's sobriety, my health, and the GRU Major's health, etc. The GRU Major excused himself to go to the bathroom, stood up and walked smack into a wall on the other side of the room from the bathroom. I caught him as he reeled away, and steered him into the bathroom, and closed the door from whence some disturbing sounds emanated. The night was over, and as TM and I were preparing to leave, the Major emerged, pale, shaky, barely coherent.

He was genuinely happy that TM and I were preparing to leave, and he led us out. As we were descending the stairs, I pointed at a framed piece of art, a litho that was interesting. The Major asked if I liked it. I affirmed, and a second later it was off of the wall and in my hands. TM and I made our departure.

During the evening's festivities, TM had brought up religion and was more interested in bringing Christ into the lives of the KGB Captain, the GRU Major, and I than in anything else. He was more interested in proselytizing than in talking to and developing a relationship with a couple of prime prospects - Soviet intelligence officers. He was representative of the new wave   [[xxxxx this portion has been censored by the Department of State and/or the CIA xxxxx]]   . [[xxxxx this portion has been censored by the Department of State and/or the CIA xxxxx]]   had invested thousands of taxpayer dollars in training him [[xxxxx this portion has been censored by the Department of State and/or the CIA xxxxx]]   and doing duties as an   [[xxxxx this portion has been censored by the Department of State and/or the CIA xxxxx]] . He abandoned that training and his duties on his first encounter with potential human   [[xxxxx this portion has been censored by the Department of State and/or the CIA xxxxx]]   sources.

Again and again, now living in a bedroom community, I hear of and learn from items in newspapers, on TV, and in magazines about the CIA's ineptitude. Were I inside the Washington beltway, I'd likely be privy to more information, much of that classified.

It's disgusting.

The CIA has a multi-billion dollar budget. The CIA, to maintain its facade of secrecy has its funding built in as a part of over a dozen agencies' budgets. It's complicated but it is supposed to work that way. Other moneys are not necessarily directly allocated to the CIA, but the CIA controls the uses of large amounts of Pentagon money for instance. So, while the CIA supposedly doesn't get billions for missiles and satellites, the CIA directs and controls how certain funds are spent on missiles and satellites, etc.

With this 44-billion dollar budget (reported in News Week magazine in November of 2005), some mistakes are possible, but the CIA screws up all too often, and a substantial part of that 44+ billion is squandered by an organization accountable only to itself, and one that is bloated with inept self-serving incompetent bureaucrats.

Subsequent to the Aldrich Ames case, the CIA leadership crumbled (or perhaps they wanted it that way) and the FBI was sent in to look for turncoats. Seemingly everyone who ever talked to a foreigner, drank whiskey, used a cuss word, didn't teach Sunday school, or looked at another person as a sex object was put under the lights with threats and intimidation that affected their careers and lives. They scrambled for cover to protect their own personal best interests, their careers and eventual pensions. They quit doing their jobs.

The FBI has exclusive rights to investigate espionage. But, who watches the FBI?

Even while the FBI's Robert Hanssen was busily and joyfully selling our nation down the drain, the FBI, or employees derived from the FBI took control of CIA operations. How many of them are ideological 'volunteers' with special sick agendas, or who are otherwise on the payroll of the Russians, the Chinese, or Moslems whose goal is the destruction of the United States. We need somebody besides, or better, in competition with, the FBI to look after our national interests.

This FBI creep, Hanssen, reportedly sold an enhanced (enhanced with back-door covert operations capabilities) version of a secret Justice Department computer program (PROMIS) to Russian gangsters who reportedly sold a copy to al Qaeda's Osama bin Laden. By exploiting this program, bin Laden and his merry band can reportedly track what the Justice Department, FBI, CIA, and others are doing to track him. And people wonder about bin Laden's elusiveness? He's dialed right in.

Arbitrariness and tyranny took over the CIA and rendered the Directorate of Operations ineffective.

CIA Facts

The 2004 CIA World Fact book listing countries in Africa with Moslem populations of over 500,000 footnoted Eritrea (which was established in 1992) citing insufficient data on its Moslem population, estimated at 2.2 million.

Insufficient data, eh? For a change, the CIA was being honest.

Chapter 9

WAVES

Ships that make no waves
make no headway.

In the Federal Government, one must regularly get promoted as one pursues his or her career. Whether it's in the Bureau of Indian Affairs, Bureau of Land Management, IRS, State Department, National Park Service, the FBI, Department of Defense, or the CIA, all face an annual review or performance evaluation. Federal Government employees' careers hinge on the written word - the annual performance review. Even nominal periodic step increases hinge on one's level of minimally acceptable performance. To actually get promoted, one is required to at least 'walk on water', if not flow above water, all of the time, and they never pass gas. In some jobs, employees are subject to a Time In Class (TIC) requirement where they must get promoted within certain time frames or they are booted out. It's that way for military officers, in the State Department where I worked, and it is also true to the CIA.

Employees thus affected seem to evolve into bureaucrats concerned only with getting certain duties done that their supervisors will reflect on, getting, or earning promotions and pay increases, and ultimately surviving until they can retire. This is a reality. Actually doing their jobs is distantly secondary to just sustaining their careers.

Our supervisors wrote our performance reports by which we (our careers) lived or died. Performance reports are based on criteria established by basic job functions; and goals and objectives established by supervisors are added on. When an employee such as a CIA or FBI officer does his job---rather the job his supervisor wants done whether it is important or not, he or she will a get a satisfactory report. If he or she sucks up to and kisses his or her boss' backsides well and avoids getting a broken nose whenever the boss turns a sharp corner, one may even get a 'walk on water' performance report with a recommendation for promotion.

If however, a subordinate while trying really hard goofs up, or even does a good job, but makes a wave or two somewhere, or worse, brings what might be perceived as undue or unfavorable attention on their office, unit, or supervisor, the employee's performance report will reflect their "imprudence" or whatever term may be applied. Two or three of these, and an ascending career comes to a screeching halt, and may even descend. So, it's better to not try to do too well.

Another aspect of these performance evaluations is that supervisors are required look at employees beyond their actual jobs and job performance. The basic performance evaluations consider several factors, covering basic job requirements, goals, objectives, etc. Some sections of the performance evaluation actually include things not in the employee's established, agreed upon cast-in-stone job description or work related duties. One of these is consideration of the employee's sex, ethnic, cultural, or racial qualifications, with reverse discrimination establishing the white Anglo-Saxon protestant male being on the lowest rung of the feeding chain with the greatest hurdles to overcome. Now, I've said that and all of the breast beaters will assuredly call me all of the names they want. Regardless of the chest thumping and wailing and whining, we all, in our little hearts know and understand this basic truth.

The other, an important subject in the performance evaluation is an item that is supposed to demonstrate that the employee is well rounded and has a life away from work. This covers outside activities, such as hobbies, involvement in the local community, community services, charitable work, etc. If misused or miss-applied, this criteria is wrong. It happens. In the case of CIA employees in particular and all others in general, much credence has been given to involvement in church activities, and that actually became an important factor in scoring, or ranking for promotion...... Those CIA employees who were not wrapped up in religious activities suffered and were passed over, and those active Christians (Mormons) got the promotions and rewards such as choice assignments. They in turn looked for what I call other clones, and that is how a puritan religious Mafia gained far too much influence in the CIA, to the detriment of not just the CIA, but the security and safety of the United States and its citizens, you and I.

Risk Aversion

Naturally, an employee with a career interest will do anything he or she can to avoid a bad performance report. It's called risk aversion.

Over the years, risk aversion becomes second nature. A lot of fine, capable, competent, energetic, courageous, honorable, and aggressive employees actually take risks, and most of them do NOT survive in the government. The majority of government employees who do survive, do so by becoming risk averse drones unconcerned with our national welfare, who base their priorities solely on their own self-interest. A rare exception was Ambassador John Bolton, a somewhat irascible, opinionated, S.O.B. who was not easy to work for, especially if one was risk-averse and challenged as to being competent. When Bolton was nominated to become the U.S. Ambassador to the United Nations (a place that desperately needed just such an ambassador to represent the interests of the United States well), the mealy mouthed, politically correct foggy bottom liberals and their champions seized the opportunity to assassinate him in political terms. His nomination did not pass Senate muster.

Federal Bureau of Investigation

The Federal Government's performance evaluation system is corrupt and corrupting. Therefore, because of the risk involved, very few federal employees, including or especially CIA Case Officers and FBI agents are able to, or are even permitted to excel, to achieve very much in the jobs they are supposed to do. Some are good enough to actually go forth and do their jobs and succeed. They are often exceptions, and work for exceptional supervisors who help them to succeed.

Before the 9/11/2001 hijackings, FBI field agents in Minneapolis became very suspicious of the Moroccan, Mussaoui, and reported their concerns to their FBI headquarters. Along with their concerns, they made recommendations. Other FBI Investigators in Arizona found some other things disturbing, and reported their findings along with recommendations. At least one person claims that the incidents of 9/11/2001 could have been stopped, or at least reduced, had the FBI headquarters leadership and management been attentive and responsible.

Senior FBI managers failed to take appropriate heed, and left the Minneapolis field agents so frustrated that they took a risk and went outside of the FBI's Byzantine hierarchy to the CIA for help.

For being diligent in serving the nation, the Minneapolis FBI field agents were reprimanded for not being risk averse. This will have (forever) an adverse impact on their careers regardless of praise from the new FBI director, Mueller. For doing their job, they in fact suffered and their names were rarely heard of again. This is grossly unfair and flat wrong.

The responsible FBI headquarters management people ought to be held to a standard, and there need to be consequences for their ineptness. In this case the fools dumped reprimands on their subordinate Minneapolis field agents. Rather than hurting their diligent subordinates, these risk-averse supervisors should have been demoted (at least three grades), and held to a tough standard before they got promoted again. In fact the FBI headquarters jackass who refused to respect his subordinates' suspicions was rewarded. This is flat wrong.

Since the CIA came into being, the FBI and the CIA have been antagonists. People joked that neither had the other agency on its auto dialer. This needs to change, and jawboning isn't the cure. One, two, a dozen or more Senate and Congressional hearing and investigations are going to make politicians feel good, but that ain't no cure.

The FBI failed to respond, to foresee, or take action to prevent the incidents of 9/11/2001 partially because of bureaucratic confusion as well as leadership and headquarters ineptitude. Another reason for the FBI's failures is because the FBI has tried in recent times to become all things – to be Super cops, and have thus dissipated themselves. There are some really splendid officers in the FBI who need to be allowed to do the great work they are capable of doing. There are really splendid officers in other agencies as well who need to be given the freedom to excel. Their headquarters need to mentor, guide, and protect them while they do their great work.

Predictably, and in response to criticism that they are all screwed up, Justice Department and FBI top management have done whatever any good bureaucrats would do to duck the heat and cover their ineptitude: Blame it on something else and reorganize. This CYA fool-the-public action was taken at the end of May, 2002.

The failure of the FBI prior to events leading up to 9/11/2001 became a partisan political issue predictably to be taken up by insignificant politicians trying to sound significant. The opposition political hacks, Daschle and Gephardt and their minions demanded to know why the President didn't intimately know all of the details.

It was because of a failure of the system, a failed system that Messers Daschle and Gephardt played a major role in creating over two or three decades. And then, these partisan side-liners tried to make something of it. When casting stones for ineptness, they needed to look into a mirror and then cast their stones at the image they see. Fortunately, neither fool survived their re-election process.

The President of the United States receives an intelligence briefing every morning, even on mornings he'd rather sleep in. The Daily Intelligence Brief is compiled from information gathered and reported by thousands of investigative agents, spies, analysts, and others. Thousands of them, generating thousands of pages. That's one hell of a lot to read and digest every day. He can't possibly do that, so a condensed digest is prepared that is just a few pages long – of highlights.

The President's Daily CIA Intelligence Brief is 3-5 pages long. Just long enough to get his coffee curdling in the morning..... It is but one of several briefs he has to deal with every day, including briefs from the FBI, and now, Homeland Security.

Chapter 10

POLITICAL CORRECTNESS
The epitome of stupidity

On July 4th, 2002, a day when America was prepared for a renewal of much ballyhooed and promised terrorist attacks, an Egyptian named Hesham Mohammed Hadayet took two guns and a knife and went to the Los Angeles International Airport. He walked past several crowded, busy airline counters, to the El Al Israeli Airline counter. Once there, he pulled a gun and started shooting at Jews. He killed two and wounded three others before the El Al security people took care of him and sent him off to roast in hell. Were it not for the rapid response of alert Israeli security Personnel (take note FBI, FAA, and others), this Islamist creep could have killed many more.

Politically correct dork Norman Minetta and the FBI (**F**oolish, **B**lind, and **I**nept) expressed puzzlement about the Mohammedan killer's motives and were very reluctant to brand this incident as a terrorist act. Why? Why not? This is bizarre thinking at best, and is simply dishonest. But, it was political correctness at its worst. How can the American public trust these types of pronouncements? It took the FBI more than 24-hours to conclude that Hadayet actually intended to hurt anyone.......??...? A week later the FBI was still uncertain that this was an act of terrorism..... And the FBI wants the public to have confidence in them with these types of statements and pronouncements? They acted like Keystone cops. The FBI needs to earn respect the old fashioned way -- by doing their job.

Let's cogitate a little here. An angry, socially challenged male Moslem (devoted follower of Islam) who celebrated when bin Laden's minions downed two tall buildings; who complained about an American flag being displayed, posted a "Read Koran" sign at his home, often and stridently expressed his hatred of Israel, and propagated anti Israeli falsehoods (Jews spreading aids amongst the Arab population); and who went out, and specifically targeted, and killed Jews. To this the FBI said there's no indication of anti-Israeli views or any other type of racial views, nor any connection to any terrorist group (that the FBI would be aware of). Several news organizations around the world have reported that Hadayet was a member of the Egyptian Islamic Jihad and has met in California with (spent time with) Osama bin Laden's deputy, Dr. Ayman al Zawahri. In another time of his employment Hadayet aroused the suspicions of El Al (which probably helped to get him fired from his job).

C'mon boys and girls. A moron could figure this one out without much problem. But then, the FBI is having trouble dealing with this, so what are they doing?

One week earlier, politically correct FBI Director Mueller (a clueless political hack) dignified the collaborationist American Muslim Council with his presence. He delivered a speech in which he soft-pedaled the issues -- to an organization that is, or whose membership and officers are, closely tied to Moslem organizations dedicated to the destruction of the United States. If the FBI is unaware of these facts, that's a travesty.

Four years after taking his office, FBI Director Mueller still was unaware (willfully ignorant) of the relationship between al Qaeda founder Osama bin Laden's long relationship with Sheik Rahman (the "blind Sheikh") who is in prison on terrorism charges (the 1993 bombing of the World Trade Center).

Being politically correct is harmfully stupid in dozens of ways. Mueller was right up there with the most blatantly stupid.

Some time prior to the attacks of 9/11, a typically risk averse career Foreign Service Officer, Wendy Chamberlin, was sent to Pakistan as the American Ambassador. [This is just as we did when sending a female charge des Affaires to Iraq which in all likelihood contributed to the 1990 Iraqi invasion of Kuwait and the thousands of deaths, incredible suffering and hardship to so may, and the billions squandered in that war.] It was another of the typical politically correct diplomatic assignments that makes little sense, sending a woman to a chauvinistic Mohammedan dominated country that has little regard or respect for women. Thus, the host country (Pakistan) should not have been expected to show a great deal of respect or regard for the United States. They didn't. We had earlier created and established Pakistan's support for the Taliban for a number of reasons, none of them truly favorable to the United States. After the United States attacked the Taliban, and things got tough in Pakistan, Ambassador Chamberlin seemingly went whimpering to her bosses asking to be returned to the United States. The frying pan was getting hot and her politically correct duties combined with her risk averseness were suddenly becoming much more than she could handle. Naturally, the politically correct State Department bowed to her whining and whimpering and brought her home. She was dysfunctional.

Now, what would happen to say, an army general who complained that his job was getting too tough or hot to handle and whined and whimpered asking for relief, running off leaving a staff behind to face the music? He'd be cashiered for cowardice. But cowardly Ambassador Chamberlin who apparently did just that got rewarded and promoted. That sends another great affirming signal to everyone else in the State Department, telling them to be politically correct, cowardly, risk averse, and whine a lot at the right time, and you'll be rewarded. Do your job well however and your career may very well be in serious jeopardy.

Ms. Chamberlin's successor was the apparently if not obviously stupid, inept, and likewise risk averse, and cowardly Ambassador Nancy Powell. She refused to allow distribution in Pakistan of wanted posters and other information advertising the $25 million reward for bin Laden. The stuff was warehoused at the American Embassy in Islamabad for over two years before Congressman (Mark Kirk) uncovered this willful act of disobedience, and only after some serious arm twisting did that moronic Ambassador get relieved of duty for her treasonous and wanton dereliction of duty. This disgraceful idiot should have been brought to trial for serving as an enemy agent, working against American interests and endangering American lives. Nancy Powell stands as an unfortunate example of what successes (promotion and appointment as Ambassador) that clueless, often useless, and risk averse public servants can achieve based on gender alone.

Subsequently, another knife in America's back from the risk-averse and politically correct cowardly Consul General in Peshawar, Michael A. Spangler, a supposed expert on Pakistan (and therefore Islam) who idiotically (he was probably quaking in his shoes) declared at a public event that the United States is "eager to promote Islam's message of peace and justice". This guy was a complete coward. We need to get these phony, risk-averse and ignorant simple minded dweebs out of our diplomatic missions and install people who will at least refrain from stupid remarks if they can't at least condemn those narrow minded barbaric pagans for what they are.

While President Bush, his Secretaries of State, Defense, and others speak laudingly about Mohammedan chauvinist Pakistan being such a great friend and ally in this war we have going against 'terror', our actions speak differently. We sent a risk averse coward, Wendy Chamberlin as ambassador on one occasion, and then a politically correct, risk averse, and inept idiot, Nancy Powell as another Ambassador.

While we speak about respect for allies and so forth, we send marginally competent or totally inept females as our ambassador to a nation that has no respect for females, and derivatively, this indicates that we really, truly have no respect for Pakistan, and we ought to expect no respect in return. This is, I guess, as it should be. It might be another story if we sent ladies with gumption who had a brain cell or two to rub together to such a place.

In a rare show of decency, American Ambassador to Yemen, Edmund Hull spoke out about extremist Mohammedan activities taking place at al-Eman University and its funding of Islamic terrorism. The rector of al-Eman, a slime bag cretin named al-Zindani, a long-time supporter of al-Qaeda has been listed by the USG as a funder and supporter of terrorism. Al-Zindani is also one of those behind the attack on the USS Cole, and one of his so-called students murdered three US doctors in 2002. I never heard about Hull again. I suppose he was reprimanded for being honest and candid.

I spent some time at the American Embassy in Asmara, Eritrea in 2005. While Eritrea is 60% Moslem, the government is controlled by nominal Coptic Christians who led in the war of independence from Ethiopia. The Christians are dominant politically and are trying to bring Eritrea forward as a modern nation. They practice religious repression, keeping each religious group in its place, and restricting non-Copt Christians. The USG is rightfully slamming them because of this, and withholding support in various arenas critical to the country's success as an independent secular nation. Rather than slam the Eritreans, we need to strongly encourage them to liberate their stance on non-Copt Christians. By being politically correct the USG is indirectly encouraging and supporting the more serious long term threat to Eritrea, Mohammedism.

The population of the capital city, Asmara is largely Christian. The American Embassy hires local nationals for many of the jobs such as drivers, clerks, security guards, and consular and administrative staff. The embassy hires from the local pool of talent and skills, which is difficult because there are few people with the language skills and other abilities that the Embassy needs to operate. Also, having a homogeneous staff is vital to the smooth functioning of the mission. At a staff meeting, the Deputy Chief of Mission (DCM) asked why there were not very many Moslems on the Embassy staff. That question made me cringe, because the implication was clear, that she wished and might soon impose hiring of non-homogeneous (Moslem) staffers to suit her need for politically correct "diversity" and to hell with effective or efficient management of the embassy. That kind of political correctness is perversely S-T-O-O-O-P-I-D!

When I was the Human Resources manager at the American Embassy at Dhaka, Bangladesh, I faced a similar issue. About 85% of the white collar Bangladeshi staff were Christians or Hindus, in a country where Christians and Hindus are less than 5% of the population. I was told, as I recruited new staff and so forth, that I should hire Moslems only, not Christians. This was an instruction that I should exercise a cultural or racial bias in recruiting in order to move towards a more "representative" staff. This requirement was wrong in that it restricted my choice of recruiting the best talent (from an extremely limited linguistic, talent, and skills pool) for the Embassy, and the fact that Christian employees were inherently more loyal and dedicated to the success of the Embassy's mission. I ignored the instructions to be politically correct and to lower standards to accommodate the stupidity in the Embassy's senior management, and I continued recruiting and hiring employees who had necessary language skills, education, talent, determination, ability, and whose loyalty we Americans could depend on. While I was doing my job, I in fact did hire a few Moslems who had the skills, talents, and abilities that the Embassy needed for its mission.

Knowing the enemy

When one is at war, it is advisable to know and to understand the enemy. Islam, our Moslem enemy has had agents in this country for a half of a century and they have studied us and know us well, and are successfully, incrementally, mounting success after success. Their goal, of course is to subvert and overturn the U.S. Constitution and establish Sharia laws and controls over all non-Moslems in America.

In America, with thousands of Mosques, Islamic Centers, Islamic Schools, and Islamic organizations, many under the guise of other often innocent sounding names like the "Institute on Religion and Civic Values" which conceal their Islamic agenda. The Institute on Religion and Civic Values has been successful (working under the blinded radar) in instilling a politicized, and untrue propaganda course on Islamic studies which is imposed on seventh grade students all over America.

Nobody seems to want to know much about this Islamic network. When the FBI attempted to organize an effort to map out Islamic organization locations in America (starting in Los Angeles), and then to catalog the nearby demographics, the Islamists successfully used their America hating agents within the USG (FBI, Homeland Security, etc) to have this halted. Thus, we have fifth columnists actively at work thwarting organizations and efforts that are supposed to be protecting us from harm. Those organizations, with significant fifth columnist activities and controls are in fact using those organizations to protect our enemy right here within our country. They are turning the FBI and others into organizations that go after prudent citizens and patriots.

An underfunded and understaffed private sector group SOCIETY OF AMERICANS FOR NATIONAL EXISTENCE (SANE) started a project called "Mapping Sharia". It is an effort to locate Islamic Centers and Mosques, etc., to determine their denominations (Shiia, Sunni, Ahamadiya, etc.), and then to identify their level of hostility towards civilization, and America.

Chapter 11

WHO'S IN CHARGE?

***When in doubt, when ducking for cover,
to Cover Your Ass (CYA),
act immediately ---- REORGANIZE!***

Can the CIA, FBI, and now the Homeland Defense Agency, and others be trusted completely with the nation's security? Is there a workable formula that will harness the huge, conflicting and conflicted bureaucracies involved, and make them into a colossal bureaucracy that will be effective?

After the events of 9/11/2001, a couple of FBI reports surfaced (in May of 2002) that caused the utmost of embarrassment for the FBI and its new director. When this inept bumbling was revealed, the proverbial stuff hit the fan. One of the reports bringing this about was from an FBI whistle blower, Colleen Rawley, in Minneapolis, whom the new FBI Director, Robert Mueller has publicly (he was obliged to do so) acknowledged and thanked (a rare first for a patriot and whistle blower) for her courage and invaluable service to the American people.

Well, look for Colleen Rawley now and see where she is in her professional career. Whistle blowers never fare well in the federal bureaucracy, and she suffered, as well as her career for doing what was the right thing. The upper echelons of FBI brass were arrogant and inept, she upset their apple cart and that wiped her career out. She "decided" to retire on or about the day she was able to retire and her dedicated service and loyalty to the American people are lost. The jerks that she blew the whistle on were rewarded for their asinine behavior and gross stupidity.

In response to some political grandstanding, FBI Director Mueller led off with a grandstand of his own, a "reorganization" of the FBI designed to take the wind out of critics' sails. His "reorganization" established "Flying Squads", and supposedly assigned or recruited 1,500 bodies into new or enhanced counter-terrorism programs. How many of these instant counter-terrorism specialists were linguistically qualified, or culturally conscious, or have the sophistication to understand the fascist Islamic opponents we must deal with?

The magnitude of this folly will be a long time coming. While the FBI may be in need of shaking up, the idea of abandoning its crime detecting operation is simply bad. Turning the FBI into a major intelligence gathering operation is questionable if not simply unwise. A new domestic intelligence agency is needed for sure, but this should not be the role of the FBI. We need an FBI that is focused on investigating crimes and bringing criminals to face justice. But, the deed of folly is done, and the American people will suffer the consequences.

Following the FBI's artful lead, President Bush announced a sweeping reorganization of the Federal Government in order to deal with these new and very real threats. The leading critics, Senator Daschle and Representative Gephardt were obliged to ante-up, to support the reorganization of institutions that failed us so miserably.

Notwithstanding that the reorganizations were good or at least a useful step in the right direction, there are many more steps yet to be taken before anyone can crow about any kind of real success. Besides, 2002 was an election year, and President Bush needed to stop the damaging hysteria coming form the opposition. This 'reorganization' was very effective. What he did was not only good election year politics, it was good for the nation, even if marginally so.

However, let's not forget for a moment that when you reorganize such as was done with the National Security agencies and move one bumbling inept jackass from one chair or office to another, the inept bumbling jackass is still there. The reorganization may delineate things a little, or differently, but serious systemic problems remain, and one is that employees of most Federal Agencies dislike and have little trust or confidence in the FBI. Within the FBI, this is also true as is evident with the Mussaoui case. That isn't likely to change with the stroke of a Presidential pen.

Inside jobs

Our own soldiers and sailors' lives are at risk daily, and sometimes (if not most of the time) it is an inside job.

A civilian Navy employee, a woman welder complained that welds were inferior on critical aircraft carrier catapult systems, a failure of which could cause loss of lives besides being very costly. The welder, Kristin Schott, screwed up her considerable courage and blew the whistle on these bad practices. She was right, very right, and these shabby welds had to be fixed at taxpayer expense (far less than a plane wreck and lost lives). What did the Navy brass do to express their gratitude to her for saving lives? Schott was demoted, denied promotion, and shuttled into a less praiseworthy position. That's retaliation. Yes, this courageous woman was retaliated against for doing an exemplary job. The risk-averse brass who screwed up were humiliated and paid her back. Those jackass bosses are still there........., and their negligence will yet cost lives of our young people.

Most government employees know and understand that if they blow the whistle they will almost assuredly suffer the consequences of their convictions.

Late in the Bush administration it came out that a very courageous official (Thomas Tamm) at the Justice Department dropped the dime on an illegal eavesdropping program. It was classified at the highest levels, but was nevertheless in violation of FISA laws. Following his convictions and loyalty to the Constitution, he revealed to news media what was going on. As of this writing, he is unemployed, under investigation, and may likely be prosecuted for revealing sensitive intelligence gathering information. What about the fact that those intelligence gathering activities were against the law?

Policy and Focus

The State Department as well as the rest of government is woeful at best. They have no policies to speak of. Their thousands of intellectuals and regional and area specialists and experts are dolts.

There are area offices and officers who are supposedly experts and focused on every nation on earth. The same holds true of the CIA and other agencies. They are well paid and are supposed to use their expertise and knowledge to help formulate and manage American policies for and with each of those nations. They don't.

It's not entirely their fault. They are often ignored by senior officials who are both untrusting of these people (oftentimes for good reason) and are themselves unfocused and unprofessional. If the political hacks have an interest or develop an interest in an area, then policy may follow. But if they don't, policy dissipates and there is a void.

For instance, after the Soviets were driven out of Afghanistan, Afghanistan was ignored. Nobody gave a hoot, and nobody did anything until after 9/11 when they discovered that America's creation, bin Laden was there and he and his Taliban had turned the country into a personal fiefdom.

If the gnat-brained secretary of State Madeline Albright and her whimsical, liberal and so very flaky Clintonites had anything operating between their ears, the Taliban and bin Laden perhaps wouldn't have been there, and perhaps bin Laden wouldn't have been able to engineer the 9/11 attacks.

The future of U.S. national security

President Bush's plan was a feeble step in the right direction of trying to make what's wrong right. However, consolidating too much under one umbrella (holding all of one's eggs in one basket) can have real risks.

A Single Engined Aircraft

Imagine this: Going to an airport (any airport) to catch a long trans-oceanic flight on a jumbo jet. OK, so far?

You board a 400+ passenger jet that has only one engine - for an eleven+ hour flight. Would you feel completely comfortable going off on a huge, heavily loaded jet headed out over the ocean and depending on one single engine?

Now, after boarding and taking your seats, the pilot (just one pilot, no co-pilot, no navigator, nor flight engineer) comes on board. The door closes and the single motor starts up, and we taxi down to the runway. The pilot comes on over the public address system (just one speaker for the whole plane) and from him we learn that he is actually a political hack and not a real pilot at all. He's a real nice guy and the position pays well. Still feeling safe?

Besides having just one engine, we have just one tire under each wing, and just one set of electrical wiring, one hydraulic system, one set of controls and cables, one radio, and no redundant systems. Feeling queasy?

And now at 39,000 feet we learn we have a bad load of contaminated fuel and no filters. Oops! The compass just failed and the single fuse powering the entire instrument panel just blew and there isn't a spare to be found, and pilot's only microphone just fell into his coffee mug.

Unh-hunh. I agree. I'd never get on such a plane or feel confident around such a mess.

I like traveling on a plane with a trained, vetted, experienced, tested professional pilot guiding it. And, the similarly qualified co-pilot and flight engineer add very welcome redundancy. The redundancy of multiple engines makes me feel good too, along with knowledge that the big plane abounds with redundant back-up systems that can take over for any system that may fail. Yeah, I'll bet you'd feel better about that too.

President Bush's reorganizations needed redundancy with fail-safe backup systems. Their need was and still is clear as exemplified by the dismal, wrongheaded performance of his Department of Homeland Security and Federal Emergency Management Agency in the wake of Hurricane Katrina. Political hack Brown, the director of FEMA did a lot to affirm that President Bush is less bright than many would want to believe.

Three years later, the Department of Homeland Security with a new, second chief, Michael Chertoff was still floundering. He brought in a 47-year veteran of the CIA, Charlie Allen to work to integrate the many disparate intelligence activities now under the DHS umbrella. Ho hum...., and so the risk-averse and proprietary menagerie continues to go off in their different ways. This is probably in fact good, but is mismanaged as different egos try to become demigods.

Come the 2008 election, and the new POTUS #44 lurched the government to the far left with his "transparent" government where he appointed an ignorant fool, Janet Napolitano as secretary of DHS. Napolitano has steadfastly been against protecting America's borders, and has thus worked to open our borders to terrorist elements and eased their access to America. Early in her tenure, she declared that jihadist and terrorist words were not to be used by officials. Soon after her appointment, Napolitano had the DHS begin compiling a secret list of patriots and free citizens, and related groups whom she and the Obama crew consider to be a threat. A threat to what? The definition of extremist is being used very loosely or liberally, and that can include a whole bunch of decent people, over 50% of Americans who voted for other than Obama. By these actions alone, she is herself a rogue who is conspiring against genuine American national safety and security, and hundreds of millions of good, decent, people.

THE CIA

The CIA can't be relied upon to serve us well. They rarely have in recent times. They didn't do it all by themselves however, They've had help in being screwed up.

The CIA has long held the responsibilities for two important areas of National Security. They are the CIA's Directorate of Operations and the Directorate of Intelligence. The CIA has thus been a two headed creature, neither always very well controlled nor coordinated.

The Directorate of Operations is, or perhaps more appropriately was the spymasters, the place where both famous and infamous covert operations were created and executed. Some were successful. Some were not. In 2005, it was determined that the CIA would remain Coordinator of Overseas spying. Supposedly it would be a coordinating, not controlling position considering all of the US agencies getting into the intelligence gathering act, but language in that left the CIA in a controlling position to assure that there would be no redundancy, a bad idea!

The Directorate of Intelligence is not covert, and the employees can even tell people where they work, and thus have little trouble getting home mortgages. Their work is nevertheless vital and what they deal with is often very secret. These folks just don't sneak around in the dark. This is the place where national intelligence gathered from all agencies was or is supposed to be sent, analyzed, collated, and disseminated. It hasn't received the cooperation it needed from all agencies that have any form of intelligence collection apparatus, especially from the FBI.

A two legged stool

The 2002 Congressional and Senate hearings focused on intelligence community failures. Was this really useful? Certainly! Various agencies had and failed to share or process information they held. But, none of the information held or not processed precisely predicted the date, the time, the target or targets, or the individual perpetrators of the 9/11 attacks. Collectively, all of that undistilled information was useless.

The intelligence failures are that the greater intelligence

community led by the CIA and with the full complicity of the Congress and at least four administrations (Carter the idiot bungler, sincere but occasionally vapid Reagan, Bush the mindless follower, and Clinton the wannabe despot) all willfully and negligently discounted the need for human intelligence. They left the security and defense of the United States hamstrung. They instead relied arrogantly on a two legged stool of imagery (pictures) and electronic signals. The two legged stool didn't stand up. It toppled, and left the American people flat on their backsides. That is a profound neglect that must be corrected. The stool needs three equally sturdy legs.

Power Corrupts, and
Absolute Power Corrupts Absolutely

The Federal Bureau of Investigation (FBI) was created to investigate crimes and prosecute criminals, including espionage, something it seemingly did well. The FBI has dissipated itself over the years by horning in wherever they could get away with it, whether they were welcome or not, invited or not. The FBI has tried to spread itself all over the place, to play the role of super cop, to amass absolute, imperial authority. They loved to grab the limelight and thump their chests at 'their' successes.

The FBI became the bully.

The FBI gathered intelligence, initially in pursuing pure criminal activities, but started getting involved overseas in what the CIA felt was its turf. Uninvited, the FBI also refused to share. So, the CIA threw up its own veils. Subsequently a turf war or conflict grew and has existed between the two agencies for at least three decades, if not longer. When pundits said that neither the CIA nor FBI had one another on their office auto dialers, they were right on.

During the cold war, a hotline was established at the Pentagon, connected with a counterpart office in the Kremlin, in Moscow. Each had a Russian and an American teletype machine, linguists on duty, dedicated redundant phone lines that were open and operational on a continuing basis, and people who made it work. Test messages were sent every fifteen minutes to assure the lines were open and functioning. The redundant systems were up, available, and ready for use if and when needed.

The CIA and FBI had teletype machines in their respective headquarters and were supposed to use these to share information over the years. The relations between the two were so completely antagonistic that they failed to communicate over their own hot line, much less actually share information. The teletype machines got dusty, and phone calls were rarely made. This was the established, failed system in effect on 9/11/2001, and while the two are being compelled to communicate and share information today, it is like two squabbling competing children. For the moment, while under close scrutiny, they pretend to cooperate. Will this continue? A very telling 2005 report depicting how, nearly four years after the intelligence community fowl-ups leading to 9/11, proprietary intelligence people are still hoarding intelligence and refusing to share it. Folks, make your own judgments.

The notoriously power hungry FBI has horned in on DEA turf as well, to the extent that the DEA has lowered its priorities on trying to apprehend drug dealers, leaving this to the FBI, who are doing a lousy job.

We often used to hear or read of DEA drug busts. Sometimes they were violent and people got hurt or died. It was kind of wild and wooly, but drugs were seized and drug dealers put out of business, put away, or killed, lots of them. No more. Nope. The FBI spends hundreds of thousands of dollars using wire taps, all too often on the wrong phones trying to gather evidence to indict a few ranking drug kingpins a year. In the meantime thousands of tons of drugs enter the United States making thousands of drug dealers wealthy, and destroying the lives of hundreds of thousands of Americans. The FBI's approach is a joke, a very costly and barely effective joke.

Big drug hauls. The Coast Guard on mostly routine patrols does better than the FBI or the neutered DEA. The Border Patrol and U.S. Customs does better than the FBI.

The FBI and Treasury Department's cooperation is marginally better than the dysfunctional FBI/CIA rivalry.

I don't know but would venture to opine that the level of cooperation between the FBI and the Secret Service, and the Bureau of Alcohol, Tobacco, and Firearms isn't too good either, as well as with other federal, state, and municipal police agencies..... The FBI is trying, and having some limited successes, but not always.

In summary, the FBI has too often abused its scope of authority and grabbed power and authority from and over other agencies to the point that the FBI has seriously antagonized just about all other federal government agencies. Some (not all) FBI officers are often haughty and lord their power and authority over others. The FBI is corrupted by its own power and is seeking and perhaps achieving absolute corruption.

An example of FBI corruption, misconduct, and abuse is a 2005 report that the FBI had conducted clandestine surveillance (this is a good idea) on some U.S. residents for over a year. However, this was arrogantly done without following well established laws, regulations and procedures in this regard, a no-no.

The FBI 'cooperates' in that they want information provided to them from all sources, but when it comes to feedback from the FBI, they stink. As a consequence, local and state law enforcement people increasingly don't bother to feed information to the FBI, because whatever they provide disappears into a black hole. They rarely get any feedback, useful, positive, negative, or otherwise.

The May 2002 "reorganization" of the FBI following revelations of its headquarters' contempt for its own field officers, gross ineptitude and mismanagement has no real meaning and likely accomplished little. It was just a CYA ("Cover Your Ass") action to cover Director Mueller's backside so that he could stay on as Director, and gain more power.

Many people in law enforcement resent the FBI, and whatever jawboning or public relations spinning is done, the FBI doesn't always receive a high level of genuine cooperation from people in the law enforcement community (some, who have been victims of FBI excesses) with which it has competed and abused for so many years. Perhaps that has an element of goodness, a leveling influence on those seeking absolute power.

For years, the FBI (FBI's Special Agents) with its unique special mandate of investigating espionage and similar crime has treated other agencies' employees with disdain. Some of these FBI Special Agents are simply jerks. But then, that's life, plenty of people (about ten percent) at all levels of any society are jerks, just not very many with that type or level of power and authority. Reorganization does little regarding imperious personalities, priggish attitudes, earned and deserved bad reputations, and other baggage, desirable or otherwise.

There are dozens of other federal agencies involved in gathering intelligence for one reason or another. They either are highly specialized, or get into one-another's turf and nobody seems to share well. There is vast room for either improvement or something new and/or different.

There are hopefully increasing exceptions on the good side, so not all are bad, or ineffective.

The State Department is overt in its information gathering, and its officials meet with officials of other countries and exchange information, working at and maintaining good relations with countries around the world. They even do their reporting job well at times. All local news papers and magazines are subscribed to, appropriate sections translated and worked with on a daily basis. And, a copy of each publication is forwarded to the Library of Congress regularly. (The Library of Congress gathers newspapers, books, and magazines from throughout the world, and is the greatest repository of public information in the world.)

The State Department's minimally funded and staffed Bureau of Intelligence and Research, is one of the smaller organizations, just a couple of hundred employees, most on rotational assignments. They are involved with analysis and reporting, and they occasionally turn out quality analytical products and reports that are valued and whose recipients are uniformly satisfied and impressed, including the White House.

The Department of Defense has its Defense Intelligence Agency which gathers information overtly through Military Attaché offices in Embassies, as well as through Military Assistance and Aid groups, exchanges with other governments, etc. The Department of Defense is involved with clandestine electronic intelligence gathering and so forth that is effective and productive for military purposes.

The Department of Agriculture overtly gathers crop information which is used to forecast world food production, demands, and needs, etc.

The Federal Aviation Administration gathers information applicable to aircraft and air travel. Some is sensitive, some is not.

The Department of Commerce gathers trade information and uses this to help American Businesses to compete.

The National Security Agency works in electronic eaves dropping, satellite imagery, and so forth along with the Department of Defense and Central Intelligence Agency.

The Drug Enforcement Agency is supposed to be involved in international and domestic drug trafficking. Restricted, they aren't doing very well.

The Treasury Department follows the money, tracks down forgers, tax evaders, and keeps up with the flow of money. It can and should be empowered to wage electronic and monetary warfare to destabilize or destroy the finances of those arrayed against us.

The Bureau of Alcohol, Tobacco, and Firearms gathers information pertinent to those activities.

The U.S. Customs gathers information on smuggling activities. The Coast Guard is likewise active, and these two have done well with the limited resources they have had. They ought to become more involved, especially in controlling and inspecting more than just 2-5% of inbound shipping containers and vessels. But, containers move on rail and on trucks too, so there is a jurisdictional dispute or turf fight involved here as to who has ultimate responsibility for containers. While these agencies are futzing around fighting their little bureaucratic turf battles, evil is happening.

The above is simplistic and omits some other activities, but paints a picture of just a part of the various and sundry intelligence gathering operations the U.S. government is involved in.

Other agencies involved in the war on terrorism include the Federal emergency Management Agency (FEMA) which has no need to gather intelligence. They should be fed intelligence data from the HDA, so they can analyze and prepare to respond, to react to inevitable attacks.

Former FEMA Director, James Lee Witt, opined that the inclusion of FEMA in the HDA has in fact hampered its ability to react to disasters whether man made or natural.

Since we drove some elements of the Taliban out of Afghanistan, the drug business is once again a thriving enterprise. This is shameful. Apparently American authorities truly desire that the drug trade in fact thrive. (After all, the illegal narcotics and drug business means job security for thousands in law enforcement, treatment, and so forth.) With our power and presence in Afghanistan, we could easily halt opium production, yet we let it thrive. There is something very wrong here, because illicit narcotics are a part and parcel of the war or wars being waged against the United States. This drug trade is a major source of income for funding terrorist activities.

National Security Council

The National Security Council (NSC) has grown and plays an important role in the White House. They've done some good things, some interesting things, and some dumb things, just like the rest of the government.

Richard Clarke got himself posted to the NSC early in the Clinton Administration, an administration made up mostly of clowns. Clarke became the so-called anti-terrorism Czar in the NSC, responsible for overseeing and coordinating various elements of the many federal agencies involved in counter-terrorism. He spent eight years in that powerful top position where he supposedly received information from all agencies, and even had the authority to task agencies to obtain information. If anyone other than the directors of the CIA and FBI can be held directly or personally accountable for the 9/11 attacks, it's Clarke.

When the Bush administration came into the White House with Condoleeza Rice as the National Security Council head, she apparently soon deduced Clarke's arrogance, his deficiencies, and his uselessness was appropriately addressed. He got the boot.

His huge but so very fragile ego bruised, Clarke ran out and wrote a book that was replete with inaccuracies in a very sick attempt to cover his backside. In it he falsely blamed 9/11 on President Bush. He even went before the Congress and lied under sacred oath. Richard Clarke is a nasty, jealous, inept and feeble minded little worm below contempt and not worthy of any further mention in history.

The Homeland Defense Agency

The new Homeland Defense Agency (HDA), or Department of Homeland Defense was apparently destined to be the focal point for all intelligence in the war on terror. That's a tall order. One of the first changes was creation of the position of intelligence "Czar" to oversee and control or coordinate all intelligence gathering activities. Bad idea! It's just like a one-engined Jumbo jet, destined to fail - horribly.

For the Secretary of Homeland Defense to be effective, the other agencies (and cabinet level Secretaries) were supposed to become subordinate to the Secretary of Homeland Defense (SECHOMDEF). It didn't happen and that's why Secretary Ridge bailed. He wasn't supported or allowed to be effective. Officers in various agencies, when offered positions at DHS refused because there was no status, authority, or anything they wanted or desired in those positions. Those who moved over were largely ineffective bureaucrats looking for a better roost.

To be effective, the Secretary of Homeland Security must have authority (and his mangers the derivative authority) to crack heads together to get independent (and they must nevertheless remain independent) agencies to perform their duties, and to relinquish and share information they gather. That's a tall order, because statutes, rules, and regulations presently exist that allow agencies to withhold valuable information from one-another. Attention legislators! You need to take serious action here. Couple this with the agencies' proprietary attitudes, turf sensitivity, and so forth, and there are tons of issues to overcome before anything else will work. How much time will pass and be wasted, and ineffective wheel spinning is to be done before things begin to really work is unpredictable.

In addition to being a coordinator, it's envisioned that the Homeland Defense Agency must receive intelligence and information from dozens of sources, collate it, analyze all of it quickly and accurately, and then disseminate this in a timely fashion and to appropriate agencies and levels of government.) By 2008, it hadn't happened and the ball started rolling to establish yet another bureaucracy with a 'czar' of intelligence.)

Things are faltering.

The HDA should task, or assign responsibilities, adjudicate disputes, and then judge performance between these competing agencies. Individuals at all levels who fail to cooperate, perform, and work towards the common goal (war on terror) should feel the repercussions. I'm not talking about a slap on a wrist, but loss of job, job assignment, rank, and pay should be actions taken, not just considered or written down on a piece of paper. The HDA should, in cases where deaths or injuries occur, task the FBI (<u>and/or others</u>) to investigate and the Attorney General should then prosecute American officials guilty of negligence. Right now, incompetence or negligence is often rewarded. Why?

The CIA's Directorate of Intelligence is a huge organization involved in the analysis of intelligence and generating reports, just what the HDA and others need. The HDA can and ought to be the main and central recipient for all analyzed intelligence. The CIA should remain the primary repository for all intelligence gathered by each and every agency, including every damned piece of paper, photograph, and electronic bit and baud that everyone [including the FBI specifically] collects, as well as all others.

The CIA must be required to share that data with other agencies so that independent analysis can be undertaken to pick up what the CIA inadvertently misses.

The Department of Homeland Security (DHS) within months of being created was already politicized. Supposedly, monies were to be allocated to communities on a priority basis depending on needs following standardized criteria. It didn't work that way. Within months, millions of dollars were foolishly and wastefully being dispensed to communities based on political clout and preferences, not demonstrable need based on threat analyses.

While all of these silly "me first" but totally risk averse fools are running around protecting their proprietary turf and trying to one-up one-another, they totally ignored the greatest threat to the United States: Nuclear weapons. They are out there. They are available, and they may already be in the United States awaiting the right opportunity to strike the most deadly, and destructive blow ever.

There's More

Nobody in the federal government, including Homeland Security elements, should be exempt from issues of waste, fraud, and mismanagement. Some proposals have included immunity from such. It's wrong, flat wrong. That's a license to steal. Nobody but nobody should be exempt from the law, especially public servants.

The Freedom of Information Act and other laws regarding privacy and secrecy must remain intact (or even be strengthened as regards government information), and be applicable to the Homeland Defense and Security groups as well. To this end, we again need strong deterrents such as mandatory forms of retribution (job and assignment loss, fines, imprisonment, etc.) to hold accountable those federal officials of high and low rank who abuse these good laws.

These laws were ignored under the Bush administration, and I have no doubt that the Obama administration won't abuse or ignore those laws as well, if not even more so to go after political and ideological opponents.

Competition

If competition is good for commerce and sports, why not for our National Security?

The principle of the seven P's (Proper Prior Planning Prevents Piss Poor Performance) would dictate that as an overwhelming priority, we should know our enemy and then try to understand his motivations and priorities so that we can deal with that enemy effectively, to survive.

We are at war, and the first battles that need to be won are right here, at home, between competing Federal Agencies and all of the accumulated baggage that lies on that battlefield. The HDA can end this if it is well organized and strongly managed.

The CIA felt that with its Directorate of Operations, it had sole authority to be the top international cowboy of spying, that its mandate gave it a monopoly. The FBI's unwelcome, forced intrusion caused great and continuing resentment.

The FBI seemed to feel that its mandate gave it authority and the power to do whatever it wanted to do, wherever it wanted, and to go whenever it felt like, a monopoly to be and do everything. The FBI expanded itself into gathering intelligence because the CIA would not share. What the FBI itself did gather wasn't shared with the CIA. That was redundancy that didn't work.

That the two got into turf battles and cut their lines of communication is well known. Neither had much confidence or trust in the other.

The CIA's Directorate of Operations can and should focus broadly on gathering raw intelligence. This doesn't necessarily need to remain within the CIA. It could be assigned to a new broad based collective agency. (By being separated from the CIA, the remaining principal element of the CIA can be free from the burden of being a two headed albatross. It can and should thrive with decent and focused leadership and management, goals, and objectives. Other agencies should likewise gather raw intelligence, and they could be more focused and task specific, or even redundant in order to pick up what others are likely (did I say likely, how about assuredly) to miss. The CIA's Directorate of Intelligence can then be the central repository of gathered raw intelligence and without the Operations Directorate, be the principal analyst of intelligence.

Wherever it lands, the Directorate of Operations should proceed with a world-wide mandate as well as domestic authority to gather intelligence aimed at protecting the United States from hostile outside forces. This should be at least 50% focused on establishing an effective human intelligence (HUMINT) operation and also involve domestic counter-espionage investigations.

The CIA of today has gone from its wild and woolly (but often effective) origin from the WWII Office of Strategic Services (OSS) to a bloated, inept, incompetent careerist centered, risk-averse operation that is badly managed. Those religious fundamentalists in the CIA, and other inept risk-averse careerist managers interested in promoting only themselves or some other misguided agenda not consistent with America's best interests need to be culled. That's a lot of culling.

About competing redundancy in gathering intelligence: The USSR had its KGB, NKVD, and GRU, three competing national security agencies, all charged with roughly the same level and scope of activities and acting with similar authority. Autonomous, they were in competition with one another, and were also authorized to conduct counter-espionage investigations. They were judged on their performance, not their hyperbole. It is the same with the Chinese, and many other nations. It worked, and continues to work well for all of them. It's a useful if not essential redundant mechanism that we could benefit from ourselves. What one may miss or omit, another will cover. Competition works.

Covert or clandestine military, paramilitary, or other named operations (as opposed to overt gathering of intelligence information) ought to be assigned to and carried out by the military. Effectively, there are four branches plus the Coast Guard, so the issue of redundancy is more or less moot. Besides, this is not the gathering of intelligence. It's in the realm of aggressive, proactive operations.

Perhaps covert operations of a non-military nature such as approved assassinations, sabotage, kidnappings, and so forth, should be within the realm of one or two other agencies. This would include the formation and support of mercenary forces, bounty hunters, and other black operations

The FBI was created to conduct criminal investigations, which includes espionage, or internal counter-intelligence. Who checks on the FBI? The FBI has been checking on the FBI, and the FBI has often failed. Who will check on the new FBI? Where is the redundancy? It has been shown that the FBI cannot adequately police itself. Neither can the Justice Department. At least one other agency must also be involved in domestic counter-intelligence and counter-espionage, with responsibility to check on the Justice Department and the FBI, to ferret out and catch fifth columnists and turncoats there, etc.

The FBI should be reined in and limited to its original mandate of dealing with criminal investigations and bringing criminals to justice. Its non-criminal intelligence gathering activities while redundant, are not very comprehensive or effective, and this should be largely eliminated and moved over to other agencies. Those employees of the FBI who are involved in intelligence gathering should be dispersed to agencies where these fine folks can find a place to fit, and do their jobs.

The FBI should be a police/law enforcement organization involved in investigations and prosecutions. They should receive intelligence from competing domestic intelligence sources as well as international sources and be allowed to analyze these bits and pieces of information to do their job of law enforcement, counter terrorism, criminal apprehension, and prosecution. That should be the focus of the FBI, not to let that present out-of-control, out-of-focus, thinks-it-is-god and thus dysfunctional and inept organization continue as it is. Intelligence that the FBI does pick up should not be held (hogged) closely within the FBI, but must be put into the intelligence pool to be shared by other analysts in other organizations.

The FBI should maintain an investigative and focused intelligence operation involved with criminal activities, INTERPOL, and other law enforcement agencies similarly involved. The investigative information gathered would, of course be used for prosecutions, but the intelligence derived (all of it) must be shared.

At the same time, the FBI using shared information from all agencies can conduct its own analysis for pursuing their criminal investigations, etc.

FBI Director Mueller has worked to move the FBI to the forefront of intelligence agencies. In fact, Mueller listed among his intentions the virtual abandonment of criminal investigations and prosecution of crimes in favor of detecting and preventing terror attacks. First, that is another gross failure of neglect of the public trust (Who will focus on detecting and prosecuting crimes?). Second, it is a pipe dream, claiming that he wants to prevent future attacks - that is the job of the WHOLE INTELLIGENCE COMMUNITY working in concert, not just the FBI hero wannabes.

Clearly, the FBI was asleep during the years when gross criminal financial manipulations, payola to politicians (Christopher Dodd, Barney Frank, and Barak Obama), theft, and more took place. The FBI's negligence led to the 2008 financial collapse.

Domestic intelligence gathering operations must be separate from law enforcement and prosecution entities. Domestic intelligence gathering must provide their intelligence into the pool for analysts to digest and then disseminate as appropriate.

There will always be some turf disputes between agencies. The Secretary of Homeland Security should be the one to arbitrate or adjudicate disputes. If he or she cannot, then the White House will have to establish some entity (a panel of ranking officials) who can arbitrate. Bearing in mind that redundancy is needed, turf disputes ought to be reduced and handled properly while encouraging competition.

Private intelligence

Because of interference from a bevy of outfits such as the ACLU, CAIR, and other anti-American fifth columnists, there is a real and genuine need for private organizations immune from FOI probes to gather intelligence. This intelligence can be "shown" to the FBI and others, but not given to them unless there is a legitimate need to release it. Thus, probes from the ACLU and CAIR can be legitimately answered by the FBI and others truthfully advising that they do not "have" such information. The private intelligence immune from FOI probes must remain sacrosanct. Their information should enjoy the same client privacy privilege as is provided to doctors and lawyers.

Domestic Intelligence

Actions have been taken that will ease restrictions on conducting investigations and gathering information in places such as libraries and over the internet.

It's hard to believe that our legislators and political leaders of previous administrations (both Democratic and Republican) placed such onerous restrictions on law enforcement agencies. While these over reactive restrictions were established in response to past abuses, they were often overdone and misguided at best. If and when someone in law enforcement or intelligence does violate the law and/or a citizen's civil rights, they ought to be prosecuted, which means they lose their jobs and go to jail. A mere slap on the hand is inappropriate. When law breaking and abuse occurs, it should not fall on just the actual abuser, but must be reflected on up the chain of command as well to his or her mentors and supervisors at least three levels up, even Cabinet level officials) who also need be held accountable, with their jobs on the line. Accountable, they should also be considered for prosecution and imprisonment under conspiracy laws when criminal acts and abuses occur.

More aggressive actions need to be allowed when dealing with non-citizens. Let the American Civil Liberties Union (ACLU) and other anti-American organizations frenetically involved with screwing things up stew in their own frenzies. Non-citizens by virtue of their not having the same vested interests and responsibilities as citizens can and ought to be more closely observed, with fewer "rights".

Whenever I hear mention of the ACLU, my hackles instinctively rise. This ethically challenged gang of ultra liberal pseudo intellectuals have been a major thorn in the side of that which is honorable and decent for decades. They make the most outrageous statements and comments imaginable or possibly attributable to responsible adults. Seemingly they often support crass, disgusting causes that leave me grasping for my antacid. The early ACLU had a long history of doing mostly good things for people, but about three decades ago, they really lost touch with reality and lost their focus on decency. I am certain that most true patriots will agree with this.

I believe that the ACLU's disgusting championing of the turncoat Johnny Walker Lindh, the Taliban, and Al Qaeda detainees in Cuba, and whatever more will come will be a major issue for the government to deal with. I once, long ago, applauded the ACLU and cheered them on when they were champions for decency and justice. I will cheer for them again when they return to moral civility, decency, and reality. We may even need the ACLU as elements of the FBI and some others may over-zealously pursue the enemies of America and wind up being incapable of distinguishing friends from foes. I do respect the ACLU when they are correctly striving to protect us and our freedoms and liberties from the occasional "jack booted thugs" wearing badges. As sure as you are reading this, there are elements of our government who would witlessly suppress the Constitution and the Bill of Rights to combat radical militant Islamic fundamentalist terrorists so that radical militant right -- or left -- wing fundamentalists can take control.........

Profiling

There are three types of profiling.

The first is racial profiling. Simple racial profiling alone is wrong. There are those who use this as a crutch to abuse those of other races. In the war on terrorism and in our life-and-death conflict with Islam, racial profiling alone is dumb, ineffective and will lead to errors that will cause deaths. Those who advocate or practice racial profiling only demonstrate the depth of their ignorance. Race or ethnicity may be a part of an overall profiling, but should never be the sole criteria.

The second, counter-terrorist and criminal profiling is a relatively new science for the United States. The Israelis (and some others) do a fine job of profiling the bad guys. This profiling activity involves reading eyes, emotions, body language, taking cultural dispositions into consideration, and other signs or signals (such as looking for prosthetic pinkie fingers on Japanese visitors to ferret out Yakuza gangsters) and so forth. We have a long ways to go in this science, and we desperately need to do this more, and well.

Let me introduce a third type of profiling that is desperately needed and ought to be put into play. It is career profiling for and within the federal bureaucracy. This would extend even to those not directly involved in the war for survival of the United States.

Some law enforcement agencies use tools such as the Minnesota multi-phasic tests and derivatives to ferret out as best they can those personalities who, when they get a badge pinned on their chest would be inclined to become abusive monsters and bullies. This is good. It does a lot to eliminate "tin star" cops. The FBI needs to use this type of profiling when hiring their Special Agents. All federal agencies involved in law enforcement need this. This should be used periodically throughout a law enforcement official's career, to rein in those who fall out of themselves and lurch over to the dark side.

There is another profiling tool called the Myers-Briggs profiler that needs to be brought into service. If not this one, another that provides similar results is needed. The Myers-Briggs program identifies sixteen basic personality profiles. One of those groups is a group of personalities who tend to be very bright and inquisitive. They are generally sparkling extroverts who are articulate and capable in many ways, and thus get good jobs, good assignments, and promotions, often to management and supervisory jobs. They have one fatal flaw. They love to be informed -- which is good. They love to gather information -- which is good. They have a never ending craving for more information -- which is good. The flaw is that they cannot make a decision without yet ever more information! They are thus nearly incapable of making a decision. It's terrible because they can't really function. These folks are incapable of reasoning things out based on adequate information and arriving at decisions. They just dither!

These are the profiles of the all too typical and often found managers typical of what the Minneapolis FBI Special Agent whistle blower, Colleen Rawley may have encountered when she wanted to go after the French/Arab terrorist, Moussaui. Rawley apparently was on to something and just wanted to investigate further, and sought approval to pursue what she knew in her inner soul to be a solid lead. The officials at FBI headquarters in Washington, D.C., were simply incapable of deciding to go forward and investigate this character. They were timid and overcautious, they didn't have 'enough' information to justify going further. They reflected the typically risk averse career centric types who garner "walk on water" performance evaluations because they are so bright that they sparkle. They badgered the Minneapolis Field Office for more and more detailed information, and asked myriad stupid questions in their quest for yet more, and ever more information, which raised further questions calling for still more information, but no decision. No action was forthcoming. (Now, years after 9/11/2001, we learn that these jerks were rewarded. Rewarded for what? What happened to Agent Rawley? No rewards, no. Obscurity was her reward for a job well done.)

When managers fit the indecisive profile, they need to be directed into jobs, positions, and assignments where there is a need for this thirst for information.

Just like the physically handicapped and the mentally or emotionally challenged of the world, the bright but indecisive ditherers have clear and distinct limitations that must be recognized and dealt with. Never, ever put these bright, indecisive people into supervisory positions, or other responsible authoritative or management positions where decisions need to be made based on a reasonable amount of information. They can't effectively perform this role. They just dither. They always dither, and always will dither. It's a part of their internal wiring. They got us killed. They'll get more of us killed.

Ditherers need to be placed into roles where they and their characters are valuable as advisors, helpers, analysts, collators of intelligence, challengers, but not as decision makers. Making sound decisions is simply not an integral part of their being.

Ditherers are not just in the FBI. They are in all agencies. I've had to deal with them in the Department of State, in industry, as a salesman, as an official, as a customer, all over the place. They are enormously frustrating to work for or to deal with because they simply fail to take action. They are however, very effective at passing along the blame for their failures to their subordinates who "fail to provide adequate information", etc. They are very effective and articulate at blaming, they get rewarded for screwing things up and hurting others who are sincere and able.

Reform and Reorganization
We trained hard, but it seemed that every time
we were beginning to form up into teams,
we would be reorganized. I learned later in life
that we tend to meet any new situation by
reorganization, and a wonderful method it can
be for creating the illusion of progress while
producing confusion, inefficiency and demoralization.
Petronius Arbiter, 210

The government's reorganization and the accompanying reform initiated by President Bush was welcomed on one hand, and dreaded on the other.

In 2008 the Obama campaign was based on just one word: CHANGE! That mantra was also adopted by McCain.

Reorganization or CHANGE! is not a substitute for real, genuine, and effective action. The Bush administration's reorganization of government was a panacea (CYA) for poor performance. Reorganization is not a true remedy and if not done well may in fact lead to even more confusion, friction, bureaucratic inertia - paralysis, and a loss of mission intensity, etc., for years to come. Obama's CHANGE! is not a good change. Obama's CHANGE is destined to fail.

Reforms and change, if sincere need to be carried out by real people, not moralists or ideological zealots such as former Attorney General Ashcroft with his fundamentalist agenda. Neither should the reforms be undertaken by ditherers or legalists who tend to be genuinely confused and contradictory.

The basic focus of the reforms must be to protect the sovereignty of the United States, and to guarantee the Constitution -- our freedoms, our liberty, and the survival - the prevalence of our society and culture.

In the government bureaucracy, there are many who have different agendas that are not consistent with what ought to be the focus of the HDA.

An example of this is in the excellent book, SEE NO EVIL where the author succinctly describes a situation where a spy was being turned over to his new CIA Case Officer by a departing CIA Case Officer. The spy was an atypical spy who was providing useful information that had not been reported to the CIA's headquarters by the (departing) CIA Case Officer. Her agenda was proselytizing -- she was a missionary -- and she was more interested in converting the spy to her particular Christian faith than in serving the security needs of the United States. While her personal agenda may have been personally worthy, she was failing to do the job she was trained and tasked to do.

In effect, the CIA Case Officer was not performing the duties (a dereliction of duty) for which we taxpayers were paying her. According to Baer's book, this had been OK'd by CIA headquarters managers as being an activity protected under the First Amendment. Those particular pinhead managers at CIA headquarters ought to have been charged with Waste, Fraud and Mismanagement (WFMM) for allowing, if not outright encouraging that Case Officer to fail to do her job. She was a functioning missionary at taxpayer expense, to the detriment of our National Security.

Based on my experiences with the CIA and within the government, Baer's account is unfortunately not an isolated incident, but reflects a continuing serious deficiency within the Federal Government.

Employing missionaries as spies is like mixing oil and water. It doesn't work!

I wonder if those pinhead CIA managers who OK'd the Paris

Case Officer's dereliction of duty would have approved an employee's getting involved in gambling, smuggling, or pornography while on duty as being protected under the First Amendment?

In the area of profiling government employees, steps must be taken in selecting, hiring, and promoting to weed-out religious (or other types of) fundamentalists, or misguided idiots who feel it is their duty to sacrifice America to their own personal agendas.

It is OK to have religious beliefs. Most people have them. It is good to have spiritual foundations and convictions, and it's OK to share them -- while off duty. It is wrong to bring them to the workplace and to try to impose this stuff on others just as it is wrong to distribute pornography, use drugs or to drink booze at work, and try to get others to booze it up at work too.

Religious proselytizing at work should fall under the same laws, rules and regulations as partisan political activities in the federal workplace. If an employee of the government does this, they ought to be fired.

Combatant Prisoners

The debate on the status and treatment of detainees held at the United States' Naval base at Guantanamo Bay in Cuba had its own issues.

Those characters, murderous Taliban religious fanatics or Al Qaeda terrorists, received protection and safety (even or especially from one-another), better food, superior medical care, housing in clean and sanitary conditions with adequate, clean clothing, and better all around conditions than in Afghanistan - with better sanitation than in their caves; and freedom to practice their religion.

Liberal civil rights advocates in the United States were seething, ranting and raving because the detainees were not held on U.S. soil. If they were on U.S. soil, the civil rights legal community would have joyfully turned the whole thing into a circus. They are bitter at being denied the opportunity of performing as ringmasters, shills, and hucksters with their walnut shells, and swindling the American taxpayers out of additional millions of dollars.

There was jabbering about the Geneva Convention, and treating them accordingly. The Geneva Convention is a treaty that provides for and protects the rights of uniformed soldiers. None of the core Mohammedan terrorists or Taliban or al Qaeda wear uniforms representing unity or membership with an organized force or a recognizable government. They therefore do not qualify for protection under the Geneva Convention, period. Their organizations or networks are not signatories to the Geneva Convention, so we do not need to reciprocate.

Other liberals demanded that they be assigned attorneys and be tried in civilian courts. While there may be merit to providing civilian representation and trying them in civilian courts because they don't fit the mold of uniformed soldiers vis-à-vis the Geneva convention, this idea is arguably moot. To face trial in a civilian court, there must be witnesses available to testify against them. The principal witnesses available are other core Mohammedans, and that is the crux of the problem. These people are not cognizant of the standards or rules of ethics or civility in a civilization as we know it, and being Mohammedans, they would not testify against other Mohammedans in a court in a Christian, or civilized nation. That is one of their core beliefs, it is a requirement of Islam. In a court they can absolutely be counted on to obfuscate (taqiyyah), lie, commit perjury, and not cooperate. They don't even know what a truth is, so any testimony would be worthless.

In a court, if they were brought into to testify, a judge would need to be prepared to throw the proverbial 'book' at them and provide long, even indefinite jail time for each act of obfuscation (contempt of court), or lying -- committing perjury.

When it came time to begin releasing some of those prisoners, we actually repatriated them back to their home countries. Within weeks, some of them turned up shooting at American troops and killing innocents all over again. A January 2009 Department of Defense report indicated that at least sixty-one of them had become involved in further acts of terrorism. But, this has no meaning for the ACLU pinheads and their fellow travelers. We should have hauled the prisoners a couple of hundred miles off shore from Cuba, showed them the direction of Mecca, and booted them from the choppers and told them to swim home.

Some liberal pinheads got the silly notion that they could call this sanitary, civilized facility in GITMO a gulag. Naturally, there were others that jumped on this fantasy, demonstrating their levels of complete willful ignorance about what a Soviet gulag was. They just want the prisoners released. If released, the prisoners should be let loose, well armed in front of the abodes (or rocks) under witch the pinheads reside, and then let's see who squeals about what is just.

Focus on Terrorism

The days of make-believe should be over.

Fact: This war that Islam is waging against us will never be 'over.' We need to understand that we need not live in perpetual fear, but we do owe it to ourselves to understand that we live in perpetual grave danger.

We are not facing a single state enemy that we can confront and deal with decisively.

We are facing what are essentially networks of fundamentalists who do not belong to a nation per se, even though most of those gangs are sponsored and supported by nation-states such as Iran, Saudi Arabia, the Gulf States, Syria, Indonesia, Pakistan, Egypt, Malaysia, and many others. When we do find a nation-state supporting terrorism, we have an obligation to deal with them as we did in Afghanistan and Iraq. We need to do so with North Korea, Syria, Iran, Saudi Arabia, Libya, Egypt, and those others who are in that rut.

We have a bunch of clowns running around telling themselves that they are waging an effective war on terrorism. They ain't doing it. They have a victory here or there and think they are winning. It's a help, but not the solution.

So far, we have tons of paper filled with sometimes disjointed reports from dozens of mostly politically correct commissions, and some containing some useful information and perhaps even representing money well spent.

Now, we need people to take all of those reports and studies and collate them into coherent sets of indexed and cross-indexed studies, recommendations, and then to create logical, workable action plans.   These action plans need to address dealing with terrorist supporting nation states on one side, and to take on the gangs on the other side. Coordination is a part and parcel of these actions whether focused on a 'big' picture, or pixels within that template.

Serious stuff includes completely eliminating (as in obliterating) threats.   Make-believe nonsense such as airport checks of little old ladies and known prominent people are a waste of talent, money, and energy.

Our national survival is in serious jeopardy because of foolishness promulgated by moronic politicians, faux-intellectuals, joined by Tinseltown weenies and others of their pitiful or simply evil ilk.

State (Islam) Sponsored Terrorism

Our national leadership of elected, bureaucratic, intellectual, and spiritual leaders have not yet come to grips with the awesome enemy that we face.

While they dither and sit on their butts wringing their hands and conduct Congressional hearing after Congressional hearing ad nausea, we remain at risk, dire, increasing risk. That risk grows every day.

The leadership want to treat all acts of terrorism as crimes punishable under existing laws. They want to treat all terrorists as criminals, either as individuals or as gangs. They have gone so far as to recognize some "states" as terrorist sponsors. Wow! That's a great move there. We're claiming that Iran and Syria are terrorist sponsor states. We took out Iraq (for now), Khadaffi and his Libya have "come in from the cold" and is now increasingly a 'friend', and of course there's North Korea.

Bin Laden is considered a clever criminal to be arrested and put in jail after a circus of a trial someplace. Bin Laden went on hiding out in an Islamic "state" (nation) where he probably got the care (medical attention for his reported kidney disease), support, and loving attention and full protection of one or more Islamic governments or Islamic government entities. While we dithered and wondered why nobody would turn bin Laden in and claim his $25 million reward, bin Laden remained free to roam, and to plot further our demise.

There are thousands and thousands of bin Laden cohorts and wannabe's out there working, plotting and preparing deeds, and most of them with the knowledge, care, support, full protection, and loving attention of one or another Islamist "state" nation. And, of course, we'd love to arrest them and try them under some law or another, convict them and send them off to jail. This is really neat stuff here, but it's hardly productive.

Seemingly, nobody has or wants to come to grips with the real fact. None of those pseudo intellectual giants, groveling politicians, or risk averse bureaucrats has what it takes to step up to the plate and begin to point in the direction and show that we are dealing with the dark, sinister political "state" of Islam. The conquest oriented "state" of Islam stretches from islands in the Philippines to the west Coast of Africa, and has growing pockets of conspirators in every other nation on earth. The cultural "state" of Islam that is harboring, funding, protecting, encouraging, sponsoring and plotting for our demise is fifty-eight or so Islamic nations as well as 'cells' in every nation on earth. Islam is not a few criminals, is not a gang, it is not some criminal conspiracy. Islam is more than terrorist, but terrorism is a modus operandi, a very effective way of hurting us, of very successfully diverting and confusing us. We need to devise whole, meaningful ways to deal with the whole enemy – the entire "state" of Islam, of Mohammedism, and its 1.5 billion adherents.......

As regards bin Laden and others like him, we should go to the financial, material sponsors and moral supporters, Saudi Arabia. Bin Laden, with Saudi money, Saudi support, and Saudi love sent nineteen of his Mohammedan cohorts to take down the Twin Towers. And our Presidents and government continue to grovel at the feet of the Saudis. This is an outrage!

Bin Laden's deputy, Abu Zubaydah was picked up in Pakistan, and under Sodium Pentothal gave some information, but not enough. He was secreted into Afghanistan into a fake Saudi type cell and then confronted with two American intelligence agents whom he believed to be Saudis, he was visibly relieved. He spun off a bunch of Saudi names and phone numbers who he claimed would tell the interrogators what to do (about him). The names and phone numbers were accurate. When American officials confronted the Saudi government, suddenly three of those named, before Americans were allowed to talk to them, died of mysterious causes within the same week. They were healthy, robust men. The Saudi government in fact executed them before Americans could talk with them. Why? To protect Saudi princes (Saudi government officials) who were and still are working to support bin Laden and to destroy the United States.

We ought to give the Saudis sixty days to deliver every bit of information they have on the bin Laden wannabes--all of them, and their supporters. If they fail, we should deliver retribution equal to or greater than the losses that occurred on 9/11 which should include the deaths somewhere in Saudi Arabia of 3,000 or so Saudis, and an economic burden equal to the billions the 9/11 events cost us. How do we do this? Use our imagination. I'd suggest that we 'vulcanize' (bomb and burn) all Saudi military facilities in Saudi Arabia, and then take over their banks and oil fields and take out oil to cover the billions we lost. The billions would not be the $100+ and increasing) or so per barrel they charge, but the $5 or so per barrel cost of extracting the oil. Then, we can take out several Saudi and Iranian Embassies delivering amounts of devastation equal to or greater than the losses they and their paid minions have done to us.

Sure this would "outrage" Mohammedans all over the world. Wonderful! Without their Saudi money, many would dry up. For those that don't dry up, we have other equalizers, called bombs.

The threat of reciprocal terrorism that will be equal to or greater than what they want to deliver to is what will work. If and when any one of them goes out and blows himself up taking several of us with him, we reciprocate. We needn't worry about the "nationality" of any particular perpetrator as long as we clobber something somewhere in the global Islamist "state", using a rolling roster if we would, of locations, including mosques wherever they are.

At the end of 2008 after several years of enduring over 8,000 rockets launched at them by Mohammedist thugs, Israel responded by crushing parts of Gaza. The Israelis used their overwhelming brain power, courage, technological superiority, and excellent military to effect success. Naturally the anti-Semites of the world went into a tizzy. Among other things, some of them demanded that Israel's response to Moslem attacks be proportionally limited. In a sense, I agree - to a proportional response based on demographics. There are about 1,500,000,000 Moslems in the world vs. about 15,000,000 Jews. For every attack launched at Jews wherever they are, the Jews should be entitled to proportionally attack Moslems. That number, unless my math errs comes down to 100. Every time a Jew is murdered, they should be entitled to kill 100 Moslems in 'proportional' response. That's fair. The body count may not be performed by Moslems because they will simply lie.

Liberalism

Liberalism is a type of deficiency, perhaps even a disease (as stated by activist, writer, and genius Michael Savage), but a useful one. We need liberals just as much as we need lunatics. Those of us not suffering from liberalism need the liberals to help keep us in balance, to keep us reminded of who we are.

203

We need to keep the soft-on-Islam liberalism willful ignorance in check. This is an absolute. Never should we elect as President someone like 'Hillary', or a Marxist communist devotee like Obama (but we did), or the hero of Chappaquiddick – Edward (Ted) Kennedy (who were it not for his father's money and his brothers' fame would be on welfare, or rightfully in prison for manslaughter), like the craven, feckless, omni-directional dolt, John F. Keary, or any other flaky liberal. These people are profoundly out of touch with all but their silliness. Sadly, they have a lot of devotees, and the reality of 9/11 did not adequately get their attention. They believe that if we try to appease the Mohammedans (as the French and British, and the Dutch, and Swedes, and the Norwegians, and the Danes have done), that the Jihadis will leave us alone and go away and play with themselves. It ain't going to happen!

Liberals in general are real, genuine, pie-in-the-sky willfully ignorant idiots, and perhaps cowards. They go out with slogans and placards in safe places, prefer to appear openly on streets with police protection, on university campuses, and other well protected places to demonstrate against America and the greatness that it is and the goodness that it stands for.   Why don't they round themselves up and go to Tehran and demonstrate against nuclear weapons proliferation, or go to Mecca or Medina in Saudi Arabia to demonstrate for women's rights, religious freedom, and civil rights. How about going to North Korea to demonstrate for free, democratic elections and a multi-party system? They don't dare to do that because they know that they'd be killed or imprisoned for having the temerity to express such opinions in those places.

A favorite of the liberal anti-war types is sloganeering out there in fantasyland. One slogan is *"War Never Solves Anything!"*

Wrong! War does indeed solve things, especially for the winner. War won America's independence, it stopped slavery in America, defeated the Nazis, saved South Korea, and can prevent the Islamists from enslaving the world.

Liberals run around insipidly bleating that we need to understand the root causes of the Mohammedans' discontent. That's incredibly easy to understand. The cause of Islam's discontent is our very existence. Duuuhh!

Retired Air Force General George Hawley spoke out with some really good common sense statements: 1) "Our country has, with all our mistakes and blunders, always been and always will be the greatest beacon of freedom, charity, opportunity, and affection in history." If you need proof, open the borders and see what happens. 2) "Violence only leads to violence." This is one so stupid, you usually have to be the president of an Ivy league university to say it. The truth is that ineffective, unfocused violence leads to more violence. Limp, panicky, half-measures lead to more violence. However, complete, fully thought through, professional well-executed violence never leads to more violence because, you see, afterwards, the other guys are dead. 3) "The CIA and the rest of our intelligence community have failed us." For 25-years, we have chained our spies like dogs to a stake in the ground, and now that the house has been robbed, we yell at them for failing us. Starting in the late seventies under Carter's Stansfield Turner, the giant brains who get these ideas decided that the best way to gather international intelligence was to use spy satellites. "After all, they reasoned, you can see a license plate from 200 miles away." This knowledge is very helpful if you've been attacked by a license plate. Unfortunately, we were attacked by humans. Finding humans is not yet possible with satellites. You have to use other humans. When we bought all our satellites, we fired our humans, and here's the really stupid part. It takes years, decades to infiltrate new humans into the worst places of the world. You can't just have a guy who looks like Gary Busey in a Spring Break '93 plop himself down in a coffee shop in Kabul and say "Hiya boys. Gee, I sure would like to meet that bin Laden fellow." 4) "These people are poor and helpless, and that's why they're angry at us." Uh-huh, and Jeffry Dahmer's frozen head collection was just a desperate cry for help. The terrorists and their backers are richer than Sean Penn, and ironically, a good deal less annoying. The poor helpless people, you see, are the villagers they tortured and murdered to stay in power. Mohammed Atta, one of the evil scumbags who steered those planes into the killing grounds is the son of a Cairo surgeon. 5) "Any profiling is racial profiling." Who's killing us here, the Girl Scouts, Hawaiians, Canadians, Icelanders, the Norwegians? Just days after the attack, the New York Times had an article saying dozens of extended members of the bin Laden family living in America were afraid of reprisals and left in a huff, never to return to studying at Harvard and using too much Drakkar. 6) Here's a resolve to keep: Never forget our murdered brothers and sisters. Never let the relativists get away with their immoral thinking. After all, no matter what some moronic political science professor says, we did NOT start this.

TURNING TERRORISTS
AND MURDERERS FREE

Barak Hussein Obama has plans to let 9/11 mastermind, Khalid Sheikh Mohammed go free.

Before I go into this, I need to go back a bit in American history to provide a basis for understanding.

CRIMINAL TRIALS

Celebrity O. J. Simpson (OJ) murdered his wife, Nicole. Of that, there is little doubt. He was brought to trial where he was not found guilty, and was set free. This was a travesty of justice committed by high officials for politically convenient reasons.

The evidence was there, the motive, the weapons, and the evidence was overwhelming. OJ was hugely popular in the black community, and the consideration that he only killed his wife, a white woman in a fit of jealousy led political leaders to make a fateful decision. It was believed that OJ would not be a threat to other people if turned free because the savage murder of Nicole was merely the result of a domestic dispute.

There was a widely felt believe, an understanding that if OJ were convicted, there would be race riots in Los Angeles, that many people would die, business would be affected, and all sorts of conjecture about the ill effects of a conviction. He and Nicole lived in an upscale neighborhood that was primarily white, Brentwood, and a trial (by jury) there would likely have brought a guilty verdict. Such a verdict was deemed intolerable because of the perceived adverse impact it would have in the Los Angeles area, and perhaps in other parts of the country.

Behind closed doors and far from public scrutiny, the Mayor, of Los Angeles, the District Attorney and others gathered to conspire and develop a strategy to pull the wool over the eyes of the public, to get OJ acquitted, and to hell with the law and justice.

First, they decided to change the venue from the mainly white Brentwood where a conviction was all but assured with an educated, informed, white jury. They decided to move the trial venue to a neighborhood where the conspirators determined that mostly illiterate people sympathetic to OJ could be loaded onto the jury.

They next decided to put together a prosecutorial team of marginal attorneys (losers consisting of one black male, one white male, one white female) who would not be able to put together or manage a strong case. Soon after the trial started, the one white male prosecutor apparently figured out what was happening, that everything had been stacked against the prosecutors, got himself off of the case. He was not replaced. The black male prosecutor became "ill" and performed his duties marginally. The burden was left to the white female prosecutor who was probably overwhelmed and thus did not do as well as she ought to have done.

A weak judge was selected to preside over the case where his control would be marginal and letting the defense set the agenda, the tone, and the pace of the trial.

OJ was acquitted, there were no riots, business continued to prosper, and OJ went free.

Trial of KSM

The following is a prediction. Let's hope that I am wrong, or that this, when it gets out there and is being discussed will cause Barak Hussein Obama to back off on what I suspect is a diabolical plan to turn Khalid Sheikh Mohammed (KSM) free. The trial of 9/11 mastermind,

Khalid Sheikh Mohammed and his co-conspirators is being carefully orchestrated to follow a strategy to get him spun loose, to set him free, to reward him for his role in murdering 3,000 innocents.

While Attorney General Holder announced his (surprising?) decision on November 17, 2009, to hold the trial in New York, the Governor of New York had been advised way back in the spring of 2009 that the trial would take place in New York. This meant that a determination to set the venue in a civilian court had already been determined, but that the American people not be informed until later when the stage was better set.

The implication of a trial in a civilian court in New York is clear. It will be a jury trial, where the process of jury selection will result in jurors who are peers – Moslems.

Barak Hussein Obama, on his Asian tour in November of 2009, carefully orchestrated a slip of the tongue (a determination that KSM was guilty and would be sentenced to death) determined to set a precedent that the defense attorneys will use to declare that the POTUS had prejudiced the case against KSM and his crew. This declaration by the President of the United States, the highest authority in the nation has set that issue up for exploitation by KSM's legal defense team. A day later, Attorney General Holder did the same thing, further "prejudicing" the case against KSM with an additional statement for the defense legal team to exploit.

Just to help things along, we can expect that the government's (carefully selected by Holder) prosecutorial team will be a cast of characters who are, like the team that prosecuted OJ Simpson, of limited competence at best. I'd like to say that the deck will be set against them, but they in fact will be a part of the deck, and will be handicapped at every turn. The same standard will apply to selecting a marginally effective judge who will preside over the case.

So, the deal has been set. The fix is in. KSM will be tried in an atmosphere where his defense team can justifiably claim that the President and the Attorney General prejudiced the case against him (KSM). The trial (by jury) venue will be in a civilian court where Moslem jurors will NOT (no way, Charlie) vote to convict, where Moslem jurors simply will NOT vote for the death penalty (it is against Islamic law to vote to kill another Moslem).

Barak Hussein Obama has thus conspired to set KSM and his co-conspirators free. Obama and Holder have set the stage. Obama has deliberately sabotaged America's national security! This is treason!

Chapter 12

DETERMINATION

It is said that there is no question to what one can do if truly determined and dedicated. We face determined and dedicated fundamentalists who are ready to die to achieve our destruction. They are dying, and they are still growing in numbers.

Are we determined and ready to dedicate ourselves to survive as a nation, survive as a culture, survive as a civilization? Are we ready and prepared to do all of what it will take in view of their absolute determination to do or die? The answer must be yes. The alternative is our demise.

Women who send their children
to blow themselves up

Many Moslem women gladly send their sons to die as Martyrs. Why? Why gladly?

Living in the Middle East for a decade, one cannot help but to see, and to observe, and to learn, to draw personal conclusions based on what one sees as I did.

Males are considered to be superior, and females inferior. That is it. That is what Mohammed, the woman hating baby rapist pederast taught his followers, and what his 1.5 billion faithful followers practice today. Women are chattel, to be used, as the narcissist woman hating Mohammed taught, as tillage (dirt) for men to use as they see fit. Forced into arranged marriages not of their own choosing women and even some men are bound in misery.

The women must suffer because they have no way out. If they abandon their marriages, their fathers, brothers, or cousins will murder them for the sake of family honor. Their feelings do not matter, it's the men's stupid sense of honor.

Men bound up in arranged or failed marriages to women they don't love or want take their anger and frustration out on their wives. They beat them, abuse them, mock them, and just make their lives miserable. The women have two choices, to suffer on, or to commit suicide because there is almost never a way out for them, other than somehow killing their abusive husbands and getting away with it. The numbers of women who die from self inflicted injuries are NOT documented in Moslem societies. Their astounding numbers would be incredibly embarrassing for those crappy Moslem governments who cover those very horrifying facts up.

In watching TV, have you observed the Moslem women cloaked

in black lamenting loudly (it's compulsory) when someone in their family dies? Have you noticed their missing, broken teeth? While they may look fifty at thirty, they don't have candy and other sweets to rot their teeth. Those broken teeth got broken in violence, what we call incidents of domestic violence. They have been beaten by their spouses, and in some cases by their sons, brothers, cousins, and fathers.

These women have children, and few of those children are love children. They are children of forced marriages, and often forced and even violent copulation.

These women are stuck with children, and in some cases are not happy with their children. Oh, yes, they take care of them, or suffer severe consequences. Some have a powerful maternal instinct that carries them through.

I have often seen spoiled, nasty little Moslem boys slap and kick their mothers, who just try to appease the little crap heads. The women are not allowed to strike back, to defend themselves. They have to do what they can best do to defend themselves. They teach their daughters how to avoid confrontations, because the little boys are also allowed to beat the crap out of their sisters, often with impunity.

So, the boys grow up to be bullies, and their sisters just suffer. That's their life style. That's their culture.

Mothers in these cases become insane in ways, and act on their insanity, sometimes committing suicide to end their tragically miserable lives.

Or, they try ways to retaliate as well. When retaliating, they must be subtle. Sometimes it's infanticide. They kill their boy babies to deny their husbands, or kill their girl babies to protect them from their inevitable suffering. They otherwise encourage their sons to be martyrs. The sooner the little jerk dies, the better off she, the mother will be, and also she will get the rare instance of secret inner joy of seeing their vile, bastard husbands suffer the losses of their precious but otherwise useless sons.

The women can encourage their daughters to be martyrs as well. In becoming martyrs, their daughters will thus avoid the suffering and misery of being a Moslem wife. Some women will even encourage their daughters to break Mohammedan taboos so that they will be killed for the sake of family "honor." The girls will die young and early, before spending their lives in abject, prolonged misery.

What motivates Moslem women to commit the ultimate deed, to blow themselves to bits and pieces?

Recently, Iraqis wrapped some mentally handicapped women in high explosives and sent them into a market, and when the poor women reached an area full of people, they exploded, murdered by their handlers. This is the most heinous, ruthless and cruel treatment of unfortunate women.

Other women willingly(?) blow themselves up. The explanations given are generally false (taqiyyah) when portrayed by

Moslems. Still, the female assassins are sad, unfortunate pawns of all that is evil in Islam. Mohammed, the woman hating baby raping pedophile taught that women were dirty and that they were inherently evil; and therefore that eighty percent of them would go to hell, that it was the law of allah. Mohammed also taught that the only way for a woman to be assured passage into heaven was to become a martyr, to die in jihad.

In this same vein, Mohammed taught that only 20% of men would go to hell, and that 80% of men would go to heaven no mater what they did nor now they lived their lives.

Chapter 13

AMERICA, THE TARGET

Europe and United States of America are the principal (but not only) targets of Mohammedan domination, led by jihad and taqiyyah in every form. The remaining countries of the world are also marked. And, or course Israel is a special case and America's unequivocal support of Israel drives the haters of civilization nuts.

The majority of Europeans, too intimidated, too frightened to support Israel like the United States does, and therefore won't even support the United States. They are cowards, perhaps genetically so.

For hundreds of years the Samurai ruled Japan with a sharp blade. Anyone who didn't go along with the program got their heads neatly sliced off. A couple of hundred years of such "culling" left a nation of people who are somewhat genetically predisposed to follow orders, and to be cooperative and respectful.

Europe has suffered through horrific wars in recent centuries that killed off millions of spirited, incredibly courageous, aggressive, men, the kind of men who are inclined to do the right thing as opposed to men who cower in fear. Thus, the gene pool of Europe has been adversely affected, or culled, and those men who avoided fighting in the great wars and thus survived to spawn more of their own genetic types have been able to spread their more dominant genes of risk-aversion, or cowardice.

The future of Islamic terrorist attacks against
the United States and the West is
not an if.
The future of Mohammedan terrorist attacks against
the United States and the West is
one of magnitude
and
when, what, where, and how.

While the Mohammed emulating terrorists who struck the USA on 9/11/2002 were determined and dedicated, they ought to have been stopped long before they struck. Due to American bumbling and the Islamists' luck, they succeeded.

While the Mohammedans determined to destroy the United States have access to sophistication in the areas of weapons and technology, they are not very good at using it. When they are successful however, it is due more to luck than to skill. For every success, there are hundreds of failures. They bumble and screw up more than the FBI and CIA combined, and that's a great (as in a lot) deal of screw-ups that work to our benefit. Practice makes perfect, and each time they try and fail, they also get a little better.

They are ideologically committed and therefore willing to gamble, and gamble again until they succeed. They are not diabolically clever or brilliant, they are however persistent. Each attempt however unsuccessful builds on their skills and abilities, and attracts more and ever more talent from the millions of human sources they can draw from.

Here are some of the things we need to consider: bombs, hijackings, cyber, chemical, biological, and nuclear, attacks.

BOMBS

At an appropriate time determined by our foes, we may see a beginning and then an increasing use of car/truck and other types of bombs in the United States.

Bombs are relatively cheap to build, are low technology and reliable, are accurate and easy to deliver to a target. Stolen and rented cars and trucks (trailers) will be one method. Motorcycles can be useful in certain circumstances although they can't carry enough explosives to cause a truly spectacular blast (unless it's a big "road bike" such as a six cylinder Honda, a Harley Davidson, or other similar capacity motorcycle with a trailer).

There will be more backpack bombs too. And then, there are booby traps.

--Here's a scenario: Every commercial or industrial entity must have their portable fire extinguishers serviced yearly. These include factories full of hazardous or highly explosive materials, hospitals, schools, stores, restaurants, government offices, everything. This process calls for removal of the extinguishers to an area where they are emptied, opened, checked and serviced, refilled, pressurized and then brought back into the facility.   Usually, this is in back of the building or otherwise away from high traffic areas. The reason for this is that when the technician is emptying or depressurizing the extinguisher, they can "pop" and blow the chemicals out. This is hugely messy (dust), and the best way to avoid inconveniencing people, the servicing is done away from them.

Extinguishers are often installed near doors, and are otherwise strategically located throughout a facility. In ballrooms, plants, and warehouses, the extinguishers are often hung on supporting columns. What if a terrorist stuffed high explosives and timers or remote controlled detonators in several extinguishers, to be set off one at a time, or all at once, and only when a desired effect is planned, possibly months after the "servicing" was done.

VIPs like the President, Vice President are on the move a lot, and they visit auditoriums, hotels, ballrooms, etc. Does the President's Secret Service bodyguard detail check each and every one of the fire

214

extinguishers, or otherwise establish some sort of control of them? One could be wired to go off when the VIP walks by.

Combined with the release of a chemical agent such as sarin gas, or flammables, or nuclear stuff, or whatever you can imagine, such an attack would be catastrophic.

Targets for bombs include nearly everything from bridges carried out by bombs in rental trucks or trailers; aqueducts and water pipelines, gas lines, fuel tank farms, power distribution lines, school busses, strategic manufacturers, subways and rail lines, chemical plants and facilities, etc. Use your imagination.

To cause maximum disruption and economic damage, bridges can make great targets. Taking down a bridge over a river is a tough job, but there are thousands of bridges over freeways and railroad tracks. Driving down roads on hot summer days, all too often you will see big eighteen wheeled semi trucks, or even rental vans parked in the shade under a bridge, presumably so a driver can get some rest in the shade, or possibly broken down there and waiting for service. Police and Highway Patrol vehicles routinely drive right on past these trucks without paying them any attention, thus giving a potential bomber a pass to take his time to do it right.

Bombs can even be used in combination with chemical, biological, or radiological stuff to raise the ante.

An enormous threat that scares the heck out of authorities consists of a radiological weapon, a 'dirty' bomb. It uses nuclear materials but is not an atomic bomb. Setting a few hundred or even a few thousand pounds of polluted radiological waste (from x-ray, or nuclear medicine sources) on top of several thousand pounds of high explosives is quite feasible. It could be placed into a 40-foot shipping container on a ship, or even made locally in an eighteen wheeled truck. Setting one off in say, Long Beach, California at three in the afternoon when a nice onshore breeze generally prevails would cause the plume of poisons to be carried into Los Angeles and inland for several if not dozens of miles affecting hundreds of thousands of people. Few people would die initially, but the long term adverse effects would have an enormous impact. The initial blast killing a few would cause crisis levels of fear and panic with millions of people. Are the civil authorities well prepared to deal with something such as this? Nope! Their heads are in the sand.

HIJACKINGS

Aircraft hijackings and other hijackings such as trains, ships, passenger and school busses are a real, continuing and present threat. They need not be much of a future threat.

In the United States, the huge expense of hiring, training, and maintaining a force of Federal air Marshals and eventually sustaining them in retirement is not fiscally reasonable, nor should it be necessary.

In fact, there are very few air marshals flying, and they are easily identifiable to hijackers.

After a long effort, airline pilots have been allowed after training to carry guns on their planes. This is good. This is another deterrent. This is a good redundancy. This is something that some insecure, risk-averse federal bureaucrats didn't want and resisted.

Using modern, presently existing technology, flight decks and flight cabins of aircraft can be remotely monitored for trouble. This can also be done with ships, trains, and busses, etc.

On aircraft, fail-safe computer systems can and should be installed that when triggered would take command of and fly the aircraft to the nearest airport for an emergency landing. While the computer takes over either on a command from the pilot, or ground personnel (based on monitoring, reports, signals, etc.), it can broadcast its plight (a hijacking for instance) all of the way to its landing. Ground based pilots can monitor the computer and/or take control and fly the plane as is done today with   [[xxxxx this portion has been censored by the Department of State and/or the CIA xxxxx]]   USAF drones, etc. If this technology is not applied to all commercial aircraft, then someone is guilty of incredible stupidity.

The USAF has a successful, tested, and working program right now to soon start building pilotless high performance fighter jets and bombers that are more demanding to control than commercial airliners.

These systems should be installed soon on all commercial aircraft so that when or if a hijacking occurred, the plane's control would be denied to the hijackers, and the plane flown safely to a landing where the hijackers would have to deal with other issues.

Air Marshals would be redundant on these planes.

Yes, idiots would still try to take over aircraft and would perhaps kill some people or make them hostages, but they would flat out be unable to use the planes as weapons, or to go where they felt they could gain an advantage.

Similar fail-safe monitoring and control systems can be installed on ships to cause them to drop anchor, or move to a certain location if something untoward were to take place. Busses and trains can be made to just slow and stall out.

Millions of truck movements take place daily in the United States. More than 80,000 of those movements involve explosives, flammables, and dangerous, toxic chemicals and poisons. It took nearly five long years for the government to just start to get around to establishing a bare minimum standard for identifying hazmat trained drivers. Still, there are no worthy screening procedures of these drivers, many of whom have Middle Eastern origins.

Fuel trucks move about airports every day. They are at small airports, medium sized, and large ones, some filled with thousands of travelers at different times. They are fuel trucks and they carry jet fuel (kerosene) and some still carry more highly volatile gasoline to fuel small planes, cargo planes, and passenger aircraft. Unguarded, it would be very easy to hijack a tanker with up to 9,000 gallons of highly volatile gasoline or fuel and crash it into a terminal building creating an inferno that could murder thousands. Authorities have largely done nothing to protect travelers from this very real threat. It would not be complex nor very costly to do so. Authorized fuel tanker operators are or should be assigned to appropriate trucks and the trucks equipped with keypads, weight sensors in the seat (trucks should only have only one seat in special, single driver cabs) and biometrics such as fingerprint or eye scanners, and only when all three (or four) screening devices agree should the vehicle engine start or continue to run, etc.

KIDNAPPING & HOSTAGE TAKING

While politically inspired kidnapping and hostage taking is no longer in vogue, it remains and will always be an option.

The United States wisely established a strong and unchanging policy of refusing to negotiate with hostage takers. We lost a few people initially, but because such acts of terrorism bore very few successes, the terrorists gave up on this approach.

At the same time, we developed and maintain, and insisted that our government officials take precautions and follow security procedures that worked, and work today. We can never back away from this and this is a continuing daily victory on our part.

CHEMICAL, BIOLOGICAL, RADIOLOGICAL/NUCLEAR

The Chemical, biological and radiological/nuclear (CBRN) threat is enormous and has some of the greatest potential for damage.

We desperately need a national health surveillance network to track illnesses and to be able to detect any such biological (germ warfare) attacks and then deal with them expeditiously. There are ongoing efforts to do this, but we are not moving along as quickly as we can. When we get clobbered, we'll know the results of our dereliction.

There are thirty-six (36) known microbes and toxins that are particularly dangerous, and not all of them are well controlled. Neither the CIA nor the FBI can confirm or deny the existence of any others, or that something new could be under development as a weapon, a nasty surprise weapon.

There are more than 1500 biological culture collections worldwide that our intelligence community THINKS they know of, but nobody knows exactly how many and where they are.

Early in 2009 about forty al-Qaeda members died horrible deaths in the Atlas Mountains of Algeria. They were diagnosed to have died of the plague. The manner in which they suffered was reportedly horrible and prolonged. Initially, people thought that they contacted Bubonic Plague from rats who shared the caves these guys were living in. Further study revealed that these deaths were not from Bubonic Plague. These men died from some form of Pneumonic Plague, and that it was likely man-made (weaponized), and that the deaths were the result of an experiment gone awry. This is frightening. This also confirms that there are people out there who are advancing in their capabilities to create a weaponized germ warfare disease that could be unleashed at any time.

More than a dozen countries hostile to the United States are known to have biological weapons programs and stockpiles. This is what the authorities know. What about that which they know nothing of? And, there is plenty that they know nothing about.

Our government has an obligation to defend us in these areas, and it is understandable that this is a complex and dangerous area to be addressed.

Without viable human intelligence, the detection of novel, advanced bioengineered pathogens is nearly impossible to determine. And, if they are used against us, the effect could be worse than any disease ever known to mankind, especially if we have no antidotes.

In 1993, the United States Government naively entered into a pie-in-the sky Chemical Weapons Convention that restricted the United States' abilities to learn and understand more about chemical weapons. The treaty calls for all countries to stop creating biological and chemical weapons, and to destroy all of the facilities they have. Pie in the sky Clinton era liberals thought this would be another end-all. If anyone truly believes for a minute that China, Russia, India, Iran and other signatories to this treaty will adhere 100% to it is a pinheaded simpleton. Further, many countries have refused to sign on, and their chemical and biological weapons programs are running on full tilt.

Yet, there are certain fools, mostly political liberals who yet insist that all we need to do is to strengthen the treaty and all will be nice and cozy. Morons!

What the treaty is actually doing is causing and enabling those countries actively involved in developing such weapons to work harder and work better. Denied access to our materials and equipment, those that are rogues are being forced to engineer and design and build their own highly sophisticated equipment and create their own materials in secret. This is good for them and their economies. But, by not knowing what they are buying or obtaining, building, or creating, we are less able to know or understand what they are doing and/or how successful their programs are.

It's a catch-22 situation. We can sell rogues the equipment and materials they desire and therefore help them develop chemical and biological weapons that we know about. Or, we force them to develop their own possibly new and more dangerous, and certainly less understood (by us) technology and not know what they are doing, therefore making ourselves more vulnerable in the long run.

This just addresses independent nations who have programs.

There are terrorist cells and privately run and funded organizations that are entirely clandestine, more difficult to find, and these can be far more dangerous.

Over the years, Syria, North Koreans, Iran, and others have sent "medical" teams to work with the stricken victims of Ebola - hemorrhagic fevers in Africa. Have they worked to cure the illness? Have these teams worked to ease the suffering of the ill? Yeah, sure! These teams have in fact collected specimens and brought them back to their respective countries. Why? We need to develop these biological agents as weapons.

Once the evil rogues and monsters manage to refine and "weaponize" virulent, communicable hemorrhagic fevers and other diseases such as Plague, Smallpox, Pneumonia, Polio, Dengue, Meningitis, Malaria, Yellow Fever, and others, there will be simple hell to pay. Durable, long lived toxic chemicals that "multiply" themselves are another horrible threat.

We should all take careful note of our government's actions of June 28, 2002, when 20,000 high tech, state-of-the-art multi-purpose gas masks were hurriedly made available to our governmental leaders in Washington. Those items are being updated and replaced regularly as they age and deteriorate. There is a deep and disturbing meaning behind this, and this action does not instill a great deal of confidence (of government actions) in me. None of these "leaders" trumpet the fact that they, their families, and their staffs are being protected while you and I are being left out here uninformed and totally defenseless.

The Center for Disease Control (CDC) says it's ready for terrorist threats. This readiness should be questioned. Coming from an agency whose managers feel it's a wise investment of millions of dollars of their limited funds to get involved in social programs that are rightfully the purview of other agencies, I find this claim to be suspect if not completely false.

First, the funding to be fully staffed, equipped, and prepared is not there. Organization and coordination all of the way down to local health department offices and groups has not yet occurred.

The CDC doesn't have in place any reliable method of quickly and affirmatively identifying an attack. The CDC must rely on a possibly astute local physician or first responder to sound the first alarm, which at the very best will or could be hours after an attack, which will be too late for many hundreds if not thousands.

The CDC has limited stockpiles of antibiotics and vaccines, all in centralized locations, often away from vulnerable population centers. When an attack occurs, it will take additional hours and hours to get these out and disbursed into useful service. That, of course is if the attack doesn't adversely affect the CDC locations first.

The CDC doesn't talk about well established plans for bulldozers for mass burials, body bag stockpiles, and **barbed wire and chain** barricades, and armed troops to "quarantine" afflicted citizens --

you and I, and our children and, loved ones.

Things do look slightly better in a couple of areas. Public health offices (epidemiologists) in Los Angeles have developed and are using (and refining) a database system that constantly gathers information (symptoms and treatments) from a variety of medical sources such as hospitals, clinics, etc. This information can hopefully spot unusual occurrences early and trigger responses. It's a vast improvement over hoping and praying that some doctor or nurse will be astute enough to pick up early on something unusual.

The CDC is also diverting some of its money from nonsense areas into a similar symptom surveillance system. They were 'shamed' into doing this.

These new and developing surveillance systems will only pick up on diseases or attacks after they have occurred. That isn't prevention! It is earlier containment though, in that it can identify problems in a few days rather than weeks, and that will save lives.

What is needed is something more. And, the technology is already available, but needs to be brought forward and enhanced. Biological detectors that can be placed in areas where a lot of people travel or congregate and can be used to pick up on a chemical or biological weapon before people are affected.

Chemical plants, refineries, and manufacturing plants, handlers, shippers, and factories that store, mix, and use large quantities and varieties of chemicals are especially vulnerable to terrorist attack. Many of these more than 15,000 plants located throughout the United States are in populated areas, and contain powerful and deadly toxins and combinations of chemicals which when combined can create powerful blasts disbursing vast amounts of deadly poisons, even mixed cocktails of indescribably awful poisons.

These are nightmare propositions! 15,000 plants, located in every city and in most towns. Potentially huge bombs! Deadly poison cocktails. What is being done to protect you and I? Less than we would expect, or deserve.

The chemical industry, including some of those who handle and use chemicals have been reviewing and updating their procedures. Impressive, eh?

The government ought to be doing more. Some legislators, both Democrats and Republicans have drafted and submitted improved terrorism-specific security requirements (Environmental Protection Agency) rules requiring these industries to tighten up. But, let's not forget that these powerful, wealthy, well funded corporations -- industries all have their lobbyists in Washington busily paying your Senators and Congressmen to NOT take action; and a majority have accepted that money, including Presidents. So, no action is being taken. These industries insist that they are doing what is necessary and that further regulation would hinder their progress. That's pure unadulterated bulls...baloney!

They are doing what is important to them -- protecting their bottom line, that of making lots of money and leaving you and I at great and increasing risk.

I'm not a great supporter of big government except when it's necessary, and here is an area where big brother needs to step in with regulations as well as criminal penalties for officers of those companies that are neglectful.

Company bosses have stated that if they received taxpayer funded subsidies they'd do a lot more. Yeah, they want you and I to pay for improvements that will make them more money.

Some corporate leaders have expressed their professional consciences in the most callous and cavalier fashion with stated or secret intentions to just declare bankruptcy should such an event occur, and then move on, leaving your rotting carcasses behind. That's exactly what an American company (Union Carbide) did in Bhopal, India after their negligence caused thousands of deaths, prolonged agony and continuing suffering for thousands more.

Many insurance companies have dropped terrorism insurance coverage, especially chemical manufacturers and users that are uninterested in doing the right thing. State insurance commissioners need to review the licenses of insurance companies to make them provide appropriate terrorism insurance.

State regulators should shut down those high risk chemical manufacturing and user associated companies that don't have terrorism insurance. Private citizens should be enabled to independently investigate and publish reports to this end.

When your Senator or Congressman runs for election again, vote not for partisan reasons for a change. Learn what their voting record is regarding your safety, how much they take from which lobbyists, and then vote accordingly.

Even better than looking at the Washington politicos, get involved with your town, city, and county politicians, who are more likely to be your neighbors and who may share your concerns.

FEMA and Concentration Camps

Sometime in 2004, the Federal Emergency Management Agency (FEMA) was charged with establishing and equipping six major concentration type holding camps at six locations (military bases) around the country. This fact did not become a factor until after Barak Hussein Obama was installed as President in 2009. The many millions of concerned Americans who are clearly fearful or apprehensive about Obama's anti-constitution socialist, even fascist agenda and close ties with people who hate America jumped on this claiming that these concentration camps were built just for American patriots. That reality could come to pass.

However, the main motivation for the establishment of the

camps is for another extremely sinister purpose. Islam! America hating Islamists are known to be working at developing and deploying infectious bacteriological or viral weapons. To protect the unaffected population from such an attack, those infected or diseased would be rounded up and moved into these camps for the purpose of quarantining them away from the healthy members of the population. It was revealed in January of 2009 that about forty Algeria based al-Qaeda had recently died horrible deaths after contacting some form of ultra deadly bubonic or pneumonic plague. Some chuckled that these cave dwellers got it from rodents. Others more realistically believe that these al-Qaeda deaths were because of a biological warfare experiment gone awry.

Those camps are also available for another type of emergency that could arise out of the civil war raging in Mexico, or possibly even in Europe. Drug gang-wars have boiled over into a nationwide conflict between the Mexican government and the bad guys. If the Mexican government collapses and ceases to function, we will have millions of desperate refugees pouring over the borders that our political leadership have refused to protect. Rather than let them run amok all over the country, these camps would be employed to control and shelter them.

A fourth consideration regarding these camps would be to take in and protect refugees from a natural disaster of major proportions. The hurricane that wiped out New Orleans clearly established the real and genuine need for such facilities should a huge natural disaster occur. It could be something like another hurricane, flooding, a really fearsome earthquake or caldera.

A fifth consideration would be to house survivors of a nuclear attack.

VACCINATIONS

We need to continue improvement of our national vaccination programs. These need to include all past as well as present diseases, and be applied to the entire population.

So far, the United States has countermeasures (we think) for a handful of more than fifty known bio threats.

What are we getting besides equivocation?

Smallpox is a major threat. It is known or understood that bad guys are working to weaponize an enhanced version of this horrible disease. We need to re-establish a vaccination program immediately to begin protecting folks. Polio vaccinations are a must for all. Outside of the United States, vaccinations against tuberculosis is a common practice, and this needs to be done in the United States, as well as for Hepatitis. Of course, we need to revitalize our Typhoid, Yellow Fever, and many other programs.

Let's cut to the quick about secret government biological weapons programs. All of the secrecy aside, the U.S. government has worked on a variety of biological weapons programs in the past. They claim to have abandoned, or closed some of these down, etc., which is all fine and good and in compliance with unverifiable un-universal, and unenforceable treaties. Let's understand clearly that besides U.S. programs, other countries have continued with their programs, and if the CIA has done its job at all, we ought to know about at least a few of these.

Cut the subterfuge and lying, dump the dumb treaties and get going on these various and sundry biological programs and develop preventative and protective programs that will protect the entire population, not just a few "important" officials. Besides, if we are all hurt or made ill, or are dead, there won't be anyone around or left over to recognize the significant or insignificant importance of "important" officials, etc......

NUCLEAR

Our nuclear facilities are vulnerable. So say many. Our nuclear facilities are safe and well protected. So say many. Someone is wrong~

I'd guess that a containment dome can be breached with a fully laden jumbo jet propelled at full speed, by a stolen bunker buster bomb, or a monster such as the BLU82.

Then, of course there are the ponds of contaminated water used to cool "spent" fuel which are wide open, and that is another point of vulnerability. There are lots of ways to cause some of that dangerously radio active material to be blown into the air, on a breezy day so the poisons can be carried by winds and affect far more people than conventional experts and wisdom want to admit.

It's not likely that bin Laden or one of those zealots could get their hands on a bunker buster or BLU-82. So they say. But, anything is possible to someone determined and willing to sacrifice all to achieve an objective.

For starters, we ought to conduct tests against domes. If the domes are proven to be vulnerable, we will have to build protective caps over the reactor domes, on which a weapon would destroy itself. That's a no brainer.

What about an eighteen wheeled semi truck loaded with eighty thousand pounds of high explosives driven into a nuclear reactor site, or into a cooling pond? Think of the possibilities....

Moslem Pakistan has nuclear weapons, and as long as the fragile but nuclear responsible Pakistani government maintains control, we're safe. How much do you want to bet that this status-quo will continue for the next fifty years? Syria, Iran, and North Korea all have active nuclear weapons programs and one or more has developed nuclear weapons. They also have very active missile programs which, when their bomb is ready, can be delivered over long distances quickly.

Pakistan is not a long-term friend of America. As long as

prominent Pakistani Mohammedans such as Abu Ala Muddy are allowed to preach and teach that non-Mohammedans have no right to rule in any part of earth, we have to be prepared for the eventuality that these hateful people will come into power over there.

Of course, the Pakistanis are working a new con game demanding in every way possible that the United States do what the Pakistanis want to 'alleviate poverty and alleviate terrorism.' The UN (of course) is tagging right along with this blackmail scheme, with the "learned experts" at the State Department close behind. The Pakistanis want money to industrialize the border areas with Afghanistan, etc., etc. Yeah, sure! Giving them money won't stop terrorism, and trying to introduce any industry will be a further waste of money because the $$$ will be stolen before the $$$ hit's the ground.

We need to flat tell the Pakistanis that if they want to hold their borders inviolate, they need to **control** their borders. They've had nearly seventy years since gaining independence to do so, and have failed. We can tell them that we will continue our hot pursuits of bad guys until the Pakistanis either kill the terrorists and take control of their border regions, or shut access to Afghanistan down to terrorists. Or, we can offer up that if Pakistanis want to stop the terrorists moving back and forth across the border, we to round up some hot nuclear goodies and seed the border with them. That will take care of the our enemies.

North Korea is well along with development of long range ICBM's which could be used to attack the United States. I for one doubt that the North Koreans (crazy Kim) would be foolish enough to attack directly. We would retaliate (I hope) and turn North Korea into a glassified wasteland if they ever did, and I suspect the North Koreans as well as their Chinese partners understand this.

For decades, the North Koreans have been digging miles deep into their many mountains with miles and miles of tunnels and huge caves. That is where 'dear leader' Kim and his cronies hide out. That is where the North Koreans are building and developing nuclear weapons facilities that we don't know about.

North Korea won't send any nukes directly into the United States. However, North Korea can use their missiles and nuclear-bombs in space to knock out our satellite systems with electro-magnetic pulse (EMP) strikes. Do you think that we'd be in deep doo-doo if our spy, weather, geodesic, communications and other satellites were blasted? You'd better believe it. Much of our high-tech society would be wiped out. That is the purpose of North Korea's missile development program, to hit us indirectly and really mess us up. Taking out our satellites would hurt us far more than nuclear detonations in one or two American cities. A good sized EMP strike would clobber us like nothing we've ever seen. Such an attack would jeopardize our society as we know it. It could be done with a simple scud missile fired from the hold of a ship a couple of hundred miles off shore from an American port.

The North Koreans, may sell these weapons to our foes. The

Iranians could attack our satellites in the Middle East and then take over neighboring oil fields in Iraq, and we would be nearly helpless. We depend on our technology too much in some cases, and in this instance our 'smart' bombs without satellite guidance wouldn't be able to find their way home. Without satellite navigation, our pilots wouldn't be able to find their way to or from target areas, or even back to their bases........

The US military is increasingly dependent on computers and sophisticated electronics and at the same time has relaxed requirements for EMP protection for its systems. This is stupid! Civilian infrastructure is likewise vulnerable to EMP attacks which could literally shut down all of the United States. Electricity grids could be crippled thus jeopardizing communications, crippling or simply shutting down food, fuel, and water supplies, etc., etc. Our vulnerability to this one threat is awesome, and the neglect of authorities in developing protection is criminal.

RESPONDERS

Decontamination plans are primitive, and we are facing an enormous challenge in dealing with just a few hundred victims.

After the Anthrax incidents of 2002, everyone was worried. Our "leaders" went on TV to assure us (accompanied by images of green clad people tippy toeing through children's wading pools being squirted from a five gallon pump sprayer by another similarly clad responder) and to show us how wonderfully prepared everyone was. That's fine for a few people.

What about a mass contamination?

Privately, our leaders have said they'd have to strip hundreds or even thousands down, ladies to one side and men to another for modesty purposes, and then traipse them through a gauntlet of fire trucks hosing them down. This, naturally only of the Environmental Protection Agency would permit the runoff. Of course, in Minneapolis in January, the victims would likely freeze and stick to the pavement.

So far, we've rightly spent millions to protect first responders. But, if they can't help hundreds or thousands of affected victims, what is the real benefit to you and I?

What about thousands of potentially contaminated and sick people. What communities have the necessary thousands of beds available to accommodate the thousands of sick and/or injured, or have the facilities to handle those other thousands of terrified and unsure people that the authorities refer to as the 'worried but well.'

Given the above scenario, the meaning of being prepared takes on new and disturbing dimensions. In cases of contagious disease contamination, being prepared means having the ability to control or restrict the movements of thousands of afflicted victims. That means barbed wire and guns, bulldozers, and mass burials.

Medications

The need for emergency stockpiles of huge quantities of varieties of fresh medications to treat thousands or even millions of people from one or multiple chemical, biological, or radiological attacks is ever present, and it represents an enormous expense and a logistical headache to sustain. It MUST be done!

CYBER WARFARE

Cyber attacks occur every day, and some have caused significant interruptions. Bad people, commonly referred to as hackers are working every day at trying to get into all manner of systems, private, government, banking, whatever. They have had many successes, some that have been detected, and which have then been countered. The more insidious problem is with the hack attacks that have not been detected.

Hackers can and ought to be encouraged to report their successes, and then be rewarded when they show how they did it, and get further rewards for developing ways to block such hack attacks. The same could be done for those who create computer viruses, and then be rewarded for developing vaccinations for those internet viruses. These talented resources could also be called on to apprehend or thwart those who do these things for criminal purposes.

While we're at it, encourage these same groups to go after the systems of those who wish us harm, and reward them for verifiable and unique successes that they report to us.

We used to have a thriving "Silicone Valley" with thousands of excellent computer programmers who earned substantial incomes for their work. That was good. Hundreds of other mini-silicone valleys sprouted that did well too.

Somewhere so-called management people 'discovered' that they could send all of these 'coding' and support jobs overseas to India, the Philippines, and other locations where they could pay a mere percentage of those high wages and get all of their work done.

This is far more than a bad idea. It was incredibly dumb.

Yes, these companies saved, bunches of money over the short term. They caused great harm to America's economy, but as long as the managers keep their salaries, perks, and bonuses, nobody cares.

The quality of that 'coding' plummeted as did the support services.

I for one changed cellular phone companies every year because none of them provide adequate service. I know that I may not get better service when I move on to the next one, but I get the satisfaction that I'm denying them my continued loyalty (and $$$) because of their lack of loyalty to me. I used an internet service provider that went belly up.

They served me well, did a good job, but were small and fell to the wayside. I saw an ad on TV for Netscape and decided to go there for service. That lasted about five hours -- the time I wasted to bail out of that very unsatisfactory deal. The process of getting my computer up and running on Netscape failed, and then several phone calls to their toll free number got me, after long wait times, connected with nice but ineffective people who could not understand my American English and my voice that does not annunciate well. I went to a service provider who charges three times more than Netscape, but have staff people whom I can communicate with.

The programming, coding, and support work for enormously huge, complex systems used by banks and the finance industry is not controlled or done by Americans. It is done in Asia by people who hold no loyalty or alliance to the United States, and in all likelihood some of these programmers are working at installing hackware, Trojans, 'back doors' or other sub-level and undetectable programs used by al-Qaeda and other terrorist organizations. These organizations easily and adroitly move their millions of dollars, Euros, or other currency units around using the 'back doors' undetected and even under the very noses of American intelligence organizations such as the FBI, CIA, Treasury Department, and others.

There are increasing numbers of anti-Islamic web sites coming into being all over the place. They provide a valuable service to civilization. Their numbers are not nearly equal to the number of Islamist web sites proselytizing and lying about the so-called virtues of Islam.

A Mohammedan successfully attacked and destroyed a wonderful internet web site operated by the Anti-Terrorism Coalition which contained and provided for perusal a famous (famous for its excellence and accuracy) database of terrorist websites. The Islamist attacker posted: I WILL CONTINUE HACKING DOWN YOUR FILTHY ZIONIST SCUM WEBSITES UNTIL THEY DISAPEER! Alahu Akbar! F**KINK KIKES!" (The language, spelling and grammar was that of the Mohammedan hacker.)

The Several countries have several thousand hackers working on American and allied computer networks. Their capability is highly advanced and the threat is real. Their purpose is to gain intelligence and develop capability to cause those systems to shut down when such a decision comes from their wonderful leader, Kim Jong-Il.

The bad guys have teams of hackers developing ways to hack into and screw up emergency services systems during a national emergency. This can cause thousands of more deaths and create additional mayhem.

Civil planning

We all understand that a failure to plan is a plan to fail.

Here's a scenario that can be played out in any metropolitan area.

A dirty bomb goes off upwind of a heavily populated area, and the mushroom cloud goes up. The talk radio guys go into hyper gear with their frenetic speculation, scary scenarios, plotting the toxic plume, and more. Everyone near or under the plume panics and hits the road to evacuate; and nobody gets out because the roads shut down in absolute gridlock due to panicked drivers causing accidents or other acts of stupidity.

Do the civil authorities have a plan to deal with this? The civil authorities have largely failed to plan and they have thus planed to fail their constituents. When (not if, but when) that type of balloon goes up the proverbial stuff will hit the fan, chaos will ensue and the civilian authorities will be overwhelmed from the very beginning. Everyone will be on their own in what will be an environment of anarchy and chaos where the police will be ineffectual. This is why every American needs to be armed and prepared to deal with what the police won't be able to handle.

Planners need to get prepared now. They need to shut gasoline pumps off so people cannot fuel up and hit the road willy nilly silly and utterly chaotic. The distribution of critical and volatile fuel needs to be put under strict control immediately. Then, on-ramps to freeways need to be blocked and closed. How? Use trucks and truckers to do this (but this takes organization and planning). Those roads will be desperately needed by responders for critical transportation needs and if they are blocked, the responders will be rendered useless and helpless. Control and limit access to critical roads -- ration access to evacuees in numbers that the roads can handle, and people will be able to move out in a timely and organized, disciplined manner.

What about beyond the plume? The vast suburbia unaffected by the plume will suddenly find themselves playing host to multiple thousands of hungry, scared, tired, and desperate refugees. Are their planners preparing to handle such a vast emergency? Those desperate refugees need to be dealt with sensibly lest they become desperados. The citizenry of those communities will not be able to depend on their own police who will be overwhelmed with the emergency. So, those citizens will need to be armed to maintain order and their own security.

American Successes

According to U.S. government claims, hundreds of Islamist or Mohammedan terror cells with more than 3,000 operatives have been disrupted. Where are those 3,000? Are they still here? Are they alive? Are they in prison? Are they still capable of pursuing their goals?

As of sometime in 2006, those U.S. government sources have charged 375 people in terrorism cases, of which 195 have already pleaded guilty or have been convicted; and over 500 people have been kicked out of America, alive too.

What happened to the many, many mosques and Islamic centers who recruited, supported, nurtured, and led these potential terrorists along? Are they still doing their filthy deeds?

The answer, boys and girls is: YES! In fact, they are thriving, and even more are being established.

Chapter 14

ASSAULTING AMERICA

Americans, particularly the elites refuse to grasp.....
that their country is engaged in war to the death with
an enemy who has warned us of his every move and
intention. Whatsoever comes next, whatever disaster befalls us,
our children, and our country, we were
warned and chose not to fight to our utmost.
Imperial Hubris, by Michael Schuer

The United States of America is feebly engaging in the struggle for the survival of civilization and political freedom and independence. A few countries recognize this and are joining us, but as our attention wanes, so does theirs. Many others would rather shirk their responsibility to the preservation of civilization and are all too willing to let the United States carry their burden. What's new?

When you become indifferent and you
lose the will to fight, some other sonovabitch
who has the will to fight will take you over!

Many countries or people for a variety of reasons are opposed to the United States in its efforts to preserve political freedom, choice, independence, decency, and civilization. They are doing this for a variety of reasons ranging from cowardice, hatred, jealousy, simple or willful ignorance, or only God knows what. Our most dangerous foe after Islam is ignorance of Islam.

They hate us because we are wealthy, basically decent, generous, caring, and genuinely wish to do that which is good or the right thing. And, they hate use because we tend to believe in a just, loving, and decent God. The Islamists are either fundamentalists (a rapidly growing side of Islam) or a dwindling number of secularists. The core Islamists are followers of and idolizers Mohammed who eliminated all but one god of the pagan Arabs, and elevated the pagan moon god, Il-Allah to a higher position. Allah is still a pagan moon god whose exaltation is a figment of Mohammed's sun struck, greedy, sex, revenge, drug, and hate addled brain.

Symbolism is important to many if not most people. The American flag stirs passions, some patriotic and others hateful. The cross is the symbol of Christian salvation, the star (stars are givers of light) of David of Judaism, and the crescent moon (a bit of light in a sea of darkness) of Islam.

Guns in the United States

We have other foes and fifth columnists, right here, in the United States who are determined to destroy this great nation and culture from within. Among them are those who are opposed to the Second Amendment to the constitution, the anti-gun crowd. And this includes President No. 44, Barak Hussein Obama who was sworn in on January 20, 2009.

The right of each and every upstanding American citizen to own guns is sacred to our Constitutional rights and must remain so. It is this proper and good proliferation of personally owned guns that guarantees, supports, and ensures the First Amendment, and every other liberty.

The socialist and Islamic fascist groups whose real intent is to turn America into an Orwellian police state have it as their first step to remove our ability to defend ourselves from their jack booted thugs. Their version of Utopia is not flower children dancing amongst the daisies. Their version is for them, the few sick minded elites to dominate the rest of us, who will be their slaves.

Those who would suppress or take away our rights of free speech and expression, our core liberty, and who would enslave us, hate each and every one of those very freedoms -- and gun ownership is the core focus of their hatred. They know, and you and I know that if and when they, the radically insane America haters, the fools, fundamentalists, the socialist and fascist enslavers gain too much power, power of the wrong kind, they will be neutralized or eliminated by gun wielding freedom protecting and liberty preserving patriots.

It is a fundamental truth that the political and cultural freedom of the world and civilization is maintained by the Second Amendment of the Constitution.

Pinheads

It took a while for some of the Pinheaded liberals to come out against the war on terrorism, to blame America for bringing it on ourselves. And, of course, they believe that Charles Manson is also a sweetheart.   While we were going after the Taliban, I was surprised that "Hanoi Jane Fonda" didn't sally forth to join the Taliban to perform as "Qaeda Jane." She probably didn't do so because she was afraid they'd (the Taliban) possibly beat some sense into her.

Millions (many coerced) have reportedly demonstrated against the United States for a variety of reasons. Billions haven't. American protesters against involvement in the Middle East are in fact one or even all of three things: (1) Simply Ignorant; (2) Willfully Ignorant; (3) Clearly not very bright.

The most liberal, pinheaded American Senator has been sworn in as President No. 44, which doesn't bode well for responsible patriots or civilized folks.

The war against America:
Allah is our goal,
the Prophet, Mohammed is our leader
the Koran is our constitution.
Jihad is our way, and
death in the way of allah
is our promised end.

The Moslem Brotherhood

Islam is at war with the United States. Barak Hussein Obama has declared that we are not at war with Islam. This is capitulation. We as well as our leaders must quit deceiving ourselves, themselves and others. We need to begin taking steps now, today, to ensure our viable future.

While I am not particularly fond of or wildly supportive of fundamentalist Christian evangelists, I will be among the first to agree when they do have something to say that is wise, wonderful, and good.

Pat Robertson has opined, and everyone with half a brain (liberal pinheads don't have room for brains in their vacuous pins) has to agree that under no circumstances should any core Moslem be appointed to a federal judgeship, and none should ever be allowed to serve in the President's cabinet, or any other high position of trust. This has happened however, and the erosion of our freedoms is moving along. The reason, of course is quite simple. No Moslem will ever, ever in anyone's wildest dreams take action in the best interests of the United States or decent, civilized people if or when an Islamic issue comes before them. It's that simple. It's a fundamental truth!

Dhimmi

Right here, at home in the United States, we have Mohammedans at every turn working to impose their will on us, and enjoying many successes. Moslem taxi drivers in certain cities are outraged because police ticket and even tow their taxis and delivery vehicles when they stop them in the middle of the roads (in particular at airports) to get out and pray at their appointed time. (In Islam, if one is unable to pray at a given time, he or she can perform their make-up prayers later in the day to maintain their good graces with allah.) These same taxi drivers in America want to refuse rides to anyone transporting alcoholic beverages (even holy wines), pork products, rides for unwed couples, etc.

These Mohammedans should lose their rights to drive taxis at the first such offense, and should be given one-way tickets back to the hole from which they came. They deserve nothing else at all.

Fifth Column

232

Seditionist Fifth columnist and dhimmi, Senator Dick Durbin stupidly likened the strict, respectful, and humane incarceration of Mohammedist terrorists at Guantanamo Bay, Cuba (GITMO) to the brutal Soviet gulags where people suffered and died; to the Nazi holocaust that worked to annihilate Jews and Gypsies; to the killing fields of Cambodia's Khmer Rouge. Durbin's pronouncements affirmed that he is not only a traitor to the memory of those innocent millions who perished so terribly, but that he is a traitor to civilization embodied in the humane, decent, treatment of the GITMO detainees.

Durbin is either incredibly ignorant (a real possibility if not a clear probability) or he thinks he's smart (not very likely). He clearly has no understanding of, nor respect of or for historical facts. Durban, with a large Moslem population in his district is just a political whore working for their votes.

In his spew, Durbin talked about America's "reputation" as though it was one of his concerns. Unfortunately, America has a mixed reputation, precisely because of pinheaded people like Durbin. Sorrowful is the reputation that America is a "sucker" nation that is all too tolerant of sick, twisted people like Durbin and his fellow seditionist Senator Patrick Leahey who likewise regularly betrays constituents with his own hate-America actions and activities. They treat those who vote for them as stupid, ignorant suckers who will re-elect them again and again so they can cause further harm to America and to American people and interests. And, they do get re-elected.

Militant Islam

We need to recognize when we are dealing with any person or organization that desires to undermine America and civilization in the name of some faux religion. In 99% of conflicts where Islam is involved, the aggressor, the invader, is always Islam. Here are some of the danger signs:

1-　　Justification of any Islamic or Moslem terrorism, or acts of terrorism, violence, or hate, Palestinian or otherwise. Encouraging the veneration of suicide bombers as martyrs.

2-　　Supporting or refusing to condemn al Qaeda, Hamas, Islamic Jihad, Hezbollah, CAIR, the Moslem Brotherhood, or other terrorists or terrorist organizations.

3-　　Promoting jihad for Moslems to fight against what they determine is "injustice" of "aggression" which is in fact our (or any other civilized people) rightfully acting to defend ourselves.

4-　　Demanding that Americans accommodate, accept, or even impose primitive Islamic laws, barbaric Moslem customs, and evil Mohammedan practices that conflict with, or are harmful to, or are against American laws, customs, and practices.

5-　　Demands for bigoted and biased Sharia law in Western

233

civilizations, or denying that Sharia forbids equal rights for women and members of religions other than Islam.

6-   Denying that Moslems were involved in the 9/11 terrorist attacks, and thousands of other terrorist attacks around the world, such as suicide bombers in Iraq, Afghanistan, or Israel.

7-   Refusing to cooperate with or provoking others to not cooperate with authorities or following standard security procedures. Refusing to report Moslem terrorists who are plotting attacks in the United States or any other non-Moslem country.

8-   Branding Moslems who are moderate as apostates. Promoting anti-Semitism.

9-   Refusal to participate in activities with non-Moslems.

10-   Demanding that Moslem females must wear Moslem garb in civilized countries; demanding that their mosques be allowed to use loudspeakers to call people to prayer; demanding the right to stop their cars, taxis, trucks in the middle of public ways to get out and do their prayers even though this disrupts and inconveniences others; demonizing Western cultural values.

11-   Denying that Koranic writings and examples or rules set forth by Mohammed are used by terrorists to justify acts of violence and hatred.

12-   Desiring to observe all tenets of the Haditha even while in civilized countries.

Chapter 15

IT'S THE MONEY, STUPID!

Our American government works in strange and wondrous ways, especially in Washington, the seat of our national government where the Congress passes laws. It must be understood that not all laws passed by the Congress are necessarily good for the American people any longer. That's a fact.

One of the greatest perks a Senator or Congressman can have is a seat of influence beyond their basic elected offices, on a committee or panel. When a Senator or Congressman is on a committee, they are besieged by lobbyists currying favors.

Did I say besieged? Siege is normally a hostile act. When lobbyists are involved, it's friendly, it's a source of money, lots and lots of money. Money for campaigns, money for trips and travel, money for leisure activities, money for things, gifts, and yes - bribes. The Arabs call it baksheesh. The Congress has made it legal for themselves to accept those "perks" and the only word for it is legalized bribe taking.....

The best funded lobbies in Washington are the Arab oil lobbies, specifically the Saudi lobby. The Saudis send billions of your and my dollars used to purchase expensive oil back to Washington to fund a host of lobbyists whose job is to protect Saudi interests (nearly all of which are detrimental to America's best interests). What are those Saudi interests? To keep the United States dependent on their (Saudi) oil, at the highest possible prices consistent with not causing a depression or runaway inflation in the United States which would make oil too costly. [This is less than they send to al Qaeda and other anti-American terrorist organizations such as Hamas, to Chechnyan terrorists in Russia, to Bosnians, to Islamic Jihad, CAIR, (four billion to fund the Palestinian intifada), and much, much more.]

These lobbyists bribe (payola, grease, wine, women and song, drugs, M-O-N-E-Y - all called 'gratuities', legal entertainment, etc.) congressmen and other appointed government officials to make sure things that happen are in the best interests of the Saudis, NOT your interests or mine. And those elected leaders and decision making officials suck it all up, the money, gifts, and other legal personalized ...ahem.... baksheesh..

An example: The Saudi/Arab money and its influence purchasing lobby played a role in the spring of 2002, influencing the Congress to NOT raise automotive fuel mileage requirements -- just so we can further remain hostage to those Arab oil interests. Far too many of your and my Representatives and Senators pocket in one way or another plenty of money, Arab money. They just suck it up, and to hell with you and I.

We Americans are being betrayed daily by many of our elected representatives who are so desperate for money to pay for both their elections as well as that which I won't mention.

The environmental movement in the United States is unwittingly (hopefully unwittingly) probably one of the oil lobby's greatest allies. When gas, oil, coal, or other energy source exploration is discussed, these freaks go nuts on us. I would suspect that they just might get some of their funding by one way or another from those holding us hostage for oil.... These same morons have played a very significant role in relegating the United States to the background regarding Nuclear Power. Again, whenever anyone thinks about building a clean, efficient, cost-effective, and non-oil dependent nuclear power plant, these same well paid environmentalists go berserk in opposition.

We need to recognize that the United States does indeed care for the environment, but bowing to the environmental extremists does not serve the American people well at all. The enviro-extremists don't care about that which 99% of Americans consider important -- jobs, food, housing, our families, or our society. The enviro-extremists, or enviro-whackos work hard to protect and preserve weeds and bugs to the detriment of people. These whackos do not care if people have trouble feeding and housing themselves and their families. They really, truly don't.

The Mohammedans have missed so far in taking America down, by causing major disruption or even destruction of our financial systems. We did that all by ourselves.

However, they have an opportunity with the insurance industry. Besides buying life insurance policies and then blowing themselves up to make claims which naturally will be denied after $$$$ in haggling. The Mohammedans could buy and insure the heck out of properties and then blow them up, and cause further turmoil.

Of course, to avoid this, the insurance industry can become discriminatory and refuse to insure certain religious, ethnic, or business groups. But, such discrimination is illegal, so the increasingly befuddled courts at the behest of the increasingly silly ACLU would strive to assert their greater-than-God authority to compel the insurance industry to continue providing insurance and thus to self destruct.

Baksheesh

For the millions of people of the Islamic cultures, baksheesh – bribery as we know and understand it is an acceptable way of life.

Early in my Foreign Service career, I had a young counterpart, a rare nice guy who lived in this Moslem culture (Turkey) explain to me that he divided his income (derived from his official compensation and the bribes he received) into four parts. Two parts (50%) was used to live on, one part, 25% was passed on up the line to his nominal supervisors, and 25% was saved to purchase his next promotion or assignment, etc.

He explained to me that people he knew who did business with us Americans at the Embassy were baffled by our not soliciting bribes for the favors, help, and assistance they received such as obtaining visas. Baffled!

Balderdash

The Palestinian intifada in 2002 sent many hashassins into Israel to blow themselves to smithereens and to murder as many innocent Israelis as possible in the process.

The responding Israeli attacks into the Arab inhabited territories of the West Bank of Trans-Jordan, commonly referred to as the Palestinian territories, brought many Arabs to the TV stations for interviews, to talk about the Israeli-Arab conflict.

The Israelis went into a terrorist stronghold, Jenin, and took out 56 Palestinian terrorists, of which fifty were armed. The Arabs ran amok telling lies and mythical fabrications to the world that 500 of them were slaughtered. Naturally, the Arabs believe their own lying myths -- their taqiyyah, and 56 murderous terrorists were transformed into 500 innocents.

Americans - those with a fundamental understanding of reality - found the sheer mendacity of most of the Arabs to be incredibly outlandish. When asked about terrorist bombers in Israel, these Arabs never acknowledged the attacks. In no way would they acknowledge reality. Their responses were always whining complaints about the Israelis killing so-called Palestinian civilians - armed Arab militants not in uniform. They refused to answer even direct questions about the deaths of Israeli women and children with one notable exception: One Arab went so far as to say that it was OK to murder Israeli, Christian, and non-believer women for they only gave birth to more Jews or non-believers, and that killing non-believer (especially Jewish and Christian) babies and children (before they could breed) was desirable too. Yeah, Mohammedans murdering women and children, even babies is fully justified, even encouraged within the 'wonderful' world of Islam.

The Arabs' ability to deny reality is astounding.

Consider the Egyptians' passionate, hysterical denial of reports that their own Egyptian Airline pilot, while driving a commercial airliner into the Atlantic Ocean was muttering prayers praising Allah and asking for forgiveness as he killed himself and all of those innocent people.

On the 4th of July, 2002, an Egyptian's anti-Israeli passions overcame him and he went to the Los Angeles Airport and killed two people, the Egyptian government ranted about America's press overemphasizing his evil deeds. They wanted at first to deny that the screwball was even Egyptian. The Egyptian government demanded that any and all reports be censored from press, magazine, and TV coverage. It didn't happen.

When confronted with evidence of their funding thousands of fundamentalist schools (Madrassas) that preach and teach only hatred of the west, the Saudis deny with stone faces that any schools they sponsor are involved in preparing (I call them "Manchurian Candidates") to become jihadis (holy warriors), or terrorists. The objective of all of these jihadis is to conquer the world and to impose intolerant Islamic Sharia law - a wholly repressive, ugly, primitive, barbaric rule on everyone.

When we rounded up Al Qaeda members in Afghanistan and Pakistan, the Saudis demanded that Saudi nationals we held be turned over to Saudi authorities to "deal with" (so the Saudis could turn them loose).

Some good news: On August 16th, 2002, survivors of people murdered on 9/11/2002 sued the Saudis, et all as appropriate for a whole bunch of money for their involvement in those murders. Great!!!!!

Hearts and Minds

Some fools in the civilized west are talking about winning the hearts and minds of the Moslem people. Good luck, flower children. Enjoy your serendipity.

The civilized world has a real challenge in dealing with the mind sets of the Moslems. Moslems thrive on living with their hatred, ignorance, lies, deceit, and myths, and will readily believe anything they are told about conspiracies.

But then, the Koran, in chapter 9 states: Allah and His Messenger dissolve obligations. That means that lying is not only OK, it is sanctioned. It tells Mohammedans that they have no real or moral obligations to keep promises, treaties, contracts, or obligations, as it suits them.

Al Jazeera TV is the most successful TV station in the Arab world because its rampant, strident anti-American and anti-Israeli rhetoric meets consumer demand. Al Jazeera TV reflects Arab public opinion. This is a no brainer, folks. They despise us.

Chapter 16

ISLAM

***"When I, a thoughtful and unblessed Presbyterian, examine the koran
I know beyond any question that every Mohamedan
is insane, not in all things, but in religious matters. I cannot
prove to him that he is insane, because you never can
prove anything to a lunatic — for that is a part of his
insanity and the evidence of it."***

Mark Twain

The word "Islam" means **submission** or **surrender** in Arabic. To be a Moslem, one must submit or surrender to the rules and laws of Islam. Submission and surrender are absolute, not partial, nor with a free choice. The mission of Islam is to obtain absolute and total submission or surrender by all humanity to Islam, by whatever the means. If that means murder, Insha'Allah.

Islam is many things:

Political Islam is rule by evil, biased, and bigoted tyranny.

Economic Islam is surrendering your successes.

Military Islam is the tool of conquest and mindless destruction.

Social Islam to live in perpetual poverty, ignorance, suffering, and humiliation.

Legal Islam is to have no God given rights of free choices and actions.

Religious Islam is the filthy beard behind which the other forms of Islam hide.

Islam is NOT like or similar to anything else.

The practice of the dark cult of Islam is itself a continuing human tragedy of incredible magnitude. Wherever Islam reigns, be it a territory, a province, or a country, it has borders that are bloody. That is the true, fundamental nature of Islam.

Here is a clarifying misconception about (imperial) Islam which some uninformed people or liars claim is a religion of peace, and that it is neither anti-Jewish nor anti-Christian. From just after its first days, Islam has been a violent imperialist movement based on conquest and subjugation. Mohammed, who 'good' Moslems are supposed to pattern their lives after conducted seventy-four military campaigns aimed at slaughtering, brutalizing, and subjugating entire groups of people. Mohammed married several times, including in his harem a six year old child, Aisha. Mohammed practiced and condoned theft, rape, murder, torture, plunder, pedophilia, violence; and debauchery was one of his favorite pastimes.

People in the west were horrified to see the pious, Mohammed imitating Taliban of Afghanistan in the way they ran the country as they emulated Mohammed and closely followed his insane, vicious, backward, medieval teachings. Those hateful, abusive Taliban men pictured beating or shooting defenseless women were merely fulfilling their primitive mission in life, to emulate Mohammed in every way, as they strove to mirror Mohammed's gross sociopathic evil.

That is Islam's principal article of faith, emulating Mohammed.

Moslem fathers in many parts of the world have their sons vow on a daily basis: "I will kill a Jew before I die!" A religion of peace and harmony? Yeah, sure!

Another clarification: Ignorant people claim that Islam is just a religion. Just? It's fundamental truth time: Islam is NOT a religion except in its claims to worship allah, a figment of Mohammed's fertile, insane imagination. Allah, in Mohammed's teachings played second fiddle to Mohammed, the creator of Islam himself. Islam is a dark, evil twisted ideology and a corrupt and violent political system, not a true religion by any sense of the meaning. An Islamic state/nation cannot exist as separate entities of a responsible, reasonable, civilized government separated from their religion. In Islam, there is no distinction between church and state. The Koran is an Islamic nation's constitution, and Sharia is its law. An individual cannot dissent, or challenge, he or she can only submit to being dominated and controlled. Islam is an absolutely tyrannical totalitarian social organization and is without boundaries. In Islam, there is NO room for secularism.

We are required to lie when it suits the advancement of Islam, and we expect the infidels to accept this taqiyyah, and in their abject dhimmitude to actually do the same. Truth and honesty will not be tolerated!

Anonymous

Umma is the Islamist statement of equality for mankind, to be clear and precise - of <u>Moslem</u> mankind. If you are not Moslem you are not equal, you are not a part of the umma, you are an inferior required to live as a surrendered dhimmi in a sub-status of perpetual humiliation and servitude.

The umma are required to adhere to the five pillars of Islamic faith. I list them here, and add a sixth which is called for in the Koran:

1 – Faith – belief that allah is the only god, and that Mohammed is his messenger.

2 – Pray five times per day.

3 – Zakat – give 2.5% of everything one owns to his Mullah or Imam every year.

4 – Fast for 28-days per year.

5 – Conduct pilgrimage to Mecca

6 – Jihad against all infidels.

In an Islamic nation, non-believers such as Jews, Hindus, Christians, Buddhists, etc., pay special, unique high taxes, [including occasionally imposed blood taxes of having their children, both boys and girls taken away into slavery - usually for initial use as sex slaves], are subjected to forced conversions, and other biased and prejudiced acts. Only a false, phony, artificial prophet such as Mohammed would feel the need to torture and murder people to forcefully convert them – to spread their ideology, their Moslem faith.

There is and will always (as in forever, and ever, and ever) be an insurmountable, permanent divide between Islam and the civilized world. Islam cannot compromise and be decent, responsible, respectful, or civilized in its relationships with non-Moslems. Anyone who says or claims otherwise is a liar or a fool.

allah

According to factual historians, Il-Allah is an ancient Arabic word meaning "moon god" that goes back to ancient times of pagan worship and rituals at Mecca and the Kabala. Thus the crescent moon is the symbol representing Islam. The Moslem calendar is lunar, and their religious events and so forth are observed in accordance with cycles of the moon. Accordingly and in reality, Moslems are primitive pagan moon worshipers.

Their inferiority complex is so deep that anything that even hints of what they define as disrespect can send them into a frenzy. A rumor of American prison guards' Koran flushing down a toilet set off world-wide protests and rampages, along with demands for retribution (such as hanging guards), etc. A depiction of Mohammed with a bomb in his turban begat a truly but atypical insane series of events.

Civilized people like Buddhists, Christians, Jews, Hindus, and others don't lash out in violent rampages when centuries' old Buddhist statuary are blown up, when a moron immerses a crucifix in urine, or some Mohammedan jerk burns a treasured Torah.

Islamic terrorists once holed up in Bethlehem's Church of the Nativity used rare antique Christian bibles for toilet paper, and nobody rioted. The Christians and Jews just recognized and accepted the simple fact that they were dealing with representatives of earth's lowest forms of life -- scum, Moslem scum.

Dysfunctional societies (Islamic) go on rampages, for any infantile reason such as a cartoon depicting Mohammed with a bomb in his bonnet.

Ignorance and Illiteracy

There are about 1.3 billion Moslem people in the world. Some estimates range up to 1.6 billion. A little more than one million of those Moslems are actually literate or well educated in the western sense.

The rest are ignorant and dependent on the teachings and proclamations of their Imams and Mullahs, teachings which generally are about hatred and murdering non-believers. True independent and honest, self critical cognitive abilities are largely mythical within the Moslem diaspora.

Is there any wonder that from all of the ignorance in those closed, willfully ignorant societies, there are people who hate us? They don't know any better. They don't want to know. And, certainly, their leaders aren't about to be honest and ready to clue them in, even if they themselves understood or had a real clue.

Former Iranian President Rafsanjani claims it is a crime for the United States and the developed countries of the west to purchase and harvest resources needed for their economic engines. Rafsanjani is a fool and an idiot. What's new? If it were not for the West's wealth and purchases, he would likely still be an apprentice carpet weaver in some backwater of his Islamic paradise.

The developed countries pay for that which they get from backward countries that benefit from those expenditures. It is unfortunate that in many cases, the wealth from those purchases fails to filter down to the people because of the corrupt leaders of those countries. Rafsanjani's whining is hollow because he and others like him are angry at their inability to plunder that wealth entirely for themselves. Rafsanjani criticizes the west for helping the poor while he and others like him sat on their hands during the Indonesian tsunami crisis which affected millions of Moslems. Rafsanjani's words are taqiyyah!

Trust the Truth

While it is OK, even desirable for imperialistic Moslems to defame Christ, Christians, the Pope, Buddha, things Hindu, etc., it is intolerable for others to defame their head poobah, the pedophile, Mohammed, allah, or Islam. In fact, the penalty is supposed to be death. The author, Salmon Rushdie ridiculed Mohammed and his Islam in a book, and a fatwa was issued calling for his death. Rushdie remains in hiding today. It is considered a crime to say anything derogatory about Mohammed, even if it is historically factual and true, and whenever one speaks of him or uses words about the prophet, they are supposed to recite some other invocation about peace and blessings being upon him, etc. Mohammed never, not once, met the criteria of a true prophet by receiving a direct revelation from God (he was visited by a myth); of prophesying the future, of any miracles.

Since Mohammed, the dark, moody, vengeful, primitive, savage, ignorant, confused, crazed, self-proclaimed 'messenger of allah' organized his band of pagan Arab followers into a fundamentally insane violent, polygamous, militant, greedy, pseudo religious cult, Islam has remained expansionist.

From day one, Mohammedan 'missionaries' were largely unsuccessful in bringing the Moslem faith to people and to convert them based on values, decency, and reason, even when Mohammed stupidly claimed that all of the world was Moslem at its creation. Yeah, Mohammed's Koran teaches that all are born Moslem. About the only way Islam could gain converts however, was and is under the threat of violence, torture, death, and enslavement --- terrorism. People living in civilized societies who knowingly and willingly convert to Islam are to be considered deranged. While its imperialistic expansion has slowed down from time to time, Islam has adapted and moved forward, and right now, like a deadly, virulent plague, it is sweeping the world in a capillary fashion.

**If there was no evil in the world,
how would we know what is good**?
My eight year old son.

Mohammed, an ignorant camel herder along caravan trails sat around campfires and listened to people talk about religion and things spiritual. There were conversational snippets of Judaism and of Christianity that the spiritually bereft Mohammed apparently soaked up. Based on these snippets, and his very limited understanding of the one true living God and other things spiritual, he began his quest for domination of the Arabs, and Arab domination of the world using his allah as his tool. His wicked mind distorted the little he learned about Judaism and Christianity and he applied that to his newly created Islam. Nowadays, of course, Moslem Jordanian (our friends, right?), Egyptian, Syrians, Saudi (and other) Mohammedan leaders preach that Jews "distorted their (Moslem) scriptures" and did so in an instant using black magic. Yeah, sure, magic, unh-hunh! Unfortunately, Mohammed's followers actually believe this nonsense.

Mohammed was a sly, narcissistic jackal. Yes, he was charismatic and was apparently bright too.

Mohammed, at the reported age of fifty-two married a six year old girl, Aisha, (also referred to as Ayesha) an adopted niece, and consummated this marriage when she was just nine years old. Mohammed was therefore a pedophile, a child rapist. He confided in her after he married her that he had dreams about her after once seeing her nude, and believed this to be a message from his god. As ideal Moslem men are expected to pattern themselves after their Mohammed, the taking of child brides is common even to this day. Recently, in Pakistan, a Mohammedan tribal counsel in Multan ordered the betrothal of a two year old to a forty-year old man. That is not only sick and immoral, it is evil!

Much of the most hate-driven violence in the world today (and over the past fourteen hundred years) is driven by Mohammedans in the name of Islam.

Religions that cherish life such as Christianity, Buddhism, Judaism, Hinduism, Shintoism, and other faiths are fairly homogeneous and largely peaceful in their proselytization. Unlike them, murderous, death loving, death seeking Mohammed worshiping fanatics and zealots have sallied forth, saber in hand to terrorize and impose the Islam or death on everyone in their path.

In some instances, recognizing their own depths of technical and commercial incompetence and non-competitiveness the Mohammedans have permitted some infidels to live on in the state of dhimmitude (slavery or servitude) where their technical skills and expertise are deemed essential. Without these technical experts, the Moslems would have absolutely nothing. They depended on and compelled these pour souls to do and perform that which the Moslems are basically too lazy, stupid, and inept to successfully do themselves.

Many Moslems cringe at the word of dhimmi when used by a free westerner because that tells them that we understand their ultimate motive -- to place us in dhimmi servitude, inferiors to them, as second class citizens without human, social, legal, or any rights or dignity.

Despite protestations to the contrary, the true face of Islam is that of a militant, brutal, ugly expansionist cult devoid of genuine civilized values. That is a very simple, pure truth. Islam will never, ever reconcile or join with that which is non-Islamic. According to Islamic teachings and laws, it is OK for Christians to convert to Islam, but it is illegal (punishable by death) for a Moslem to convert to Christianity. Under Islamic (Sharia) laws, a Moslem can testify against a non-Moslem in court, but a non-Moslem CANNOT testify against a Moslem in a Moslem court. A Moslem who murders an infidel cannot be punished with death, while a civilized person, an infidel, who merely offends a Moslem can be killed.

Non-Moslem females in many Moslem countries are compelled to wear a veil at school and on the streets. In fact, one must recognize that it is actually wise for non-Moslem women to hide, to protect themselves -- from the rapacious followers of Mohammed.

Iranian President Ahmadinejad claimed that there were no homosexuals in Moslem countries. Yeah, following the narrow Moslem definition of homosexual - oral sex between people of the same gender is gay. However, everything else sexual between men in particular goes.

Fundamentally, Islam divides the world into two parts, the house of Islam -- Dar al Islam, and the house of war -- Dar al Harb. Dar al Harb is everything beyond the borders of Islamic dominated and controlled areas. If you're a Mohammedan, you're in. If you're not a Mohammedan, you will be the subject of warfare or some form of subjugation sooner or later.

All (infidel) countries that have freely elected, democratic, or even dictatorial but non-Islamic governments are in the category of Dar al Harb, the status of war, or enemy -- to eventually suffer defeat at the hands of the imperial Mohammedans.

Islam, for most of its 1,400 years of existence has been dominated by brutal, ethically challenged and morally bankrupt leaders who pattern themselves after their idol, Mohammed, intent on stealing everything they can and enslaving the world. This continues to this day and will not change at any time in the future. Not ever.

Under centuries of leadership of this long chain of mostly brutish, selfish, self-centered, intolerant, lying, fearful and fearsome men, the Moslem world, the nations of Moslem culture are and will forever remain the most impoverished and backward countries on earth, as they should be. The only exception is wealth from the oil they sell. When their oil is gone, they'll only have their ignorance to rely on and will fall back into poverty bringing everyplace they dominate with them. The only other times they have enjoyed any other forms of wealth, has been when they could steal it. They have never, ever created anything of true, lasting value themselves.

In recent centuries of rapid world economic and scientific growth and achievement, Arab economies with an abundance of that which is needed to generate wealth, have grown at a paltry 0.5%. That is relative stagnation if not real, factual regression. Their labor productivity has actually declined while the world's has increased dramatically. Unemployment remains at a constant 15+% and underemployment at another 50% or more.

The dark but sadly true historical record of Islam is that the rule of Islam has always (ALWAYS) promoted and perpetuated poverty. This is what destroyed greater India, the Moghul invasion and the imposition of Mohammedan rule which destroyed much of Hindu and Buddhist civilization that thrived at the time. The Moslem savagery took millions of lives. The Moghuls simply destroyed all non-Moslem art, temples, statuary, literature, and they stole everything else, raping and enslaving children, both boys and girls. The magnitude of Moslem massacres in greater India/Hindustan dwarfs the Nazi holocaust and the Spanish slaughter of South American Indians.

When the Islamic forces entered and seized control of Hindustan (India), the horrific, systematic slaughter of Hindus and Buddhists raged on for years, decades. Most of the Buddhists were killed off. The weaker minded, weaker willed Hindus more willingly succumbed and submitted to accept dhimmi status. [This is where Afghanistan and Pakistan (east and West) evolved.] The remaining Hindus were subjected to paying the jizya (poll, and land taxes) that supported continuation of the harsh Mohammedan Mogul domination.

Of fifty-eight countries with a Moslem majority, none has a stable democratic system of government, a comprehensive educational system, religious freedom or religious tolerance, women's suffrage, and none have any great thinkers, scientists, etc. The only things these places have are abundant self-pity, anger, and ever growing misery and impoverishment. A 2004 United (Useless) Nations Arab Human

Development Report naturally blamed the creation of Israel and U.S. support for Israel as the cause of Arab/Islamic nations' impoverishment. This Moslem inspired claim is insanely mythical and quite typically Moslem. Those countries were that way long before modern Israel was created.

A few quasi-civilized, educated, thinking, responsible, caring Arab leaders and scholars have identified parts of the problem behind this widespread impoverishment: Three of the identified deficits are freedom, empowerment of women, and education. Others who are not Arabs or Moslems, naturally, have identified out a fourth Islamic deficit -- absolute religious intolerance.

Before the Mohammedist empire building expansion began 1400 years ago, the Near East and North Africa were the heart of Jewish and Christian civilization, and succumbed to Islam after centuries of jihad in which nearly all infidels (Jews and Christians) in sight were slaughtered, enslaved (placed into various forms of servitude), or forced to convert to Islam. The rape, enslavement as sex slaves, and forced conversion of Jewish (and Christian) women was a common practice. (Thus, actual Jewish blood runs deep in the veins of Arabs, something they apparently have in common with Adolph Hitler.)
The victors in round 1? Islam.

Centuries before the Crusades commenced, imperialistic Islamic expansion proceeded into the Iberian Peninsula, Sicily, Sardinia, Greece, the Balkans, and Eastward into Asia.

The Crusades were in direct response to continuing and expanding Islamic barbarities. The Mohammedan conversions of Asia Minor, Turkey, Palestine, Persia, Lebanon, Syria, and Alexandria in Egypt which were important Christian centers was nothing less than cataclysmic. The barbaric horrors the Mohammedans inflicted on conquered peoples were indescribable. Typical was the barbarity of degenerate Moslem Turks in 1453 when they conquered Constantinople, butchering infants and the elderly, and then fighting amongst themselves over the boys and young girls (sex prizes), and enslavement of everyone else. Nobody survived.
The victors in round 2? Islam.

Yet, in 2005, the jackass, Sheikh Fawzi Zafzaf, president of the Interfaith Dialogue (Trojan Horse Charade) Committee of Al-Azhar (the highest ranking religious authority in Egypt and reportedly the most respected Sunni authority in the world) had the temerity to demand that the Roman Catholic Vatican apologize for the Crusades. This is another example of unrealistic imperialistic Mohammedan balderdash. This demonstrates that the Al-Azhar and its leadership deserve no more respect from the civilized world than the scrapings from the bottom of a cesspool.

In fact, Pope John Paul II did make some apologies. He even

attended Islamic services at Mosques and held his tongue. This is regrettable and foolish, and while he lived, this acting the part of a dhimmi or useful fool was not often or much questioned in or outside of the Roman Catholic Church. Subsequent to John Paul II's passing on, realists and pragmatists are bringing this foolish activity into question, which is appropriate.

During the reign of Pope John Paul II, the Vatican had an ambitious outreach program to Islamic countries that brought absolutely no relief or benefits to subjugated Catholic and Christian minorities in Moslem countries. Nothing was said about the horrors regularly being delivered to Christian Assyrians, Chaldeans, Maronites, or Copts, or the daily murdering of Christians in Pakistan, the Philippines, the Balkans, Turkey, Lebanon, and Indonesia. Under urgings of the Vatican, Moslem minorities received additional benefits and privileges in civilized countries, and still there were NO reciprocal goodwill gestures or actions from the Mohammedans. Why should the Mohammedans have reciprocated? The Pope was in fact helping them to further their goals. In fact, attacks against Christians and Catholics were even stepped up because the Pope's conciliatory actions were seen as clear signs of weakness to be exploited, and the vilification of the Pope and the Christian world continued unabated.

Pope Benedict has come out demonstrating that he knows and understands Islam, and seems at times to have pointed out that Islam is evil, uncivilized, and useless.

The earliest Christian wars (long before the Crusades) against Islam were waged **in defense of Christendom**, or to liberate and re-conquer lands that were originally and rightfully Christian. Some of these activities took place after the dark ages in Europe and as Christian Europe emerged and started becoming a coherent civilization capable of driving the Mohammedan fundamentalist invaders and occupiers of Europe back somewhat. The Mohammedan Moors were finally driven out of Spain in 1492, the year Columbus reached the Americas.

<u>Round 3? One for the good guys.</u>

Imperial Islam went on the strategic defensive for about three hundred years after being driven back from Iberia and Eastern Europe. That strategic defensive move ended early in the 20th century, and since then more Christians have been slaughtered than at the time of Roman persecutions.

One example was the Turkish pogroms against Orthodox Christians - mostly Armenians during (1915-1916) and after World War I in 1922. Between a quarter and a half of a million Christians were slaughtered in just one campaign. The Turks were performing their Koranic duties. Those Christians weren't just killed either. They were butchered alive, and left to suffer terribly before they died. Women and children were split from breastbone to pelvis and their intestines spilled, and then they were left in their agony to suffer. Naturally, many of the women were repeatedly raped first. Men were first sexually mutilated and then, with hands and feet on opposite sides chopped off, and their remaining hand and foot crushed by clubs, were left to die. Yeah, those Turks are such wonderful people!

In 1966, I visited a historical sight in Istanbul where Christian Armenians went to a Roman Catholic Church seeking sanctuary. Naturally, the Mohammedan Turks cared not a wit about a Christian sanctuary and went in and conducted their slaughter of hundreds in a small courtyard. The property was never painted over. In 1966, nearly fifty years later, blood stains still showed faintly nearly three feet high on the courtyard wall, all along the wall. Yes, bodies and gore were stacked three feet deep. The Turkish government were then and remain today (especially with the increasing Mohammedan influence in government) one of the world's greatest violators of human rights. Now, in the new century, the Turks are starting their version of taqiyyah with a propaganda campaign wanting to change the historical facts in history books about their genocide. These incontestable truths are not merely Armenian historical facts, but hundreds of independent scholars and historians agree that this genocide took place. Further, while the horrors that befell over a million Armenians were being unleashed, there were thousands of newspapers around the world reporting on this on a regular basis.

As recently as 1955, the Turks rampaged against Greeks in which their homes and businesses were destroyed, their property stolen, their women raped, and men butchered. This is not ancient history, but represents modern Turkey at its very core.

When Arabs and Moslems whine and fuss about their grievances against Christianity and the Crusades, we must not ever, never, ever forget that their grievances are unfounded. The Crusades were simply a payback that didn't succeed in driving the Mohammedans back to where they came from, to where they belong. The Mohammedans have always been the violent, militant aggressors. We, in fact must confront them each and every time they bring this up as a grievance -- that their grievances are pure and simple balderdash – lies, taqiyyah. In the civilized west where democracy and the rule of law prevails, the Mohammedans are learning and teaching their followers to take advantage of liberal laws to further their unrelenting dark, evil cause.

Steeped in the primitive self-delusional Moslem cult's crude core ideology is their claim or belief that all lands once Moslem are therefore Moslem forever. So, they claim that Spain is Moslem, and they dream of a re-conquest of Spain. The present Spanish government seems to be accommodating them.

In recent centuries, the British and the French have been the standard bearers in the conflict with Mohammedan barbarians. They won some and lost some, but gained control of and maintained control

of much of the Arab world for many years creating a sense of stability. This stanched Islam's aggression and expansion for a long time.
<u>Round 4 to the French and to the British.</u>

Hitler was anti-Semitic. Hitler was insane. (Had he prevailed, he would have started on the Arabs after completing his extermination of Jews and Gypsies.) Mohammedans sat it out letting Christendom beat itself up (but they did help Hitler in killing Jews). Closely on the heels of Hitler, the Cold War became the focus of our lives in the West, and Islam found itself facing a common enemy with the West - Communism. The Arabs were nevertheless able to capitalize on the rivalry and benefited from this with support from the Cold War antagonists.
<u>Round 5 was a draw.</u>

Round 6 began with the establishment of the nation of Israel and the Arab-Israeli wars in 1967 and 1973 in which the Israelis scored significant military victories against stupid, incompetent Mohammedans.
<u>Israel won round 6.</u>

However, polarization followed the establishment of Israel, and civilized Western powers were driven out of, or their influence was greatly diminished in Islamic countries. The Arabs discovered and exploited the technological benefits of modern forms of terrorism, and have used those skills both openly and stealthily with significant effect.
<u>Round 7</u> ended with the beginning of the new millennium, and <u>the winner was Islam.</u>

Let's not putz around here! Terror is a tool that has been used liberally by Islam since its inception. We are not by any means facing a new enemy or threat, just a fresh wave of Islamic empire building expansionism that we cannot accommodate in any way if our civilization of independence, political freedom, rights, and pursuit of decency and happiness is to endure.

Today, Christians in Cyprus, Turkey, Pakistan, Armenia, Sudan, Egypt, Nigeria, Timor, Malaysia, and other places are daily at risk of extraordinary Mohammedan brutalization. They are being brutally murdered and 'ethnically' cleansed in Libya, Syria, Iraq, Iran, Saudi Arabia, Bangladesh, Turkey, Bosnia, Indonesia, and other places.

Islam has won four of the preceding seven rounds of which one was a draw.

Round eight opened on 9/11/2001, and Islam is prevailing. Round 8 has promise of becoming a knockout round, and Islam is in a position of opportunity and strength, and is in a position to prevail if we let them, or unwittingly help them.

Their principal tactic in countries where they are not in power is the use of stealth jihad, and with so many stupid useful fools around in leadership positions, the Mohammedans are gaining daily.

250

War on terror

I believe that President Bush was fundamentally a good, decent man, but not very bright. In the war on terror, Bush was by reason of Saudi influence over him confused at best. He was essentially if not willfully blind to the effects the Wahabis had on him and his administration, and the control the Wahabis exert in the United States Government. He has done good things, and then he has done really dumb things.

Early in the Obama administration, there are no improvements in dealing with Islam at all, except that a pacifist and delusional Obama (who has repeatedly emphasized his allegiance to Islam) is even more willfully ignorant than Bush, and Obama's teams of dhimmi minded sycophants will weaken civilization further.

ISLAM: Fundamental Truths

***Islam should be the only religion
permitted on earth, and the
Koran the only law in America!***

> 1998 proclamation by a leader of the Council on American Islamic Relations - CAIR

The Koran is Islam's centerpiece the so-called infallible word of allah as it was came from the befuddled mind of Mohammed. Either Mohammed was befuddled, or his allah was whimsical. The result is the same. I do not believe that allah is a genuine deity. Allah is a figment of Mohammed's feral mind. However, in order to understand the 'infallible' word of allah, one needs to study the Hadiths. These are yet more miscellaneous ramblings and blatherings of Mohammed which are supposedly indispensable guidance for Moslems, enabling them to understand the pure, 'infallible' words in the Koran. If this leaves you confused or befuddled, then you've started to understand what lies between the ears of Moslems and what makes them tick.

We need to understand that the Torah, the Old Testament, the word of God is the living word put into writing by men, fallable men who may have gotten their messages wrong.

The Koran, according to Islamic doctrine is a perfect text that is eternal and cannot ever be reinterpreted, so Islam cannot ever progress out of the dark ages. It is not allowed to do so.

Islam's American Agenda

-        Turn America's freedom of speech into a series of hate crime laws that will eventually eliminate the first

Amendment. Yell, rant, rave, accuse any detractors of Islam to be racists, Zionists, etc.
- Maximize Moslem immigration. Practice no birth control. Mary American women and Islamize them; then divorce them after 3-4 children and mary again and have more children.
- Take over American medicine by getting Moslem doctors involved in every facet of medical care.
- Convert angry, alienated American blacks to Islam. Form groups to riot demanding Islamic Sharia laws in place of America justice.
- Befuddle simple minded Americans by falsely claiming that Islam, Judaism, and Christianity share the same identical virtues.
- Demonize individual who are outspokenly against Islam, intimidate them with messages, and imposing messengers. Seek to eliminate or even to kill them however it can be done.
- Establish Moslem enclaves in cities and communities and let Islam grow and take control of these places.
- Nominate and get Muslim sympathizers elected into office where they can enact legislation favorable to Islam, ultimately to incrementally overthrow the American Constitution, and begin imposing Islamic laws on America.
- Baksheesh American politicians with generous legal and illegal political contributions, donations, funding PAC's that we will control, trips to the middle east where we can BS them about the wonderfulness of Islam, and make them dependent on us and subservient to us like Dick Durban.
- Make big Moslem grants to universities and get Moslem directors in control of universities and colleges.
- Get Islamist operatives into the federal government in key national security positions in the FBI, CIA, State Department, Congress, DHS, the courts and law enforcement agencies at all levels where they can protect Moslems, and work against others within the system.
- As a tactic, occasional acts of violent terrorism, and then whine and claim victimhood if anyone looks sideways at us. American fools fall for this propaganda easily.
- Modify American school textbooks to condition and prepare American children to accept that Islam is superior to other cultures, religions, and ideas. Take over the minds of American children.
- Promote the falsehood that terrorists have hijacked Islam.
- Take control of Hollywood to make sure movies are pro-Islam, get control of the press, TV, radio, and the internet by buying corporations or controlling stock. Muzzle popular

hosts such as O'Reilley, and drive Michael Savage out of the airwaves.

- Appeal to ignorant but compassionate and sensitive Americans for tolerance towards Moslems.

Abraham (Ibrahim)

Moslems often open discussions with Christians claiming that both religions began with Abraham. That's true, but soon after Abraham's mistress, the whore, Hagar bore Abraham a son, Ishmael, God saw fit to bless Abraham's wife, Sarah with a son, Isaac. Hagar plotted against Sarah and Isaac, and her willful son Ishmael reportedly was a lying, immoral, thief. Abraham kicked Hagar and Ishmael out of his tent. Hagar and her illegitimate son, Ishmael were the beginning of what eventually became the followers of Mohammed.

We westerners need to understand clearly that Islamists do NOT operate or function with the same logic as do western or civilized people, nor do they believe in or accept, or even tolerate the same or even similar moral codes, values, or ethics. This is a fundamental truth.

The Koran and its Sharia law (accompanied by the Hadiths, the Sunah, and the Moslem principle and practices of dhimmitude) is a dark enemy working against the Constitution of the United States. Islam is an ideology that is the avowed enemy of the United States (and all of civilization), a dedicated and devoted enemy. Islam today and every day acts against and presents a real danger to the United States and our Constitution - our laws, and our cherished liberties, liberties that Barak Hussein Obama disapproves of.

Mohammed's Koranic teachings include crap like: Everything Moslems do is predetermined, predestined, even commissions of evil, that Moslems have no free will to determine their actions. This means that vile, evil deeds are committed by the will of allah, Insha'Allah! Might this explain why so many Moslems have personalities similar to that of amoebas devoid of human sensibilities? They feel that whatever they do, whenever they do it, and however it is done is the will of allah, Inch' Allah.

Dhimmitude is living in a permanent state of subjugation. If Christians, Jews or other unbelievers are permitted to live, it is to be a sub-human life of humiliating dhimmitude and for most, terrible impoverishment and suffering. People allowed to so live are merely useful, if not essential to the survival of Moslems – that's why they are allowed to live.

There are variants of Islam who claim to be the purest forms and consider other forms to be apostates. While they dispute one-another, all want to put Islam in control of earth, to subjugate all people to the rule of Islam, preferably their form. All reject democracy and any form of republicanism or freedoms of choice in government, of thought, of religion, of life. Any Islamist claims or declarations to the contrary are

253

simply lies, taqiyyah.

Islamists use nice words for what they tell us that they profess. It's takiyyah. They do it in English. What they say or declare is merely to befuddle us. They lie. Lying (takiyyah) is permissible, even preferential in fooling us. They tell us what some of us (willfully ignorant useful fools) want to hear and to believe. Mohammedism, the dark, primitive, evil cult, and its practice leads directly to crimes against humanity.

Like some other religions, Islamic holidays fall at particular times of the lunar year. But, Islam is different. The exact day for some holidays cannot be determined because their occurrence may be subject to the appearance of the moon. There is no assurance that the moon will be there, scientific proof be damned. Accordingly, village "A" in Pakistan may celebrate on one day because someone there saw the moon between clouds, but village "B", a mile or two away can't celebrate that day because nobody saw the moon. Confusing? Yeah!

Because Islam refuses to accept the scientific reality of a 365-¼ day year, they rely on their lunar calendar, so their holidays constantly rotate with about ten days' variation per year.

When I lived in south Asia, there were periods of constant monsoon cloud cover for weeks on end. I asked how anyone could celebrate a holiday that depended on the appearance of the moon when the moon couldn't be seen for weeks on end, nor for that matter, the sun. No Moslem could answer that question for me. I did learn that with the application of modern western technology the problem had mysteriously and miraculously been solved. No Moslem will agree to this, but it's a simple fact. It is now an 'event' where some Imams in Saudi Arabia (if it was cloudy in their location) board a passenger jet, fly above the clouds and the 'miracle' of the appearance of the moon is excitedly be broadcast throughout the Moslem world. This persists today. So, in fact, it is now pre-ordained by mere mortals when the moon would miraculously appear, but for planning purposes, nobody can be certain until some wild eyed bearded Imam determined that the 'miracle' of the moon's appearance occurs.

Wahabism is the fastest growing sect of Mohammedism. Based in totalitarian Saudi Arabia and blessed with prodigious reserves of oil which they prostitute for money, they are able to buy the expansion and influence of Wahabism.

Take a look at the Saudi flag. It is green with Arabic writing and displays a sword, or cutlass. The cutlass or sword symbolizes how Islam is spread -- by the sword -- used to subjugate non believers, or to kill us. The inscription on that Saudi flag is the most "sacred" phrase of the Koran, the shahadah: *There is no god but allah, and Mohammed is his messenger.* The sword depicted gives the clear message that death awaits the non-believers.

The first object of Islamist "missionaries" is to spread the word through good deeds, and pleasant words but if anyone obstructs this form of spreading the word, it is then a duty to kill those who obstruct or refuse to convert, thus the sword. The sword, or the knife is used to cut one's throat and remove their head.

It is known and understood to most (civilized) people in contact with them that those westerners who have converted voluntarily to Islam are bizarre, soulless people to start with. There is no other rational explanation. The only exceptions would be some American Blacks, many who have converted for the simple reason that by belonging to a disciplined organization they were offered a life that was an improvement of sorts over the chaotic lives of disarray that so many came from. These tragic people do convert for what seems to them to be a good reason. Their group, the "Nation of Islam" is nevertheless another separatist, racist group whose goal is the undermining of the Constitution of the United States.

In Florida, an ignorant convert to Islam attempted to impose her personal version of Islam on the American people by refusing to let her face be shown for a photo on her drivers license. Her actions merely demonstrated the depth of her stupidity and arrogance. Apparently unbeknownst to her, Moslem women worldwide remove their veils for passport, visa, identification photos, and drivers licenses (in countries where they are permitted to drive). Notwithstanding, her pious refusal, her visage was already a matter of official record -- in a police/jailbird booking photograph. Ah, such ignorance is truly blissful.

Imperial Wahabism's goal is first to seize ideological control of global Mohammedism, and then to establish themselves dominant in the world. They are having immense success.

In proselytizing their faith, they use phony (taqiyyah) themes of peace, tolerance, and civil liberties copycatting the old Soviet Union's tradecraft of false propaganda. They have taken their time to systematically study us westerners and our civilization to find weaknesses to exploit. They have done this well, very well for fourteen centuries. Of course, our thirst for oil is one of those exploitable weaknesses, and that is why they have invested so heavily (more than three billion dollars per year) in their legal lobbies and in buying the votes of your and my naïve, sometimes incredibly stupid, greedy Senators and Representatives in Washington. They spend additional millions in every state buying the votes of state senators and assemblymen; and even on politicians in major cities.

In addition to the criminal organization, the Council on American-Islamic Relations (CAIR) discussed elsewhere, the Wahabis have established vast networks of other like minded social and political institutions and organizations such as the lead organization, the Moslem Brotherhood of America and its many subsidiaries and franchises, the American Muslim Council (AMC), the Muslim World League (MWL), the World Assembly of Muslim Youth (WAMY), the Islamic Society of North America (ISNA), the Global Relief Foundation (a terrorist organization that has been shut down by USG authorities), and hundreds more.

These all operate under the guise of being mosques, charities, educational foundations, youth and/or student organizations, investment firms, tax-exempt foundations, holding companies, etc. They raise money to fund their purchases (bribing) of lawmakers, to screen their funding of terrorist groups, to fund all manner of Mohammedan/Islamic activities. When any one of these outfits, or their leadership becomes too notorious and gets too much exposure as a lying anti-civilization front of fundamentalist Islam/Mohammedism, and their activities are found to be illegal, they just shift themselves or their resources to another, and yet another far faster than cumbersome government law enforcement institutions can move to keep up with them. The AMC had as its coordinator for lobbying (buying politicians) the very same Sami Al Arian who was finally caught up in his absurd lies and was indicted on fifty counts of terrorist involvement.

The AMC founder, Abdurahman Alamoudi has declared: "We are all supporters of Hamas and Hezbollah", both of which are violent terrorist organizations.

Moslems in mosques in the United States pursue a political agenda that is anti-United States, and anti-Constitution, therefore anti-American. This is a fundamental truth. Nowhere will anyone find a mosque classifying itself as non-Islamist. Therefore all mosques are Islamist (Mohammedan) in their fundamental nature and, they believe and promulgate Sharia as the desired law of the land. There does not exist a Moslem system that teaches to Moslems the acceptance of the principles of political and religious pluralism and to live in true, genuine harmony with non-Moslems. This is another dark but fundamental truth of Islam.

Mohammedans in Quebec, Canada attempted to force the Canadian (Quebec) government to recognize Sharia laws. This was hotly debated, and after due consideration, wisdom and sensibility (as well as decency, honesty, and character) prevailed and the Quebec legislature decided to disallow discrimination with Moslem (Sharia) tribunals in the province. Self-respecting Moslem women had been holding their breath and secretly praying to the real God that the Quebec government would do the right thing by disallowing Sharia; to permit continued liberty, decency, freedom, happiness, and so forth for people equally. Naturally, the Mohammedan men are seething over this rejection of their evil stupidity. For example the Canadian chapter of the mafia-like Council on American Islamic Relations whined claiming that the Canadians (those of a civilized mentality) didn't understand what faith-based arbitration is all about. Balderdash! The Canadians understood too well what it meant and rejected it. Good for them. What it meant was that the Mohammedans will be further limited in their efforts to isolate and control Moslem people in Canada.

In England however, British libel law is being exploited by Mohammedans. American author, Rachel Ehrenfeld has a book, FUNDING EVIL, that documents (among other things) how a Saudi charity owned by a Saudi billionaire (Sheikh Khalid bin Mahfouz, a Wahabi Mohammedan) funneled millions of dollars to al Qaeda. He sued Ehrenfeld in British court where her book is now banned, and were she cannot easily defend herself. Now, she therefore cannot travel to England where she faces arrest and incarceration for her decency and good work. The U.S. Department of State ought to put Mahfouz on the terror lookout list and keep him from traveling to the United States, should impound his money (he is in fact a terrorist supporter), and issue a warrant for his arrest. But, he's rich, connected (he has American politicians in his pocket), and can therefore get away with his crap. This is insane!

While the British are playing host to some of the most evil beings on earth, they are rejecting some of the most decent people on earth. Their wild-eyed Moslems have so intimidated the British that the government has disallowed travel to England by great intellectuals such as American writer and radio host Michael Savage, and Dutch parliamentarian Geert Wilders because they are honest and outspoken about the evils of the true Islam.

The British have stupidly (their Archbishop of Canterbury is about the most stupid, ignorant religious leader in the world) determined that they can allow Sharia laws to be practiced in Mohammedan enclaves. Those Mohammedan enclaves in Britain are so evil, that British citizens are not allowed to enter them. Britain is on its way to losing its freedom and becoming another bastion of stupidity, evil, and poverty.

Wahabist Mohammedans have infiltrated U.S. government law enforcement and intelligence institutions as well as our law making bodies themselves, the Congress of the United States. In so doing they buy and even control legislation and insert loopholes in laws that permit them to keep operating without being monitored or stopped. Former Senator Edward Kennedy, greedy and in need of lots of money to buy his re-election campaigns, inserted such a loophole in the USA Patriot Act and the Foreign Intelligence Surveillance Act. This guarantees that carrying out instructions of a foreign intelligence officer in support of political objectives in the USA is not covered under the law. The cowardly hero of Chappaquiddick, Kennedy, a treasonous traitor has become a fifth columnist, has sold us out and provided protection for those involved in subverting the constitution and laws of the United States. This really means that the U.S. government has been intentionally crippled from within by being very poorly equipped at best to monitor foreign covert political influencing operations against Americans and especially against U.S. lawmakers. If it weren't so scary it would be laughable how the dragging of dirty Saudi money through a greedy politician's field of view is like a $20 in slick Willie Clinton's childhood trailer park.

Under the Patriot act, the authorities can secretly check on and monitor activities of people in the United States (including American citizens) for acts of subversion. They have done this with thousands of people per year, and often have violated the simple regulation governing this. This is wrong. As a loyal American, I understand, accept, and even welcome properly undertaken extra national security precautions without resentment. However, our Mohammedans resent, resist and work to thwart these efforts at every step.

Renowned and highly respected experts have urged that the United States government start monitoring Moslem employees in American law enforcement, military, intelligence, and diplomatic services for subversive activities. They have a valid reason for this. There are evil Mohammedan subversives in government who hurt us daily. We have got to stop them. We don't need any more major Hasans, but they are being permitted by continue as they have for years, right here in our back yards:

> Amal Kasi, Pakistani, CIA HQ, 1993
> Hassan Mohammad Hadayat, Egyptian, 2002
> Sgt. Hassan Akbar, U.S. Army, Kuwait, 2003
> Mohammed Reza Taheri-azar, Iranian, NC, 2006
> Naveed Afzal Haq, Pakistani, Seattle, 2006
> Omeed Aziz Popal, Afghani, San Francisco, 2006
> Suleyman Talovic, Bosnian, Salt Lake City, 2007
> Abdul Hakin Muhammad, American, Little Rock, 2009

An example of their powerful influence: They have caused (perhaps with the help of the naive Bush Whitehouse) an FBI probe into terrorist ties of the World Assembly of Muslim Youth's (WAMY) Virginia office, headed by Abdullah bin Laden (yeah, Osama's brother) to mysteriously be dropped. The Wahabis have wormed their slimy way so far into the FBI so as to have helped to propagate a culture of extreme political correctness silencing the likes of the FBI's very own, very professional counter terrorism expert, Robert Wright, for exposing how his bosses inserted their power and influence to block or stop investigations into Islamic terror networks in the United States. They worked hard (but without success) to prevent information from surfacing that a Mohammedan traitor in their midst, Special FBI Agent Gamel Abdel-Hafiz refused to wear a wire in an investigation because he declared that a Moslem doesn't record another Moslem. Was he disciplined or fired for his act of treason? No. He should have been shot or exported to a country that would appreciate his treachery.

The FBI reportedly had about 800 officers devoted to counter-terrorism activities. Fifty percent of them are Mohammedans, a majority of whom are sworn enemies of our Constitution. I am concerned that should I come across information about terrorism, I fear that I would compromise myself if I contacted the FBI.

Wafa Sultana, a very courageous woman of Syrian descent who humbled Islamic clergymen in televised debates received a number of vile death threats. When she contacted the FBI about these, a Moslem FBI agent came to her, behaved rudely and in a very intimidating manner. He scared her so badly that she went into hiding. This courageous American citizen is fearful as well as distrustful of the FBI!

Undue Islamic influence and even controls exerted over the FBI, CIA, DHS, and others in gathering, analyzing and disseminating intelligence and other valuable and useful information are having a seriously detrimental effect on American national security as well as it is detrimental to civilization.

The Wahabis even conduct pro Mohammedist brainwashing operations (sensitivity training classes) at the FBI's Quantico training academy, and the Pentagon's National War College. This is outrageous! We need patriots to train our law enforcement and military people, not anti-American propagandists. The Wahabis control all Islamic chaplains in the U.S. Military and in the U.S. prisons where they indoctrinate as opposed to teach or preach. One such Army chaplain, Captain James (Youssef) Yee was caught at the prison facility at Guantanamo Bay carrying classified documents out. We can only guess at the purpose of his purloining of those documents. Charges of espionage were later dropped, and of course Yee and his fellow Mohammedans claim that this was because those documents had no meaning or intelligence value. One need not induce much imagination to see the Saudi hand behind this. Major General Miller, the commander of the Joint Task force at Guantanamo simply announced that the government dropped the charges because there were national security concerns that would arise from a release of the evidence (the sensitive classified documents) in a trial. Then, of course Yee and his pals later insisted that the Pentagon apologize for going after him, a thieving slimy, treasonous fifth columnist lowlife.

The Wahabi Mohammedans are getting their stuff together and are in fact censoring Islamic topics at universities and colleges, and are controlling or preventing Islamic education in public schools unless they are the ones providing for the evil brainwashing of our children. The Mohammedans recognize and understand that public schools are fertile grounds for their evil brainwashing program. In this connection, there are all too many American parents totally ignorant of the evil propaganda being fed to their children, and sadly, who could really care less about what their children are being taught. History books being used in American public schools teach that jihad merely means a struggle for a Moslem to do one's best to resist temptations and evil. This is an example of taqiyyah at its best - indoctrinating (brain washing) American children about that which is not true, and that which will in fact eventually hurt them. American history books don't teach history anymore, not honest history complete with warts. The teachers themselves don't even know the truth about history because the history books have been misadjusted. To counter this, we need to organize civilized parent groups to monitor in, and after class activities at schools, materials used in teaching, newsletters, videos, films, etc., to protect young children's fertile minds from the depredations of evil fundamentalist religious cults such as Islam.

Moslem schools in the United States (and Canada) actively teach hatred of Jews and Christians, and even emulate the extremist Madrassas compelling students to memorize the Koran, segregation from non-Moslem Americans and Canadians, gender separation, and other sick Mohammedist crap. When there were reports in the mainstream press about these activities, the typical taqiyyah came out of people like Islamic school principals and leaders of Moslem community councils, groups, etc., claiming they were "shocked". A student in a Saudi funded Islamic school near Washington, D.C. expressed his feelings that being American is just being born in America. Saudi published books (propaganda) used in the United States and Canada indoctrinate young American children that all religions are false except Islam, etc.

Teachers at those Saudi Mohammedan schools are Saudi government employees, some with diplomatic credentials. They are in fact preaching hatred and the violent overthrow of the American constitution. Sixteen arrogant Saudi nationals holding Saudi Diplomatic passports and accredited to the Saudi Embassy were recently kicked out of the United States because they were teaching Islam outside of the Saudi Embassy and were therefore in violation of their status. Thankfully, someone was aware and took action.

When Secretary of Defense Rumsfeld started an excellent but legally questionable operation to try to influence Islamic populations, one of his own, a DoD spokesperson, Torie Clarke reportedly leaked lies and disinformation designed to wreck the plan to the New York Pravda (Times). Rumsfeld wanted to do this operation to establish something akin to the cold war's anti-communist Voice of America/Radio Freedom to spread the truth to the Islamic world, to counter their lies. We still don't have anything to do this, and Hanoi/Mecca Jane's former squeeze, Ted Turner's CNN sure as hell wasn't performing the role.

We need a "RADIO FREE ISLAM." Assuredly, Chappaquiddick hero, Kennedy (now deceased), the Wahabis, Turner, Obama, and other fifth columnists and useful fools of their ilk won't allow that to happen.

We in the civilized world need to better understand the evil depth and breadth of both Islam in general and Wahabism in particular's influence in our countries and institutions and then to take action to counter them.

FUNDAMENTAL TRUTH: Islam is NOT compatible with civilized societies.

The Mohammedans like to do a form of forked tongued Islamic rope-a-dope called 'taqiyyah' and 'kitman' when challenged in order to turn aside their opponents. It does take some skill, knowledge and understanding of Mohammedism (illogic) thinking to handle some of these guys. One of the most skilled Mohammedans, a jerk in Europe, Tariq Ramadan had for a while successfully convinced people that he was a moderate scholar. Ramadan and his "kitman" eventually ran out of room in Europe (Geneva) and he decided to move his sorry, emissive, prevaricating, lying, deceitful operations to Notre Dame in the United States but was wisely denied admittance to the United States because he is in actual fact a terrorist. Ramadan worked at it but ran out of room when he met with Islamic expert Nicolas Sarkozy (who is now the President of France) in a public venue and was shown up for the phony that he is. Well educated, expert at circumlocution and articulate, Ramadan is an associate of known terrorists and is simply a slimy immoral Mohammedan pig scum bag who ought to be exiled back to whence he came. Ramadan is one of those Mohammedans who want to cure Europe's 'spiritual' deficiencies by imposing Islam on the Europeans first, then on the United States.

The American people need to learn more about the other Ramadan types who have managed to slip through and are in the United States disbursing their subversive messages of hate.

Federal, State, and local government officials need to be honestly appraised of what Islamist organizations are tied to or affiliated ideologically, materially, financially, or in any other way with identified terrorist groups (Anything Islamic is technically terrorist). CAIR would fall at the top of this list. The CAIR has as its main goal in the United States, the stifling of the right to free speech, which is guaranteed by the First Amendment. This is sedition!

CAIR is engaged in acts trying to enforce censorship of what Americans read: When two books were advertised in the conservative *National Review* magazine, the CAIR launched a campaign of intimidation demanding an apology and removal of advertisements for the books. The books were *The Life and Religion of Mohammed* by (missionary) Fr. J. L. Menezes (an accurate research written eighty years ago), and the excellent, historically accurate and truthful *Sword of the Prophet* by Serge Trifkovic. CAIR ranted about the books (which clearly depict unfavorable truths and facts about Mohammed's posing as an Apostle of God, his innumerable marriages, licentiousness, deeds of rapine, torture, warfare, thievery, butchery, claiming that all was done with divine guidance) claiming the books were virulently Islampohobic hate speech, etc. The books were the truth, factually, and historically. Clearly CAIR differs with what others want to say about Mohammed, but they have no right to censor what freedom loving people have a right to say.

CAIR apologists freaked when a TV series that came out depicting some Moslems as terrorists, and whined about how people may (negatively) view Moslems. That's OK. Mohammedans are in fact, in deed, in act after act, in fact our enemies, our very worst enemies.

Saudi Embassy (in Washington D.C.) spokesman and snake oil purveyor, Adel al-Jubeir has claimed with one side of his forked tongue that the Saudis are fighting terrorism and that they support "peace" with Israel while funding and supporting several terrorist organizations engaged in daily acts of terror against both Israel and the United States.

A reporter investigated and then reported on how a Saudi billionaire, Sheikh bin Mahout has been stalking and suing (its called intimidation) reporters or writers who have reported on his funding of terrorists and terrorist organizations. This creep needs to be placed on the list of those not allowed entry into the United States, and more, that the federal government get off of its arse and properly and thoroughly investigate this guy's involvement and then impound his billions, etc. Perhaps a true patriot somewhere will take stronger action......

I have borrowed some details and facts from one of, if not, the very most respected and arguably best informed experts on Islam on earth, among them Stephen Schwartz, whose factual, honest, and insightful writings I have and continue to read whenever I get the chance. Mr. Schwartz has testified repeatedly before the Congress and Senate lending his well informed insightful analyses and expertise. He is very highly regarded by good people.

American Foolishness

Our American liberals need only to look into a mirror to see a major enemy of our freedoms, and an ally, a useful fool of the Islamists who wish to subjugate America. The liberals need to look inwards and see what they are doing to contribute to the demise of that which they treasure, their own freedoms.

Blasphemy

In Islam, blasphemy includes the definition that freedom of thought, freedom of conscience, choice of religion (outside of Islam) are unpardonable sins.

In Pakistan a man was sent to prison for seven years because he insulted Islam's holy book, the Koran. The man admitted (anyone who would admit in an Islamic court that he insulted the Koran is not too bright, if not nuts) that he used the Koran for a leg rest whilst sleeping, and that he tore out pages on which he would write magic spells that he would hand out to others. Under Sharia law he could have been sentenced to death. Under Islamic laws anyone who insults the Koran (me, for instance), who throws it on the ground, slamming one's hand down violently near or on the Koran, touching it with feet, etc., can be sentenced to death for such blasphemy and desecration.

The American news magazine, Newsweek, published a fantasy about American interrogators flushing a Koran down a toilet at a detention camp at Guantanamo Bay, Cuba. They retracted their tale after Moslems in a few countries rioted about the so-called desecration and several people reportedly died although their names were never released(?) nor details about how they died. The red faced Newsweek brass confessed that the story was a fabrication, and expressed some regret that their falsehood caused some people to lose their lives. Notwithstanding the Newsweek brass' confession that the story was a fabrication, a bunch of Saudi "scholars" went on a rant demanding that those responsible (those who did not perpetrate the non flushing in the non toilet of the non existent Koran) be tried in an Islamic court. Yeah, sure! Some real justice there, eh?

Later, after a sane investigation, Newsweek published an article affirming that acts of desecration in most cases were in fact committed by the Mohammedan inmates themselves, not their guards. (No Mohammedan rants here.) Among these incidents was documentation that Moslem inmates have themselves flushed pages torn from their Koran down toilets. American guards' handling of the Koran have been respectful and any 'touching' of it has been respectful and never intentionally disrespectful. While bibles are tossed around, American guards are required to handle the Koran delicately so as not to offend criminal murderers. This cockeyed nonsense is plainly over the top.

On the other hand, Mohammedans have often used pages torn from the Christian bible for toilet paper, but that's OK, in fact it is an article of faith for Moslems to erase the past by destroying burning books, in particular bibles, and those contrary to their twisted beliefs. And, naturally, holding the Koran in one hand, reciting its verses while holding a knife in another and then hollering "Alahu Akbar" while slowly and torturously butchering a bound and defenseless person by slowly and purposefully slicing through his or her throat until the head rolls free is just fine.

In response to Mohammedan outrage, President Bush went on with atypical simple minded and foolish platitudes: "We respect and admire the religion of peace and tolerance." Hey, Mr. ex-President: Have you heard that Islam is an evil cult?

When the pitiful South Korean Kim Sun-Il was slowly butchered by Mohammedans in Iraq, the South Korean people sadly surprised me with their cowardly Spanish like reaction, demanding that the South Korean government pull out of Iraq. I had hoped that the South Koreans would get their hackles up and sack or burn a couple of mosques in Korea. That would have been the appropriate thing to do. Cowards!

I know and understand that the President of the United States (Bush) thought that he had to act out to appease a billion or so jerks. I wonder what he really and truly thought..........

In March, 2005, a Saudi writer was sentenced to 275 lashes (of a whip or a cane) and several months in prison for questioning the method for determining the beginning of a holy day (subject to the appearance of the moon) and intelligently suggested that this was being primitive. Another Saudi (a rare civilized man, but one of questionable sanity) criticized the commission that imposed the 275 lashes and jail time, and that fellow was put on trial by the very commission of evil, ignorant Saudi morons that he criticized.

An Italian writer, a seventy-year old woman named Oriana

Fallaci, was hauled into Italian court by an Islamist for exercising her rights to freely express herself in telling truths and facts about Islam in her best selling (in Europe) book, *The Force of Reason*. An Islamist, Adel Smith accused Fallaci of defamation. Yet, when he himself was found guilty of gross defamation, he whined like a baby. In her book *The Force of Reason*, Fallaci asserted facts which are historically accurate and correct but obviously because of their truthfulness, accuracy, and correctness were found to be offensive to Moslems. One of these historically accurate assertions discusses the Moslem sacking of an Abbey and then sacrificing the virginity of a nun every evening on the altar. Fallaci spoke of the yoke of the Islamic creed that spreads hatred instead of love; an Islam that extols slavery over freedom; of decrying the Islamic practice of the sexual mutilation of young girls which she called female castration. Fallaci complained about the five times daily imposition of howling of Moslem meuzzin from loudspeakers calling their Mohammedans to prayer. For speaking the truth and speaking her mind, the Mohammedans wanted to muzzle this fabulous woman. They failed.

Sir Winston Churchill was very wise and had this to say about Islam in his 1899 book, THE RIVER WAR: "*How dreadful are the curses which Mohammedanism lays on its votaries! Besides the fanatical frenzy, which is as dangerous in a man as hydrophobia in a dog, there is this fearful fatalistic apathy. The effects are apparent in many countries. Improvident habits, slovenly systems of agriculture, sluggish methods of commerce, and insecurity of property exist wherever the followers of the Prophet rule or live. A degraded sensualism deprives this life of its grace and refinement; the next of its dignity and sanctity. The fact that in Mohammedan law every woman must belong to some man as his absolute property (either as a child, a wife, or a concubine) must delay the final extinction of slavery until the faith of Islam has ceased to be a great power among men. Individual Moslems may show splendid qualities. Thousands became the brave and loyal soldiers of the Queen; all know how to die; but the influence of the religion paralyses the social development of those who follow it. No stronger retrograde force exists in the world. Far from being moribund, Mohammedanism is a militant and proselytizing faith. It has already spread throughout Central Africa, raising fearless warriors at every step; and were it not that Christianity is sheltered in the strong arms of science (the science against which it had vainly struggle) the civilization of modern Europe might fall, as fell the civilization of ancient Rome.*"

Chapter 17

APOCALYPSE
(Greek for "Lifting the Veil")

Before the attacks of 9/11/2001 and when I was inspired (my outrage was a kick in my own pants) to reconsider Islam and then to write this book, I confess that I was ambivalent about the true, dark, evil culture of Islam and the Arabs even though I had lived in Moslem countries for over a decade. I had espoused an opinion (actually a misguided hope) that Islam is basically a peaceful religion. I have known and liked a few people from this culture and religion, and still like them, some of them, a few. But there aren't many of them.

I realize now that those rare few whom I can still really like and feel genuinely and comfortable being around are definitely not devout practitioners of Islam. Neither are they agnostics any more than I. They, like I, believe in a greater, universal God of decency, love, charity, and goodness, but eschew fanaticism and the destruction of others (people and societies) based on a preferred, brutally arbitrary, evil method of believing in, and primitive forced or false worshipping of allah.

Following the 9/11/2001 attacks, I had to reflect on my views, and consider more than my own narrow, limited understanding prior to that eventful day. I had to go out and study and learn more. I did.

**The world is too dangerous to live in,
not because of people who do evil but
because of people who sit and let it happen**
Albert Einstein

I pulled out my copy of the Koran and actually, conscientiously reviewed the writings. Much wording attributed to Mohammed is indeed very hateful towards non-Moslems as well as women. The time I have spent studying and learning has led me to become less narrow minded (pro-Islam). In studying and learning I have come to understand the honest, true, dark, evil side of humanity called Islam.

You may read in different books, articles, web sites, quotes from the Koran citing chapter and verse. If you check them in a copy of the Koran, you may become confused. The chapter and verse may vary according to version and interpretation. So, a Shiia version may differ from a Sunni version, as will they vary from a Wahabi (conservative and regressive Sunni), or Ahmadiyya version, etc.

Current English language offerings, mostly of Saudi origin have been carefully translated to soften down or evade truthful, factual writings and teachings of the Koran. They are just Islamist propaganda.

We must all be reminded that Mohammed was ignorant. He

was possibly charismatic. There is little doubt that he was very sly and deceptive. Mohammed did not write the Koran. He just babbled. He couldn't read what was written when and if it was done. So, nobody is absolutely certain that his every utterance was accurately transcribed. His solution to most problems seemingly was to attack and subjugate or kill his opponents. Mohammed was in fact a thug. His failures are not trumpeted, but assuredly he and his minions rightfully got humiliated on occasion, and that humiliation is the root of his hatred. In true Moslem tradition however, just about anything, any truth along this line is and always will be patently denied. The Koran speaks of charity and forgiveness (but only to those who converted to, or are followers of Mohammed). It is possible if not probable that Mohammed was mentally unable to deal well with or to cope with reality, and that is why his many utterances seem to be confused and inarticulate in nature, often garbled and undefinable, and hateful in particular. Maybe he was stoked up on Qot, a still popular narcotic

Here is an attempt to describe the differences between the two major factions of Islam, the Shiia and the Sunni who have little compunction in their hatred of one-another: The difference dates back to when Mohammed died, and involves who should have taken over that mob. Mohammed neglected to set an orderly succession, so a feud erupted and goes on today between those who claim to be blood descendants of Mohammed, and others who claim to be the more devout followers.

A high ranking Palestinian (Attillah Quiba) has claimed that the pig, Yassir Arafat, was poisoned by high technology of some sort (Israeli or western, of course). This is but one of hundreds of grossly stupid and ignorant mutterings of senior level Arabs. It is sad, but very typical stuff. Arafat died of AIDS. And, he didn't get his HIV from a blood transfusion either.

**Read not one book and follow,
but read two or more and decide.**

Scholars have studied and dissected the great religions of Judaism and Christianity for centuries, including their histories and all that has been written and recorded. Our knowledge of these religions is great.

There are almost no comprehensive modern non-Islamist studies of Islam's 1400 years, of Islamic of jihad-holy war conquests of non-Moslems. There are very few if any thorough, balanced, critical examinations of Islam at all. The Koran has never really been subjected to scrutiny following the proof demanded by rational standards of modern archaeology and historical scholarship. Most recent so-called scholars of Islam are Islamist proselytizers or apologists who fail or refuse to consider all of the Koran or any of the Haditha (more garbled mutterings and pronouncements attributable to Mohammed). Any

Islamic scholars or experts who are not apologists are roundly denounced, ridiculed, or rejected outright by Islamists who are terrified that anyone will discover any real truths of Islam. Fearful Islamists with clouded minds strive at every turn to prevent honest examination or exploration into the soul of Islam. In fact, critical investigation of the Koran or other Islamic writings attributed to or about Mohammed are in fact expressly forbidden. In reading or trying to study the Arabic Koran, one will find that a lot of what it says does not make any sense (Mohammed's garbled mutterings), and any serious intellectual attempt to explore this inconsistency and confusion is not welcome. After all, the Koran is held by Islamists to be the literal word of Allah. So, gee, we've got to believe them at their good word, right?

Well, over the eons spanning human history, there have been many texts that their various believers declare were handed down by God. The Koran is just another of those, nothing, absolutely nothing more, especially in consideration of the evil degenerate responsible for it.

Some few scholars who know well, have studied some of the earliest renditions of the Koran and have even claimed that parts of it were derived from Christian Aramaic texts. This is more than plausible. Other historical scholars agree that the first evidence of any Koran at all didn't even appear until close to sixty years after Mohammed died.

My studies and reflections have been an epiphany for me. I have read some books, followed the news, listened to Islamists speak, and done additional research on my own. I have studied, digested, analyzed and determined that because of my own earlier ignorance, I had been too soft on Islam.

I find that modern Islam is without a doubt hostile to modern civilization. Islam is determined to destroy our culture and replace it with Islam in a new dark age of hate, fear, repression, torture, enslavement, and ugliness. That, sadly is the true face of Islam.

Fundamentally, Islam divides the world into two parts, the house of Islam -- Dar al Islam, and the house of war -- Dar al Harb. That's it. There is no room for or consideration of anything else. War against or conquest of the unbeliever is a central doctrine and practice of Islam. Islam is nothing more than a religion of war and conquest. The principal belief of Islam is killing, eliminating, subjugating, or destroying non-believers - civilization.

The founder of Islam, Mohammed was a man with real serious limitations.

Islam is considered by some Christians to be the New Testament's Antichrist (Revelations).

Islam has almost always been dominated by ethically challenged and morally bankrupt leaders intent on enslaving the world. This continues today, and will not likely change in the future (1000+ years). These ungodly leaders of Islam would install ugly totalitarian Sharia based laws and punish everyone on earth, including or even especially the dwindling numbers of moderate (lax) Moslems for any and all transgressions, real and perceived.

We must also recognize that there are decent, good people dubbed Moslems who are really nominal Moslems, who are compelled to pay lip service to Islam to preserve their very lives. They deserve recognition and protection. They are nevertheless a distinct and probably a doomed minority.

Under the centuries of leadership of this long chain of intolerant, fearful and fearsome men, the Moslem world, the nations of the Moslem culture are the most impoverished and backward countries on Earth. In recent years of rapid world economic growth, Arab economies with an abundance of that which is needed to generate wealth, remain in economic stagnation.

More than thirty thousand Imams (Moslem preachers) from over sixty (60) countries take their lead from Saudi Arabia every week for their sermons. Fifty-two times a year, sermons that savagely attack Christianity in most disparaging terms. When referring to the Pope, the accompanying term "may Allah punish him as he deserves" is usually included. This was even done regarding Pope John Paul II, even when he was striving to improve relations with Islam.

Another Example: Secretary-General Kofi Annan of the United Nations was often referred to (in Saudi mosques) as the "Betrayer-General", who the Imams call a combined Jew and Christian. I wonder what they call the useful fool and willfully ignorant apologist Korean Secretary General, Ban Ki-Moon

A common theme of these sermons is jihad, contextually used to motivate Moslem children in the hatred of infidel Christians and Jews. Underlying this is the bedrock theme that a true Israeli-Palestinian peace will never, ever be accepted. This is what comes from Saudi religious leaders as an instruction to all other religious leaders. There is nothing very much different said in Syria, Pakistan, Iran, Iraq, Lebanon, Egypt or other Arab and Moslem countries.

In Sarajevo, the Saudis offered money to rebuild a mosque provided the Imams of that mosque would begin preaching Saudi (Wahabi) style fundamentalism. The Saudis were rejected. Wow! Here we have an Islamic group with a sense of independence and feelings of responsibility who were unwilling to be exploited. Neat! Rare!

Islamic front groups (in fact, almost ALL Islamic groups) in Europe, Asia, and America regularly and repeatedly raise funds in support of terrorist groups under the guise of humanitarianism. In all of those non-Mohammedan countries, restrictions on conducting intrusive investigations should be, must be lifted.

Chapter 18

WHAT KIND OF A CULTURE ARE WE DEALING WITH?

INSHA' ALLAH
(The will of God)

Wherever one travels in the Moslem world, the phrase, "Insha'Allah" is heard again and again as well as being written in many places. "Insha'Allah" translated into English means: "It is the will (or wish) of allah," or invokes the meaning: "Allah made it happen."

When a person sneezes, it's Insha'Allah" as in gesundheit.

When a dish is dropped and breaks, it's "Insha'Allah" as in oops!

When a farmer complains about the lack of rain, it's Insha'Allah".

When someone hijacks a plane and it is flown into a sky scraper, it's "Insha'Allah!" as in "It is the will of Allah!"

The phrase "Insha'Allah" is written on the front bumpers of trucks, buses, taxis. Its purpose is to absolve the driver should the vehicle cause damage somewhere.

When a bus driven by a hashish besotted driver runs through a bus stop and kills a bunch of pedestrians, it's "Insha'Allah" – the mayhem was the will of Allah. It was Allah's desire, not the moronic driver's fault. When a truck driven by some egomaniac speeding down a narrow, crowded lane or alley crushes a child, it's "Insha'Allah", as in God made it happen. The goofy driver had nothing to do with being a reckless, careless, uncaring ass.

Blame the pain, mayhem, and suffering on someone else, it's the Arab/Moslem way - to find a scapegoat for their own idiocy.

In Bangladesh, a pedestrian, looking the other way walked out from between parked cars (at the middle of the block) in front of a bus the American Embassy operated and got himself killed. Soon, the ambulance chasers (local lawyers) seeking big bucks from the "rich" Americans showed up at my office clamoring for money. The bus was from the Embassy motor pool that I ran, and I had to deal with them. I met with the group, most of whom were shouting and brandishing their outstretched palms demanding instant wealth, I refused them. They clamored louder. Concluding that I couldn't deal with them rationally, I responded "Insha'Allah" and walked away. I heard no more, and we didn't fork over a penny.

A rickshaw zoomed out of its traffic lane and sideswiped my car ripping the rickshaw's wheel off and spilling its passenger into the street. I drove on to the Embassy compound (it's unwise, even foolishly dangerous, especially for an infidel foreigner to stop and wait for an

Islamic mob to assemble and go nuts in these types of circumstances). After the expected crowd of wealth seekers assembled at the compound gate, I met with them (guards at my back), I pointed out that the rickshaw had hit and hooked the rear bumper of my car and had in fact caused damage to my car. My next statement was "Insha'Allah", I make no claim on the rickshaw driver, and I walked away. The crowd dispersed.

"Insha'Allah" is cultural. It is fatalistic. It represents both an excuse for those who "do" and acceptance by victims.

Long ago, a gardener (working in the grounds of an American Embassy in an Arab country) who had never driven a vehicle, climbed into an Embassy truck, got it running and drove it into a pool. When asked why he did it, his response was "Insha'Allah" and a shrug. When Arab workers complained to the American supervisor who fired the man, the American shrugged and responded "Insha'Allah.", meaning that Allah had fired the man, their complaint ended.

Insha'Allah - it's the will of Allah, it's Allah's fault. Allah screwed over you. Allah killed your family member. Allah stole from you. Allah is why you're ignorant. Allah gave you AIDS. Allah made you hate everyone and everything.

"Insha'Allah" represents one aspect of what we in our culture must understand and deal with. It depicts a culture who, if they kill one of their own are fatalistically accepting of death as Allah's will. However, when an infidel such as an Israeli or American kills one of them, it's not accepted as the will of Allah, "Insha'Allah." Revenge is however an "Insha'Allah" inspired response, and they view killing us as Allah's will, and refuse to acknowledge that killing any infidel can in any way be wrong. Insha'Allah, a Hindu in Bangladesh walked past a Mosque after services and the Mohammedans were so enraged at this transgression that they beat the poor guy to death.

Insha'Allah, it is their goal, their mission, their sacred duty to destroy our society, our culture, us. This is according to the Koran.

When the world trade center was taken down millions of Mohammedans celebrated along with bin Laden who declared "Insha'Allah". Most Moslems in America celebrated the downing of the World trade Center. This, we must all remember.

Jerry Fallwell, another zealous religious fundamentalist didn't use that Arab phrase Insha'Allah, but he opined that the attacks of 9/11/2001 were the will of, or an act of God. According to Fallwell, God did it because we have become a nation of fornicators and abortionists. In this, Fallwell and bin Laden were two of a kind.

Then of course, there were thousands and thousands if not many millions of silly Mohammedans who actually believed Mohammedan preachers who claimed the 9/11 attacks were caused by Zionist hooligans, a conspiracy theory, one of thousands of outlandish conspiracy theories based on whim and imagination.

Love, Gentleness, and Charity

Moslems the world over, especially in western societies, profess the love, charity, and the peaceful intentions of Islam. For instance, Islamic laws (some stemming from the drug besotted, deceptive, out of control ego, and anger induced rambling musings of Mohammed) mandates death for apostates, anyone leaving Islam, such as the unspeakable act of converting to Christianity. That's real love, charitable thinking, and forgiveness, isn't it?

During the war between Iraq and Iran, both sides in this Moslem-vs.-Moslem conflict charitably and lovingly used women and children by herding or stampeding them across minefields, to clear mines by detonating them. It was not important to these so very caring, charitable leaders that women and children were slaughtered and maimed, and left to suffer and die prolonged and agonizing deaths in those awful minefields. Of course, they didn't use women and children of their own tribe or religious faction, they used innocents of the other's tribes and religious factions. Thus, the Sunnis of Iraq were eliminating Shiia women and children before they could further breed or reproduce more of the despised Shiia. The Iranians, of course used Sunni women and children. Both sides of course used Kurds, Turkomen, Jews, Bahai, Zoroastrians, and Christians as well, all therefore expendable.

Moslem boys at play have as a basic objective in their games, to make the other, weaker children cry, all else is secondary. To bully and hurt others, especially those who are defenseless or lack the strength, will, or ability to resist is a desirable Moslem pastime. Responses are such as when Saddam Hussein dispatched his trusted troops against Iraqi citizens (Kurds and Shiia Moslems in different areas of Iraq) who were not of his Sunni sect, and dispatched them with chemical weapons, poison gas, nerve gases. No quarter was given to women, children, infants, the old, the infirm - none, no mercy. This is genocide. This is Islam. Reportedly close to 200,000 Kurds were 'cleansed' under Saddam and not one Arab objected to this. This is an acceptable practice among those primitive willfully ignorant Mohammedans going back centuries.

In February, 1996, following a series of suicide bus bombings, an American-born Islamic militant drove his car into a group of Israeli citizens waiting at a bus stop in Jerusalem, killing one and wounding 25. After Israelis opened fire and shot the terrorist dead as he tried to flee, the American based Muslim Public Affairs Council (MPAC) issued a press release accusing Israel of a "terrorist" act because they killed the murderer.

That is atypical Moslem thinking at work.

A Traveler's Tale

Traveling with my pregnant wife from Paris to North Africa on an

Arab airline, we found ourselves moving from an organized civilized operation to a typical Moslem/Arab operation. There were no reserved or assigned seats for passengers. The rule is to fend for oneself. To get a choice seat, or even side-by-side seats with their family members, people needed to rush the boarding door as soon as it opened, climbing over, jostling, elbowing, and pushing others in order to get in and secure seats. My wife was pregnant, and I was not very appreciative of this foolish chaos. When I slowed and leaned backwards rather than push my pregnant wife into the people in front of her, the jerk behind me started jabbing his thumbs into my ribs. His intention was to prod me to act like an Arab and abuse my pregnant wife and force our way into the aircraft in front of others. Weighing over 240 pounds, and wearing boots, I looked down and saw a sandaled foot belonging to my tormenter. I set my heel on his toes and leaned backwards, grinding down on his toes with all of the force I could muster. He quit jabbing me, moved away and left us alone. I moved around my wife and had her hold onto my belt, and I used my size and strength to get us onto the plane where we shared seats along side of one-another.

Another Travel Tale: Crowd Control

I was traveling from Baghdad to Cairo on an Egyptian Airline. I was booked on a "laborer" return flight and was flying from a Baghdad terminal which was basically a warehouse. I had checked in early and was in a seat patiently waiting for the flight to be called.

There were two flights scheduled to go out within ten minutes of one-another, one a Pakistani Jumbo airliner and the other an Egypt Air Jumbo flight that I was booked on. The two large aircraft were configured to carry regular passengers (no first class seating), so they had over 750 seats between them.

The hundreds of excited, returning Egyptian and Pakistani laborers had assembled in the area and were nervously milling about. The terminal had one single pedestrian door from which passengers would pass through as they went to their respective airplanes. The door was a single, not a double. When some sort of announcement was made, all 750+ stampeded towards the one door at one time. It was a real melee to see with wild men clamoring and climbing over one another in their efforts to reach the door first. After a moment or two, I could hear thudding sounds and a few people came reeling out of the crowd holding onto their heads as they staggered away. Soon, the crowd fell back as uniformed Iraqi (I assumed they ware police of some sort) officers wielding wood clubs whacked and walloped those laborers beating them back and away from the door, and forcing them into two queues, one for each destination aircraft. They were told to sit (or squat) and wait. Every couple of minutes, one of the poor laborers would jump up and take off towards the door, and would be clubbed back by a police officer.

When the actual time came for boarding, an offer approached me and asked which flight I was on, and then escorted me to the plane, let me pick my seat and then stood guard over me and my seat when boarding was permitted. Again, I could hear the sound of clubs meeting skulls and wails of pain as the police allowed twenty at a time to leave the terminal building and board their respective flights. On board the plane, a couple of fellow travelers lunged for my seat and the police officer "persuaded" them to turn back and find another seat. The last man to board, with a bandage on his skull was allowed the remaining seat alongside of me. Needless to say, at the end of my flight to Cairo, I waited patiently while the mob deplaned.

Responses

Until now, the civilized world has seemingly had no way to deal with or to counter this concentrated level of sustained Mohammad inspired insane hatred.

What can we do to deal effectively with the likes of the "Osama bin Ladens" and the host of other militant backward Islamic Mohammedan fundamentalists who would destroy the entire Western civilization?

Should we consider the use of tactics and follow practices typical of, uniquely tailored to, understood by, useful, and effective within their culture? That of course is to destroy them. That is too draconian however. It would be better if we could inspire their own to kill them – to kill one-another. But, in reality, we really need to assure that they be limited to feeding off of themselves, one-another only, and cease being the blood sucking parasites that they are to the rest of the world.

We should consider monitoring Mullahs and Imams, and those other leaders (be they corner soapbox politicians, kindergarten level teachers, politicians, scholars, all who advocate extreme violence against us--the overthrow of our civilized governments, societies, and culture. Our monitoring should include public, private, religious, and other schools (Madrassas especially) and colleges throughout the world, and whenever a teacher advocates violence against us, do whatever may be necessary to neutralize him or her.

We're not ugly, savage brutes however, so we naturally won't attack innocents--the children.

Here, in the United States, we have or should enact laws that if enforced would deal effectively with these characters when they land on our soil. We can and should on a quarterly basis list all overseas organizations that have been involved in violence against American citizens or other civilized interests, and indict their US organizations and affiliates. We must monitor their members, and when they become involved in any way with subversive activities, or show their affiliation to listed and indicted organizations, prosecute them under established federal racketeering laws. This would include professors who espouse hatred in their classrooms and who openly or secretly support those who would destroy us. It is obvious to those of us who are thinking, responsible and civilized that many of these professors are prime examples of "Manchurian Candidates" of their own Moslem brainwashing excesses. These professors are a fifth column of seditious collaborators

I find it disturbing if not offensive that American political leaders continue to soft pedal Islam pointing to terrorism as being the problem, not Islam. This what Barak Hussein Obama claims. He feels that we need to seek out the problems that Islamists have with us and to deal with those problems, our problems, that we need to cater to the Moslems. **The problem that Islamists have with us is that we exist**. Our political leaders need to recognize the simple and clear fact that Islam is and always has been hostile to us and to our culture, hostile to any culture that is not Islamic. It has been this way for more than a thousand years, and will not change, ever. Reportedly, there are plenty of decent, civilized, moderate Moslems who do not espouse the overthrow of our western societies and cultures, but these people are a minority without hope of succeeding. There are others who are ambivalent, but these are also rare. So rare are the moderates, that few if any have spoken out against the terrorist acts of 9/11/2001, the blasting of American Embassies in Africa, the attack on the USS Cole, and the 2002 bombing of a nightclub in Bali, Indonesia that killed 200. This includes the governments of so-called nonsectarian Moslem nations. Where is the outrage???? To me, this overwhelming silence amounts to tacit approval of those terrorist, anti-western acts.

Yes, hundreds of Arab-Americans have joined the armed forces and the U.S. government and are doing what Americans do best – serving their country, and in many cases in an exemplary fashion. Some of these people may not even agree with U.S. policies in the Middle East, but still, they do their duty. Not all of these Arab-americans are Moslems, and many of those who were born into Moslem families, are not steeped in their religion, but are just regular Americans and are good, decent people. Because of the events of 9/11/2001, Saudi Wahhabi and other Islamist activism, militancy, extremist foolishness, and interference in America, the Aarab-Americans (which includes to all intents and purposes Iranians, Afghanis, Turks, Pakistanis, Bangladeshis, etc.) are suffering repercussions from many quarters. This is unfortunate, but a fact of life that they need to deal with.

One way to deal with this would be to take offense against those Moslems who are causing the troubles. Others have done this, and can be an example to follow. My mother worked in the city jail (as a Matron, dealing with women and juvenile prisoners) of a major Midwestern city. She observed one of the black jailers handling a black prisoner and he was pretty firm, taking absolutely no guff from his prisoner. The prisoner asked why he, the black jailer was being so rough on a black brother. The proud black jailer's response was to tell the prisoner that his trashy, degenerate, criminal behavior caused whites and other to look down on all blacks as being low class. He went on further to tell the black prisoner that he was disgusted with people who brought discredit on their race and culture, and that was why he was harsher on them than on whites because he wanted to cause black men to want to avoid doing the things that got them into jail, things that discredited black people.

This black police officer's example is one that many need to heed.

The Council on American Islamic Relations (CAIR) claims to be moderate and further claims that all Moslems in America are peaceful, etc. Liars! In the spring of 2005, there was a much ballyhooed rally in Washington, D.C., where moderate Moslems were to march for peace, and against terrorism, etc. It was sponsored by the Free Muslims Coalition. About fifty people showed up! Half of them were there to note and report on the moderates. Absent were the false moderates, the rank liars such as the CAIR who so often claim to be moderates, and dozens of other phonies. The obvious statement here is a deafening silence of moderates, if there are any.

We have become so tolerant
that we tolerate those who will
not tolerate us

In fact, all that has ever been heard from the vast majority of Moslems throughout the United States following 9/11/2001 were whines of outrage that Moslems who danced in celebration in the streets in the USA were being treated unfairly. In fact the American people (non-Moslem) were and are shining examples of tolerance, too much so. The tolerance expressed by Americans is based on their ignorance of Islam. Americans already go way too far to tolerate the hatefully intolerant – the mainstream Moslems.

It seems that whenever the issue of Islam and violence or terror comes up, the propagandists and ignorant apologist fools tell us that the vast majority of Moslems in the world are peaceful people. They tell us that the Moslems don't engage in terror, etc. This is irrelevant. By not resisting those who espouse such intolerance and terrorism, they are in fact tacitly supporting the bad guys.

The sadly misguided apologists ignorantly claim that poverty encourages radical Islamization. They are flat wrong. The pure and simple fact is that Mohammedism, Islam itself facilitates moves to poverty.

During the summer of 2002, the Islamic Society of North America held it's 17th convention. Uncharacteristically (not like the previous sixteen conventions) the rhetoric was toned down, moderated -- because of media presence and attention, etc.

However, some moderate Moslems such as Sheik Kabbani (a genuine moderate according to some knowledgeable sources) were excluded from participation. When the few genuine moderates are shut out, that should be telling if not completely damning.

At the conference, radical groups pretended that they are now moderate. Nevertheless, they showed their true stripes by their refusal to condemn al-Qaeda, Hamas, Hezbollah, and other murderers, etc.

Some quotes and thoughts that emanated at or from the radically toned down convention:

---Continued U.S. support of Israel will bring down the wrath of allah.

---Moslems who voted for Bush won't do so again.

---We buy our place in paradise with the blood of Jews.

---Moslems should not be prejudiced against American Hispanics because they (the Hispanics) are a potential Moslem base.

An unscientific poll of attendees revealed the most disliked Americans including Rev. Franklin Graham, Attorney General John Ashcroft, FOX news' Bill O'Reilly, and FOX news.

I will find my own way to enlightenment.
My path does not involve insane
religious fundamentalism.

Islam is not just a way of worshipping for Moslems. It is their way of life, the dominating, all controlling force in their life. It is the very air they breathe.

The constitution of Islamic nations such as Saudi Arabia is the Koran. Church and state are an inseperable one. There is no room within those sectarian church-states for religious tolerance, freedom of choice, decency, laws of man, independent political will, civil or human rights, nothing. These regimes forbid certain access to the internet, movies, TV, a free and independent press, open education, other religions, civil rights, and so much more that represent decency and true civilization.

Mohammedan media such as the Islamic Radio and TV Network prohibit infidels to even appear on its shows. It would be a sacrilege. Besides, they might slip and tell the truth, something Arab audiences can't bear to hear, because it would portray what abject losers they truly are.

In 2004, Saudi religious police went out and checked many of the homes of 30,000 Americans in Saudi Arabia making sure nobody had any Christmas or New Year decorations, inside or outside of their homes. The Saudis blocked Christmas cards from being sent or received.

Modernity is breaking through with computers and the world wide web, satellite TV, radio, and other ways for people to become educated about the civilized world. Unable to fully control or limit access of people, repressive Islamic regimes such as Saudi Arabia and other fundamentalist nations are possibly facing a demographic time bomb, and if they don't join the society of civilized nations, they will (hopefully) cease to exist.

Some so-called foreign policy experts in both government and academia who think they know everything wise and wonderful are soft peddling Islam to the American people, erroneously claiming that the problem we are facing is terrorism, not Islam. They are doing all of us a disservice. But then, they are mostly vapid pinheads, and all of us see through their idiocy easily enough.

The simple fact is that greater Islam is and always has been hostile to us and our culture. This will not change, ever. The problem IS Islam!

Islamic cleric and leader Siraj Wahaj declared: "If only Moslems were more clever politically, they could take over the United States and replace its constitutional government within a few years with a Caliphate."

Omar Ahmed declared: "Islam isn't in America to be equal to any other faith, but to become dominant."

Mohammedans teach methods of taking over America. One is telling Moslems to invest and take control of as much of Hollywood, the press, TV, radio and the internet as possible by taking control of those corporations. Another method and strategy is to yell "foul, hate crime, Zionist, out-of-context, personal interpretation, un-American, inaccurate interpretation of the Koran", etc. whenever Islam is criticized or the Koran is analyzed in the public arena.

Cleanliness is next to Godliness

Where have we heard this? It's often repeated in our Judaeo-Christian culture, and it is applicable in Moslem societies as well. However, its application is not always the same.

When we Americans (and Europeans, and Oriental Asians) talk about cleanliness, we talk about personal hygiene, keeping our homes, work places, neighborhoods, schools, parks, cities, and our nations clean.

In Islamic cultures, cleanliness applies to oneself, keeping one's body clean, etc. Keeping clean includes keeping a home clean. In many places, you can enter a Moslem person's home or apartment, however magnificent or humble it may be and it will be clean. I have seen people in larger cities where they live in multi-story apartments clean their apartments. When done, they just open the nearest window and toss their trash out of the window. Wherever it lands, they don't care. Insha'Allah!

Keeping one's body clean or free from dirt is important. Nasal and throat mucus is expectorated, on the stairs, on the elevator, on a wall in a hallway, wherever? I can't describe how my stomach has

turned when mounting stairs in an office building in a Moslem country.
I've seen phlegm "oysters" sliding down marble walls......, on banisters.
A friend once described how, after a very pleasant vacation in Thailand,
he knew he was returning to the Middle East when he got onto an
airliner and took off. He observed a man (turbaned) a couple of seats
ahead of him as the man leaned over, plugged one nostril and blew his
snot into the aisle, and then with a finger expertly cleared the drip from
his nostril and with a flourish snapped it from his fingers onto the floor.

Missionaries

Arabs and Moslems have established a demographic base in
the USA behind which evil, hateful anti-civilization Mohammedan
fundamentalists hide.

Moslem missionaries are very, very active in the United States.
They have mosques, are engaged in aggressive programs involving
ministering to Moslems, for recruiting people to Islam, and myriad other
programs offering propaganda, lies, and raising millions of dollars, a
great deal of which is returned to the Middle East.

That they have recruited American citizens not only to Islam, but
to the causes determined to destroy the United States is beyond doubt
to all but the mentally challenged, and those living in denial. Further,
funds raised are used to kill us, and will be used again to kill more of us.

Islamic organizations, mosques, charities, etc., are granted all
of the advantages and benefits of legitimate religious and charitable
organizations. They are exempt from taxation, and enjoy privileges the
same as Christian, Jewish, Shintos, Buddhists, and other religious and
social organizations, including Mormons and the Church of Scientology.

Christian missionaries in Moslem countries are forbidden. Yes,
there are a very few Christians who operate under the guise of charities,
are active in health, education, and food programs, etc. If they are
caught proselytizing, they are very often prosecuted, and sometimes
this is severe, such as public floggings in Saudi Arabia.

What are the Mohammedans afraid of? They are intolerant and
bigoted, and incredibly fearful of competition for the hearts and minds of
people. Non-Moslem missionaries are persecuted. They enjoy no tax
free or related benefits, and are prosecuted for any violations.

Egyptian Christians (Copts) are openly persecuted and biased
laws are in effect and are practiced. They pay extra high taxes and
fees, are robbed often, murdered for their property, their children are
taken into slavery, they are forbidden to speak their ancient language
(the original language of Egypt) in public, etc. This also occurs in other
Moslem countries such as the Sudan, Iraq, Iran, Syria, Pakistan (and
other 'stans'), Indonesia, etc.

In Bangladesh, for example, there were American missionaries
involved in feeding and providing medication and training to the poor
and disenfranchised. There are few, if any western style outlets in

countries such as Bangladesh. There are no hamburger shops, pizzerias, drive-ins, clubs, beaches, parks, or much of anything else available for recreation, rest, or relaxation.

In Dhaka, there was a small group of missionaries, about eight members in all, and their activity was devoted to helping the most desperately poor, the disenfranchised not even considered human by the elite Bangladeshis, Moslems. At the Embassy, we had allowed them access to our small American Embassy recreation association where we served the occasional hamburger made of local beef, Coca-Cola, had a small pool, a video library (cartoons, PG, and G rated movies, in English) and a tennis court. The club was a very welcome refuge for them and for the Embassy's staff.

The Bangladeshi government learned of this and had a conniption fit about our providing tax-free soft drinks to people not on the diplomatic, duty-free list. They threatened to disallow any duty-free imports for the entire embassy, until we kicked the missionaries out of the club and denied them access to anything.

We, at the American Embassy were thus compelled to disinvite those few decent missionaries from any facilities that we had. Needless to say, the risk averse American Ambassador lacked the basic gumption to tell the Bangladeshis to go to hell, and remind them of the millions and millions of dollars we were providing to feed everyone in Bangladesh, and to keep that government of beggars in power.

Recently, when on a two month contract assignment at the American Embassy in Asmara, Eritrea, I stayed at a big named international hotel and repeatedly suffered from food poisoning. After several bouts, one of which left me seriously dehydrated and nearly bundled up and shipped out on a medical evacuation, I figured out what was making me sick - the dismally poor hygienic practices of the hotel's kitchen. I learned that this had been a repeated problem of American officials staying at this hotel, but it was the only otherwise decent hotel offering any other amenities. This hotel was basically the only game in town, and they knew it. When embassy officials, including health professionals had previously complained to the hotel's management, the hotel's manager more or less told the embassy officers to go stuff themselves. I wrote up a warning note and had it delivered to incoming American officials destined to stay at the hotel, outlining what would make them sick. Eventually a copy of my notice got to the hotel manager. Rather than contacting me to apologize for my many bouts of food poisoning, or to otherwise take action to protect the health of visitors, the hotel's manager complained to the Eritrean Tourism Ministry (I was an Embassy official). The Eritrean Tourism Minister then proceeded to lodge a complaint with the ambassador. I guess the Tourism Minister already knew and understood that he could bully the wimpy, useless American Ambassador. The gutless ambassador, rather than defending me, caused me to stop circulating the health warning notices. The ambassador, had he any gumption at all should have pointed out that the hotel had a problem with repeated cases of food poisoning of guests, was garnering well over a hundred thousand dollars a year of lodging fees from the US Government. Instead, he went after the fine officer that I was assigned to work for (the ambassador didn't have the guts to confront me). The ambassador, being very, very risk averse, generally spineless, and not wanting to offend any local entity, compelled that fine officer I was working for to wallow and write, and deliver a letter of apology to the hotel's manager. The Ambassador was a twit not worthy of his position. How would he react in the face of a serious issue? He'd roll over and screw anything American to satisfy his clients, but surely not defend his country or countrymen.

Decency and Humanity

Not ALL Moslems are Mohammedan fundamentalists, and that is where God, not allah is casting his blessings.

Like the Sarajevo Moslem leaders who rejected the Saudis who wanted to pay for rebuilding their mosque provided they become fundamentalist fanatics, there are Moslems who try to be decent and civilized.

These Moslems who reject fundamentalist trends are the ones deserving of support for they are the vanguard of few Moslems determined to be honest, truly civilized members of the world, and beneficiaries of God. I fear that their numbers are diminishing.

Reciprocity

I offer a challenge to the elected officials of the Congress, especially those who are so keen to follow international precedent:

A)	Using the latest census figures on mosques in the USA, compare them against Christian Churches, Jewish synagogues, Buddhist and Hindu temples, etc., in the Islamic nations of the world.

B) Figures will show a numerical bias. We should then disallow immediately the establishment of any new Islamic centers, mosques, schools, institutions, etc. in the USA until there is parity in the Islamic governed countries. When Islam/Sharia governed countries encourage, support establishment of non-Moslem churches and other entities, and protect them as we do, then we can relent once parity is reached, and as long as parity is maintained. They need to welcome missionaries, permit the importation and distribution of religious literature, to encourage and welcome proselytization, and conversions.

We should demand that the Saudis, Iranians and every Moslem nation permit and support fully the building of Christian churches and Buddhist Pagodas, etc in Mecca, Quom, Medina and other cities. They must welcome and protect Christian churches and Synagogues in Medina and Isfahan, Christian cross memorials along the Khyber Pass and in Islamabad. Yeah, sure!

Who They Are

What kind of people are the Arabs/Moslems? These are but a few examples, some common knowledge, and some anecdotal.

In the south and west of the Sudan, it is a fact that non-Arab African Sufi Moslems, Christians, and Animists have and routinely continue to be slaughtered, especially the males in a government sponsored program of "Arabization". The horrid extent and level of the brutality and barbarity is only confined to the limits of your imagination. Women and children are enslaved, sold, and forcibly converted to Islam. This is happening today, and has been going on for quite a while. A new (yet another) treaty and cease-fire between the Saudi funded Mohammedan Sudanese government and the largely NON-Moslem south has promised a change, to take place over two-and-a-half years. After that period of time, the Mohammedans will probably find a fault someplace, probably a fault that they will create so that they can abrogate the treaty and begin their slaughters again. [In 2007, the U.S. Department of State reported that they had documented (proven, not rumored) more than 800,000 cases of human trafficking – slave trading world-wide. More than half of that is the Arab and Moslem enslaving of non-Moslems in the most horrible manner, and in the traditional manner: Castration (using a thin rope to drive the fact home – to affirm the slave's complete humiliation) of males, and raping and often female circumcision, mutilation of the female captives.]

The real reason for the Moslem dominated Sudanese government to agree to this treaty with the Christians was to enable them to move their resources to the western area of Sudan, to Darfur where they can continue their slaughter of Africans, many who are Sufi Moslems and to consolidate their power. When done with the Darfurians, they will return to the task at hand - of slaughtering Christians in the south. This they will do with impunity and probably with the support of the UN – Useless Nations.

It is a fact that an (Egyptian) airline pilot took the controls of an Egyptian airliner and aimed it into the sea while exclaiming again and again: "Insha'Allah! Insha'Allah! Insha'Allah! (It's the will of God). This was roundly denied and disclaimed by Egyptian government authorities and clerics as untrue. In the face of honest, factual evidence, they claimed that the in-flight recordings were faked, etc. Applying their taqiyyah, they said that no Arab would ever do such a thing. This is just one more example of denial of reality common to Moslems.

A passenger in a vehicle moving down a rock strewn dirt road in a Moslem country, I observed far ahead a man with a stick flailing at the legs of a beast of burden loaded high with wood and sticks. I thought the man a barbarian for mistreating a poor, lame, limping donkey in such a manner. As we came closer and then passed, I noted that the beast had but two legs, and was in fact a barefoot woman....... The Moslem men I was with thought it was OK..... The terrain was littered with small sharp stones.

I observed a group of young Moslem men who had caught two feral dogs on the streets of Istanbul. They had lashed the two dogs' testicles together, and then threw stones at the two screaming, tortured animals, driving them to inflict pain and agony on one-another. These fellows thought it great entertainment as they laughed and tormented the dogs further.

On a frigid morning with snow and ice still on the streets Istanbul, I saw a poor man, a beggar dressed in rags stumbling down the ice encrusted street in his bare feet, slipping and tripping along on the ice. When he approached open doors, merchants and others denied him entry into warmer buildings, beating him and stomping on his tender, reddened feet as they harassed the crying, begging man and sent him on. I witnessed some really wonderful, charitable Moslem people, eh? The lesson: In Islamic places, if you are poor, downtrodden, cold, and desperate, expect no relief.

Many years ago, a friend of mine was driving home from the American Consulate one afternoon in Istanbul. Traffic was heavy. It was the rush hour. Everybody seemed to be in a hurry, the normal stuff, with every driver trying to be in front of the other guy. Traffic islands in this city, with curbing about a foot high keep drivers in their lanes (if there were no islands, absolute mayhem would prevail, because few egomaniacal Moslems would obey the lane laws. Such lanes are meant for someone else – typical Moslem reasoning. Anyhow, traffic was moving slowly and at one point my friend swung into the left turn lane – naturally to turn left onto the street where his apartment was located. Before he could turn, he had to stop for oncoming traffic. Another driver, a Turk had followed him into the left turn lane assuming it was an opportunity to get ahead of others by pulling a quick one and running around a few cars. My friend had stopped, and the Turk jerk plowed into him. My friend's small, rear engined car was destroyed, and the big Mercedes Benz that hit him suffered serious front end damage.

They eventually went to Turkish court regarding the damages. My friend, who was rear ended while obeying traffic laws got stuck for 60% of the damage to both cars. Here's how it broke down: 20% for being there, the Islamic reasoning being that if he was not there, he wouldn't have been hit. Insha'Allah! Duuuhh!! He was held responsible for another 20% of the costs just because he was an American, and Americans are rich (his car, by the way was an old Chevy Corvair, and the jerk who hit him was driving a top of the line Mercedes). The third 20% allocation for damages was just because he was black, and that wonderful, fair, unbiased Turk judge openly declared that he didn't like 'niggers'......

A few years later while in Bangladesh where I ran the Embassy motor pool, we had rebuilt the engine in a fifteen-year old truck. Before sending it off on a road trip, I drove it around town on a Saturday to get some miles on it, to break the engine in. At one point, I was following about twenty other moving vehicles, all of us moving slowly. A driver came up behind me in a van, and started honking his horn and flashing his lights. We were all moving along at about fifteen miles per hour. When we came to a turn out lane, this guy swung out and passed me and then cut in. Sorry dude! The truck I was driving was old, already well aged and battered, and it was much bigger. I didn't jam on my brakes. I just kept my pace, and the VW driver just swung in, and lost that encounter -- the whole side of his van got ripped. I just trundled along. He followed me for another mile or so, trying to wear his light flasher switch out, and burn out his horn. When we reached a police station (near my office/shop area), I pulled in and he followed, just shrieking like a madman. It turned out that he was a minor government functionary of some sort, and I should have realized this and gotten out of his way because he was important. Besides, I was an infidel. I really sent his tender ego to new heights when I had a belly laugh at his antics. The police at this station laughed at him too. I had earlier made friends with them, and worked to maintain a very cordial relationship. I got back into my truck and drove off, and never heard another thing.

In Algiers, the last obstacle to homebound commute was a congested traffic circle where five streets intersected. It was a block from my house, and I could see the house from the intersection. I was in a usual traffic jam. I spent about twenty minutes creeping along an inch or two at a time towards the traffic circle. When I arrived, I observed a small break where I could have gotten my bumper in front of the car to my left. Observing that cars behind him were aiming to exit the circle (and thus allow traffic to circulate) I paused and waved the fellow through. This, of course opened things up and allowed everyone to proceed. However, the guy behind me completely lost it because I had let someone else go first. He got out of his car and started banging on mine. It was as though I had taken away his virility. This is the typical mentality of Arabs, they must get their bumper in front of the other guy just to prove something, and to hell with courtesy and allowing traffic to flow. That kind of reasoned courtesy is secondary.

Back to when I was in Istanbul, I was driving (alone) out towards a suburb one Sunday evening. It was a major road with three lanes going one way, a broad traffic median in the middle, and three lanes heading the other direction. In this location, the island curbs hadn't been built very high, but the median was forty feet wide.

The inbound traffic was heavy and backed up. I was moving along in the left lane at about forty miles per hour when a car came bounding and bouncing over the median and into my lane, heading towards me. There were cars to my right, so I couldn't move over and let him by, so I slammed on my brakes and skidded to a stop just feet from him. As the dust cleared, I looked out and he was sitting behind the wheel of his car glaring at me. I laughed, thinking stuff I can't repeat here. He exited his car and came around to my door, glared at me and said: "Me, Turk!" " This Turk road!" "You, American infidel – in my road!" and then he swing his fist hitting me so hard that my glasses flew from my face and into the back seat of my car.

I reversed and started to pull over to take off, and he jumped in front of me. I ran into him. He came flying up, over the hood of my car as I accelerated, and then he rolled off as I took off.

He jumped up and got back into his car and turned and came after me. I had noted as I drove by his car that there were three other men in the car with him. I didn't feel good. [I was thinking of an incident in Istanbul a few months earlier where a Turk had run into a Consulate colleague's car, rear ending him. When my American colleague got out of his car, the Turk clubbed him with a tire iron. When my colleague's smallish, slender wife got out of the car to help her husband, the Turk kicked her between the legs so hard that he fractured her pelvis. Nice, lovely people, them Turks.]

I sped down the road and when I had reached the turn off to where I was headed, I swing into the turn and took off down the road. It was dusk, and after a block on the dirt road, I realized I had made a wrong turn and that I was on a dead end street. I skidded to a stop, turned and headed back towards the highway, only to see the jerk who I was trying to get away from come around the corner and block the road. I skidded to a stop a few feet from him.

I was now in a position where I could do but one thing. Confront the animal. I had been living in this culture for nearly a year, and had observed and learned. I had come prepared. I reached under my seat and grabbed a stout four foot section of loggers chain, the ends linked by a heavy padlock, and exited my car. I went at the four Turks as fast and as furious as I could and my first swing caught the Turk driver, the guy who'd punched me, on the side of the head as he exited his car with a big knife in his hand. I heard a rewarding crunching sound and he went down.

The next guy was not yet out of the car and I slammed all of my 220 pounds into the rear car door and crushed his leg. His screams told me he was neutralized, and I jumped onto the roof of the car and the third guy received about three shots with the iron padlock end of my chain before he went down, and the fourth had wisely jumped back into the car and locked his door.

I proceeded to smash all of the windows, and managed to get a few shots in on the creep who'd locked himself inside. I smashed the lights, grill, and the radiator doing myself proud as I just wrecked the car, and then took the first man's knife and slashed the tires of his car.

When done, I drove around the car and over the semi-conscious driver's legs, and leisurely on my way. My heart was pounding. I could barely catch my breath. I was on a crazy adrenaline rush. I felt so damned good.

I was pleased with myself, not only because I had survived, but because I prevailed and they hadn't. Had they gotten the upper hand, there is absolutely no doubt that I'd have been thoroughly and methodically beaten to within an inch of my life and maimed, if not killed.

They were Moslems trying to deal as Moslems do with an uppity infidel who challenged their rights of superiority. I am proud to be a kafir who didn't submit.

Here, at Home

Here, in the United States, there are professors of Middle East studies at colleges and universities all over the country. They teach the languages, history, and cultures of the countries of Islam. Most also teach young Americans how to begin the process of submitting to the status of dhimmitude.

The National Security Agency (which intercepts voice communications but lacks the staff of linguists to translate these), the FBI and CIA, and others have awakened to the need for linguists. Their many years of neglect had caught up with them. Millions of dollars have been put forward to fund and encourage students to learn these various languages and then to pay the USG for their studies by working for the USG for a few years afterwards.

However, most of the professors of these courses and languages are, of course Moslems from those same countries, presumably target nations for the gathering of intelligence. Most of these professors are members of the Middle East Studies Association (MESA) and have obtained United States citizenship, or are permanent residents of the United States therefore having some sort of obligations as citizens, or as guests. Many of these MESA members refuse to participate in the programs and are refusing to teach languages and cultures -- because they hold no loyalty or obligation to the United States. They remain loyal to others. These MESA members are therefore agents of the sworn enemy - Islam.

We're good,
They're evil.
Nothing is relative.
General Richard Hawley, USAF, Retired

I don't think it would be unreasonable to revoke the permanent resident status of those disloyal MESA professors who are not citizens of the United States, and send them to the countries or regions where their true loyalties lie. Those who are citizens should reconsider their loyalties, and if they feel their loyalties are indeed against the United States, should go to the countries where their loyalties are rooted. Their disloyalty should in fact be addressed with one-way tickets and revocation of their United States citizenships.

Why is it that so many Arabs are so difficult to like? Are they all so unlikable? Or, is it just my unreasonable expectations that people ought to start out friendly and reasonable and then build relationships from there. Why does one have to begin a relationship built on hostility and distrust? It's their hostile attitude......

Western women who marry Arabs or Moslems

For decades, thousands and thousands of Arab/Moslem men have come to the United States (and other civilized countries) to attend colleges and universities. They come to obtain educations not available in their countries, and to learn and develop skills that they bring home with them.

Some of these men discover that there is more to the world than the crap where they've come from, and stay on illegally, or legally if they can work it. Some of these men even become civilized and go on to live rewarding lives that benefit everyone around them. They marry, have children, and do wonderful and good things that civilized people do. I applaud them.

Others get their technical educations, but genuine civilization does not really rub off on them because they simply are willfully ignorant and prone to do evil. They are usually moneyed, and can enjoy themselves in many ways. Often, they meet, court, and capture the hearts of western women, and marry them. Like married couples, they have children. When these guys return to their home countries, they bring their western trophy brides and children with them.

Of those trophy brides, half (or perhaps more) are treated to indignations and even cruelties beyond imagination soon after they get off of the plane. In Arab/Mohammedan countries, women have no rights, and both they and their children are property of the husband/father. They are chattel, to be used, even sold or given away. The women and their children may not travel out of the country without permission of the husband/father. Too often, after arriving in their new homes, these foolish, tragic women learn that they are merely one of their husbands' wives, and are lesser ranking. They are treated poorly, and are often compelled to become lowly servants to the senior wives, and to the families of the husband. If they get angry and want to leave, this may in some cases be allowed, but their children must remain.

How many responsible, civilized women will abandon their children? Not many. So, they remain in awful situations just to remain with and to try to protect their children.

I'll agree that not all women are subjected to this. A few are allowed to retain their dignity, but they are a minority.

There are other (and admittedly more rare) cases where the women wanted a divorce (women are rarely allowed a divorce is the Islamic world), and in response their husbands have divorced them (very easy for men to do), and immediately sold them into slavery.

These cases are hard to document and prove, but they are real. Because of limited language abilities, the women often don't even realize until too late that they've been sold. Those women usually vanish from the face of the earth, so there are few tales to tell.

The steady numbers of these forlorn, broken, destitute women arriving on the doorsteps of American and other Embassies tells a grim tale of abuses. A great deal of it is documented too, but the information and details are often classified or hidden by the Department of State so as to not embarrass those Islamic countries.

What happens when these women show up asking for help is that American (and other embassies) actually turn them away. Yes, we abandon them to their fates.

Their passports have usually been confiscated and often even destroyed by their husbands. Lacking a passport, there is no proof that they are Americans. Naturally, their children's passports are not available either. They are invariably destitute, and taxpayer funds are not permitted to be used to help them.

At this point, all that the embassy can do is to take information and contact relatives to notify them of the situation. If the parents or families haven't written them off, they may even respond affirmatively and possibly even send money. The embassy can pass the money on to the woman, if she's still around the doorstep after waiting for a few days for the process to be done. With the money and other relative information, she can possibly get a passport for herself, but without a birth certificate or other appropriate documentation to prove that the child or children with her are Americans, no passport can be issued for them. Without passports, the children can't accompany her.

She's stuck.

Most Embassy officials are aware of these instances, but can only be sympathetic and officious. Anything else would be in violation of American, or local (native) laws, and could result in discipline of or possibly imprisonment for the American official.

It's a dilemma, an ugly one at that, and it happens all too often. The poor women are abandoned to their savage, brutal fate, and it isn't promising.

Thousands of American, Asian, and European women witlessly get involved in these situations every year, and it goes on and on.

More needs to be done at colleges and universities to educate women of these concerns so that they can be aware of their probable (not possible, but probable) fate before they commit. By more, I mean mandatory information guidelines and so forth to let women know that there is an issue here that they need to be aware of. Let the Moslem professors protest, pontificate, lie, and hyperventilate to their endless eternal pleasure, but let the truth be known.

I am aware of one instance where a woman, in her late twenties or early thirties came to an Embassy seeking help. She was, of course, married to an Arab, and was the second ranking wife. She had two daughters. Her nose was crooked, she was missing teeth, had scars on her face and body (whip cuts and burns). Her hair was gray, her back stooped, she limped, and she looked like she was fifty or more years old. She was physically and spiritually broken and desperate, and at the point of killing her daughters and herself to end this hell they were in. She couldn't prove the citizenship of her daughters.

An Embassy officer arranged for three American passports to become "damaged" and removed from the official inventory, and then he artfully fixed them so that they were to all intents and purposes valid. Using money sent by her parents, he arranged for her and her daughters to be transported (smuggled) Europe where they were met by her parents. The false passports were then destroyed (to protect the Embassy official who could have been imprisoned for this act of decency, mercy, and kindness). The woman presented herself at the nearest American Embassy along with birth certificates (newly minted) for the daughters, and they all flew home. The Arab husband was enraged.. He demanded that the Embassy round up and return her and the girls -- duly noted. And, when he got physically abusive and aggressive, a truncheon found its mark right between his eyes. Wonderful!

In 2003, there was a much publicized case (there are many that go unpublished) about Sara Saga, a 23-year old woman with two children who fled to the U.S. Consulate in Jeddah, Saudi Arabia. She was seeking shelter from her abusive, wife beating husband. She was so terrified and absolutely desperate that she signed an "agreement" forfeiting her rights as a mother. This after absolutely stupid American diplomats allowed Saudi officials to enter this American sanctuary to confront and bully the terrified woman into signing the lives of her children over to her Saudi husband. At one point, she was given a choice -- to abandon her daughters to their fate or be murdered. She was forced to flee Saudi Arabia for her life, and the Embassy and State Department had helped the Saudis, not the American.

Heidi McClain, a child, a U.S. citizen was (with the complicity and direct aid of the Saudi Embassy in Washington) kidnapped by her so-called father and brought to Saudi Arabia without her mother's permission. The State Department's high ranking Assistant Secretary of State for Consular Affairs, the office responsible for handling kidnapping cases just wrung his or her risk averse hands claiming that the office did all that it can to help the children. Balderdash! That is a stinking lie! That official and his staff never did anything more than whine. It is unlikely that Heidi's mother will ever be able to bring her daughter out of that stinking hell hole.

Saudi Arabia is in fact and for a long time has been the principal epicenter of anti-American terrorist funding. After September 11, 2001 when the USG started its campaign to cripple al Qaeda by having countries freeze terrorist organization funds, the Bush administration exempted Saudi Arabia. Saudi Arabia exempted? This should raise a huge question mark. It did for me. In the so called war on terrorism, President Bush (43rd) seemed to continuously be bending over backwards to appease the Saudis. Was President George W. Bush another Lord Chamberlain?

A decade earlier an American woman was tossed out of the American Embassy in an Arab country when she showed up beseeching American officials for help. Assistance was denied by the American officials and she hasn't been heard from since.

The former Saudi Ambassador to the United States, Prince Bandar (yeah, a Saudi royal - a royal liar) when queried about these human rights abuses blithely stated (taqiyyah) that such is not the case. This royal bribing paymaster to fawning, begging Congressmen and Senators was treated royally in Washington. The man, Prince Bandar, the former Ambassador to the United States is still a lying low life pig….. as is his replacement, former snake oil salesman and embassy propagandist (spokesperson), Adel A. Al-Jubeir,

Saudis are officially prohibited from hiring non-believers as servants, tutors, and so forth because such exposure might be dangerous to their children's upbringing. The children might also learn something about civilization, decency, ethics, and respect, and that's not allowed.

Racial targets

During a 2001 visit to Australia, I picked up a Sunday newspaper and in perusing it, came across an article that I found disturbing, but not surprising.

The article discussed a series of gang rapes of young (age 14-18) blond, fair skinned, blue eyed women in Sydney. It told how young Moslem men actively seek out and befriend these attractive young women (sometimes they are runaways) and gain their confidence. It may take a few days, or just minutes. Whatever the case, at the first opportunity they lead them off somewhere secluded and then they send broadcasts over their cellular devices to their groups who arrive quickly, and then the girls are brutally gang raped, often for days on end by up to twenty of these cowards.

A part of the rape includes beatings, the use of very hostile, racially derogatory, culturally hateful language directed at the girls. The newspaper article very carefully mentioned this concern.

The article discussed the police being concerned at the frequency and sheer brutality of the numerous rape cases. The police said that they were very conscious of racial and cultural issues that they really didn't want to specifically identify any racial or cultural group perpetrating these attacks, etc. the article was very politically correct. But, at the end of the long article, buried in the last paragraph, the police admitted that the rapes were being conducted by young immigrant Moslem men of Lebanese and Palestinian origin living in a specific

Sydney neighborhood.

In August of 2002, a leader of this gang of young Moslem rapists was sentenced to fifty-five (55) years in jail. The article quoted testimony that the unlucky lady was told she was "getting f---ed Leb. style" and that she deserved it because she was an "Australian white pig!" Along with the rape was a terrible beating that left the girl terribly mutilated and scarred externally as well as internally.

He really deserved a lifetime sentence without parole, and castration. An Australian Mohammedan leader, Sheik Fail Mohammad, however declared that rape victims (those raped by Moslems) are accountable for being raped, blaming it on their attractive good looks and attire.

The Australian state of Victoria has established a law to protect freedom of speech by limiting what people can say. Eh? Yes, two pastors were sent to prison for asserting that Islam is inherently violent and hateful. Yes, in Australia, one can be sent to prison for speaking freely........, where there is no freedom of speech anymore.

In Great Britain, a pair of depraved sexually sadistic Mohammedan jerks named Maqas Riaz and Mohammed Irfan took it upon themselves to go out and first rape and then savagely beat a couple of hookers, Irfan declaring in one instance that he couldn't stand prostitutes. While they couldn't stand prostitutes, it was still OK for the slime bag low life hypocrites to commit rape.

Heaven and women

It is a sin to look upon a naked woman. That's what young Moslem men are taught.

It's a sin for a woman to show herself, even a spot of skin, and as was shown all too often on Afghani TV, the Taliban enforced this with clubs and guns, punishing women for any perceived infraction. Women are forbidden to go out without some related male to boss them around, to 'protect' their virtue. Moslem men don't trust their women out of sight as though they were a bunch of wanton harlots. Any Mohammedan man can brand a woman (including his mother, sister, or wife) a harlot and have her shot or stoned to death.

Early in the 21st Century, a really pretty Afghani woman (I have had had the privilege of meeting her along with Ms. America) participated in a beauty pageant where, like other contestants she wore a swimsuit. She can not return to Afghanistan now. If she did, she'd be killed for her transgressions.

Moslem women who are victims of rapes are often murdered because they are no longer 'virtuous'. All too often, the rapes are committed by their fathers or relatives who are the so-called guardians of their virtue.

Moslems are taught, are indoctrinated that women are sinful, untrustworthy, dirty.

Young Moslem girls are often circumcised -- mutilated. This is one of the sickest practices on earth. Moslem men who treat women in such a manner are primitive, uncivilized beasts and cowards. That is a simple and unequivocal truth.

We in the civilized world ought to have female doctors conduct medical examinations on Moslem girls to see if they have been sexually mutilated (female circumcision) or subjected to incest. The Norwegian parliament has taken steps to see that such is done, because it is a fact that many female children are being sexually mutilated. When such vile crimes are detected, a legal case should go forward against the fathers of those girls, and those beasts who call themselves guardians should be convicted and sent to hard time prisons for lengthy periods of time, and then kicked out, back to their homeland pits. Yet, in the face of these crimes, there are weak minded, cowardly useful fool apologists (liberals of course) arguing against protecting young girls from such sick, brutal, vile, uncivilized assaults and abuses. A large number of Moslem marriages are to girls who are underage, and this therefore constitutes a sex crime.

When an Arab hashashin goes forth with a bomb strapped on and murders innocent people, he or she does so under the confirmed belief within Islamic teachings that he will immediately go to the highest level of heaven. Therein, according to those Islamic religious teachings he will be treated to an eternity of debauchery starting with a stable full of waiting virgins and young boys.

I would like to opine that Moslem heaven is perhaps more appropriately a different kind of place where Jihadists, women beaters, child rapists, slavers, and hashassin bombers go: It is where they find their 72 virgin girls and 28 pre-pubescent boys but hopefully a place where they themselves are incapable of performing their debauchery.

Teachings

Islamic teachers instruct that the four common freedoms of the Oriental and Western cultures (of faith or belief, of speech, of ownership, and of personal freedom) are in conflict with the laws of Islam.

Mohammedans say that the Koran is sacred and valuable to all mankind. Taqiyyah! It is not sacred to non-Moslems -- the majority of decent mankind, just to those fools who follow it.

**All of our problems
are caused by America**
*Inscriptions on billboards
in the Middle East*

Arabs-Moslems are thoroughly indoctrinated into a mythology or ideology that denies the fact that they are pitifully non-competitive and willfully ignorant. Therefore they need scapegoats for their being abject failures incapable of properly exploiting or reaping the benefits of modernization or of being civilized.

Here is the greatest example of how much of a non competitive failure Islam is today. Take South Korea for example. After World War II the terribly backward and largely medieval nation was devastated by the Korean war. The tallest structure in Seoul was a three feet pile of rubble. Korea had no natural resources such as the fantastic oil wealth of part of the Islamic world. Two thirds of Korea is up and down, steep mountains and some valleys fertile for growing rice, but not much else. The South Koreans had a desire to compete, to join the modern civilized world and applied their incredible self-motivation to pick themselves up by their stockings (they didn't even have boot-straps) and make a go of it. The South Koreans have become one of the greatest and freest wealth producing nations in the civilized world through their own awesome effort.

Why can't Moslem countries do something like this? The simple fact is that the Islamic culture is a failure incapable of succeeding!

Saddam Hussein arguably had the greatest armed force in the Islamic world outside of Turkey. Twice in ten years his army was crushed by smarter, better motivated and disciplined forces. He had some pretty good imported weapons. None were created or made by Arabs. The Iranians have a large army, but none of their weapons or machines are Moslem creations. The Saudis have probably the most sophisticated weaponry in the Islamic world. The Saudi armed forces are poorly led and feeble; and without foreign technicians to maintain those systems probably won't function more than a few days if ever called into service.

The Americans have brought a renewed focus on the abject pitifullness of Moslem military and technical abilities and thus caused their greatest frustration and rage. Islam is and will always be technologically retarded, incapable of competing and developing anything meaningful. The only way the Mohammedans can deal with this is to sneak around and stab their opponents in the back. They lack the ability to successfully confront us up front. The Saudis and all of the others use surrogates and deception as their tools.

Ecstacy

The ultimate goal of fanatic Moslem assassins, hashassin, is the ecstasy of death. We ought to grant them their wishes, but not on their terms, on our terms.

Dark Ages

Islam is considered by some apologists to be mired in its own

"Dark Age" and may soon emerge and become civilized. No! Islam is by its nature and dogma a permanent Dark Age on all who 'submit'. The Koran will not ever permit Islam to move out of its primitiveness.

Islam in America

One of the things that makes the United States so mighty, is its freedoms. This is what the Mohammedans hate the most about us. This is also what the Moslems are taking advantage of to destroy us.

We have as one of our bedrocks the freedom of religion, where we are free to worship (or to not worship) as we please. This is the greatness that fundamentalists loathe, regardless of their orientation. They are determined to change this

We have amongst us millions of people from Moslem countries, some who are fundamentalist Mohammedans who are striving for the day that Islamic political systems and laws can be imposed in this great nation. On the day that happens, we will cease being great, or civilized. It is imperative that we guard against this.

Tragically, many Americans from Moslem countries are being coerced or compelled to be active participants in Islamic social/political/religious and criminal activities (it's all one and the same thing) here in the United States. A large number of these people came here to get away from ugly, depraved Islamic dominance, and have fallen into a trap here that some may desperately want to get away from. They're stuck. They are bound into this for a number of reasons, all of them tragic.

We Americans who are free need to assure that these people from Moslem countries are assured the opportunity to be free, to not participate in a despicable system that they fled and fear. We must prohibit and not permit at any time in any place or corner of our great nation the imposition of Sharia foolishness or any vile Islamic social controls on any of our citizens or residents.

Notwithstanding the need to let people practice or to be free from the imposition of Islam, we must also recognize reality and facts as they are today, and insist that Islamic dominated countries not only permit, but encourage, protect, and support the establishment of Christian, Jewish, Buddhist, Hindu, and other religions and their places of worship in those countries. Further, when a pagoda, temple, synagogue, church or other edifice is burned or destroyed in an Islamic country, that the Islamists designate a similar sized Moslem facility to be taken down in each of their nations.

Religious education

All too many of our political, social, educational, and even religious leaders are complete fools when it comes to religion, and to avoid, actually to evade controversy, they have buried their proverbial heads in the sand deeply. This can be our undoing.

Religion plays a pivotal role in all of our lives, and we need to recognize this and work with it, not shirk our responsibilities to our future.

There are those who want to avoid at all costs the discussion of religion in our schools. Those who are in this category are fools, fearful of fundamental truths of life. There are others who want to impose religious indoctrination in our schools. These folks are narrow minded bigots. Presently, the debate centers around the teachings of creationism and/or evolution in schools, and by avoiding this as an important educational issue, they are denying children important elements of their education. The creationists want to deny evolutionary facts. The evolutionists want to deny the value of religion in our society. Both extremes are foolish.

And, while these chumps are busily bashing one-another, the Islamists have sneakily slipped in, rewritten textbooks used in seventh grade all over the country, and are indoctrinating our (your and my children and grand children) into accepting the supremacy of Islam.

The power that created us (by whatever name) is so great that we cannot understand or yet begin to fathom this. So, many want to deny in one way or another that which they do not understand or comprehend.

The world was not created in a flash-bang as it is today, or will be tomorrow. It wasn't 7,000 years ago, or 6,000 years ago.. Neither are we an accident of nature.

This should be taught in schools. Both sides should be taught. One, that God established the building blocks of the universe and they have evolved and continue to evolve creating planets and star systems, and breaking them as well as they evolve and change. The other, that we are a freakish evolutionary accident.

Religion must be taught in schools. The manner in which religion is taught must avoid indoctrination into one faith (theory) or another. Children need to know and to understand this as it affects today and will affect their lives tomorrow. This cannot be done in an hour. There should be semester long courses devoted to paganism, Judaism, Buddhism, Christianity, Islam, and later fringe or non-mainstream religions such as Scientology, mysticism, Mormonism, Unitarianism, and others.

Special attention should be given to Islam as it is practiced today, not only a religion, but an Orwellian totalitarian social/legal/political system seeking total domination over all lives on earth.

Other education

A friend pointed something out to me that is very poignant: One of the great things about Communism (my friend had grown up in a

Communist country) was the broad opportunity for education of the masses, and the high quality of education provided regardless of social status. He pointed out that because of this great educational system, people learned, developed curiosity, and learned more and well. This, he opined is what caused the demise of Communism. It's hard to disagree.

Conversely, the continuing fourteen century success of Islam is the consistent lack of educational opportunities for the masses, and their continued ignorance and poverty, which holds everyone in the Moslem world in perpetual subjugation and misery.

Dhimmitude

The status of dhimmitude in a yet-to-be conquered nation does not develop all at once. It is a process of mental conditioning. It starts with compelling a city government to allow loudspeakers to disrupt a neighborhood to blare the five times daily call of Moslems to prayer. It begins with establishing Sharia rules in a Moslem community. Dhimmitude is used to suppress or compel the all too willing liberal (and foolish) media to not print or speak out honestly with truths or facts about Islam. Dhimmitude applies to people who foolishly and willfully deny truths about Islam and submit to the false claim that it is a religion of peace.

Chapter 19

THE UNITED NATIONS

With the best of good intentions, the United States and its World War II allies created the United Nations (UN) following that horrible war. We tried to do the right thing. We screwed up terribly. It turns out that this was a bad idea. The UN's continuing existence is an absurdity. It needs to be abolished.

What we wrot has evolved into an unaccountable, irresponsible, useless, morally bankrupt, corrupt and corrupting UN bureaucracy dominated by beggar nations not particularly concerned with civilized decency such as saving lives or helping folks, but only in maintaining its status-quo as a gross, inept, overpaid bureaucracy of politically correct but incompetent, corrupt elitists.

We Americans and certain other responsible nations rightfully refuse today to accede to some of what the UN wants because it's wrong. That is good. What we need to do is to either abolish this useless pit, or radically alter it. However, we don't own the UN, so we can't alter it. However, we do fund most of it, and if we cut the funds off and take other actions that we have the right to take, we can end it and much of the terrible suffering that the UN has brought.

The ineffectual, genocide supporting UN increasingly is demonstrating that it is utterly worthless to all intents and purposes as a meaningful, fair, or responsibly effective organization. It represents and supports or encourages in its membership nations that support terrorism in all of its ugly forms. The UN welcomes corrupt and dangerous despots, criminals, torturers, slave traders, terrorists, thieves, and more. Former UN Secretary General and useful fool, Kofi Anan wanted to recognize Hezbollah, the Iranian run, Iranian controlled, Iranian funded band of murderers, thieves, rapists, and things mostly evil as a good deal. Morally bankrupt himself and bereft of decency, Mr. Anan probably pocketed (indirectly, of course, through several money launderers) bloody bribe money for offering this up.

Members of the Organization of the Islamic Conference (OIC) are demanding a permanent seat on the UN Security Council. If that happens, the UN Security Council will be rendered totally useless from that point forward. There is no way that such a change should take place. This Useless Nations entity is working hard to ban free speech, freedom of expression, and they want to ban anything critical of Islam. The OIC is despicable, and anyone who supports it is likewise below contempt.

When Kofi Anan's efforts to thwart the United States in the war on terrorism (and corruption), by setting his sights on causing the defeat of President Bush in the 2004 election, he demonstrated his true self.

This champion of corruption and slime, Anan was an unmitigated disaster. Anan actually, seriously believed that he could set himself up as the world's greatest dictator overseeing all of the UN, and subjugating every nation, especially the United States to his capricious, corrupt, incompetent rule. He probably had visions of appointing himself Secretary General for life. What a horrible disaster and joke of a 'statesman' he was.

Anan and his pals even wanted to place the United States under UN domination. Of course, his highest priority was to disarm America and make all gun ownership illegal, and to follow this up with eliminating our First Amendment. This would have paved the way for world dictatorship, just what the Mohammedans want.

Kofi Annan worked against everyone involved in removing Saddam Hussein from power in Iraq (and further padding the Annan personal treasury). After the war ended, he refused to acknowledge even the personal sacrifices of coalition soldiers, and continued to refer to the Iraqi invasion as illegal, and gave aid and comfort to those who daily blew up and murdered thousands of their own fellow Iraqis.

Worldwide, a quarter of a billion children are being horribly abused in situations of child slave labor, where their pay is meager, a few cents per day, health and safety conditions are deplorable, and children die daily having never known what it is like to play or to laugh. These conditions have prevailed since the UN was created, and have in fact grown with UN support. This is well known to the top leadership of UN who barely does more than pay lip service to the existence of these uncivilized horrors.

Further, sexual exploitation of children has increased, and the UN has all but denied this fact.

If UN travelers, especially so-called VIP's reduced their first class airline travel to coach class, and started staying in three star hotels rather than five star hotels, and gave that money to non-UN children oriented private relief agencies, half of these children could be rescued from indescribable horrors within just weeks.

Don't hold your breath for this to happen.

The United Nations ought to be sent, today, to join the League of Nations, the Maginot line, the AXIS, the COMINTERN, and the Warsaw Pact in the ash heap of history.

Recognition

The Arab territories called Palestine are NOT a nation or a country. Palestine technically remains a territory, and is in fact a corrupt, lawless territory populated by fools. Yet, Arab maps show a Palestine, but do not include Israel. The UN only recognizes 'Palestine'. The UN is acting illegally. Therefore the UN is in fact kowtowing to the Mohammedists, is not being neutral, is irresponsible, and this further affirms its uselessness.

Human Rights

The United Nations Commission on Human Rights has five members. The purpose of the commission is to sit and review reports and charges of human rights abuses, and then to pass down judgments and make recommendations or condemnations. That's a good deal, right?

In 2005, three countries were elected to the Commission: Cuba, a dictatorship known for imprisoning, torturing, and murdering people for political reasons; Zimbabwe, a horribly corrupt dictatorship renowned for the imprisonment and murdering of political opponents, seizing private property without compensation, and God knows what else; and Saudi Arabia a corrupt, feudal monarchy that denies rights to women and minorities, that burns bibles, murders missionaries, and imprisons and murders dissidents.

These three countries rank among the worst, most vile human rights abusers on earth. These countries sat in judgment of themselves as well as countries charged with minor offenses. I wonder what happened to those charges, great and small?

This Commission was a sham, and is a sham today.

It is but one example of many truly illegitimate, useless UN functions.

To be effective

The United Nations, to be effective and representative of what was originally envisaged needs to become an exclusive club. It would be open to membership by all nations but: A criteria for membership needs to be established. Only nations with representative elected governments and established, functioning laws of and for the people should be considered for membership. Self-appointed dictatorships and/or military governments with 'presidents for life' by whatever name would be excluded. Single party governments could however be eligible so long as their leaderships are chosen by an elective body, not self-appointed. They must pay their dues annually, or their membership will be suspended. They must obey the laws of the nations that house them, and they need to pay their bills and park legally.

The United Nations would be expected to step up to the plate regarding reprehensible governments harmful to the common good of mankind. For instance, the UN has long tolerated rogue nations involved in slave trading, illicit narcotics trafficking, severe political repression and torture, genocide, including testing of toxins on human beings, etc. Idi Amin, Saddam Hussein, Kim Il Sung and his freaky son, the little Kim, Jean Bedel Bokassa, the Taliban, Iran, Pakistan, Saudi Arabia, and others like that should have been taken out by the UN, a responsible UN.

When horrible African tribal wars start, the UN should go in and stop the horrors riki ticki quick. When the Tutsis and Hutus in Rwanda were chopping one another up, the UN forces in their little blue beanies stood by and watched. That was simply criminal neglect.

Vestiges of colonialism

An effective United Nations would need to let some of the last vestiges of colonialism drop into the dustbin of history. Artificial borders were useful only to the colonial powers and are now often at the root of countless deaths, suffering, and persistent mayhem, especially in Africa.

Colonial era borders drawn on African and Asian maps often ignored differing cultures, societies, tribes, customs, and more. Pre-colonial tribes had their own conflicts over territory or whatever and the losing tribe either perished or was absorbed by the more dominant tribes or cultures. It was like this since Cro-Magnon man eliminated the Neanderthals.

The residue of colonialism is a root cause of the Nigerian civil wars, Rwandan genocide, perpetual conflicts in the Congo, Sudanese conflicts, the Eritrean civil war with Ethiopia, and on and on. The Sahara and sub-Sahara regions have ongoing conflicts between competing tribal groups that refuse to end. The conflict in former British India is still ongoing between Moslems vs. Hindus and Buddhists.

Yugoslavia's Tito was clever and ruthless and was thus able to maintain continuity within the former Yugoslavia. When those inheriting coalitions fell apart, the United States and Europe stupidly tried to hold them together.

In Europe, Belgium has conflicts between the Walloons and The Flemish, but they are civilized and enlightened enough to work out their differences and leave the conflict largely to jawboning. Belgium could easily break up and be absorbed into France, the Netherlands and Germany and all would be fine.

The robust East Asian cultures and civilization consisting of Japan, Korea, China, Taiwan, the Philippines, Thailand, Singapore, India, and several others all have cultures that are largely congruent with Western Culture. This is why they are all successful, because they are strong, dynamic, self disciplined, and are able to absorb from others, and give back that which is beneficial. They are competitive and able to learn and grow. Hopefully Cambodia, Nepal, Sri Lanka, and Burma have the strength and character to move forward too, as well as non-Moslem parts of Indonesia.

Oil for Food

After the first Gulf War where the Coalition forces led by the United States, under United States' initiative easily drove Saddam and his Iraqi forces out of Kuwait, an embargo was placed on Iraq. Its goal was to weaken Saddam and cause him to fall from power. That embargo failed.

During the embargo, Iraq was allowed, under an Oil for Food program to sell oil and use the proceeds to provide food, medicine, and basic necessities for the people of Iraq. From day one, that program was plagued by fraud first, and mismanagement second, all at the hands of, under the supervision, and with the consent of the United Nations.

Then Secretary General Butros Butros Ghali bowed to pressure (bribes = pressure) to approve of shaky, slimy deals, and the use of banks and companies prescribed by Saddam Hussein, etc.

Ghali's successor, Kofi Anan approved (his approval was purchased and paid for) a continuation of this fraud and theft. His faux claims that he was unaware of these misdeeds by his hand picked administrator of the programs, Benan Sevan is a lie. Sevan, a slick, slimy, greedy lying 40-year veteran UN administrator knew and adroitly used all of the loops, hoops, tricks, and flim-flam to funnel money from oil into many pockets such as French President Chirac, as well as his own. He was nearly perfect in this, but got caught in at least one area, which blew his cover. Sevan was the main pipeline, the bag man for Saddam's buying of influence. Another influence peddler was Kojo Anan, Kofi's corrupt son who readily accepted blood money in supporting this fraud.

We should have no doubt that Kofi Annan himself profited very handsomely from this, although his stash is well hidden.

All of this corruption and filth was known to President Clinton and his administration which chose to let this slip and slide (sic) by. After all, it was the Clintonites who worked to put Annan in as the Secretary General.

After months of outcry, Annan appointed Paul Volker to investigate. Volker was given sharply limited powers, was unable to subpoena documents, files were locked to him, and he was unable to compel anyone to testify under oath. Most of the documents and contracts were not executed on U.S. territory and therefore were immune from subpoena. Most of the acts took place overseas, were not done by American citizens and therefore are not prosecutable under U.S. laws. The whole thing was a charade.

This oil-for-fool scandal is but one in a long, a very long list of UN acts of corruption and greed. Al Capone should have been so lucky.

Indonesian Tsunami

As the enormous impact of the December 26, 2004 Indonesian tsunami disaster unfolded, the United States generously responded with men and material beyond what anyone else did. The Western Nations, or as I refer to them, the Civilized World likewise responded, and this was not just governments but thousands of private organizations, institutions, and individuals without precedent. Individual American and Australian diplomats, military personnel, and locally active businesses and their employees gave up their vacations and spent their own money, lots of it, to help relieve the misery of those thousands of victims. Most victims were Moslem. Where was the outpouring of support from oil-rich Arabs, their brothers in Islam? Where were the ruling, established elite of those affected countries? What outpouring of generosity and largesse came from the rest of the Islamic world, the Arabs? Nothing!

The affected countries' leadership: The Indians told us to stay away. While Sri Lanka was somewhat receptive, they let us do their work for them. The Indonesian government fearfully aware of their impotence soon started dictating to the Americans and Australians, giving a time period for us to 'get out'. Oh, let's be fair. None of the most affected, Indonesia, Sri Lanka, or the Maldives is dirt poor. The simple fact is that their leadership and elite really didn't care or want to be bothered too much with the suffering of their own people, but the presence of Americans and other civilized (non-Moslem) workers exposed their neglectful attitudes.

Then, of course, unfortunately ignorant American officials such as Condoleeza Rice and Colin Powell among others applied wishful thinking and declared that the tsunami relief would show Moslems that Americans are really nice people, etc. All that we really did was reaffirm the impotence of those governments, the impotence of other Islamic nations, and thus further annoy the uncaring Moslem leaders. Imams and mullahs all over the place preached that the United States in particular, and Christianity in general caused the tsunami. The chumps actually believe this, their own taqiyyah.

This whole tragic event clearly and unequivocally demonstrated that Western civilization is morally and culturally superior to Islam in every way.

The UN? Senior UN representatives along with their entourages flew (first class) from all over the world into where they could get five-star accommodations. Then, they flew into the disaster areas for photo opportunities, sniffed at what they perceived as a lack of perfect coordination and bitched about the US airlifting of supplies. They accomplished all of this while staying in five star hotels between their shuttles to and from photo opportunities and having to put up with the thumping whoop, whoop, whoop of those so very annoying Australian, American and Singaporean helicopters; and rumbling Australian, New Zealand, and American military transport planes. An Indian hospital ship off of the coast of Sumatra made a great photo-opportunity backdrop. The best the elite, politically correct, overpaid UN vultures could do was start, three weeks after the event, to talk about sending in assessment teams, and to put out a bevy of jibber-jabber press releases.

The UN reportedly claimed as theirs, the work done by the

United States, Australia, and several European countries --- who just happen to be UN members.

Next, the UN demanded billions from the civilized Western world so that they could build roads for their top of the line Land Cruisers and Mercedes limousines, and haul materials for the construction of their luxurious top of the line housing and offices before they could start their 'development' programs. Little, if any of the money destined for the suffering poor ever got to them. It was diverted to the UN elite whose unique titles inevitably were Coordinator for Coordinating the Coordination of the sub-Coordinator for the sub-sub-Coordinating for the lesser sub-Coordination of.....some totally worthless, corrupt, ineffective and mismanaged whatever.

The UN's title for the event: <u>United Nations Deputy Emergency Relief Coordinator and the Secretary General's Special Coordinator for Humanitarian Assistance in Tsunami-affected Countries</u>. Note "coordinator" twice in that title, so that's a really important and elevated position.

Now, the European Union (EU) eschewed emulating the action oriented 'cowboy' Americans, New Zealanders, and Australians, and adopted the UN model by making arrangements to send in a bevy of Senior Planners, Project Planners, Event Planners, and Area Planners, and Coordinators to study and write reports ad nauseum.

Two weeks after the tsunami disaster, Singaporeans, Japanese, Koreans, and others started to sign on to join and help with the Australian-American effort, but wisely and prudently avoiding at all costs being "coordinated" by the UN or EU who remained fully occupied with their first priority of establishing and refining their 24-hour catering services at their five star hotels. UN "coordinators" began focusing and declared that the Australians and Americans should switch to UN uniforms and "go blue", so that the suffering masses would know where their relief was coming from....... They needed to have something to show for their efforts.........., and to impress their so perfect, selfless boss, Kofi Annan whose significant singular contribution nearly two weeks after the disaster was to state that the question of fund raising was "looking up".

The United States' contribution to the disaster was the immediate diversion of a US Navy battle group of twenty ships, hundreds of aircraft, and thousands of Marines and Sailors, some of whom were on the ground literally within hours of the disaster. And, the Useless Nations (UN) bitched that this multi-million dollar American response was inadequate. Before it was over, the Americans provided not just millions of dollars, but billions.

The Moslem/Arab donations? Zero!

Silly Stuff

The UN sponsored Arab Human Development Report (AHDR)

publishes an annual report on Arab economic development. It has detailed how the entire Arab region is falling behind economically, discusses at length its knowledge (educational) deficit, and real lack of freedom and development. This is all fine and good, but then the reports cite the creation of Israel as the major reason for the Arabs' being so stupid and backward, and weeps, wails, and whines about United States' support for Israel.

No, the real, true reason for Arabs being backward and primitive is their willfully Ignorant pagan ideological Islamism and gross intolerance of civilization.

Chapter 20

IRAQ

Iraq is OK, or rather, some of the people of Iraq are, but like a bad or failed marriage, they probably don't really belong together.

Created in 1917 out of the ruins of World War One in the Balfour Declaration and the broken Turkish Ottoman Empire, British and French victors sat down and divvied parts of the world up. Taking a ruler and a pencil to a map, they created modern Iraq without very much or realistically serious consideration to, or of cultural, religious, linguistic, tribal, or natural boundaries.

Perhaps it was by design, to establish within the borders of Iraq a nation that would be in constant strife with one or another group trying to dominate or control others, and those not in control just striving to survive.

The Assyrian Christians were sacrificed in one of the most brutal events in modern history. Scores of thousands died, and thousands more were forcefully converted to Islam. First raped, then striped naked and marched in front of soldiers, Assyrian Christian girls were bound and laid on top of Christian holy books and bibles used as fuel to burn them alive. The perpetrators of this were the wonderful Kurds whom the Americans call "friend" today.

Out of that eventually came Saddam Hussein and his regime who ruthlessly and effectively controlled Iraq for a quarter of a century. Lacking the finesse or humanity to do so rightly or decently, they managed with brutality and fear, establishing their indecent primitive tribal dominance over other tribes.

Ruthless is a mild term for the way Saddam ruled. The rule of Saddam was vicious and brutal, aside from being insanely egotistical, which is almost atypical for Moslem banana republic dictators.

The United States supported Saddam in his war with Iraq only because he was the lesser of two evils following the Ayatollah's takeover of Iran (with Jimmy Carter's blessing) and the taking hostage of the American Embassy. Saddam attacked Iran and started a prolonged and ugly war. When it became apparent that he was not doing too well, the United States stepped in -- to maintain the status quo. The United States had determined that it was not in America's best interests to let Saddam lose the war allow the Iranians to take over Iraq's oil.

Had the idiot, Jimmy Carter not torpedoed the Shah of Iran and ushered in one of the most evil and tyrannical regimes in history, 2.5 million innocent Iranians and Iraqis lives would not have been wasted in that war.

After the Iran - Iraq war settled down and Saddam had time to lick his wounds and recover, he started looking for more trouble assuming that we Americans would let him do as he wished. The United States had no real idea of what or whom it was truly dealing with in the form of Saddam Hussein. While it was politically correct American politics, the sending of a woman as Charge des Affaires of the US Embassy in Iraq was a wrong message, a stupid move. But, it was politically correct. Never mind that it was absolutely stupid and naive.

Saddam Hussein possessed an enormous but primitive ego in a society that considers women to be inferiors. Lacking the education, intellectual capacity or urbane understanding, Saddam simply saw this as an insult.

Saddam started rattling his saber over Kuwait which he claimed to be another province of Iraq, threatening to take it over.

The United States' Department of State sent this otherwise capable Foreign Service Officer a message to deliver to Saddam that was typically foggy bottom 'diplomatese' in nature -- equivocal, convoluted, and unclear. Saddam with his limited abilities took the message as an OK to attack Kuwait.

So, the logical next step was for Saddam to do what he did, and suddenly he was in deep doo doo. When the United States raised a fuss over the attack, he believed this was just America's way of doing business, making noise.

At the time he attacked Kuwait, the United States apparently had no intelligence assets on the ground in Iraq, and in fact only had a very few fluent Arabic speakers, few of whom could even walk the streets of Iraq undetected.

When the United States rallied forces and actually attacked and drove him out of Kuwait, he was genuinely surprised. He was even more convinced of America's treachery. Our Department of State's elite 'experts' were treacherous by being just incredibly naive and dumb, and stupidly caused that terrible disaster.

After Saddam's forces were driven out of Kuwait, President Bush (the 41st) did not fail regarding the removal of Saddam Hussein. The decision at the time was to leave him (Saddam) in power because there was nobody who could fill the vacuum if he was removed, except for the Ayatollah's of Iran which were a more insidious evil than even Saddam.

America did not want to take over Iraq and we recognized that an attempt to do so would be disastrous. It was deemed prudent to leave Saddam there and to just try to contain him.

He slaughtered Kurds. He slaughtered Shiias. We established a no fly zone thinking that would hinder him.

For a dozen years, Saddam thumbed his nose at the United States and its allies. He shot at us and went about his business of satisfying his ego.

Saddam needed to intimidate Iran and his neighbors. He supported terrorists in ways we will never know.

Our intelligence remained feeble, almost obviously so. The CIA had a dozen years to do something about this deficiency, and totally neglected to do so.

Saddam by his actions led us to believe that he was working at obtaining new weapons of mass destruction (WMD). We were unwilling or incapable (or both) of learning what he was really doing. He did a good job of fooling everyone, the CIA and FBI, the Israelis, the Germans, the French, the Russians, and even his neighbors.

If he didn't fool them, then he did a hell of a job of concealing what he was doing, and we don't know that yet.

Along the way, he tried to have President Bush (41) killed. That pissed a lot of people off, the wrong people. So, when President Bush (43) was elected President of the United States, Saddam found himself in the Bush administration's cross hairs for whatever of a myriad of reasons or reasoning. Claims to the contrary, revenge for trying to kill his dad was a part of the process that led the new Bush administration to remove Saddam Hussein.

President George W. Bush asked his advisors to justify taking Saddam out and owing to a dearth of good, honest, real, or useful intelligence, the Director of the Central Intelligence Agency, George Tenet, seeking to be held over from the Clinton administration sucked up to and lied to the President of the United States. Based on speculation as opposed to facts, George Tenet gave bad advice to President Bush and his senior advisors who were by the most part all too willing to bow to the winds of George's whim and who went with the flow. The only one with the courage and convictions to stand and be counted even a little was Secretary of State Colin Powell who himself even succumbed to an avalanche of intelligence community hooey and balderdash.

President George W. Bush had surrounded himself with loyal top advisers. They were loyal to the point of being willfully naïve and blind. Were they competent? NO! Sycophants? Yes!

National Security Adviser and later Secretary of State Condoleeza Rice reportedly possessed one of the finest minds in the world. She was supposedly far from being stupid. She reportedly knew more than any one person in government about the former Soviet Union, Russia, and the former Iron Curtain. It is obvious however that her understanding of the convoluted Middle East and Islam was not on a par with her knowledge of Russia.

When it comes to Islam, Rice was and remained clearly a neophyte. She spoke saying that Turkey was a 'model' nation. Turkey, is nothing more than a recidivist, backsliding nation of all that increasingly represents the worst evils of Islam. One of the most vicious of all Mohammedan terrorist organizations, Hamas, enjoys Turkish hospitality for its terrorist training camps. Yeah, our pals, the Turks. With pals like these, we need few enemies.

President Bush's unrealistic advisor on Arab stuff, David Forte, did not speak Arabic or any other Middle Eastern language, had never studied the Koran, the Hadiths, nor Sharia laws. Forte at least admitted that he was a well intentioned amateur. This was Bush's principal advisor however, and it was acceptable to Bush. Shame on Bush for being such an utter moron!

CIA Director George Tenet, a smart, conniving, charming, and a superb self-promoting salesman was little more than a self-serving sycophant. The Intelligence service that he led, controlled, and commanded for over a decade failed dismally. In February of 2003, Tenet spoke about his efforts to "rebuild" the CIA from the time he became its Director in 1995, six years before 9/11. He had six years to fail, and fail he did. Tenet was a world class flim-flam man. During my decade of service in Islamic cultures, I learned one thing if nothing else: When a man of that culture declares "trust me" when he tells me something, I understand that in all likelihood what I am being fed next is going to be a lie. Tenet had no resources in Iraq and he and his CIA willingly trusted Ahmed Chalabi and his fellow travelers who said "trust me." Tenet & Co. were lied to, and they lapped it up. They were played for chumps.

Secretary of Defense Rumsfeld culled generals who asked too many questions and had sincere reservations about making war on Iraq. He put in place a team of generals who planned and executed magnificently the conquering of what was at best a third or even fourth rate military force.

Saddam, by virtue of his thumbing his nose at over a dozen Useless Nations (UN) resolutions gave sustenance to the Bush administration. His intransigence and actions at thwarting weapons inspectors affirmed that he was to all appearances very active in the WMD arena. Using oil for food funds, he had purchased high ranking French (President Chirac in fact), Russian, Chinese and German government leaders, as well as top leadership at the UN (Kofi Annan, professions to the contrary aside, knew even if he didn't also participate, pocketing some of the largesse himself). Literally owning all of those people/governments, Saddam knew with an absolute certainty that the UN Security Council would never, ever sanction military action against him, that one or another of his bought and paid for minions would cast a veto in his favor whenever the issue came up.

In all likelihood, the Bush administration somehow (perhaps one or two of the CIA's clandestine operations was still functional -- after all a third world language wasn't necessary at the UN) knew that the Americans would be thwarted at every turn within the UN Security Council. Given this, anyone who is surprised that the United States took unilateral action is a simpleton.

Convinced beyond any uncertainty of Saddam's awful plans, President Bush with the Support of the British and a few others sent the greatest military force in the world to attack and remove Saddam Hussein. Saddam, ignorant and unsophisticated was again surprised by the United States.

None of the Bush Presidency advisors or Executive Department officials and their hundreds of staffers adequately understood how to deal with the aftermath of conquering Iraq and how to win the peace.

Our 'good' friends the Turks, who denied us the use of their territory in preparation for the invasion of Iraq soon sent their own special forces troops into Iraq. Of course, they did this after we had defeated Saddam. The Turkish forces were not sent into Iraq to help the Americans, they were there to do mischief regarding the Kurds. However, these clandestine Turk forces were apprehended by Americans. The Turkish government who regularly abuse American forces in Turkey, screamed and wailed about the 'injustice' of a NATO partner detaining another NATO partner's troops without any warning, and even demanded an apology from the United States (for catching their illegal forces and rightfully humiliating the Turks).

The idea of establishing a lasting democracy in Iraq is a wonderful but simplistic notion. It could work if the people of Iraq were homogeneous, like the Germans in Germany, and the Japanese in Japan were after World War II. Democracy in Iraq will fail. The people contained within those borders of post World War I Iraq are not homogeneous in any sense of the world. They are at best a bunch of primitive tribes who loathe and fear that which they do not understand, and that is one-another. They are culturally, linguistically, religiously, and tribally different.

For over six hundred years, the (Sunni Moslem) Ottoman Empire Turks ruled over the area. They savagely and ruthlessly wielded the proverbial big stick to maintain a sense of order satisfactory to meeting their ends. The Turks continued a bloody pattern that had earlier been established by Genghis Khan and followed by Mohammed, a pattern that included decapitation of enemies. This pattern was followed by Tamerlane, who expanded on the beheading to include not just a few enemies but entire populations.

Following World War I, British and French victors without a great deal of consideration or conscience set out dividing the spoils of the Ottoman Empire. They took a pencil and straight edge to a map in creating some of the borders of Iraq. They did not consider tribal, ethnic, cultural, linguistic, or religious differences. They installed a Sunni regime that continued the bloody rule of the area, a regime that Saddam later took over and that he himself ruled for a quarter of a century.

Soon after Saddam's vaunted but in fact useless army ran for the hills, er.... Sand dunes, the war ended. The United States was ill prepared for the peace.

In Shiia areas, some fat 'holy' man called Sadr, with bad teeth (his black teeth looked so bad, I felt that I could smell his fowl pig manure breath from the TV) exploited American vulnerabilities and established his own little raggedy army of the Mahdi to challenge the

United States.

A former Mahdi pretender a couple of hundred years ago rounded up a large band of fellow lunatics and managed to defeat the British in the Sudan. He sent his disciples charging to their death again and again until the British ran out of bullets and were finally overcome.

Stupidly, the United States let this Iranian supported creep, Moqtada al Sadr, run his rampage for a while. He had stashed his "Mahdi" army's weapons in Mosques and the risk averse political bosses of the American army were afraid to go after him. This was incredibly 'stupid' political correctness derived from some moronic level of the State Department or the Pentagon. Sadr should have been killed, but was given a 'bye' even though there was a warrant out for his arrest for murder, we let him go. This risk averse stupidity would later bring about a major, major pain in our backside, one that we actually earned.

During earlier wars the United States had no qualms about bombing and shelling churches, cathedrals, and monasteries. We didn't hesitate to destroy temples in Japan, or Buddhist temples and monasteries in Asian wars, but we became timorous of taking out Mosques turned into armories. By showing our fearfulness of taking out armories that were formerly mosques, we encouraged all of these Mohammedans to turn mosques into armories because they now know that we stupid Americans are afraid of going after those so-called holy places. This is stupid thinking! Whenever a Mosque is turned into an armory, it is now an armory and it MUST be destroyed just as we would do any other armory. Any general who stops taking an armory/mosque ought to lose his stars and be sent to jail. How many American soldiers lives have been sacrificed, squandered because of this moronic political correctness? Too many!

The Israelis have it right. During their January, 2009 confrontation with Hamas, they started taking out Mosques that were being used as munitions storage facilities, armories, command and control facilities, etc.

When lying beasts use hospitals and schools as headquarters and armories such as Hezbollah does in Lebanon, those facilities should be treated only as armories and destroyed. Any tragic subsequent collateral deaths of patients and/or children is the responsibility of the Moslem cowards who hide behind skirts, and under diapers.

Proportionality

During the 2009 Israeli confrontation with Hamas, a new term arose where the defenders of Hamas [including leading morons at the Useless Nations (UN) demanded proportionality from the Israelis. Hamas was being confronted with overwhelming Israeli military force in response to the 7+ years of daily barrages directed at innocent Israeli women and children. The Moslems wanted a tit-for-tat response from the Israelis: A rocket for a rocket.

The Israelis and others who have sane brain cells rejected this proportionality demand as foolish nonsense. They missed a great opportunity.

Proportionality ought to be considered for adoption on a population-wide basis based on the number of Jews on earth (about 20 million) and the population of Moslems (about 1.5 billion) a ratio of 2-to-75 can be determined. Then, use that ratio in an Israeli response (others could adopt this system as well) to every Palestinian Arab attack on Jews. Two Arab explosive attacks beget a barrage of 75 responding bomb, rocket, or artillery hits. Two bullets fired over the border at a Jew would beget 75 rounds fired back into Arab population centers. This is proportional reciprocity.

Iraqi Insurgency

After the fall of Saddam, the "Sunni Triangle" of Iraq erupted in conflict. We called those guerillas insurgents. They were savage and the toll they exacted on Americans and others was terrible. They attracted and welcomed (in some cases reluctantly) to their ranks al Qaeda and any number of others (even including despised Shiia volunteers) willing to fight and kill Americans. Those Sunnis knew beyond any doubt that being the minority tribe in a Shiia dominated Iraq, they would be subject to revenge taking for the seven hundred years of brutal Sunni dominance and their killing of millions of Shiia over those centuries.

The careless and thoughtlessly stupid, abysmally ignorant American leadership failed in many ways. Trusting the Iranian backed criminal, thief, conspirator, and confirmed liar Ahmad Chalabi, Ambassador Brenner stupidly surged disbanded every semblance of remaining Iraqi government and administrative management. This simple act confirmed to the Sunnis that they were completely disenfranchised and they were thus encouraged (by Ambassador Brenner's actions) to start their battle for survival immediately. Their battle for survival was dubbed an insurgency, and the stupid Ambassador (Brenner) failed totally to recognize the scope of its meaning and minimized it, calling the Sunnis criminals and failing completely to recognize why the "insurgency" was happening. In his ignorance, Brenner became a pawn of the wily Shiia in Iraq and created a climate of distrust among the Sunnis. It took months before the Americans recognized that Chalabi was bad news and was in fact a total piece of crud and a very serious enemy. Brenner and the Administration's stupidity caused the unnecessary deaths of hundreds of Americans. But then, the CIA and the rest of the intelligence community deep in their dream world couldn't even begin to figure this out, so a very stupid, ignorant Brenner was just winging it on his own out there in his fantasyland.

The Americans guesstimated the number of "insurgents" at 5,000 from the beginning of the fighting, and held to that number for well over a year. It was only a guess. After reportedly killing and arresting about 5,000 "insurgents" the Americans revised the guesstimate in late 2004 to about 12-16,000. Those numbers were for those in Iraq, not the ones in transit, in training, or sheltered and hiding out or resting in sanctuaries in Iran, Jordan, Saudi Arabia, Turkey, Lebanon, and Syria.

Given this intelligence and intellectual void, it was relatively easy for the so-called insurgents to use the media as a propaganda arm. Undetected collaborationists abounded in their broad support of the Sunnis. These collaborators included Shiia who relied on and used the Sunnis to broaden the split to the great if not overwhelming advantage of the Shiia who ultimately garnered American support as they engineered their lopsided victories in the election.

In 2003, retired U.S. Ambassador Edward Peck lambasted the Bush administration for going to war in Iraq without UN support and for not trying other diplomatic methods first. (In fact, forty members of the UN openly supported the United States, more than the number who openly opposed us.) Peck was just another of the intellectually feeble diplomats who wanted to continue jabbering ineffectually while Saddam continued his provocations. Peck believed that the politically correct risk-averse approach was the best way to deal with this. He himself had served for 2-½ years in Iraq and ought to have known better. But, by being a lifelong risk-averse butt kisser and advocate against U.S. interests, he eventually became an Ambassador.

Peck did predict that the Middle East would become more unstable after ousting Saddam. Given Saddam's age, health, and myriad enemies, he would have soon been killed or died off anyhow, which would have had the same net effect, except that U.S. forces would have been in less of a position to thwart Iranian intentions.

In late 2004 and before the Iraqi elections, I wrote and distributed to several media outlets an opinion piece contrary to the Bush administration's simplistic and perhaps ill informed ideals. I wasn't against an election or democracy, I just opined that the Bushies didn't know what they were doing, and that electing a lasting modern democracy within the post WWI borders that created Iraq would likely be doomed. Of course, being a relative nobody, my piece was not widely used by the press if at all.

I urged breaking that place into at least three parts:

A Kurdish nation - Kurdistan. Of course the Turks would never willingly agree to this. Half of the world's Kurdish people occupy a substantial part of Turkey and they would no doubt move to join their fellow Kurds in an expanded Kurdistan at Turkey's expense. It was the treacherous Turks who disallowed their long time NATO partner and benefactor, the United States, the use of their soil in staging a northern front in the invasion of Iraq. Those corrupt Turkish legislators who voted against the United States 'mysteriously' became, one and all, substantially wealthier after casting their votes and betrayed any trust that the United States had in them. They were bought and paid for by Saddam, just as he had bought French President Chirac and more than a few others.

Speaking of Turks and Kurds. During the Korean war, the 'Turks' garnered a fierce warrior reputation in battling against the North Koreans and Chinese. Those so very fierce 'Turks' were in fact Armenian, Greek, and mostly Kurdish conscripts who were followed into battle by machine gun wielding Turkish noncoms and officers to shoot any who faltered. Those Kurds, Greeks, and Armenians were fighting fiercely for their very lives.

In my article, I suggested that an enlarged Kurdish nation would likely be joined by their fellow Kurds resident in Iran, which would serve the world's best interests by shrinking Iran's territory. The northern Iraqi oil fields would thus fall into the new Kurdistan guaranteeing their economic future.

An independent Sunni area (the Sunni triangle) would have forestalled the 'insurgency' and saved thousands of lives because there would have been less reason for their rebellion.

Of course, the Bushies, still thinking along the lines of keeping Iran away from those southern oil fields couldn't contemplate creating an independent Shiia republic. It was feared that the Shiia of Iraq would stampede into the arms of their Shiia brethren of Iran taking that huge oil reserve with them. I suggested that such would not be the case, long term. A large number of the Iranian Shiia Moslems are in fact Arabs, not Persians with whom they share little. The Iranian Arabs would perhaps be more inclined to reject the Persians and join their Arab cousins, further destabilizing and shrinking Iran leaving a smaller, less significant, and less threatening Iran.

The United States would then have been held in higher esteem and regard by three new countries populated by homogeneous peoples who would be inclined to be friendly towards and trusting of the United States. Senator Joe Biden (one of those to whom I mailed my piece) even brought this up at one point and was pilloried for expressing such a thing. He is now the Vice President.

The Iraqi elections took place after a sustained Sunni insurgency that murdered thousands of people in an ill fated attempt to disrupt the elections. The Sunni insurgents caused most of the Sunnis to stay away from the polls further weakening their political future within the elected government of Iraq. This would only lead to further disenfranchising of the Sunnis within the Iraqi federation and a continuing insurgency in a battle for Sunni survival.

Following Shiia leadership guidelines, most of the Shiia voted, and we all know how they voted, don't we.

Kurds voted too, but while they voted in the Iraqi elections, they also held their own referendum on independence, and 98% voted for independence - separate and apart from Iraq. They didn't get it, but we know how they feel.

For the internal pre-election conflict, our ally, Saudi Arabia, sent the greatest number of "foreign" fighters to kill Americans and others in Iraq. The Saudi chief justice (a "royal") by the name of Sheik Saleh Al Luhaidan declared that Saudis' going to Iraq to kill Americans is permissible/desirable. This is just another example in a long list of examples depicting clearly the true face of the Saudis, and it definitely isn't pro-American.

Within days of the election, the Shiia majority began asserting their claims and establishing their dominance of Iraqi politics claiming that they would militarily defeat the Sunnis. This implicitly established the fact that the Shiia would commence in several insidious ways their revenge taking to pay the Sunnis back for their over six hundred years of abuses.

Naturally, the formerly disenfranchised Shiia have determined that the new Iraq will in fact be a Shiia based theocracy using the Koran as the constitution and Sharia as the basis of their laws, not a democracy. The Bushies were complete fools and idiots.

Chapter 21

NUCLEAR OUTLAWS

North Korea, Iran, and others are striving to develop nuclear weapons. We are sure of those facts, aren't we? Does the vaunted CIA tell us this, or are we learning about this from other, more reliable sources? Who??

The CIA told us that Iraq was working to develop nuclear weapons. Now, the CIA says the same about Iran. Can we believe this? But, the CIA played a role in declaring that Iran had halted their nuclear weapons program. The UN has independently verified this, that Iran is working on a weapons program. How about that, better, more reliable information from the UN than from the CIA. Even Iran has confirmed this, and then the CIA said it wasn't true....

North Korea has confirmed that they have nuclear weapons. Can the CIA confirm that the North Koreans are telling the truth?

Discredited after Iraq, the United States is not trusted anymore by some countries. The US's screw up has made the outlandish UN look good.

How do we - - - how does the civilized world deal with Iran and North Korea and their nuclear weapons? Nobody has an answer other than to jawbone, hold meetings and wring their hands. Barak Hussein Obama's approach to Iran's nuclear weapons program is simply to acquiesce, and demand that Israel submit itself to a new holocaust. But then, Obama is a Moslem following his Koranic teachings.

Can the United States be trusted to deal unilaterally with Iran and North Korea? It seems that the will is lacking.

Does the United States have the military resources to deal with them? The answer is yes! It's called overwhelming nuclear force, that if pressed, the United States will use. But, does the United States have the will to that force? With Obama in the White House, nope!

North Korea and Iran need to know unequivocally that if the United States or an ally suffers a nuclear attack, that we will respond in kind - reciprocate. In fact, Iranian President Ahmadinejad has vowed to use nuclear weapons against Israel first, then the United States. And, Obama is sitting on his backside letting this come to fruition.

In October of 2008, an Iranian freighter loaded with a mysterious cargo was hijacked off of the coast of Somalia, and many of the hijackers became ill or died after coming into contact with the ship's cargo. Reportedly, it was nuclear waste, or byproducts that the Iranians intended to disburse into the air via a massive explosion off of the coast of Israel, or in a European or American port.

Chapter 22

CHRISTIANITY

**America is the greatest nation on Earth.
One of the reasons for this is the
freedom of religion – to worship
(or to not worship) as we please.**

**Another reason for our greatness is our
freedom FROM the imposition of religion.
We may soon lose that freedom.**

I do not believe in or support publicly funded religious schools. Most private schools are very good, giving kids a secure place to be and offer a good education. Others are less than good places that develop healthy or well-informed minds. Those are the religious schools such as Moslem schools which by whatever name are fundamentally Madrassas where the children are indoctrinated in a biased, one-sided religion and political system of bigotry and hatred. There are some so-called Christian schools that would fall into similar categories when they also teach bigotry and hatred.

On June 27th, 2002, the Supreme Court handed down a wrongheaded decision that paved they way for taxpayer funds to be used for educational vouchers which can be used in religious (Moslem, Christian, Hindu, Mormon, Buddhist, etc.) schools. Our taxes are being used to fund fundamentalist religious schools right here, in the United States. This is flat wrong whether they are extremist fundamentalist Christian, Islamic Madrassas or any other extremist religious form of brainwashing and indoctrination.

My wife and I did send our children to a parochial school for a few years while living abroad, but we were very careful to ensure that the curriculum included education about, but not indoctrination in religion. Yes, we ensured that they learned that God is God and that there is one true, living God. We taught our children that it is not important how, when, or where they worshiped, prayed, or paid homage to God, as long as they did so.

We taught our children that there are good and evil people in the world and that some practitioners of evil cloak themselves in religion. We taught them that good people are good whether they are derived from Judaeo-Christian cultures or others such as Hindu, Buddhist, Shinto, Taoist, Confucian, or even Moslem. We also taught our children this basic, fundamental truth: The greatest danger to society, civilization, and freedom throughout the world as well as in the United States is religious extremism. Radical Christian fundamentalism can be just as evil as radical Hindu Thugism, fundamentalist Islam, cults such as the holly Rollers, Jehovah Witnesses, and Mormonism, or any other cult because any belief or philosophy that has as its goal the establishment and imposition of onerous, arbitrary biased fundamentalist restrictive laws or rules on others.

In studying the Holy Bible we can find some pretty harsh wording where God, in the Old Testament, tells the Jews to do a pretty fair amount of bloodletting of Philistines whom God disapproved of, and who had offended God. As the Jews and Christendom have grown and matured, this Savagery is no longer fundamental to their modern culture, which just wants the world to let the Jews have their little corner on earth – Israel. Unfortunately, there are those who wish to deny God's chosen people, the Jews this respite, and who suffer the consequences of their actions.

The New Testament that is a guideline for much of modern Christianity is more about life, decency, love, respect, and caring, and not about hatred and murder. Nevertheless, there are Christians who use select portions of the (highly and tightly censored at its assembly) New Testament to do evil.

Based on my sojourns among civilized people outside of America, I find that I came to disagree with Christian proselytizers who proclaim that if a person does not absolutely accept Christ as their savior, they cannot go to heaven, or attain life after death under any circumstances. This is sick fundamentalism without a shred of decency, love, or charitable consideration. They readily condemn out of hand all of the decent, gentle, charitable, good, loving, people of the world who follow other faiths, beliefs, or philosophies (yes, I include some few people of Moslem origins). These fundamentalist so-called Christian proselytizers of their own narrow forms of belief are stupid, uncharitable, and unforgiving. They are therefore themselves forsaking the teachings of Christ. Theirs is a loathsome political agenda of hatred, fear, and subjugation just like Islam, not a generous or hospitable life agenda.

Christian Terrorists

Some so-called Christians or Evangelists are terrible racists. They used to and still use the Holy Bible to justify slavery, to justify claims of white supremacy, racism, to condemn and torture and burn witches alive, to murder Jews and others, to condemn decency, and support all of the ugly things they themselves are often known for. Fortunately, these extremists are a minority, a fringe who have forsaken their humanity.

One such extremist fringe group who call themselves Christian Reconstruction, which is very similar to an idiotic, racist, and bigoted anti-Semitic but sometimes benign outfit calling itself British Israelism. The British Israelism reportedly is the root system for the American Christian Identity Group, of which some adherents later changed their name to the Church of Jesus Christ Christian (CJCC). The CJCC has as its followers groups such as the American Nazi Party, various Hammerskins groups, Jubilee, National Association for the Advancement of White People, The Order, Aryan Nation, Posse Comitatus, the KKK, the New Order and the Covenant, Sword, and Arm of the Lord. [Their names, their behavior, and their doctrines remind one of other groups of bigots such as Hamas, Hezbollah, Taliban, CAIR, al Qaeda, PLA, Black September, MSA, and dozens of other Moslem hate groups who likewise share the common belief among these very twisted sick groups that Jewish people are descendants of Satan.] These bigoted groups have adherents such as Atlanta bomber Eric Rudolph, arsonists who reportedly torched synagogues in Sacramento, California; various murders of gays, Buford O'Neal Furrow, jr., shooter of Jews at a Los Angeles Jewish Community center, and many other such barbaric acts. Former South African Calvinist groups who preach that the collapse of apartheid and black majority rule is a punishment of God because of some perceived form of Afrikaner disobedience.

Just like Islamists, there are those who would readily destroy everything in pursuit of their own insane goals.

Idiocy in the name of God

At a 1990's American southern Baptist convention, a pronouncement was handed down obliging all women of this order, sect, cult, or whatever that its member women are obliged to submit to men.

Texan, Andrea Yates drowned her five children, was tried, and found guilty and sent to prison for life. Andrea Yates was a good Christian fundamentalist's wife who dutifully submitted to her husband and his desire to have lots of babies. By so doing, she was compelled to stay confined more or less to her home to keep producing and taking care of those children, more children than she could reasonably handle. Her fundamentalist husband had even been warned that Andrea ought not have more children after her third child, but no, her good, devout, fundamentalist husband knew better and kept knocking her up. Overburdened by her husband's dominance and over-the-top religious horsepookey, she cracked and killed her children. She is not alone in being culpable for the deaths of those children. Her idiot fundamentalist husband should likewise have been held culpable because he compelled his wife, Andrea, to produce more babies than she could handle. That is a large if not the compelling reason for her going nuts. But, Andrea's husband walked, and then good, loyal and faithful Christian fundamentalist that he was, he quickly divorced her – he abandoned his wife so that he could start another wife off with another batch of yet more babies. The guy is a major league fundamentalist jerk.

Fortunately, Andrea was later ruled to have been temporarily insane, and was later released from prison. God bless her! She has suffered terribly.

Many purist "Christian" creationists seem to be a bunch of ignorant cultists as willfully ignorant of the world as are the Islamists and the Flat Earth Society.

Evangelist, Billy Graham said it best when he opined that **in the beginning**, God said: 'BANG!"

Homosexuality

Many religious groups are having fits over gay rights. These wonderful, generous 'Christian' folks have roundly and consistently condemned homosexuality even though that has been a part and parcel of humanity as long as history has been recorded, since our ancestors dismounted the trees. These folks want to deny something that is human. Homophobism is not a charitable answer.

A likewise irresponsible response to this homophobism has been a huge gay pride push for homosexual marriages, and the disunifying furor that this has brought to America.

Responsible homosexual couples desire access to civil rights such as hospital visitation, medical benefits of couples, inheritance, and a host of others.

If the anti-gay groups want to threat their human brothers and sisters with charity even though their sexual orientation may be disagreeable, they need to start behaving like civilized people and agree to civil unions (not full marriage which is clearly between a man and a woman) so that gender confused couples can live in our society.

Abortion
[Killing babies by whatever name]

When Roe V. Wade was handed down, it was the right thing to do. By legalizing abortions, the then supreme Court halted some of the most barbaric practices in Modern America – 'back alley' abortions. The "Christians" sole political focus seems to be a complete reversal of this law that not only gives women a choice, put actually preserves lives. Anyone who wants to reverse Roe V. Wade without a civilized alternative is essentially a barbarian.

A truly civilized Christian people would look at this issue responsibly and reasonably and take measures to do what is right, to both protect unborn infants from abortions but still assure women the right of choice. Flaky, silly, irresponsible women who wake up one morning and decide to abort a viable fetus should be prohibited from this barbarity. However, women (regardless of age) who wake up in the morning after they have realized they have done something stupid or foolish should be, regardless of age, able to go to a pharmacy and obtain the RU486, or similar drugs, to abort within the first week or two of a sexual encounter that was a mistake. This is a civilized and responsible measure. This, I believe is what Jesus would want us to do. What a woman chooses to do is between her and God, not some mere mortal making his own preferred interpretation of God's desires.

Fundamental Christian fanatics, if allowed to pursue this as far as their black hearts would let them go would very likely go beyond stopping abortion to even outlaw masturbation claiming that 'wasting' seed would be tantamount to taking pre-born lives.

Perverts and the cloth

During the feverish pogrom against Catholic priests involved in sex scandals of all types, a Roman Catholic Archbishop in the Honduras blamed the scandal on Jewish media (yep, blame it on those pesky Jews). The Cardinal, Oscar Andres Rodriguez Meridiaga was obviously an anti-Semite, and probably a pedophile himself. People like him who are active in Christian communities are just as bad as Islamic leaders involved in pedophilia as they strive to live down to the low standards established by Mohammed.

Pope Benedict to Moslems:
True religion is rational, peaceful, and non-totalitarian

Pope Benedict is head and shoulders above his likeable predecessor in addressing the realities of Islam, the most irrational, violent, fascist social institution on earth.

I wish that Pope Benedict could talk to all of the Christian entities of the world and bring them together regarding Islam. But, the vast array of disparate Christian groups irrationally seem to want to remain disparate, and this will seal the doom of Christendom which will fall under the totalitarian domination of Islam if these Many Christians fail to wake up and see the writing on the wall.

Our tolerance of Islam
is based on our ignorance of Islam

Historically, the Christians have not done well in the face of the persistent, continuing Islamic assault.

In eighth century Arabia, Mohammed went after the Christians who were unable or unwilling to stand up to him and his rapacious armies and either succumbed in death, or capitulated as abject dhimmis and within generations became Moslem themselves. The Jews who were stronger in their faith also succumbed in the most part with a few thousand remaining in Yemen in the 21st Century.

Tolerance of Islam is tolerance of Satan

The Christians who once dominated Egypt saw that the

Christians of Arabia who chose to fight the Mohammedists failed. So, they tried to accommodate Islam as it swept into North Africa, and we can all see the abject misery that the Copts live with in and around Egypt today. The then greatest repository of information in the world, the libraries of Alexandria which contained thousands of one-of-a-kind scripts and scriptures were destroyed by the Moslems. It took six months to burn all of those precious manuscripts. This is what Islam brought to civilization – destruction and destitution.

In the rest of Mediterranean Africa, the Christians ceased to exist as most were killed off, were enslaved (to soon die), or compulsively converted to Islam.

South of the Sahara in present day Ethiopia, Eritrea, and the Sudan, the Christians lived on and preserved their own Coptic religion apart from the Egyptian Copts. In the face of the Islamic assault, the southern Copts were cowed and did not support their northern brethren, and the two Coptic groups hardly talk to or support one-another to this day.

The failures of the Northern and southern Copts is symptomatic of the remainder of Christendom which has fractured itself and has left Christians more interested in fighting one-another than in uniting in the face of the assault of Islam.

The Chaldeans (Iraq) don't work with or support the Copts (Egypt) or Assyrians (Syria, Turkey, and Iraq), who have opposed the Armenians (Central Asia) who have remained apart from the Orthodox Catholic Christians (extending from Greece into Russia) who have warred against the Roman Catholics whose approximately one thousand separate protestant factions have warred against one another for centuries and encourage factional rivalries today.

One should ask why they don't organize, unite, and fight. They are dhimmis, that's why – they are cowed. They are doomed.

The Culture of the Dhimmi

Dhimmi defined: The word "dhimmitude" as a historical concept, was coined by author, Bat Ye'or, to describe the legal and social conditions of Jews and Christians subjected to Islamic rule. The word "dhimmitude" comes from *dhimmi*, an Arabic word meaning "protected". *Dhimmi* was the name applied by the Arab-Muslim conquerors to indigenous non-Muslim populations who surrendered by a treaty (*dhimma*) to Muslim domination. Islamic conquests expanded over vast territories in Africa, Europe and Asia, for over a millennium (638-1683). The Muslim empire incorporated numerous varied peoples which had their own religions, cultures, languages and civilization. For centuries, these indigenous, pre-Islamic peoples constituted the great majority of the population of the land. Although these populations differed, they fell under rule by the same type of Islamic laws, based on Sharia laws.

A dhimmi in Moslem countries is a brutally subjugated second class citizen with few rights or privileges. In confrontations, dhimmis are not permitted to fight back, and if they do, they can be imprisoned or killed just for trying to exercise their basic human rights. A dhimmi may not testify against a Moslem in a Moslem court. A dhimmi can be lynched or killed by a Moslem and in most cases the Moslem will not be prosecuted, because abusing a dhimmi is not considered a crime. Dhimmis pay extra usury taxes, including blood taxes (their first born). They can be, and often are ripped off and cannot defend themselves. Their daughters are often raped and left in their shame, and their fathers, brothers, uncles, or husbands are unable to take action against the Moslem rapists.

After a thousand years of struggling to survive in Moslem dominated cultures, those Christians have evolved a survivalist culture (Stockholm syndrome) that is difficult for free, civilized westerners to understand or comprehend.   Here, in the United States, Copts, Chaldeans, Armenians, Assyrians (even second or third generation), etc. are frightfully cowed by the mere thought of confronting a Moslem. It seems that this is a part of their genetic make-up, this dhimmitude. They choose flight over fight, surrender over defending what's right. When speaking of their homelands or peoples, all they seem able to do consistently is to lament their collective miserable fate. They need to get away from this.

Divide and Conquer

Islam has taken advantage of this non-Moslem divisiveness as Islam has grown. Islam has encouraged self-destructive rivalries as they have incrementally advanced again and again. For fourteen hundred years, Moslems have been able to advance and grow as a basically unified force as they have incrementally taken over and brought Islam and all of its accompanying totalitarianism, uniform ignorance, poverty, and suffering onto the heads and shoulders of 1.5 billion souls. Islam's borders remain bloody on all fronts as loathsome Islam seems inexorable in its spread.

To welcome Islam is to welcome Satan!

Writing on the Wall

Students of anthropology have learned and continue to teach the fundamental fact and truth about the strong and the weak.

Ever since God created man, we have formed ourselves into tribes and social groups for the purpose of providing mutual benefit and support. Throughout history we have seen groups come into being. Grow, become soft or lazy, and vanish, often under the treats of those who were stronger and tougher.

The writing is on the wall. We of the modern civilized world have the technology, sophistication, competence, and capability to prevail against Islam. Do we have the will?

In Europe (including Russia), China, and the Americas there are growing numbers of people who are rising out of their stupor and beginning to awaken neighbors to the dangerous fascist (Islamic) totalitarian threat thundering down the road at us. This is wonderful, and needs to move forward as a gathering swell.

We need to promptly establish cooperative interfaith dialogues that exclude those who wish us ill, the Moslems, all Moslems. In these dialogues, we need to come to terms with our differences which pale in comparison to the mortal Islamist threat, and know we must unite to become strong in the face of this assault on everything that we hold precious.   We must know that being atheists, agnostics, Jews, Catholics, Shintos, Buddhists, Confucians, or Protestants is very secondary to the coming train wreck named Islam.   There is one alternative to joining together against Islam: Perish!

In this conflict, pacifism is cowardice!

Courageous Minority

There are some Christians who hail from Islamic countries who are not cowed, and they do indeed speak out.   They can do this because they have no known family members left "back there" who the Moslems can round up and make to suffer terribly for the offenses of their family members.

One such hero is an Egyptian Coptic Priest, Father Zakaria Butros who has a TV program that is circulated in Egypt and other places. The program's focus is on Mohammed, and Fr. Zakaria really upsets a lot of Moslems with his candid discussions of Mohammed. He uses the Koran and established Islamic literature and dissects all of it to ridicule Mohammed. He has also caused a great number of Moslems to question their beliefs, and in the process hundreds of them have converted to Christianity.

Fr Zakaria lives in hiding. There is a sixty million dollar price for his head.

To be anti-Islam is to be anti-Satan
To resist Islam is to resist Satan
To fight Islam it to fight Islam
Defeating Islam is defeating Satan

Chapter 23

COMMISSIONS, STUDIES, HEARINGS, AND REPORTS

Since the 9/11/2001 attacks, there have been hearings, studies, commissions, and studies of commissions, and so forth to the point that it was nearly impossible to keep track of all of them. Have they been effective in getting at the real root of the problem, and putting forth viable, honest solutions?

Almost three years after the 9/11 attacks, the CIA was shown to have no, none, zero agents in Iraq prior to the 2003 invasion of Iraq. The CIA was just plain derelict.

Saddam's "bunkers" were bombed based on CIA information. After the bombs dropped, neither Saddam nor even the "bunker" was found. The CIA's information was often bogus, based on a bunch of often dysfunctional analysts trying to cover their useless backsides and hoping for the best. The CIA again played America for suckers.

The best that the CIA has been able to come up with based on their multi-billion dollar feed trough has been stuff like: "we believe", or "we think", or "there is no conclusive evidence...." and they were still able to sell folks, including the Bushies, me, and even the liberals on viable Weapons of Mass Destruction (WMD) in Iraq.

Mindless legislators from both parties focused on rearranging chairs and calling it reform.

9/11 Commission

The 9/11 Commission was a failure at the outset. Its investigations, hearings, findings, and determinations were almost meaningless.

Prior to the 9/11 Commission, a Joint Congressional Intelligence Committee released a report on its findings about intelligence lapses prior to 9/11. It was helpful in that it was more focused and concise, and accurately depicted some issues not in the 9/11 Commission report.

To start with, the 9/11 Commission was 'bi-partisan' with equal numbers of Republican and Democratic members and co-chaired by a Republican and a Democrat. In this context, bi-partisanship meant that neither Democrats or Republicans would be faulted, that both sides assured that the guilty were protected.

The commission's recommendations were based on an assemblage of hold-harmless, no fault findings. Useless! That's about what one could expect.

Further, the commission members were obviously bewildered and befuddled by the baloney generated, much of it their own.

Because they couldn't honestly make heads nor tails out of all of the various intelligence agencies and their functions, the commission decided that the next time around, they'd like to look at just one agency. So, they recommended establishment of a Director who would coordinate all activities, so as to have blanket coverage of everything in the world. That would hold one entity culpable. They wanted one entity that would direct information collection in prescribed ways, and offered a prescription for analysis. This is all like the one-engined, 650 passenger super jumbo jet with no backup systems: A disaster waiting to happen.

The new 2009, version of Director, an ex-Admiral (Dennis Blair) has promised to do his job well, and to respect and welcome independent monitoring. Can a citizens group with appropriate security clearances be allowed to independently monitor intelligence gathering activities? What is the criteria for doing well?

The 9/11 Commission failed to provide a real hard nosed report with genuinely critical analyses capable of leading to generating real meaningful recommendations to address the very real threats we must deal with. In short, it was a failure.

The intelligence services that failed us so terribly got a wash. If the Commission had the real interests of the United States (as opposed to covering their respective partisan political parties' backsides) at heart, they would have recommended wholesale firings of those many who failed, and prosecution of the dozens if not hundreds of criminally negligent senior officials.

Over three thousand people were murdered, and nobody was found culpable besides the Islamists? Every bureaucrat in every agency involved performed flawlessly, eh? None were found to be negligent? Who in the CIA decided to not inform the FBI or State Department about two of the hijackers (Khalid Almihdar and Nawaf Alhazmi), known by the CIA to be al Qaeda operatives who attended an al Qaeda meeting in Malaysia. Those failed individuals and their treasonous supervisors all of the way up to George Tenet need to be hauled before a judge and jury of well informed citizens.

The 9/11 Commission itself (every member, whether a sitting elected official or lesser member) should be ashamed of themselves for neglecting to do comprehensively and honestly all that they were commissioned to do. That was to not just wave a finger around, but specifically to name the guilty. Every last one of them failed.

The 9/11 Commission report is valuable for what it represents and some of what it points out in general, but is also a failure to comprehensively, honestly, and forthrightly serve the American public. The fortune in taxpayer money spent on that report is a waste. The report itself gathers dust in the National Archives.

Competition is Good

My recommendation is to establish actual competing

intelligence services, not one huge failure prone organization prepared to reward risk-averse employees for not doing good jobs, for not doing the right thing. Let the policy and decision makers such as the Cabinet and the President define and decide which or what serves America's interests best. Don't worry about overlapping efforts and redundancy. Worry about one service finding and filling gaps that another invariably misses. That's how to get comprehensive and useful intelligence as opposed to continuing useless balderdash generated by risk-averse nerds. Reward successes and risk taking when justified, and don't condemn those who try and do their genuine best. At the same time, when people fail to serve U.S. interests in a professional manner, fire them at the minimum, and prosecute them if such is justified.

HUMINT is the most volatile and complex part of gathering intelligence. The traditional CIA manner of hoping for walk-in defectors, or relying on other governments is clearly a high risk, low yield venture. Nevertheless, we need to continue obtaining this intelligence whenever we can.

Using competing intelligence agencies and being more resourceful using 'spooks'   [[xxxxx this portion has been censored by the Department of State and/or the CIA xxxxx xxxxx this portion has been censored by the Department of State and/or the CIA xxxxx]] who are genuinely under deep cover, we need to go out, work, and recruit (including blackmail) a variety of sources as well as simply purchase clandestine information. Then, when this more useful information is shared with other intelligence agencies (yes the competitors), those other intelligence agencies can set out to independently verify the viability of that information.

Inevitably, by taking on risky operations, we will assuredly get good, useful, valuable information. At the same time, there will be inevitable situations where our deep cover 'spooks' operating without diplomatic immunity may get caught. When this happens, we will need to be prepared to get heavy handed in protecting or getting those 'spooks' home. This would include black operations using third country (including mercenary) forces in what may even be embarrassing situations.

If we want to succeed we need to take risks. Winning does not come without taking risks. If we don't take risks, we'd better get our little prayer carpets out, learn the direction of Mecca and how to stick our asses up into the air five times a day.

The Joint Congressional Intelligence Committee had in its report some interesting information:

There was a very large section in their draft that was taken out because it would have been too damaging to Saudi Arabia. It would seem that the Saudis were standing by if not actually present, and had their checkbooks out and readily stepped in to help the commissioners and their staffs along with their retirement nest eggs. However, some of the   [[xxxxxthis portion has been censored by the Department of State and/or the CIA xxxxx xxxxx this portion has been censored by the Department of State and/or the CIA xxxxx xxxxx this portion has been censored by the Department of State and/or the CIA xxxxx xxxxx this portion has been censored by the Department of State and/or the CIA xxxxx xxxxx this portion has been censored by the Department of State and/or the CIA xxxxx xxxxx this portion has been censored by the Department of State and/or the CIA xxxxx xxxxx this portion has been censored by the Department of State and/or the CIA xxxxx xxxxx this portion has been censored by the Department of State and/or the CIA xxxxx xxxxx this portion has been censored by the Department of State and/or the CIA xxxxx xxxxx this portion has been censored by the Department of State and/or the CIA xxxxx xxxxx this portion has been censored by the Department of State and/or the CIA xxxxx xxxxx this portion has been censored by the Department of State and/or the CIA xxxxx xxxxx this portion has been censored by the Department of State and/or the CIA xxxxx xxxxx this portion has been censored by the Department of State and/or the CIA xxxxx]]

There are indications that the White House, the Bushies, were not very cooperative with the committee, but still got a wash from the committee. The White House should have been blasted for their unwillingness to cooperate fully and completely. But then, Porter Goss was one of these committee members and he later got the White House nod (payoff) for CIA Director.

The report mentions FBI management failures to follow through on such as recommendations of a skilled, professional investigator's suspicions about Islamic flight school attendees in San Diego. Those failed, risk-averse managers who shut that portion of investigative expertise down should be in jail. They aren't. In fact, their careers have moved forward, while the diligent, patriotic agent who brought this up has been shafted.

Republican Senator Richard Shelby opined or asked if the recommendations (of this committee) should be followed through? He hoped so, but commented that if it's like things in the past, not much will happen. A year later, the report was mostly gathering dust. Senator Shelby was correct.

Then Democratic Congresswoman Nancy Pelosi indicated that this committee's inquiry was not about assigning blame for 9/11 (a deficiency as far as I am concerned), but about better protecting the American people in the future. Well, if you're not going to blame a failure, I guess you want to repeat history by protecting or rewarding the guilty, so they can continue, eh? That ain't protecting the American people, Tootsie, it's your stupid protecting those who failed to protect the American people before 9/11.

The Commission reportedly discussed classified materials that they weren't able to provide in their report. Some of the classification and withholding of certain information was sensitive in that it would have compromised names, methods, and ongoing investigations. Fine! What ever became of those investigations?

Other holding back of so called classified information was not for anything more than to protect certain bureaucratic and politicians' reputations, derrieres, and useless careers.

Chapter 24

CONCLUSIONS and RECOMMENDATIONS

We are at war and our sworn enemy is Islam in all of its forms, and all of the dark, regressive evil that it stands for!

The sooner we recognize and accept this simple, well established historical fact, the sooner we can move to protect and preserve our civilization of pursuits of happiness, of freedom and choices, of independence, political freedom.

The fascist political system that is Islam is on the march! It is powerful, much better organized than many understand or can comprehend, and it is without conscience or pity. The tens of millions of deaths of the great wars of the 20th century will (not might -- will) pale by comparison if the evils of Islamist expansion are not halted or turned back.

American authorities have been long ignorant of true Islam. An example was when American Moslems, the most famous, Black Moslem and great boxer Mohammed Ali shirked induction into the armed forces claiming that his new religion forbade the killing of other people (?????). That was one of Ali's phony claims, and if he was being honest in his claim -- he had never in fact even read the Koran, but just listened to lies of his Moslem handlers. Worse, the entire Justice department, Army Department, and others with their vast resources were also ignorant of the Koran and Islam which indeed instructs Moslems to kill, to slaughter others, especially non-believers, which in this case (the Vietnam war) were the Buddhist or Christian Vietnamese. Mohammed Ali shirked his duty both as a citizen and as a Moslem.

Osama's Biggest Win

Osama bin Laden, with Saudi money, Saudi moral support, and generous Saudi backing started killing Americans the day that the Soviets left Afghanistan. He has been successful in some of the most significant terror acts or acts of violence against the United States that have ever occurred, including the 9/11 Twin Towers incident.

Years after 9/11/2001, and with a multi million dollar bounty on his head, bin Laden continued to tweak the United States with near impunity. Nobody has taken the $25 million offer to turn bin Laden in. When questioned, President Bush and others in the Bush cabinet have downplayed their failures to capture bin Laden claiming that his capture while important was not a major priority. Duuuhhh!!!!

While the 9/11 attack was incredibly successful, bin Laden's continuing encouragement of terrorist acts against the United States in particular and Western Civilization in general continue. More importantly to the Islamic world, bin Laden's status as a free man able to thumb his nose with impunity at the United Sates is the mightiest recruiting tool the terrorists and extremist militants have ever been handed. This has meant that every day bin Laden went without being killed or apprehended, he was thus an inspiration to millions of Islamists. Our ineptitude has encouraged and enabled hundreds if not thousands of Moslems to become jihadists in the cause against the United States and Western Civilization. Every day, thousands of Moslems make that commitment based in bin Laden's inspiration to them that the United States is indeed a paper tiger.

Islamophobe

There will certainly be some who will condemn me as an Islamophobe. Phobias are irrational fears. I am not irrational. I do not have a phobia regarding Islam. I do not fear Islam.

I am Islam-aware! I know and understand Islam's frightfully evil goals and objectives.

I am rationally Islam-averse.

I find Islam in all of its forms to be repugnant and uncivilized.

Some Islamists, Moslems, Mohammedans may want me dead, and some may even try to impose a fatwa against me with a price for my death. They surely want me to be quiet. It ain't going to happen! I am a civilizationophile. I'll say that again: CIVILIZATIONOPHILE.

Most certainly, the Islamist Mohammedans would prefer that the many and growing numbers of people like I who are aware of and discuss the true goals of expansionist Mohammedism's oppressive fascism would prefer that we tell people to be kind to Moslems while they prepare to cut our throats, and in turn that the Moslems will be kind to us. This is pure nonsense. I am prepared to be kind to individual Moslems on a reciprocal basis. I will reciprocate to their genuine kindness, but phony, false gestures won't sway me.

Mohammedans declare anyone who raises issues or serious questions about the spread of Mohammedism and its bigotry to be a bigot, a racist, etc. That's all that they can do, because Islam is indefensible. When Moslems strive to emulate Mohammed in every way, they are as racist as he was when he called black Africans "raisin heads" and other derogatory names.

I support the survival and even peaceful expansion of nonsectarian governed civilization as it is practiced in the western Judaeo-Christian societies, where people are free to worship (or not) as it suits them.

Freedom as we know and understand it to be is not a part of Mohammedan vocabularies or understanding. Secularism is anathema to Islamists.

Since the murders of 9/11/2001, there is a rightfully increased awareness in the United States (and around the civilized world) of the vile depredations of Islam. One item arising from this are 'interfaith groups' which so many ignorant Christians are getting involved with. In most cases those 'interfaith meeting groups' are tools of slick Mohammedans engaged in dawa, using them (the ignorant, foolish Christians and Jews) to successfully pull the wool over Infidel eyes. Any interfaith group that would be worth its name must include Coptic Christians, Maronites, Jews, other Orthodox Christians, and then some Moslems. Many infidels are in too many cases allowing themselves to be played off as fools, or worse.

Increasing numbers of us – civilized people - are educating ourselves because all too many of our political, and especially our willfully ignorant educational and religious leaders don't have the courage to speak out or do what is right. In so doing, we in the mainstream are in fact becoming wiser and rightfully aroused and are moving forward to confront Islam --Mohammedism. We are not initiating a war on Islam. We are just responding Islam's war on us countering Islam's sinister and never ending war on decency and civilization.

A Forecast

The real battles are yet to come. They are not the present "war on terrorism", nor the earlier scuffles with Mohammedists that date back to the times of Presidents Jefferson and Adams, of the Barbary pirates who demanded jizya taxes from us, etc.. They will be the wars of conquest focused Islam versus non Moslems defending the civilized world, a clash, a monumental clash of civilizations that began fourteen hundred years ago.

The present skirmishes have already started, and do not consist of great armies clashing in remote fields of battle. Yes, armies will be involved, but the wars are also stealthy cultural conflicts involving a civilized society that cherishes liberty, freedom, creativity, challenge, progress; and an Orwellian totalitarian cult that hates, that despises and wishes to destroy all that they cannot subjugate and control. The Mohammedans want to do to Europe and the United States what they wrot in the Middle East, parts of Asia, and in North Africa. They want to create ever more loathsome poverty, slavery, disease, and subjugation, and a wasteland of fear and ignorance. That is what Islam is all about!

In this, the United States will have natural allies, if we survive the initial Mohammedist invasions. I suspect that Europe, at least parts of Western Europe may already be lost.

Turpentine Shoes

God hates sin.
Cowardice is a sin.

Far too many American Christians are unwilling to confront Satan.

Satan is operating under the guise of Islam. Islam is Satan's masterpiece. Even when Christians know and understand that Islam is the embodiment of evil they are totally derelict in confronting this embodiment of evil. These Christians in denial are cowards hiding behind the biblical proclamation that 'the meek shall inherit the earth'. They misunderstand that those who shall inherit the earth are those who are meek before God, not cowards in the face of Satan's tool, Islam.

I have talked to "Christians" about the onslaught of Islam, and their atypical response is: "God is in control." Then, they blithely wander off happy in their own fog of self-righteous denial. They flat refuse to consider confronting evil.

I receive lots of mailings asking for everyone to pray for our national leadership, but neither offer nor ask that anyone become active in confronting evil, Islam.

I refer to these cowardly Christians as *turpentine shoe Christians*. They need to pour turpentine on their shoes to keep the ants away from their cowardly candy asses.

People of all philosophies and faiths need to understand and to come to grips with the fundamental truth that any accommodation to or with any form of Islam is an agreement, a submission in support of evil.

Russia and the USA

The world has three super powers. The USA is no longer the gorilla in the room. It's just another monkey.

China and Russia are still fearful of the United States, but not for the same reasons that existed during the cold war era.

Through squandering our wealth and goodwill in Iraq and Afghanistan, we have lost the respect and trust of many, and our prestige as a responsible government is gone.

President Jimmy (Pea brain) Carter stabbed Iran in the back and allowed the prince of evil and hatred, Khomeini, to take Iran out of the realm of nearly civilized and drag it back to medieval times.

How do Russia and China see this? They see that the USA favored primitive, barbaric Islam over a leadership that was determined to bring civilization to a nation.

Later, President Reagan tucked his tail between his legs after he permitted Islamists to murder 241 Marines in Lebanon without retribution. The Mohammedans went off on a field day with more atrocities – murdering Americans and bombing Embassies with impunity. Reagan and later, Bush (41) failed to respond.

How did Russia and China view this? They saw the USA as being unable to deal with a dedicated pack of Mohammedan rabble who have a focused goal based on hate.

What did we do when the USSR invaded a primitive, hostile

Afghanistan where for decades Moslem terrorists had been taking refuge, and a country that refused to try to stem the obscene levels of illicit drugs and other contraband being smuggled into the USSR?

First, Carter tried to embarrass the USSR by screwing their Olympics up. U.S. olympians denied the opportunity to compete were hurt, not the USSR. Then Reagan threw in with the Mohammedan Taliban and al Qaeda to defeat and humble the USSR in Afghanistan.

How do Russia and China view these actions? They see the USA as taking advantage of a weakened USSR, and as providing large scale support of savage, barbaric Mohammedans against an ideologically opposing but otherwise culturally civilized nation.

President Clinton did a tail tuck in Somalia to again show that the USA couldn't deal with a rabble. What Russia and China thought of this is too obvious to explain.

Serbians got fed up and responded after a decade of Mohammedan ethnic cleansing with thousands of attacks and repeated outrageous atrocities directed against Christians. When the Serbians responded with a justified large scale push back, Clinton attacked and killed thousands of Serbians. Clinton clearly supported the Mohammedan instigators of this Balkan conflict.

How did the Russians and Chinese see this? They clearly saw the USA siding with a barbaric, hostile Mohammedan culture and working against a society based on civilized values and morals.

Our elected American leaders are themselves a rabble of ignorant pinheads who fail to see that the Russians are in fact a natural ally in this civilizational conflict. The Russians have Mohammedan states at their doorstep and know it, and they, better than us understand that threat all too well. The Russians have a headache today with the Moslem Chechnyans who are waging a continuing brutal war against the Russians. We Americans have stupidly tried to intervene to protect the Chechnyan animals who have murdered thousands of innocents with really brutal, savage acts of barbarism, Such includes the violent raping, torturing, and then murdering hundreds of innocent children at a school in Beslan. Why protect such barbarians? Yet, we stand mute, wringing our hands about Putin creating a more stable Russia better able to protect its citizens while we foolishly whine about effective Russian actions regarding Chechnya.

The Russians are waiting hopefully for the United States to come to grips with this fundamental truth about Islam being our greatest mutual foe, and then we can join together. We share more than our witless leaders understand or will admit.

The Russians are aggressively re-establishing themselves as a nation to be reckoned with. They have rekindled their nuclear weapons program in a big way. What reasons do we give them to not follow this track?

Nuclear Options

I opine that one of the reasons the Russians are doing this is out of fear, fear that the inept, stupid American leadership will allow Islam to take over America within the next 20-40 years. At that time the Russians (and the Chinese) will find themselves confronted with a nuclear USA under fundamentalist Mohammedan domination. When that occurs, neither the Russians nor the Chinese plan to lose.

Another natural American ally is India, which has been in perpetual conflict with feral Moslems ever since the Moghuls invaded and destroyed the great culture and civilization that was Hindustan India and began forceful conversions, conversions which created Pakistan, Afghanistan, and Bangladesh. In that Islamization process, an estimated 50,000,000+ (fifty million or more) Hindus and Buddhists were slaughtered during decades of savage, brutal conquest, a holocaust dwarfing what the Nazis did to the Jews.

Another natural ally of America is China, but this alliance may never materialize if the United States becomes too closely allied with China's arch foe, India. An ancient culture, China has long been an inward focused nation, it almost always has been so, working to repel outsiders and to go their own way. True, they have absorbed some of their attackers, such as the Manchurians.

With the rise of the USSR and America as superpowers (the USSR, allied with India nearly had China surrounded), China felt compelled to move to establish defendable frontiers, and establish a regional hegemony of their own. This move took in the ethnic (Uighur) Chinese of Xinjiang, China's western frontier, and on her southern flank, Tibet. The Uighurs could never have defended themselves from a Russian takeover, and China prevented that. Similarly, the Tibetans could not defend themselves from a hostile, expansionist Indian takeover, and China has prevented that.

In recent years, the USA has involved itself in China's internal affairs in two ways:

1) The Mohammedan Uighurs want to assert – to impose, to force themselves on the Chinese, or to assert their separatism, a first step towards declaring another independent fascist Islamic nation. The Chinese aren't about to let this happen, and when Moslem Uighurs act out (with Saudi funding, and support from many Islamic countries), the Chinese rightfully and promptly respond in an appropriate manner. Good for China!

China and Pakistan have been strangely allied for decades against their mutual foe, India, a cultural and religious foe of Pakistan, and a political/religious foe of China. These two are strange bedfellows. Many of the Uighur Islamists in China have received their terrorist training in Pakistan, and also received earlier training in Pakistan supported Taliban camps in Afghanistan. This anti-Chinese support is continuing, even growing. The Chinese tolerate this Pakistani interference because they can use the Pakistanis against the Indians.

2) Tibet is predominantly Buddhist and its people are by their very nature and culture non-militant. China cannot spin Tibet off as an independent nation. China has worked hard to provide as much autonomy to Tibet as they reasonably can, but not total independence. An independent Tibetan nation would fall quickly to Islamist invaders from neighboring Pakistan, Afghanistan, Tajikistan, Kyrgyzstan, and Kazakhstan. The good but vulnerable, Buddhist Tibetans would be slaughtered within a decade or two and their culture destroyed; and they would simply cease to exist. The Dali Lama understands this fundamental reality. The so-called Free Tibet movement receives substantial support and funding from Islamists, most of it secret for obvious reasons. China does not want or need a huge, aggressive, violent nutcase "Tibetistan" on her southern flank, and we need to wake up and side with and support China in both of these issues. Under Chinese governance, the people of Tibet enjoy far, far more personal and religious freedom and regional autonomy than they would ever have under any form of Islamist rule. This is a fundamental truth.

Newly affluent China has launched a major campaign to upgrade their military to super-power status quickly. Like the Russians, they fear the silly ignorance of American leaders, and that the Americans may allow Islam to soon govern America, and the world altering consequences which would result. Like the Russians, the Chinese do not aim to lose.

We Americans need to work with the Indians and the Chinese to encourage that they bury their differences. India needs to accept that Tibet is racially and culturally a Chinese Province. China needs to support India in securing India's northwest frontier and Kashmir. Once done, China and India can focus their energies and resources on their real enemy, Islam.

We nevertheless must try to remember that all Moslems are not bad, just the very many who are sly Islamist Mohammedans, who absolutely support the Islamic goal of worldwide domination. Faux moderate Moslems who remain passive are de facto supporters of Islamic fascism.

Recommendations

We must demand all manner of political, economic, legal, cultural, and religious parity with every Islamist nation or entity. We must halt the establishment or construction of any more mosques, Moslem or Islamic centers or schools, or whatever facility or organization of any kind in any civilized nation, especially in America. This should remain so until Christian and all other religions are permitted to establish schools, churches, centers, libraries, and organizations open and available to the public in every Moslem majority country on earth without any form of dhimmi status, and that the Moslems fully guarantee their freedoms to live and operate, and that they are protected by those countries' laws and police, etc.

Until the Moslems reciprocate fully and completely, and until parity is reached in every way, they should be forbidden to expand in our countries. This must include ceasing any further immigration until they permit non-Moslems to emigrate and to thrive in their countries.

Islam – The Consummate Enemy

Why do the countries comprising Western Civilization not understand or comprehend the true threat, the true enemy confronting us? I repeat, the enemy is not terrorism, the enemy (Islam) uses terrorism as a tool, a weapon, a threat to kill, to intimidate, to dominate, and to rule.

Western political, academic, religious, and business leaders seem to be unable to grasp the breadth and depth of the enemy that is coming after us, stalking us, who hates us, and has as its overarching sole objective the end of our very existence. Those leaders are at the top of the Islamists lists to perform the Daniel Pearl gurgle when Islam takes control.

These same pathetically ignorant political, academic, and religious Benedict Arnold/Lord chamberlain styled leaders act as apologists, even as defenders of the vile Mohammedan enemy. This is just plain insanity! They are one and all suffering from various levels of the Stockholm syndrome. In their total, blundering ignorance and Chamberlainesque desire to please or to appease, these leaders parrot the politically correct, risk-averse and incredibly stupid and naïve phrase: "Islam has been hijacked by extremists." These nitwits need to spend some time bringing themselves up to speed on the true facts about Islam. Islam is extremist! Mohammed was an over-the-top extremist lunatic, and his followers are working hard to emulate him in every way possible. Emulating Mohammed is their fundamental duty, their destiny. Mohammed was a pedophile and rapist, a greedy, vengeful, bloodthirsty and consummately insane beast. Mohammed's hundreds of millions of devoted followers all work hard to emulate his absolute sociopathic attitudes and behavior.

These western apologist leaders are focused on their personal egotistical goals of getting re-elected, promoted, tenured, or other self-agrandizing actions. Few seem to really care about identifying (other than superficial pronouncements about a hijacked Islam) or speaking out about this terrible, frightful, hate consumed and utterly determined enemy. Many of these leaders by virtue of their narrow focus lack the attention span, intellectual or cognitive abilities needed for their roles. In terms of experience, most have little more than a few minutes per day to observe and to learn, and that is just a little more since 9/11/2001. In terms of knowledge, few show any real understanding at all of the Koran, the Hadiths, the Sira, or Shari 'a law. Few seem to even care. In terms of motivation, their motivation is limited to themselves, but not to the preservation or continuation of civilization.

And, those leaders are at the top of lists being prepared today for their capture, humiliation, public torture and brutal prolonged deaths which will be recorded and used to intimidate others into submitting to Islamic supremacy. This is a fundamental truth.

Traditionally, when confronting an enemy, a traditional style enemy, western civilization has faced and dealt with a hierarchical structure usually with a singular leader, and his team of followers or henchmen such as Saddam Hussein, Pol Pot, Tojo, Hitler, Stalin, the King of England, etc. We understood and therefore could deal with that. Those foes have been relatively short-term as in a war of a couple of years, or a structured organization such as Nazism or Communism whom we could compete with over a couple of years or decades and ultimately eradicate.

This enemy, this foe, Islam, does not have such an easily identified structure with a titular head, one whom we can easily identify and target, to kill or subdue, and then move on as we have over our short history. The consummately singularly focused and totally determined enemy facing us, Islam, is miles ahead of their weak, confused, ignorant prey, the civilized west and the country at the top of that list is the USA. We need to get going. NOW!!!!

Islam's sole political, economic, and social agenda is world domination and control to be achieved by any and all means. Their deception is working well right here.

While we in the west have had conflicts from time to time and gotten over those spats, Islam has steadily been going at the business of conquest and domination for fourteen hundred years. While they have been dealt setbacks, they have never, ever sued for peace and given up. A treaty according to Mohammed is just a tool to be used until they, the Islamists have the upper hand and can renew their attack. Treaties to Moslems are absolutely meaningless. They only back off, regroup, develop new strategies and tactics based on a new and evolving consensus, and then move forward. Mohammed set the tone and the objective, and his followers, like mindless ants, follow on his path, striving to fulfill his mission.

Having never, ever dealt with such a determined, long-lived foe, our collective leadership are unwilling to admit or are incapable of admitting that this is a new challenge and that they are not (yet) really up to meeting this challenge. This must change! This is a new and harsh reality, and if the western civilization's collective leadership pursue neglecting their duties and obligations to civilization, our world, the civilized world will come to a grinding halt within this century. THIS IS A FUNDAMENTAL TRUTH!

We need honest, hard headed and clear thinking people to step forward and deal aggressively with silly risk-averse political correctness, which all too often comes at the expense of reality. We cannot survive doing anything less than facing the truth and dealing with it.

Deal with it: Islam is NOT a religion of peace. THIS IS A FUNDAMENTAL TRUTH!

Islam is not even a religion. It is a dark primeval cult, a political and social system more evil than were Hitler's Nazi cult or Communism.

Jihad is the Mohammedan doctrine of conquest, killing, and warfare against all that is not Islam. Jihad has no other real meaning. All other claims regarding jihad are simply bogus and are intended to dupe those who are stupid.

There is no kinder, gentler version of jihad except in the pitiful, weak minds of submissive apologists and fools.

Jihad is correctly defined as a duty involving unrelenting hostility towards, and violent conflict against those who do not submit to the vision of Mohammed.

FUNDAMENTAL TRUTHS: Islam is anti-civilization. Islam is evil.

Reality: Many in the civilized world cannot truly fathom the depth of the real Mohammedan hatred for all that we are. Fact: The Koran calls for the death and destruction of all 'non-believers' -- a non-believer is not a Moslem.... The Koran will not change, ever. The Koran IS cast in stone. The Koran is not a living, evolving document.

Once our leaders do accept these fundamental truths and facts, they and we can deal with the fundamentalist evil that is Islam. Striving to be politically correct as well as maintaining their risk-averse postures, our diplomatic and intelligence community hasn't a clue about what is needed. Some in our military are more open minded and receptive to the fact that we must face this enemy, but the military is not sure how to deal with the Mohammedans.

The Mohammedans, Islamists, Moslems, or whatever they want to be called, or anyone wants to call them, will never, ever engage in this conflict following our rules or any civilized rules (except when they can take advantage of them). They will make up their own rules as they go. We must learn and to understand their rules and even follow and use them when it is appropriate to do so.

Terrorism in every form is an instrument of Mohammedan policy. Terrorism has been a part of Islam since the day that Mohammed conceived it. They use it at every level they can to intimidate, to rule, and to take control.

Terrorism must become an instrument of American policy. We must use it against Mohammedans/Islamists/ jihadists wherever and whenever we can do so effectively. We are technologically superior to the Mohammedans in every way and we need to apply this tool successfully, effectively, wherever and whenever we can to instill such respect for us amongst this real enemy so that they do not dare to come after us, our women, and our children. We must compel them to back off, relinquish their false claims, and to beg for peace -- on our terms, again and again, every time they renew their attacks on us.

It must become American public policy and doctrine that the

very hour that the Iranians (or the Saudis, or any other Islamic government) are known to have a nuclear weapon, we must use nuclear weapons of our own against every one of their facilities involved in creating their nuclear weapons. Turn those facilities into uninhabitable wastes. We can of course let one of our allies do the deeds, but doing this ourselves will re-establish America's reputation as a nation that means business.

We should do this to North Korea the minute that the North Koreans export a weapon, or sell the technology to do so. We can send an armada of low yield nuclear tipped bunker buster cruise missiles into North Korean tunnels and caves, and eliminate that despicable monstrosity of a so-called government as soon as possible. Yeah, sure, we will have to help South Korea and China to "deprogram" and educate thirty million tragic North Koreans who have been brainwashed from they day of their birth.

We need to work with the civilized world to limit their ability to acquire weapons of any sort.

Information war

We engaged in a very effective if sometimes bewildering propaganda war that worked to defeat Communism. This worked because by getting the truth out there and countering communism's deceit and lies, people realized that communism was a farce and a failure.

We must counter Islamist propaganda with the truth, the real truth, the simple truth, all of the truth. Each and every time an Islamist speaks out or publishes something in this country, we need to respond, to rebut with the truth, with simple facts. These truths and facts are quotes from Islam's own Koran, from the Hadiths, and from Sharia texts; historical facts need to be brought out and disseminated showing how evil Islam really is.

For example, when Moslems falsely claim that Islam is merely a religion of peace, we need to reply with the clarification that their sentence is incomplete. Islam believes only in peace under the domination and control of Islam.

Objective (honest and based on fact) studies of Islam and Mohammed need to be conducted and promulgated to Moslems.

We must remove and eliminate the Islamist missionaries in our military who only work to subvert our civilization with their deceitful false truths, lies, taqiyyah, and acts of treason and murder. Member of the Obama presidential transition team and Fort Hood shooter, Nidal Malik Hasan was just one of those monsters, and there are more of them in the military, and they need to be found out, isolated, and removed, each and every one of them. We must do the same in our prison programs. We need to educate members of the armed forces about the truths of Islam, especially officers and other leaders who have been brainwashed into believing that Islam is somehow something other than consummate evil.

Before the gun smoke cleared at Ft. Hood, droves of befuddled pinheads started with the mantra that Nidal Hasan's attack was not an act of Islam inspired terror. Chief among them was a morally cowardly but politically correct 3-star general named Casey who tripped all over himself trying to deflect that he was the culpable overseer of a facility where he and his staff allowed a Mohammedan terrorist to plan and execute an attack.. DHS Secretary Napolitano took immediate steps protect Moslems from what is in fact justified patriotic American outrage about an act of hatred that had been committed by a devout Moslem. This monster was alive and well and acting out all over the place. His Islamist insanity was reported again and again to superiors who, one and all shirked their duty to take action. Their cowardly inaction has resulted in thirteen dead and dozens wounded in a horrific act of terrorism. And what about the hundreds who were 'counseled' by this evil Moslem terrorist? As with the misbehavior at Abu Ghraib, each and every superior of Hasan, up to three grades above needs to be hauled in and cashiered for dereliction of duty. They were, one and all inept officers, deserving of being cashiered and nothing more for allowing this terrorist to fulfill his self imposed mission. Naturally, his defense attorneys indicated that they would claim insanity in his defense. Hey, he's a Moslem, and insane and Moslem are synonomous. [If he is allowed to claim any form of temporary or permanent insanity, every other Moslem terrorist can cop the same plea and then claim exoneration from their crimes.]

What was Obama's response to this terrorist act? He took a pleasure weekend at Camp David, and only agreed to lower American flags to half staff after patriots raised a ruckus. Obama is a major pinhead and twit. But then, his crotch groping during November, 2009, ceremonies at the tomb of the Unknown Soldier further indicated his unpatriotic disdain and lack of respect for things important to Americans.

In our prisons we must disallow books and literature that espouse violence. That must include the Koran, which should be taken out of prisons, because it preaches violence, encourages killing, rape, and murder again and again. If the Koran is not taken out, then there need to be classes (mandatory attendance) conducted along with Islamic teachings that teach the truths about Islam.

We need to teach one and all about the true evil that is Islam, corrupt, with no civilized values, morality, or decency. Islam is a sick, twisted social, political, economic, or belief system. We can cite Islamic controlled countries themselves as representative examples that they are -- to show and demonstrate that Islam ultimately offers only darkness.

We must not permit Mohammedans to teach anything about their false propagandistic Mohammedist Islam in our schools or other institutions, ever. They are doing this now, in textbooks, to depict Islam as being other than what it really is. Neither should we permitquisling dhimmi apologists to work to indoctrinate our society into a defeatist attitude of submission to things Islamic.

We need to establish counters in our newspapers, television, radio, and all media to Islamic balderdash. We must at every opportunity teach one and all that Islam is morally corrupt. Wherever Islam prevails as a social or political system the economies crumble and poverty, suffering, sorrow, ignorance, and disease prevails. We must teach that Islam has nothing but avarice for others, and that Mohammedans are ugly, indecent parasites who live off of the wealth, talents, skills, abilities, and blood of others, offering only pain, humiliation, and suffering in return.

We need to acknowledge that any Moslem concentrations are a real security threat to western civilization. We need to halt immigration from Islamic countries, all of which should be considered threats to American national security. The same holds true for Europe, Australia, Asia, the Orient, and other civilized nations.

We in fact need to conside expulsions - repatriations of devout Mohammedans back to and into the self created cesspools they came from.

Cease now all so-called aid to Moslem countries, especially to the Egyptians, Palestinians, Indonesians, Somalis, Sudanese, Bangladeshis, and Pakistanis. There is absolutely no evidence that any of this wasteful dispensation of our treasure to them has ever been beneficial to the rest of humanity. Not one cent of taxpayer monies and wealth should be delivered to those whose aim it is to destroy and subjugate us. Poverty is not the problem. The ideology they follow is the problem. Islam will remain what it is until the Moslems themselves learn, and acknowledge that their political, social, intellectual, and economic failures are attributable only to themselves, not the infidel, and then take action to join the civilized world.

The next time a natural (or other) disaster occurs in one of those places, we should let the Saudis take care of the suffering people. If the Saudis ask us to do anything, we do so only by charging the oil Arabs $500+ per person per day, plus all expenses (thousands of dollars per hour for aircraft, ships, and helicopters, etc.), and for every nail, syringe, gallon of jet fuel, or whatever, we mark the item/s up about 500+% as they do for the oil they sell us @$50-$200+ per barrel while oil extraction costs are about five dollars per barrel.

Spotlight individual Arabs' wealth, especially to the poorer Moslem populations both within and outside of their countries. Class warfare will only benefit us.

When Arab/Mohammedan nations inevitably get hostile with one another, let them have at it.

Prior to the 2005 G8 meeting in Scotland, hundreds of entertainers staged a series of concerts aimed at spotlighting Africa's plight. This was an effort to pressure the wealthier nations to give yet more, to shovel yet more money into bottomless pits where it would be squandered yet again, and ripped off by so-called leaders yet again.

Oil rich Nigeria should receive not one cent. The money for the poor there ought to be drawn out of the Swiss or other banks where billions of graft and theft have been deposited.

If we provide yet more money to the impoverished of Africa, we need to change the way we do it and the terms. We send the money through American or European banks and control it closely, purchasing materials and supplies but not providing even one cent to the African nations' government leaders, or to so-called national banks. Then, the workers, including or even especially Christian missionaries doing the spending need to be vetted, and closely scrutinized at every step to make sure the money is getting to the needy. We should not send a cent to Islamic controlled nations, except to the non-Moslem victims of Mohammedism.   Let the oil-rich Arabs provide funding to their Mohammedan brethren.

The very moment one of those despots begins to wrangle for a cut of the money, the spigot ought to be turned off immediately, and the workers pulled out.

Letters to editors have been published urging people to kill Moslems in retaliation for the deaths of Americans.   The right of newspapers to publish such letters to editors has been upheld under freedom of speech laws even though such letters incite violence.

Markets and Economies

The oil-Arabs, mainly the Saudis have bought into nearly every corporation in America.   They have done so freely and without constraint.

They are imposing Islamic Shari'a banking rules on financial institutions and banks. Shari'a financing compels these institutions to make annual donations to so-called Islamic charities which are in fact organizations, including terrorist organizations working against us, killing us.

American companies and non-Moslem American citizens are not allowed to own companies or businesses in Arab nations, except only in (dhimmi) partnership with Arabs who earn plenty from all such enterprises, and who also can exert controls, but otherwise do little if anything at all in the line of real work.

We need to change our laws regarding Arabs' (or non-Americans for that matter – be more generalized) ownership in things American (the same can and should be applied in all civilized nations). We should demand reciprocity in Arab countries and compel them to take on non-Moslem American/Asian/European/Latin/African partners who will likewise earn 51% of all profits, and exert the same levels of controls over their businesses and enterprises in our countries.

Any Moslem who refuses to participate should be immediately

expelled and sent back to his origins, and the business enterprise and all of its assets expropriated and sold off at auction to non-Moslem buyers.

We need to outlaw any and all political lobbies at every level involving non-citizen entities or funding of any type, and establish strict and severe prison terms for violators, either those who shovel money and bribes to politicians (even foreign diplomats for this would be in violation of law, and therefore their diplomatic immunity would not apply), as well as politicians and their minions who accept or take possession in any way of such largesse. Jail the rich Arab bagmen, too.

Test the blood of every Moslem entering a civilized nation, and when HIV or other sexually transmitted diseases are found, refuse their entry, and publicize our findings, giving names and nationalities, etc.

Make it very expensive and difficult for Moslems to acquire western technology and educations, including medicines. Charge 500% more in university tuitions and use that money for non-Islamic apologist scholars to subsidize Islamic studies and research, and to publish their findings, including factual televised documentaries in 170 languages for worldwide dissemination. These studies would be about terrorism, the mistreatment and subjugation of women and religious minorities, the Arabs' historical role in slavery, how they view art (such as paintings and sculptures), music, etc.

Reciprocity

Demand reciprocity in everything. If they want to send one of theirs to a school or university, demand that we send one of ours to teach in their schools or universities.

If they want a Mosque or Islamic center or whatever, demand that we can also build a church or religious center in their respective country.

For every Koran or religious text they send off to one of the civilized nations, we can also promulgate something like a poster, flier, distribute Christian scriptures and religious materials or whatever in their countries.

Why is it OK for a Mohammedan to denigrate a bible, but a travesty when a Koran is denigrated? The travesty is requiring our soldiers at GITMO and other places to handle Korans with special gloves, great reverence, etc. That is pure and simple balderdash and playing stupid dhimmi to the Mohammedans. It must stop.

If one of them straps on explosives and detonates himself or herself in a public place killing innocents, we should pop an explosive off at one of their gatherings.

More Reciprocity

The OPEC nations are nailing us big time. We need oil and

they know it, and thus charge us way beyond decent prices for oil. While the cost to extract oil in most of their countries is about $3-5 per barrel, they charged us (in 2008) upwards of $130 per barrel.

Well, the OPEC countries need products that we produce, and we should likewise charge prices with several hundred percent mark-up. Or, we can just establish reciprocal commodity values:

A barrel of oil for a vial of insulin;

A barrel of oil for a pound of chicken;

A couple of thousand barrels of oil for each semester of higher education one of theirs gets over here;

A hundred barrels of oil for a surgical tool;

Charge a barrel of oil for each pound of machinery that they get, including luxury sedans.

Just make them pay like they make us pay. If we don't reciprocate, we are stupid. We have been stupid for a long time and need to wise up.

Can we end this war?

According to Islamists, this protracted conflict between our civilization and the Mohammedan system of evil will not end until their Allah ends it. However, we can bring about a truce (which Mohammed permitted – but truces are valid only for ten years), but it must be on our terms and renewable every year on our terms again, not theirs -- no way can it be on their terms, ever. We must accept and use the true God's blessings and recognize that this is World War IV in process and end the silliness of calling it a war with or on terrorism, and trying to deal with it on a stupid self-limiting basis, as though we were dealing with a few criminals, etc. We are in mortal conflict with an entire culture consisting of about 1.5 billion people.

We can not end the conflict with Islam because Islam will never, ever reconcile to live peacefully with or to respect us. They just can't do this. It's against their laws.

The war we are engaged in now is what will determine the earth's future, as a civilized world of rights, freedom, opportunity, goodness, charity, and civilized decency, or one of Moslem oppression, subjugation, hatred, death, ignorance, and abject poverty. That is a fundamental fact and truth.

But we can win by using that which God has given us. We can, should, and must use far greater levels of ferocity on the Mohammedans than they can imagine and drive them back to their origins, leaving them too fearful to do anything against us. They are like a pack of beasts who, when sensing a weakness will attack, but when confronted with superior power will back off. We can and must impose our will on them, or we will lose. Period!

Osama bin Laden

347

Osama bin Laden, years after he came to the attention of the American authorities as a grave danger, after he blew up American Embassies in East Africa, and the Twin Towers on 9/11 went around un-captured, and with relative impunity. When asked, President George W. Bush foolishly said that getting bin Laden was important, but not all that high on the list of priorities. Bush's Secretary of Defense agreed with an opinion that the killing of bin Laden would make little difference in recruiting jihadists, and those wonderful intelligence analysts reportedly considered him largely peripheral. Duuuhhh! Bin Laden by doing what he did, and being left alive became one of the greatest inspirations for Islamist jihadists in the world, if not the absolute greatest. Mohammedans write and recite poems to his greatness and he is held up as an example every day in Madrassas and mosques around the world. The now legendary Osama bin Laden has become a lasting inspiration to Mohammedan jihadists around the world to continue to wreak havoc of the greatest magnitude possible on the civilized world. Bin Laden's aim is to radicalize and mobilize the Islamic world, and he is enjoying immense success on a daily basis, and will continue to do so even after his demise.

When President Bush delivers his State of the Union Message, bin Laden delivers his State of Islam message -- to a much larger and more attentive audience.

AID and Education

The nations of the civilized world must tie all foreign assistance, including payments to the United Nations who ought to echo civilized guidelines, to the needy (especially Islamic) nations to certain educational performance criteria. They may NOT include religious indoctrination in schools that we fund. This would include rejection of Madrassas.

Madrassas throughout the world should be forbidden to exist, until and unless they teach things other than Mohammedism and jihad – hatred, bigotry, and warfare.

Arabs claim Jerusalem as a "Holy" city. These claims are phony. They only became popular claims after the establishment of modern Israel. Jerusalem has been Jewish for thousands of years - just read the Old Testament and learn about world history. Before the establishment of Israel, Islamic sites at Jerusalem were hardly utilized or honored by Moslems.

The Temple Mount in Jerusalem is considered by the Jews to be their most holy place on earth, but it is in Eastern Jerusalem and Christians and Jews are forbidden to pray there because it might offend some idiot Moslems. The Temple Mount is not highly ranked as a holy place in Islam. It is controlled by the Israeli government, yet Moslems are allowed to worship there while such practices are forbidden to others. The Israelis ought to establish reciprocity, permitting anyone who wants to worship there to do so, and any Islamist chump who takes offense should be dealt with accordingly. It should rightfully be annexed it permanently, and throw all of the Mohammedans out of the area and tear down their mosques. They are usurpers, nothing more.

During the quarter of a century that I spent living overseas, I managed to learn two languages with some difficulty and which I speak poorly. Nevertheless, in every country where I served, I tried to learn a few of the fundamentals and basics of host country languages which gave me a window into their culture. Words the people use and their meaning are important windows that enable one to begin to understand the thought process of people one must deal with. For instance, in one culture there is no word for hygiene. Thus, there is no conceptual understanding of hygiene as we westerners know and understand its meaning. Regarding Islam, some of my colleagues and I have been working on the below piece which we believe that you will find interesting and useful.

GLOSSARY

Arabic/Islamic words and terms that we kufar, non-dhimmi,
non-Moslem infidels will find helpful and clarifying.
Understanding Moslem values and ethics will remove
your confusion and inability to comprehend them.

ABED

Arab word for negro and slave. There is no differentiation in Arabic for slave or for black African. The two are synonymous. Mohammed derisively referred to black Africans as raisin heads.

CALIPH

Title of Islamic supreme leaders following the death of Mohammed. There is no Caliph today. A goal of Islam is a restoration of the Caliphate, a harsh and unrelenting ruling the world <u>WITHOUT</u> the consent of those governed, i.e. world-wide slavery.

DARABA*

In Koran 4:34 – Mohammed tells Moslems to "beat" one's disobedient wife or wives. This is a divine sanction established by Mohammed who in his Hadiths gives lessons on when, why, and how to beat a woman, generally (but not always) using a firm, freshly cut branch.

DARURA (see also taqiyyah)*

"Darura" in Arabic means "necessity." The Arabs and Muslims understand this idea. "Necessity" can even justify violating explicit prohibitions. A Moslem may, if starving, eat pork, according to some. A Moslem may, to protect the faith or his/herself or any other indiscretion, lie to Infidels -- lie about Islam itself, lie about their own belief in Islam, even lie about Mohammed. It's called Taqiyyah, and it's used to seduce us.

DAR-AL-HARB*

Lands of war, or arena of battle. Regions or peoples not under Islamic rule.

DAR-AL-ISLAM

Lands of Submission/peace. Regions or people under Islamic rule.

DAWA*

Moslem missionary efforts to convert non-Moslems to Islam.

DHIMMI (The Insulted Ones)*

In Darb al Islam it is the inferior, second-class status of non-Muslims. Dhimmis are oppressed. They are compelled to be servile and are subjected to separate rules, special taxes, confiscation of property, including children (such as conscription into military service such as the Iranians and Iraqis have done with Jews and Christians – used to clear mine fields), forced marriages of children (girls only) to Moslems, fewer rights and very limited privileges, etc.

In Darb al Harb: Many people outside of Islam seemingly have already begun accepting dhimmi status to Moslem superiority or dominance which will eventually lead to Islamist dominance whereby the dhimmi status means the acceptance of oppression – of forsaking the will and dignity to resist. These dhimmis are often ignorant liberals such as Britain's Prince Charles, and others who seem to remain willfully ignorant of Islam. A political dhimmi outside of Moslem territory is a useful fool. This would include any non-Moslem politician who parrots the Darura and taqiyyah that Islam is a religion of peace, and that Islam has been hijacked by a very few violent terrorists.

EID

There are several 'eid' festivals for a variety of reasons. Most are subject to the appearance of the moon, etc. This practice dates back to early pagan Arab worship of the moon, and seems to have been adopted by Mohammed to become Moslem festivals.

FATWA*

An Islamic religious ruling, issued by a Muslim clerical leader (mullah). Often a condemnation of an individual who does or says anything insulting or offensive about the Koran or Mohammed. It may include a sentence of death upon, and include a bounty for that person's death. Such was the case when the Ayatollah Khomeni issued a fatwa calling for the death of Salmon Rushdie who wrote a book in which he ridiculed Islam and Mohammed. This very glossary is probably offensive to Islam, the Koran, Mohammed, Moslems, etc., and may be worthy of a fatwa.

HADITH (AHADITH is the plural)*

The collected anecdotal (but treated as gospel) reports of words, pronouncements, and deeds of Mohammed. There are five major collections, one numbering about 7,000. The ahadith are secondary in importance to the Koran, but are used to support the Koran and Shari laws. They are basically the rules governing all Moslem thinking, behavior, law, economics, warfare, etc.

HAJJ

Mandatory once-in-a-lifetime pilgrimage to Mecca and the Kabba. The Kabba is a black stone.

HALAL

Sharia approved. Halal meat must be killed in approved fashion (usually a slow death) by slitting the animal's throat and letting it bleed to death. Halal cooking is special. Halal banking is Sharia approved discrimination where Moslems get banking privileges, interest rates, preferences that non-Moslems don't get. FYI: Moslems have taken a controlling interest in many, many U.S. and European banks and are installing elements of Sharia financing. Sharia is seditious in that it promotes a violent overthrow of the U.S. constitution and government. Sharia finance does not meet standards of accountability and transparency with traceability. Some profits from Sharia finance are required to be sent to Islamic charities, which in turn support terrorist acts directed against the united States.

HARAM*

Forbidden. Many things in Islamic societies are Hiram, a term not to be taken lightly because Haram is enforced, and can be justification for harsh forms of discipline such as public flogging, prison, even hanging or being beheaded.

In Moslem countries it is haram for Christians to study the Koran.

It is haram to question or criticize Mohammed, the Koran, the Hadiths, or Allah.

It is haram to express one's free thoughts or exercise one's freedom of expression. Under Islam it would be haram to exercise one's rights of expression as laid out in the First Amendment to our Constitution.

HASHASSIN

Assassin. Usually under the influence of drugs such as hashish, thus the root of the word hashassin - assassin. Today they are mostly suicide bombers. Highly recruited are those found to be HIV positive, so their blood spatter and debris can infect others, etc.

HIJRA

Also hejira or higra. Mohammed's hasty night time skulking departure from Mecca in 622 A.D. to avoid being put to death. This date marks the beginning of the Moslem calendar.

HIRABAH*

The term *Hirabah* refers to public terrorism in a war against society and civilization. In legal terminology it is defined as "spreading mischief in the land," but its precise meaning, as defined by Professor Khalid Abou el Fadl, is "killing by stealth and targeting a defenseless victim in a way intended to cause terror in society." This is the Islamic definition of terrorism.

Hirabah includes filing lawsuits against Americans for any deed they proclaim is hurtful to them. Anything that offends them is something they can and will file a suit over, calling honest discussions hate speech, referrals to historical facts are hate speech, etc.

HURRIYYA

Slave to the will of Allah – The real but complex meaning of this is Hurriya is the so-called freedom to be a totally mindless (and willfully ignorant of other things) follower of Islam in all things, religious, cultural, political, emotional, etc.

IBLIS

Arabic for Satan

IMAM

Spiritual leader of a Mosque.

INFIDEL*

Unbeliever, Non-Moslem, Kafir, Enemy of Allah, such as Christian, Jew, Buddhist, Hindu, etc.

INNOCENT*

According to Islam, only Moslems can be innocent. All infidels are unclean and cannot be considered innocent under any circumstances. Thus, when an infidel (Jewish Christian, Hindu, Buddhist, Shinto, etc.) child or infant is murdered by a Moslem, it is OK, because the victim was not innocent in any case. Or, when an Afghani, Iraqi, Arab, or any other Moslem carrying a rifle and shooting at American soldiers is killed, the Moslem is an innocent civilian - according to Islam.

I add a modern term: **INTERFAITH DIALOGUE**

Anything referred to as an Interfaith Dialogue is a beguiling Trojan Horse charade to be used to advance the cause of Islam.

ISLAM*

Defined as submission, or surrender: The people who have completely surrendered their free will as thinking, reasoning, moral human beings, and who are wholly and completely submissive to the harsh, unrelenting rules that Mohammed claimed were handed down to him by Allah.

JANISSARY

Established by the Ottoman Turks. Janissaries were sons of conquered people (Christians, Jews, etc.) who were forcefully recruited (jizya blood tax, below) from the dhimmi class of Christians and Jews into a military force serving the Sultan. They were then trained from childhood to become efficient, brutal fighters in a disciplined military force reportedly renowned for their loyalty and fervor (vicious savagery) which earned them privileges, respect, and acceptance when they eventually became (a requirement) Moslems.

Moslem Turkish officers and noncoms in fact followed the Janissaries into battle and any who faltered were killed by their "leaders". So, the Janissaries fought savagely for their very lives. This is the same tactic that the Turks used in Korea with Kurdish (and Christian) conscripts who likewise earned reputations (as Turks) for being fearless, formidable, and ferocious. The Turkish Kurds/Christians knew that if they faltered their Turkish superiors would shoot them in the back. Like the Janissaries, the Turkish Christian, Jewish, and Kurdish conscripts were desperately fighting for their very lives.

JIHAD*

Refers to the struggle one must undertake to impose Islam on all non-Muslims by hook or by crook; by the sword if necessary. This (military jihad) is a requirement of the Koran. Jihadists who kill or who are killed in war are promised immediate acceptance into paradise, with its' ever-flowing rivers of wine, milk, and honey, lovely young virgins and a luxurious existence. Some of the hadith specify 72 ever virgin maidens, plus 28 pre-pubescent boys. Jihad also but secondarily means the "struggle", one deals with to control his desires, passions and natural impulses.

JINN

Arabic for angel.

JIZYA*

A special tax (protection money – much like the early American Mafia/gangsters required of shopkeepers – the precursor to modern insurance) levied against non-Moslems who have chosen to submit to the domination of Islam rather than to fight and/or die.

Typically this is about 20% of one's annual earnings. A blood jizya can also be collected. This is the surrender of one of a family's children for forced conversion to Islam, to be a servant (slave), forced into an undesired marriage (concubinage), forced military service (such as the Turks' janissaries), etc.

KABBA

The stone cubical building in the heart of Mecca, the holiest site of Islam which contains the sacred black stone. Draped in black curtains, the Kabba has been around much longer than Islam. Some claims state it was built by Abraham, or even by Adam. In Mohammed's day the Kabba featured 360 pagan idols and was regarded as a holy site and destination of pilgrims. When Mohammed conquered Mecca in about 630, he destroyed all of the idols except the sacred black stone representing the moon god, Il-Allah.

KAFIR (Kufaar is plural)*

Soiled or dirty person. A Christian, a dog, a pig, a Jew, a Hindu, Buddhist, etc. An Infidel. Defined: The usual translation of this Arabic word is unbeliever, but unbeliever is only a very small part of its meaning. It is the Koran that defines the word "kafir" and it says the most terrible things can happen to them. The Koranic doctrine about kafirs says they are hated and are Satan's friends. Kafirs can be robbed, killed, tortured, raped, mocked, cursed, condemned and plotted against. The Koran does not have one good thing to say about kafirs. For over the last 1400 years, 270 million or more kafirs have died as a result of the political doctrine of Islam. It is the biggest single source of suffering in the history of the world. The word kafir is the worst word in the human language. It is far worse than the n-word, because the n-word is a personal opinion, whereas, kafir is Allah's (Mohammed's) decree. Nearly two thirds of the Koran is devoted to the kafir. Islam is fixated on the kafir and the moderate Muslim thinks that you are a kafir. How moderate is that?

MUJAHIDDIN

Jihad fighters

NAKBA*

A Catastrophe: Example: The establishment of the free democratic nation of Israel in 1948, the only truly free nation in the Middle East.

NIKAAH*

Islamic rules of marriage which permit (**MUT'A)** paid for sham marriages for a single night, a few hours, or a couple of days. This is legalized prostitution where brokers (pimps) arrange the liaisons ('marriages') with girls as young as five years old. This is slavery, pedophilia, and prostitution, plain and simple as it also includes human (slave) trafficking. In this activity, the "groom" provides a "dowry", which may be money, jewelry, fabrics, etc. The marriage is ended by the groom proclaiming "I divorce thee" three times. The bride gets to keep the dowry and is free to marry again. This sanctioned form of prostitution makes forbidden out-of-wedlock sex and prostitution unnecessary. Very often, these sham marriages are with young girls, some just children. In this light, most of those sham affairs are rapes committed by pedophiles.

NASKH*

Abrogation, Cancellation. All religious faiths that existed before Islam are Naskh, and their existence today is corruption, an abomination.

QUR'AN

Pronounced koran by westerners. It is a non-chronological collection of fanciful 'revelations' by Mohammed that he claimed were passed down to him by his god, il-Allah, through an angel, Gabriel. This is regarded as the actual words of Allah by gullible Muslims. There were riots in Islamic countries because non-Moslem (civilized) American military prison guards at Guantanamo Bay reportedly mishandled Korans. The American guards are kufar and their handling of the Koran was in itself considered offensive. But, it's OK for Moslems to abuse Holy Bibles, Torah's, and other scriptures. Many in the civilized world believe that the Koran is merely Satan's response to Christianity. The Koran is basically the anti-thesis of Christianity.

RAMADAN

A month-long period of sunrise to sunset fasting. Ramadan falls on a different date each year because the Moslems follow a lunar calendar of twelve 28-day months which create a 336 day year. This is a further affirmation of Islam's roots in moon worship.

SALAT

Five daily prayers recited by Moslems always offered facing Mecca. They are supposed to do these at certain times, but if they cannot do this, Koranic law permits that they may perform make-up prayers. When Moslems claim that it's a must that they knock off from work or other duties to "pray" at certain times, it's really balderdash on their part.

SHAHADA

A statement which makes one a Moslem forever when spoken three times in Arabic in the presence of a witness. This contradicts another claim that all Christians and Jews are Moslem at birth but just don't know it. In fact as Mohammed taught that we were all born Moslems, so one does not "convert" to Islam; one "reverts" to Islam.

SHARIA

Sharia are derived from the Koran and the Sunnah (precedents handed down by Mohammed) which establishes the legal code of allah for all of mankind. There are no options. Sharia is Islamic laws which boil down to a codified form of the most crude and brutal laws of the jungle and the survival of the fittest or most savage, which treat Moslems differently from non-Moslems. The best definition of Sharia is Jim Crow law.

SHIRK

Idolatry or blasphemy against Allah or Mohammed.

SURA

A chapter of the Koran (which contains 114 suras), each representing a specific "revelation" recited by Mohammed.

TAQIYYA (see darura)*

Practice of deception or concealment to fool, beguile, or to confuse the enemy, the infidel, the kafir, etc. It is an encouraged and approved tactic of Islam to lie, to conceal, to cheat, to misinform, to mislead, etc. when dealing with non-Moslems. This is a well established, even desirable practice of dawa (missionary efforts) and is conducted on a regular basis in the USA and elsewhere in the non-Muslim world.

When a Moslem is subjected to a polygraph, their core belief in the fundamentals of taqiyyah can let them lie and to actually defeat the polygraph.

A Moslem can pretend to be friends with non-Moslems in order to gain advantages.

Moslems will dispute this because this is required of them. They may say that lying is permissible in only three circumstances, one of them being war. Well, anyone/anyplace that is not under Moslem control (Dar-al-Harb) is a field of warfare, Darb-al-Harm.

ULEMA

The Moslem people.

WUDI

Ablutions such as the washing of one's feet, hands and face before Moslem prayers or attending services in a mosque. .

ZAKAT

Similar to tithe. An obligatory contribution of alms in the support of Islam. Zakat is generally considered to be 2.5% of one's net worth, each year, excluding the value of one's home.

This means that all Moslems in the United States are required to fork over at least 2.5% of their net worth every year in support of Islamic causes. In most cases, this goes to local Moslem organizations that support the jihad/wars against America and non-Moslem civilization.

FOOTNOTES

Moslems often agree that Christ was a Prophet, but Christ is ranked a far distant second from Mohammed. They agree that Christ was a messenger from God, but his messages of love, peace, decency, humility, and charity are perverted and are thus worthless and meaningless; that Mohammed's Koranic messages of hatred, lust, greed, and savagery are more true and reliable and important.

The secular separation of church and state is a conceptual distinction for which there is no vocabulary in Arabic. If there is no vocabulary or words for a term, there is no conceptual understanding, and thus no acceptance. Thus, Islam does not comprehend nor will Islam accept or tolerate any separation of church and state.

The very first Christian Crusade was in response to an 846 C.E. Moslem expedition from Sicily which sailed up the Tiber River, attacked and sacked St. Peter's in Rome. Following this act of barbarity, Christians organized the first of the Crusades.

Moslem depredations have not ceased. Why should the Crusades not continue?

*Terms, practices, or words used regularly in Mosques in the USA, in dealings with Americans, Christians, Jews, Hindus, Buddhists, etc.

CHECK THESE OUT

memri.org
islaminaction.com
revolutionmuslim.com
familysecuritymatters.org
fatherzakaria.net
oathkeepers.org
politicalislam.com
formermuslimsunited.org

Jewish World Report – Insight
The Sword of the Prophet by Serge Trifkovic
El Plan Espiritual de Aztlan
Saban Center
"How to Identify Friend from Foe" by Melanie Phillips, Nov. 17, 2009

Recommended Reading:
INFILTRATION, *BY Paul Sperry*
STEALTH JIHAD *by Robert Spencer*
WHAT WENT WRONG? *By Bernard Lewis*
MUSLIM MAFIA *by Paul David Gaubatz*
SEE NO EVIL *by Robert Baer*
FUNDING EVIL *by Dr. Rachel Ehrenfeld*
THE AMERICAN HOUSE OF SAUD *by Steven Emerson*

4259800

Made in the USA
Charleston, SC
19 December 2009